COLONIAL TRANSACTIONS

- 60% pop live in Poverty. (32)
- 1/5 households have access to potable water (32)
- Economic stagnation in early 2000s.
  ↳ Lack of Connectivity.
  ≠

- Anecdotes of Bernault's own multiple visits to Gabon.

Clan expansion using slaving and marriage
  ↳ Slaves had no other Clan than their masters - Masters asserted control over slaves as wives and offspring.
    ↳ Rich men used this to accumulate offspring → Creating matrimonial competition between Clans. Weaker groups would form Alliances. (39)
Use of Matrimonial "eating" or "swallowing" of other Clans for Expansion purposes
Use of Slave trade for clan expansion.

(40)

THEORY IN FORMS

A Series Edited by Nancy Rose Hunt and

Achille Mbembe

COLONIAL
TRANSACTIONS

⁚⁚⁚⁚⁚

Imaginaries, Bodies, and Histories in Gabon

FLORENCE BERNAULT

DUKE UNIVERSITY PRESS
Durham and London
2019

© 2019 Duke University Press
All rights reserved
Printed and bound by CPI Group (UK) Ltd, Croydon, CR0 4YY
Designed by Amy Ruth Buchanan
Typeset in Arno Pro by Westchester Publishing Services

Library of Congress Cataloging-in-Publication Data
Names: Bernault, Florence, author.
Title: Colonial transactions : imaginaries, bodies, and histories in
Gabon / Florence Bernault.
Description: Durham : Duke University Press, 2019. |
Series: Theory in forms
Identifiers: LCCN 2018047203 (print) | LCCN 2018059396 (ebook)
ISBN 9781478002666 (ebook)
ISBN 9781478001232 (hardcover : alk. paper)
ISBN 9781478001584 (pbk. : alk. paper)
Subjects: LCSH: Gabon—Colonial influence. | Gabon—
History—1839–1960. | Gabon—Religious life and customs. |
Magic—Social aspects—Gabon. | Witchcraft—Social aspects—
Gabon. | France—Colonies—Africa—Administration. |
Imperialism in popular culture—France—History—19th century.
Classification: LCC DT546.175 (ebook) | LCC DT546.175 .B47 2019 (print) |
DDC 967.21/02—dc23
LC record available at https://lccn.loc.gov/2018047203

Cover art: Malangatana Ngwenya (1936–2011), *Untitled*, 1967. Oil paint on
hardboard, 1095 × 1902 mm. © Fundação Malangatana Valente Ngwenya.
Photo: © Tate, London 2019.

TO SUZANNE AND ROMAN, WITH LOVE

CONTENTS

Preface ⁘ ix

Introduction ⁘ 1

CHAPTER 1 ⁘ A Siren,
an Empty Shrine, and a Photograph ⁘ 27

CHAPTER 2 ⁘ The Double Life of Charms ⁘ 69

CHAPTER 3 ⁘ Carnal Fetishism ⁘ 96

CHAPTER 4 ⁘ The Value of People ⁘ 118

CHAPTER 5 ⁘ Cannibal Mirrors ⁘ 138

CHAPTER 6 ⁘ Eating ⁘ 168

Conclusion ⁘ 194

Notes ⁘ 205
Bibliography ⁘ 293
Index ⁘ 321

One day in Brazzaville (Congo), witchcraft filled my heart with anger. I was very young and very inexperienced, and this was my first stay in Equatorial Africa. At a dinner with friends, Guy, a young Congolese man, told us that, as a boy, his parents had sent him away to the care of relatives in the big city. He had been a sickly child, and a local diviner had diagnosed his ailment as a result of mystical attacks by a jealous uncle. Guy worked at a local school for students with special needs, managed by Catholic nuns. He was a devout Christian, and a very good friend of ours. That night, my young mind became irritated by these apparent contradictions. I asked Guy, rather brutally, why he and his parents still believed in witchcraft since they were Catholic? I do not remember his response, but I still sense the embarrassment that I later felt about my brash, idiotic reaction. I later came to grasp that, beyond a personal failing, the impulse was also shaped by the colonial past. Historically, I was the descendant of men and women who had invaded Africa and had also, in their time, been baffled and angered by local ways. This study of Gabon is thus written by an outsider coming from the colonizing world, aware of, but not freed from, weighty politics of representation. To a large extent, this book is an effort to stitch together Guy's life story and my multilayered anger—not to smooth over my awkwardness but to use the story to get into the murky space where African and European imaginaries about power, agency, and misfortune clashed, overlapped and combined.

Scholars tend to reflect on the historicity of modern witchcraft by reaching out to precolonial patterns and beliefs and comparing them with contemporary ones. By jumping over the colonial moment, they obscure how colonialism restructured the field of practical and mystical agency. This book offers a thick description of these reconfigurations over the last hundred years. But its main argument is to revisit how domination worked, showing that colonial agents *transacted* power, creating *transgressive hegemonic processes* that were shaped, across the racial divide, by *conversant* and *congruent imaginaries.*

While writing this book, I experienced major geographical and intellectual displacements. A few years after the conversation with Guy, the raging civil war in Congo-Brazzaville forced me to switch my research to Gabon. Although I knew the country from my first book, it took me years to appreciate how much it differed from the Congo. In both locales, I retained a close friendship with Joseph Tonda, himself tragically displaced from Brazzaville to Libreville. Our ongoing collaboration has been crucial to conceptualizing this book: for this and much more, I want to thank him. I owe a huge debt to the friends who welcomed and helped me in Gabon: Jeannette Angouang for her hospitality and generous friendship, Lionel Ikogou-Renamy, Florence Ilama, Monique Koumba Mamgoumbi, Raymond Mayer, Guy Rossatanga, Mesmin Soumao, André Fauster, and finally, for guiding me in the city politics of Lambaréné and Mouila, Agathe Nginguena, Daniel Baboussa, and Joseph Massala.

The shift was also analytical. My first book touched only lightly on the moral principles and spiritual benchmarks that informed electoral and ethnic politics. After moving to the University of Wisconsin–Madison, I immersed myself deeper in this history and found a unique mentor in Jan Vansina. Although I cannot give justice to twenty years of friendship in a few words, I want to thank him for all he did for me. Jan's rapid talk in French and English never left one of my ideas standing still. In 2004, I bought a house just a few blocks from his, and visited often. I came out of these meetings shaken, dizzy with possibilities, and strangely satisfied. Part of it was Claudine's tea and cakes, perhaps, and her way of joyfully standing her ground with her husband, while I lay beaten to a pulp. Countless times, nimbly taking the phone to ask Jan about a vocabulary issue, I felt what privilege it was to be able to benefit from his greater mind. In 2017, he left us, and things will never be the same.

In switching to the English-speaking world, I learned to use important analytical devices, especially from Peter Geschiere and *The Modernity of Witchcraft* (1997), a seminal book that opened entirely new views on the moral economy of African politics. I had the fortune to befriend Peter and benefit from his constant inspiration and generosity. Then a residence at NIAS, the Netherlands Institute for Advanced Studies in 2013–14, procured many a wonderful time with him in Amsterdam, while I was writing the first draft of the book. Birgit Meyer and Nico Besnier invited me to present my hypotheses at the Amsterdam Institute for Social Science Research, as did Stephen Ellis at the African Studies Center at the University of Leiden. At NIAS, I formed a close friendship with Kenda Mutongi and Laura Fair, whom I thank for being such a source of fun, mischief, and companionship. I am also grateful to Natalie Scholz (Amsterdam), who shared her house and her work on objects and politics of postwar Germany. At many crucial junctures, Nancy Hunt gave me incomparable intellectual support.

In Europe, colleagues and friends helped and encouraged me: John Parker (London), Joost Fontein (University of Edinburg), and the late Jan-Georg Deutsch (Oxford). After gracing the History Department at UW-Madison with a semester of teaching, Patrick Harries (Basel) became an important presence in my life before he passed away, too soon, in 2016. Across the Atlantic, and throughout the years, Catherine Coquery-Vidrovitch (Paris) and Luise White (Gainesville) have remained constant inspirations.

Despite the difficulty of adapting to a new language and a new scholarly environment, the move to the History Department and the African Studies Program at UW-Madison offered unique resources, with the collegiality, friendship, and support of Tom Spear, Teju Olanyian, Aliko Songolo, Emily Ngo Nguidjol, Jim Sweet, and Neil Kodesh. The Graduate School generously financed the field and archival work on which this book is based. The John Simon Guggenheim Foundation, the Virginia Center for the Creative Arts, NIAS, and the Institute for Research in the Humanities at UW-Madison provided me with invaluable time for writing.

Finally, I want to thank the close friends who helped and accompanied me in all sorts of ways: Anne Ruel, Sylvie Couval, Nevine El Nossery, Preeti Chopra, and Kristin Phillips-Court. Isak Niehaus (London) offered unparalleled guidance and love to help me write this book.

Introduction

In mid-nineteenth-century Gabon, a vortex of bodily assaults and magical warfare brought Europeans and Africans together in strange pursuits of power and knowledge. In the name of scientific curiosity, foreign visitors often snatched human remains from graveyards and shrines. Explorer Paul Du Chaillu so frequently stole decaying limbs and skulls from a village's cemetery that women claimed that "he [was] a leopard coming to eat them."[1] Other white men preserved the remains of exotic animals in arsenic, decapitating monkeys and pickling the heads for curio shops abroad.[2] Such rapacity resonated with African ideas about the agency of human and animal substances, and fears that outsiders could kill and absorb the life force of a person to get empowered.[3] Later on, French colonialists murmured that thieves opened their graves and stole white body parts to compose charms.[4] They also painted grisly pictures of Africans' horrific cannibalism, and their inextinguishable hunger for human flesh.

A hundred years later, in the 2000s, most Gabonese assume that politicians preserve their influence by working with magical charms made with human substances. Articles routinely claim that deputies at the National Assembly can be reelected only if "pygmies," *nganga* (ritual experts and healers), marabouts (West African fetish-men), and other "butchers" deliver human body parts to them in time.[5] A local artist compares the witches who travel today in mystical airplanes to precolonial rulers who crossed the Gaboon Estuary by flying over water: "I am not talking of the physical world here, but of the spiritual world." His grand-daughter jumps in: "When I was eleven or twelve, I saw white people flying in a plane. They got out of it and sat around a table to eat. But when they saw high dignitaries of Bwiti (a local healing cult) approaching with lighted torches, they disappeared." A visitor confirms, "There is God and there is Satan, they sit side by side."[6]

The first aim of this book is to enrich our knowledge of mystical agency and practical power in West Equatorial Africa, and to explain why, at the beginning of the twenty-first century, witchcraft attacks and the traffic in body parts constitute one of the most powerful ways for the Gabonese to talk about politics and personal affliction.[7] Anthropologists and political scientists approach witchcraft beliefs in contemporary Africa by uncovering the main economic, social, and cultural reasons behind them.[8] I argue here that modern witchcraft is first and foremost a historical phenomenon, and that its contemporary manifestations cannot be understood without taking into account the long and intricate battles between Africans and Europeans over physical and mystical agency.

The second aim of the book is to revisit the history of colonial domination and to wrestle with established ideas that, on the eve of the colonial conquest, Africans and Europeans belonged to "heterogeneous regimes of historicity," and that Europeans did not interfere in the domain of magic and witchcraft.[9] I show that in Gabon, French colonialists did intrude in and profoundly change these realms, including the broader field of political agency. Indeed, they held mutually intelligible ideas, praxis, and symbolic systems with the people they colonized. In turn, the colonial engagement exposed their own contradictory ideas about power and agency (*pouvoir*), tearing apart their practical explanations and speculative philosophies.

Understandings of agency were at the core of the colonial encounter. The ways in which Africans and Europeans thought about power and the ability to act underwrote foreign rule and Gabonese reactions to it, shaping innumerable decisions in everyday life. Far from being reduced to abstract forces or mental drives, these ideas guided people in a myriad of concrete strategies. They served to protect individual capacity, to reproduce communal regimes of choice and opportunity, and to open new channels for action. Yet "agency" is a clumsy term, and one that nobody used in Gabon. In vernacular languages, *ngul*, from the Bantu root *-gudu*, glosses the idea of force and talent, the capacity of a person to act successfully, and the power of mystical entities such as spirits and ancestors. In this book I concentrate mostly on extraordinary agency, or the ability of individuals or institutions to exert "out-of-the-ordinary," transformative acts over people and things. Equatorial Africans had historically seen extraordinary agency as ambivalent, associating destruction with replenishing.[10] Coming to Gabon, French colonialists also hold specific ideas about extraordinary forms of power (*pouvoir*). They often justified their mission in Africa by boasting about Frenchmen's extraordinary moral and political capacities. This relational imaginary needed to confront African forms of agency and denounce them both as hateful and ineffectual. Africans, meanwhile, borrowed the French term *puissance* (power) to express new problems and new possibilities.[11] At the crossroad of these engagements, this book proposes a genealogy of modern power and *puissance*, and the intellectual, linguistic, and practical transformations that made this reworking possible.

Indeed, my purview is pragmatic, contingent, and opportunistic. Rather than providing a definitive translation or definition of agency, or disaggregating the notion into neat sets of relations and causal effects, I take it as the ability to make extraordinary things (if repetitive and predictable) happen, and the causes that people imagine behind unusual action and change.[12] When colonialists and Africans speculated about agency, they employed a rich and complex vocabulary that defies simplification. The Gabonese used older words for "talent" and "capacity" while changing their meaning: for instance, the talent to speak out and to debate (iNzebi: *misaambe*), the ability to curse (iNzebi: *mundoghe*), or to accumulate wealth (iNzebi: *mabwe*; Fang: *nkumkum*) survived in the twenty-first century, but with a host of innovative senses.[13] The Gabonese also started to use foreign terms such as "seduction" (*séduction*), "force" (*force*), "elegance" (*élégance*), and "refined cruelty" (*cruauté raffinée*) to describe the qualities and power of politicians and leaders.[14] To talk about the conquest and its consequences, the French relied on *pouvoir* (power), *force*, and *génie* (genius). They described African ideas about mystical and human agents by comparing them with dark figures of evil borrowed from French mythologies, calling them vampires, fetish-men, and tyrants, and later bringing *charlatanisme* (charlatanism) and *fraud* to the colony. I thus transcribe vernacular and French terms, when appropriate, in combination with English glosses for agency, power, and capacity. The transformation of these ideas was complex and elusive. But following them over time, and the reasons and unreasons that made people turn and twist their speculative views and practical actions, yields rich insights in this history.

Taking vocabularies of power at face value, moreover, allows me to move away from the Western divide between human and nonhuman agency, and look at Gabonese ideas about the actions of spirits, ancestors, or physical charms much as I consider French opinions of the kind hailed by the French governor of Gabon in 1912, when he claimed that "the spectacle of our creative force and our organizational genius" would impress and educate the natives.[15] Indeed, the main divide between African and European representations of agency did not pass between the secular and the divine, the rational and the irrational, or the visible and invisible, even though some of the harshest battles in the colony were fought about the very meaning of these words and ideas. It ran along and between the question of the physical or intangible nature of agency.

Westerners glossed the action of spirits and ancestors as "unreal," "immaterial," "invisible," and "supernatural."[16] The Gabonese understood, however, that these entities had a very material existence and interacted with people in both tangible and spiritual manifestations.[17] I thus avoid as much as possible labeling the realm of spiritual agency as "invisible" or "immaterial." Nor do I follow a strict Durkheimian separation between "profane" and "sacred," even when I investigate how colonialists tried to create and enforce a strict separation between these domains in the colony.[18] In rare occasions, I use the adjective "sacred" or "divine" to loosely qualify the domain of extraordinary forces and entities, whether Christian or African.

Disagreement and doubts undermined everyone's views of efficacy and agency. Colonialists could not empirically measure the efficacy of their efforts to "civilize" indigenous people. Nor did most of them understand their own technology, the phonographs and the chemical reactions they used to impress African audiences.[19] Conversely, Gabonese ideas of agency left considerable room for discord. For instance, people believed that an autopsy could reveal whether a witch had cursed and killed a person. But they rarely accepted the diagnosis of the diviner without debates and hesitation. Hence the changing ontologies that helped French and Africans to act and to interpret actions allowed a fair amount of disbelief and suspicion. These doubts belonged in the broad imaginaries of *puissance* and agency that rose throughout the twentieth century, but did not significantly weaken their hold.

Last but not least, this book connects a history of agency and capacity with a discussion of new forms of *value* that emerged at the heart of colonial engagements. When the French believed in the power of civilization, and the Gabonese called on the invisible forces of ancestors and spirits, they assigned considerable worth to the agentive devices (charms, money, human substances) that made these actions workable, and to the hierarchies (of status, possibilities) that derived from them. During the colonial period, both groups increasingly measured these values in money, a process that social scientists usually explain as a by-product of commodification and the breaking down of moral economies.[20] In contrast, I demonstrate how Equatorial Africans and Europeans, independently of these pressures, had long invested in the commensurable and transactional value of human beings, objects, and currencies. In the colonial context, domination and power, too, became matters of transaction.

Beyond the Racial Paradigm

Indeed, I argue that *proximate, conversant* and *compatible* imaginaries of power existed across the racial divide, and that Equatorial Africans and Europeans situationally relied on rich intellectual, political, and cultural formations that can be compared at deep levels or particular junctures.[21] Africans worked with a cultural and historical legacy often referred to by specialists as the West Equatorial African tradition. Likewise, French colonialists in Gabon came from, and used, specific imperial formations and deep national histories. Yet, in the realm of collective power and individual agency, rulers and ruled not only infringed on and clashed with each other's worlds, but also held mutually intelligible ideas, projects, and fantasies.[22] These imaginaries, and the startling moments of recognition and awareness that colonial agents experienced on the ground, were central to the machinery of colonial domination and the world that came after it.

Imperial ideologies codified the differences between Europeans and Africans in racial and evolutionary terms. In the 1950s, academic historians opened several fronts against these prescriptions, seeking to recover Africa's complex past and to understand it in its own terms.[23] They highlighted colonialism's limited and uneven influence on the ground and, in the aftermath of Jan Vansina's interpretation of colonialism as a moment of "cognitive rupture and cultural breakdown," they insisted on the survival of African worldviews and their fluid combination with colonial repertoires and practices.[24] In the wake of this paradigmatic shift, we relativized the destructive power of imperialism, and learned how cultural mingling went both ways.[25]

Yet the effort to recover African voices and to write narratives from the viewpoint of local societies tends to essentialize "indigenous" and "emic" worlds in opposition to European or Western ones. Indeed, one of the most widely shared assumptions among historians of Africa today is that, at the time of the conquest, colonizers and colonized belonged to starkly disparate worlds, and that even their most intimate interactions engaged dissimilar views, vocabularies, and agendas.[26] By showing how such practices and representations came together in productive processes of hybridization, bricolage, and "working misunderstandings," historians sometimes forget to criticize the dichotomies enforced by colonial racism.[27]

Critics will perhaps suggest that, misreading or succumbing to the bias of colonial archives, I make up a racial commensurability that, historically, French colonialists often used as a thwarted political agenda.[28] Others might think that talking of congruent imaginaries is another way of positing universals (money, freedom, love) that never existed on the ground.[29] Yet, attention to compatibilities and resemblance does not erase disparities among historical actors, or flatten them into universal "human beings." My point is not to say that considerable historical divergences and asymmetries of power did not exist between Europeans and Africans, but to argue that these differences often obscure deeper and more subtle correspondences. Social actors separated by racial injunctions and historical experiences did not always differ in drives, affects, knowledge, or imagination: this fact is essential to retrieving the history of Africa during colonialism.

The notion of "imaginaries," conceptualized in France by social theorist Cornelius Castoriadis in the 1980s, and widely used on the European continent today, is central to my argument.[30] Far from being confined to mental or abstract manifestations, Castoriadis shows that imaginaries condense social conflicts and cultural representations: they crystallize in embodied norms and tactics that make the prime material of social institutions.[31] In Gabon, converging and conversant imaginaries emerged as much from the colonial context as from propinquities that preexisted it. Neither immobile, stable, nor univocal, they shifted according to historical circumstances and the changing power relations of the colonial situation. Nor were they homogenous and continuous: porous, full of holes and growths, they harbored contradictory meanings and ambivalent images.[32] In the convulsive context of colonialism, the French and the Gabonese experienced muffled concerns and fleeting moments of discernment and recognition, but also denial, projection, and antagonism. Colonialists' fierce racial aversion to the Gabonese, for instance, derived in part from the desire to mask any congruence with the natives and to render racial and cultural contiguity unthinkable.[33] Africans sought to mask and protect their autonomy and political agenda. These strenuous efforts, and the unevenness of power between colonized and colonizers, augmented the volatility of imaginary formations. Both answered, embraced, or concealed a resemblance that they alternatively experienced as alluring or repulsive. Hence the task to trace this history is rarely straightforward.

Marriage, for instance, was hardly a solely French or African preoccupation: both saw it as a central vehicle for social reproduction and economic exchange. Nor were patriarchal impulses to aggregate kin and followers for domestic and public influence confined to either side of the racial divide. Again, this is not to say, emphatically, that we should erase the relations of domination and subordination that operated in the colony. On the contrary, a better attention to compatible imaginaries makes us attend to the ways in which the colonial regime enhanced historical and cultural discrepancies between rulers and ruled, and ranked them in racial hierarchies. Simultaneously, we can see how this project kept being altered by myriads of moments and experiences when mirroring concerns and ideas came into plain view. New funerary laws, for instance, tried to address the simultaneous, nervous concern that both Africans and Europeans had about dead human bodies.

Most historical actors did not consciously recognize these similarities. Partly because of the powerful hierarchies imposed by the colonial regime, they positioned themselves relationally as *blanc* (white) or *noir* (black), *européen* (European) or *africain* (African).[34] This is why, keeping in mind their heterogeneity and instability, I often rely on the broad aggregate "French" or "colonialists" when talking of foreign people in position of power, and "the Gabonese" when referring to individuals and communities who experienced colonial domination in the region now encompassed in modern Gabon.[35]

In this book, I track and conceptualize four major congruent imaginaries across the racial divide. Both colonized and colonizers understood that the travail of social prosperity and power was based on *transactions* between people and numinous entities or higher principles (ancestors, spirits, science, and technology; chapter 1). They thought that people, objects, money, and power relations held commensurable value and efficacy and could be exchanged (chapter 2 and 4). In turn, transactional imaginaries encouraged practical fantasies of *kinship* and *affiliation* across races (chapter 1), expressing the new, intractable intrusion of white people in the realm of magic and power, along with fears of intimate betrayal and social death. With the imaginary of *carnal fetishism*, French and Africans reconceptualized human flesh as a fetish, for example, a material entity suffused with self-contained efficacy and agency (chapter 3). Yet carnal fetishism was riddled with deep ambivalence and anxieties, including the possibility that intimate outsiders might capture one's flesh and life force for their benefit: the alarm coalesced in a mutual imaginary of *cannibalism* (chapter 5 and 6). The cannibal imaginary underwrote social reproduction and social interaction, predicting the doom of white domination and explaining the reign of destructive witchcraft.

Transacting Power

If Africans and the French held congruent imaginaries, then we need to rethink how colonial domination worked. One of the ways in which I propose to do so is by using the heuristic device of *transaction*, a concept that with a few exceptions, has been rarely applied to colonial history, and even less so by historians.[36] Transaction elucidates how singular units of exchange arose on the ground, bringing together colonized and colonialists in active and transformative relations. I use it here as an operative idea rather than a strictly constructed concept: my aim is not to describe all colonial interactions and their causes, but to insist on the ways in which colonial domination made people come together in processual and dynamic moments of exchange and transformation. Transaction, moreover, espouses the field: in Gabon, Africans and Europeans held congruent imaginaries that interpreted the normal labor of social reproduction and exchanges with the spiritual world as so many forms of transactions.[37] Both of them also experienced colonial rule in terms of *transactions gone wrong.*[38]

Since the 1990s, to interpret colonial interactions, historians have used scenarios that tend to privilege unilateral agency with little or no reciprocity, and without the knowledge of the other party.[39] By adopting a Western dress code, for instance, Kuba city dwellers in the 1940s did not need to enter in direct relation with the Europeans who lived there.[40] Many transformative actions in the colony, often glossed as borrowing, appropriation, and reworking, could happen while avoiding close interaction with dominant or subaltern groups. Yet it is useful to think beyond self-actional initiatives of colonial individuals and groups, and to find a language that is able to analyze how reciprocal and co-constitutive relationships worked among people, especially in creating capacity and power. Avoidance, indifference, and planes of life undisturbed by foreign rule were part of the colonial experience. But transactions can retrieve another, crucial dimension of colonial life made of moments of exchange and negotiation in which people came together in singular units of historical agency and transformation.

The word "transaction" comes from the Latin verb *transigere*, "to end a conflict or contestation," and the meaning is particularly apt in the antagonistic context of colonialism, although, as we will see, transactions often embodied and triggered conflicts, instead of settling them. One of the benefits of transaction is that it presumes agency in all partners and the possibility that they enter in effective (and transformative) exchange. While "bricolage" insists on unilateral action, transaction describes dynamic and relational operations, whether indirect, illegal, or imposed under duress. Yet the concept of transaction should not sanitize or flatten these moments of contact. In the colonial context, most transactions ended in considerable loss and harm for one party. Colonial troops, for instance, could attack a village, take prisoners, burn houses, and destroy the fields. The result of the confrontation, although forceful and unwanted, opened a transformative relation in which villagers lost political independence, and human and economic assets, and the French gained sovereignty, land, and reputation. Thus colonial hierarchies, rather than preexisting these exchanges, were partly produced and shaped by them. Yet the patterns of exchange were never determined only by cultural, economic, or racial differences. Instead, they occurred between, across, and among races, social groups, genders, individuals, and spiritual entities.

The concept of transaction, moreover, follows the shape and design of local imaginaries that Africans and Europeans used to think about the colonial situation, and the normal labor of social reproduction. As this book will narrate, both rulers and ruled hold transactional imaginaries that applied to colonial interactions. The French imagined that colonialism could improve social and political reproduction among the Gabonese. They saw free commerce, taxes, and forced labor as ways of facilitating individual and collective transactions to augment communities and their material assets. The colonial "mission" was also a transactional affair, one that incited white men to invest their personal life in Africa, and use immaterial forces called science, *pouvoir*, and civilization to bring progress to the natives.[41] Colonialists thus justified the civilizing mission by computing the "sacrifice" of fellow colonialists and the alleged benefits received by the Gabonese. Likewise, the view that Africans should pay for the gift of progress and enlightenment explained the task of extracting labor and taxes. In the eyes of the Gabonese, colonial transactions had darker meanings. By the 1900s, they saw how white colonialists had taken control of economic exchanges, increasingly intruding in the realm of social and domestic transactions. They felt how taxes, male labor, and the criminalizing of polygamy and bride payments were upsetting exchanges between communities, and transactions with ancestors and spirits.[42] Moreover, they experienced the ways in which French targeted power objects that contained agency and sacred forces, destroying shrines, and confiscating human remains and charms as destructive transactions.

Indeed, the concept of transaction brings better attention to the "things" that mediated exchanges. Whether French or African, people believed that circulating and exchanging assets (material and immaterial) was instrumental to domination. When a missionary confiscated the charms of a Christian convert, he diminished the power of the convert and attached new value to the object. In this case, the Gabonese believed that stolen charms added to the mystical capacity of missionaries. Here power resulted from the exchange, but was also the transacted item itself. This book will look at a number of instances where people, bodies, currencies, charms, and commodities entered transactions for mobilizing power, agency, and social reproduction.

In the context of colonialism, using the concept of transaction allows to see how, across the racial divide, power and capacity existed as relational realities produced by active or passive forms of exchanges. Colonialism not only worked as a field of power, where people battled for sovereignty and survival, but as a transactional field in which myriad of deals, exchanges, and transfers determined, each day, subtle or major reordering of hierarchies, status, wealth, and knowledge. In its rawest formulation, colonialism was enacted when Africans and Europeans entered in relation with one another, taking something and paying for the cost, or losing assets and survival options.[43] In the colony, more often than not, transactions were suffered as moments of loss and disempowerment.

Indeed, transactional imaginaries took a consistent dark side in colonial Gabon, making the Gabonese and the French experience the power of colonial rule in terms of *transactions gone wrong*. Soon, colonialists and the Gabonese imagined transactional dynamics as contaminated by harmful effects, reversing the flow of exchanges necessary to sustaining and reproducing life, and social orders. By the 1900s, the Gabonese believed that whites had significantly disrupted the normal circulation of spiritual gifts and social investments, and were feeding on the destruction of local charms and relics. They could still attack white people or try to avoid them, moving away from colonial stations, but as colonial forces increasingly saturated physical and social spaces, the Gabonese found themselves trapped in an economy of exchanges that forced unequal and extraordinary transactions upon them. Although spurred by specific historical factors, these dynamics resembled existing representations of destructive magic that blamed greedy individuals intruding in the flux of spiritual exchanges and reproduction. Ancient hopes for exchange and reproduction became fears of physical destruction, spiritual deprivation and social decline. The French (openly or secretly) lamented the deleterious effect of their rule, debating metaphors and projections that staged them, the colonialists, as forcing local people in lethal exchanges.

Transactions unfolded in the colony as a congruent imaginary: whether French or African, people believed that circulating and exchanging assets was instrumental to domination, to social survival, and to producing power and agency.

Transgressive Hegemony

This book suggests that, in the colony, hegemonic processes did not derive only from normative understandings and explicit opinions. Instead, they stemmed from Europeans and Africans' broken norms and betrayed principles, and their frightened, parallel recognition of them. These transgressions, real and imagined, were crucial for weaving hegemonic dynamics in the colony.

In the 1970s, English-speaking scholars hotly debated the notion of hegemony in the field of colonial history, asking whether any could arise between groups separated by considerable social, cultural, and linguistic differences, and split up by brutal coercion.[44] The Subaltern Studies group articulated the most radical critique of the concept in the colonial context.[45] Yet hegemony retained considerable traction, not least because it offered a relational and dialectical model of power that ask subtler questions in place of diagnosing the "collaboration" or "alienation" of African middle classes.[46] It also deconstructed colonial rule as a monolith, shedding light on the "productive weakness" of imperial domination.[47]

This book bends the idea of hegemonic processes further. Power relations in the colony were not just incomplete and uneven: they were also made of indirect recognitions steeped in the deviant and the transgressive. To my mind, it was precisely colonialists' inability to impose a viable fiction of symbolic authority across the racial gap—in short, to sustain a real hegemony—that left room for vibrant, if concealed and occult, interracial conversations about power and transgression. These exchanges throve in the realm of the unconscious, the inarticulate and the criminal. If some hegemonic formations failed in open alliances or disagreements, some could occur in mirroring feelings of guilt, desire, violation, and fright.

Better than language, lexicon, or idiom, the concept of the imaginary is able to convey how people inject social operations with meaningless, inverted, and sometimes destructive ideas and impulses.[48] This is the reason why, in this book, I pursue the history of power and agency in the "underneath" of domination, a term partly borrowed from Mariane Ferme in Sierra Leone.[49]

Although we know that colonialism worked as "a machine of fantasy and desire," we have failed to pay enough attention to the criminal, the delinquent, and the abnormal.[50] Although we study colonizers' and colonized's "regimes of truth," we assume that these programmatic agendas were mostly normative and constructive. As we insist on the projects, competencies, prescriptions, and desires of historical actors, we remain unaware of undercurrents of betrayal and remorse.[51] The forbidden, the faulty, the illegitimate, and the transgressive, whether they linger in people's repressed yearnings or become translated in practical action, remain unseen. Yet in the colony, hidden fantasies and fitful passions were not just abstract speculations; they were also conducive to physical and institutional interventions. Some passionate actions burst out in fleeting impulses, like the one overcoming a Catholic missionary in front of a pile of pagan charms he had ordered Gabonese converts to destroy, suddenly pushing him to steal a few.[52] The extraordinary profits that the French derived in the colony openly corrupted the moral norms that, back home, informed their political tradition.[53]

Africans experienced similar moments of guilt, transgression, and vulnerability. Witchcraft accusations often offer a glimpse into these feelings. One day in 1920, a grown man accused a twelve-year-old boy of cannibalism. He claimed that the boy had offered him a piece of meat from the forest and, allegedly, had asked the man "to give him somebody in exchange," implying that he wanted to taste human flesh.[54] The fate of the young suspect is unknown, but the historian can use his story to track how the language of witch hunger and cannibal yearnings suffused interpersonal tensions and conflicts.

Understanding colonial engagements means that we need to look, underneath everyday transactions and engagements, for the repressed emotions, morbid impulses, delinquent actions, and perverse yearnings that underpinned everyday forms of power and agency. Europeans and Africans also met in these neurotic and painful spaces, and thought fright, desire, denial, guilt, and remorse shaped imaginaries of power.

Terrains 1: Gabon and the Gabonese

In the early nineteenth century, the region now encompassed by modern Gabon was home to small-scale communities of farmers, hunter-gatherers, and traders. Cosmopolitan hubs and trading ports on the coast had been in contact with Atlantic traders since the sixteenth century. Throughout political and social changes, including the slave trade, local societies had long contributed to the celebrated "equatorial tradition," a set of social and cultural traits crafted by inhabitants of the western Equatorial African rainforest

Catholic and Protestant missionary outposts started to attract small groups of converts. After 1885, French military troops invaded and occupied the land, imposing forced labor and tax collecting on the territories they controlled.[62] By the early 1920s, they had managed to crush most of the large-scale armed resistances, executing or exiling local leaders. From then on, opposition to French invaders occurred mostly in isolated attacks and religious initiatives. The Bwiti cult rose in the 1920s as the largest and perhaps the most innovative spiritual movement of the time. Borrowing elements from local ancestors' cults and from Christianity, Bwiti offered healing and social reformation against colonial devastations.[63]

Meanwhile, French colonialists bundled up indigenous healing practices and beliefs under the negative concepts of *sorcellerie* (witchcraft) and *fétichisme* (fetishism). Ad hoc *indigénat* ordinances and decrees indicted healers and ordinary individuals who worshipped ancestors and used therapeutic devices. Although the French never recognized or codified *sorcellerie* (as British colonial legislators did with witchcraft ordinances), their attacks criminalized local beliefs and actions under this umbrella notion.[64] The colonial notion overlapped awkwardly with local ideas about *dogi*, the malevolent use of extraordinary forces that destroyed people for the egotistic benefit of an individual.

In 1910, the French attached the colony of Gabon to the Federation of French Equatorial Africa, and moved the federal capital from Libreville to Brazzaville.[65] The political importance of Gabon diminished. With perhaps 450,000 inhabitants in the aftermath of World War I, the colony had one of the lowest population densities of West and Central Africa. It specialized in products from the rainforest and the ocean.[66] Most white people resided in urban areas, in the capital, or in newly created outposts in the interior. In Libreville, Port Gentil, and Lambaréné, they lived near a majority of African urbanites, pushed to town by poverty in rural areas.

In the 1940s and 1950s, a black political elite schooled in French culture gained jobs in governing institutions, where they compromised on political alliances with white *forestiers* (timber plantations owners) and colonial bureaucrats.[67] After formal independence in 1960, many white expatriates remained in the country and continued to staff important economic firms and the national administration. President Léon Mba's influence, like the compositional tactics of most local politicians, relied on opportunistic deference to French interests, albeit with a dose of anticolonial communist training, the patronage of religious networks (Bwiti and Christian churches) and urban migrants, and territorial alliances throughout the country.[68] After 1967, his successor, Omar Bongo, refined the system in unprecedented ways. Hailed abroad for its political stability and relative wealth, the country suffocated in the regime's regional compromises and haphazard alliances to preserve itself, while failing to lift the bulk of the population out of poverty.[69] At the time of Bongo's death in 2009, Gabon was a rich nation with a poor citizenry, and a country ridden with grave social and political tensions.

Yet these tensions often operated below the purview of foreign observers. As sociologist Anaclé Bissiélo said in 2002, "Ideology drives people here. Conflicts are fought and solved in the realm of the ideological. And this is the realm that every Gabonese seeks to conquer."[70] Indeed, to weaken an opponent, defeat a competitor or explain some extreme vagaries of life, many people invoke "the domain of the night" (French: *le domaine de la nuit*) and the intervention of ancestors, spirits, magical experts, and witches.[71] Few politicians shy away from spreading rumors about their own special powers, or from gossiping that their rivals are witches. In 2008, Père Mba Abessole, a well-known opponent of the regime, publicly boasted that he was able to target President Bongo with "Kapa missiles," massive witchcraft attacks. In August 2009, André Mba Obame, a contender for the presidential election, overtly complained that he was the victim of a *fusil nocturne* (English: "nightly gun"; Fang: *eluma*), another mystical weapon that people can use against their enemies.[72]

Such stories are not abstract metaphors or figurative interpretations, alive only in the minds of people, and we cannot approach them as such. Rather, we must listen as people talk of embodied powers, "fetishes" (*fétiches*), and dreadful attacks that redirect peoples' lives, amalgamating long-standing beliefs in spirits and ancestors, witches and their organic-mystical force, new global figures of enchanted power (Mami Wata), the Christian God, its saints and nemeses (the Virgin Mary, the Very Bad Heart of the Devil, vampires), Western technology, knowledge, and money.[73] Neither remnant of precolonial ontologies nor the result of late global capitalism, these stories have been partly created by the Gabonese's engagement with the theories and technologies of power that French colonialists deployed in the colony.

Terrains 2: French Colonialists

At the end of the nineteenth century, Europeans had a long history of mutual interactions with people on the Gabonese coast.[74] The slave trade had brought many disasters in the region, yet they paled in comparison to the colonial conquest. Colonialists declared the inhabitant savages and the region legally vacant, and they devastated the land to an unprecedented scale.[75] Yet despite their victories and dominant status, white rulers remained quite insulated. The French government discouraged white migration to the colony, giving priority to indirect forms of economic exploitation on the ground. Most administrators stayed in Gabon for only a few years. Racial regulations severely restricted social mingling. From the neighboring colony of Moyen-Congo, the great chronicler Mary Motley recorded her feeling of frustration and restlessness in 1950: "This little white world turned inward upon itself . . . Africa was all around, pulsating, vibrant. But I could not reach it. I was looking at a landscape from behind a glass plate."[76]

Yet Europeans and Africans pursued considerable forms of intimacy and interaction, often in awkward and clandestine moments never free of power hierarchies. Up until World War II, most white men hired a Gabonese *ménagère* (a mixed concept between "housewife" and "cleaning lady") to provide them with domestic and sexual services.[77] Masters and servants, clients and suppliers, managers and workers interacted daily, and these interactions continued after colonialists' families came to the colony in the 1940s. White *forestiers* (timber industrialists), in particular, often came from mixed-race families and lived in close contact with their employees and surrounding communities.[78] In other groups, a range of socially sanctioned venues allowed Europeans to pursue myriad forms of economic and social partnership with Africans. In the 1950s, private settlers increasingly entered into political alliances with Gabonese activists and leaders.[79] In daily life, ideas, objects, dreams, and fantasies also circulated across racial barriers, making an intricate tapestry of conversations, monologues, orders, silences, incidents, thefts, gifts, contracts, hearsay, and performances that, to some extent, made colonial Gabon a single—if uneven—unit of experience and analysis.[80]

The people I call "colonialists" broadly included men and women who derived considerable privileges from their dominant position in Gabon. Because these privileges were based on the color of their skin and a sense of cultural rather than national superiority, these people called themselves Europeans (*européens*), more rarely colonialists (*colons*) or whites (*blancs*), and almost never Frenchmen (*français*). Most were male, and, to borrow from Luise White's expression, highly "peripatetic."[81] With the exception of missionaries, administrators, managerial employees, and settlers, civil and military servants never spent more than a few years in the colony. All together, they remained a tiny, if powerful minority in Gabon. In 1936, the administration counted 1,223 Europeans (among approximately 450,000 black inhabitants). They numbered perhaps 3,000 in 1950.[82] Among them, a few dozen white *forestiers*, owners of local lumber and mining companies, born in the colony and often married to Gabonese wives, constituted the most stable and rooted part of "European" families.

Frenchmen in Gabon—and even missionaries among them—thought of themselves as rationalists and secular thinkers, marveling at the scientific progress and industrial discoveries that proved their cultural and racial superiority.[83] Yet, alternative orders of causality and meaning provided rich undercurrents in their imaginary of power and agency. Like their metropolitan counterparts, enormous curiosity about spiritual matters and the capacity of the mind and soul agitated them. Many subscribed to esoteric institutions such as Freemasonry. They revered spectacular inventions equally: the power of steam engines, the magic of electricity, the energy of speaking ghosts, and the turning tables of spiritualists. On the eve of the conquest, in the 1880s, new findings fostered popular fascination with the marvelous and the irrational. Dr. Jean-Martin Charcot's public diagnoses of female hysteria at the Salpêtrière Hospital in Paris put neurosis at the core of modern identity. In 1894, Gustave Le Bon, who had claimed the superiority of white intelligence based on cranial volume, wrote an influential study that showed how "crowds" were moved by irrational emotions.[84] A few years later, the educated public could read Sigmund Freud's early works on the unconscious.

Life in the colony often forced these intellectual and moral contradictions to surface uncomfortably, sometimes surging in acute crisis. Although colonialists arrived with specific historical and cultural legacies, and a personal story, too, dealing with the Gabonese involved complex processes of recognition, acceptance, invention, refusal, and denial. Power is an ambivalent experience and is not confined to one side only: it is essential to the formation of the historical subjects who occupy various positions in society.[85] Colonialism was a regime of coercion, but also a regime of production of historical agents.

Writing through Gaps and Knots

Historians of Africa, like others, need to work through gaps and holes, tenuous evidence, and the fierce elusiveness of the past. Many of the imaginaries that I track in this book were not audible in open discourses or articulate doctrines. They operated in transient experiences and non-discursive forms, often crystallizing in denial, transposition, and projection. Some laws first came to life in volatile dreams and unruly legends: in 1923, colonialists passed a decree against Gabonese cannibalism that reflected a long history of obsessive prejudices, bathed in reminiscences about the witches' Sabbath and the recent European craze for novelistic vampires. Likewise, Gabonese speculations about occult power frequently appeared in accidental and impulsive frights. The increasing role of blood in charms and witchcraft, for instance, appeared in isolated, fortuitous episodes. In 1931, angry parents in Libreville accused a young man of making surreptitious cuts on their baby's knees to collect his blood and put it in a charm to become rich.[86] The scene resonated with earlier animal sacrifice and the use of human substances in charms, yet the blood was an innovation. The position of the suspect was also a new element: a friend of the family who visited daily, he was both an insider and an outsider, a liminal status that increasingly characterized how people imagined witches.

In seeking empirical groundwork for this book, I often found myself teasing out the poetic power of odd sources and eccentric findings. In the colony, imaginaries and the underneath of domination often crystallized in swift moments that left no tangible traces, or only faint ones.[87] Some appeared in fictions, stories, and hearsay, others only in visual representations. As much as I could, I tested my findings by cross-reading written archives (fiction, administrative reports, diaries, trials, and essays), oral histories, objects, and visual sources. Sometimes patterns appeared; sometimes they did not.

Other sources, by contrast, are thick with meanings and outbranchings. They seem to conceal a deeper idea, like a bulging lump of rope hiding a single, precious treasure. Yet in these lumps of time and reveries, no unique or absolute meaning exists, one that we could reach by cutting through. The knot is the meaning, one that we can extricate only by re-forming it, creating new ties of interpretation and sagacity. Look, for instance, at the following vignette (figure I.1) in Paul Du Chaillu's *Lost in the Jungle* (1875).[88]

Although the artist's drawing closely followed the explorer's narrative of the incident, that of a male gorilla killing an African hunter, it also built on the expectations of the European public. The vignette thus reflects broad cultural constraints that spanned across Africa and Europe. Yet local colonial imaginaries are present as well, and their layered and contradictory meanings show through.[89] Working like a primal scene, the vignette shows the fallen huntsman watching the wild beast bite apart his gun, an obvious symbol of emasculation and a representation of homoerotic desire for the lying figure of the black man.[90] Maintaining Africans at a distance, white people often depicted them as infantile and feminine. And yet they often projected their ego

I.1 "Gambo's friend killed by a gorilla." Engraving in Paul Du Chaillu, *Lost in the Jungle. Narrated for Young People*, New York: Harper & Brothers, 1875, 133.

upon them, and upon the great apes of the rainforest. Hence the engraving expressed at least three different fantasies: the desire to castrate Africans (the gorilla standing here for colonialists), the fear that Africans could emasculate and destroy Europeans (the gorilla standing for the Gabonese), and an ambivalent lust for lethal sexual intercourse.

The Gabonese archive abounds with similar scenes of transgressive domination and magical power, ripe with images and ideas, in which we can sometimes read the congealing of new imaginaries. The 1968 emblem of the ruling party (Parti Démocratique Gabonais), for instance, reveals how governing elites violently ensnare mystical power by destroying the life of other Gabonese. The image in figure I.2 reputedly features the hand of a murdered Catholic priest, complete with the ropes that had restrained him and captured his miraculous powers.[91]

The Gabonese tell the following story about the emblem: one day in 1968, Father Jacques, a Catholic priest of Fang origin stationed in the mission of Saint Francis in Lambaréné, went on a tour on the Ogooué River. In the house of an

I.2 Emblem of the Parti démocratique gabonais (P.D.G.), featuring a disembodied hand.

agonizing patient, a group of men jumped on Jacques and asked him to relinquish his priestly power so they could use it for their own agenda. After he refused, the men killed him, brought his body to the forest, and dismembered it. The investigation failed to indict any suspect, although the police found the priest's left hand in a smoking house. A few weeks later, Omar Bongo accepted the presidency of Gabon, soon changing the name and visuals of the ruling party. For the public, his promotion to the highest charge in the country could have been made possible only by securing the higher magic of the priest's tortured body. The party's emblem thus pointed at a changing imaginary of sacred power and severed body parts.

In this rich tapestry of fantasies and fears, full of chasms and knots, I have found that interpretative devices from psychoanalysis provide a helpful hand. I am not the first to use the method, or to ruminate about the risks and benefits of the approach.[92] An open, pragmatic use of such learnings does not flatten historical agents into undifferentiated psychic subjects: rather, it reveals the creative work of the unconscious (whether individual or collective) in circumstantial moments, as well as social pathologies, strategies of enchantment, and repressive modes of action.[93] Transgressive imaginaries often worked as desires and experiences "too shameful for words."[94] In chapter 6, for instance, I use the idea of "projection" when studying the cannibal and gorilla imaginary among colonialists. Similar methods suggested rich interpretations of debt and loss among the Gabonese (see chapters 2 and 7).[95]

A final word about the geographical and temporal scope of my sources: evidence for this book comes from the whole extent of modern Gabon, with occasional forays out into the broader region, specifically Congo-Brazzaville and Southern Cameroon. Between 1998 and 2012, I consulted archival materials in Aix-en-Provence, in Libreville, and in various missionary deposits, and I conducted six summers of field research in Gabon for up to seven weeks at a time. This tactic augmented my findings while letting me compare a wide range of symbolic patterns, social actors, and parallel histories. Focusing on a particular locale might have yielded a richer and more consistent harvest, but it would have run the risk of essentializing bounded cultural and historical entities. Nonetheless, the possibilities of localized history attracted me so much that I made four extensive visits to the province of Ogooué and Ngounié in 2002, 2006, 2007, and 2012. Chapter 2 presents the results of this work, mostly based on oral sources and field research in Lambaréné, Mouila, Fougamou, and Sindara. Many of my insights into the intimate textures of power came from media: watching TV, listening to the radio, and reading the local press, along with conversing with friends about the latest scandals and urban legends that never fail to spice up life in Gabon. I made extensive use of oral histories and interviews, and of multisited ethnographies in Libreville, the estuary region, central Gabon, and Ngounié Province.

Because imaginaries evolve unevenly and unpredictably, and because they are often traced in unusual clusters of sources and evidence, the book is not organized along a strictly chronological timeline. Instead, each chapter focuses on a particular stepping-stone in the history of power and agency from the 1860s to the 2010s. Chapter 1 traces how colonial technology replaced a water spirit in providing riches and power to communities in southern Gabon. Chapter 2 focuses on the power of fetishes, and looks at the ways in which the French and the Gabonese charged agency in physical containers, while investing them with multifarious value. Chapter 3 concentrates on the body as a key ingredient of power, investigating how human flesh became reenchanted at the crossroad of French and Gabonese tactics of power. Chapter 4 asks how the power of the body became priced in money, and how French perceptions of the value of the person articulated with Gabonese imaginaries of wealth-in-people. Chapters 5 and 6 delve into the imaginary of "eating-as-power," monitoring how Africans and Europeans reworked it into cross-racial ideas of cannibalism as failed reproduction. Chapter 5 looks at French cannibal discourses as an expression of major anxieties about the nature of domination and the doom of the colonial project. Chapter 6 uncovers the transforming of Gabonese power imaginaries of eating, and how procedures of "cooking the bones" of ancestors and kin became progressively replaced by unregulated acts of tearing up the flesh and drinking the blood of anonymous victims.

A Note on Sources

To avoid giving a picture of well-organized, organic empirical sources, I describe here how the materials supporting my narrative and argument came into place. My research seamlessly rose from my monograph on Gabon and Congo-Brazzaville from 1940 to 1964, which provided the empirical groundwork for this new project. I then visited, or worked again, in several archives. Three main sites preserve the written sources for the colonial period in Gabon: the National Archives for Overseas (Archives nationales d'outre mer, or ANOM) in Aix-en-Provence; the French National Archives in Paris (Archives nationales, or ANF); and the National Archives of Gabon (Archives nationales du Gabon, Fonds présidentiel, or ANG/FP) in Libreville. In France, the central archives of the former French Ministry of Colonies (or ANF) contain important documents on World War II in Gabon, including letters from the postal control in 1939–45 (Dossier 2097-2) and African requests for citizenship, as well as on French native policy (*politique indigène*), surveillance of political parties, and elections in the colony since 1945.

Then at independence, French authorities in Libreville triaged, destroyed, and repatriated some of their documents (called *archives de souveraineté*) to Paris. A smaller part of this shipment—mostly concerning elections and political parties—ended up in the French National Archives in Paris and Nantes (ANF). The larger portion, dealing with judicial, economic, political, and social issues, went to the ANOM in Aix-en-Provence. There I worked on the series 5D on French Equatorial Africa, and the H Series on Labor and Work Force (Travail et main d'oeuvre). The most important dossiers for this book included Intelligence on Individuals (dossiers 5D 211 and 214), Racial Discrimination (5D 253), Police and Intelligence (5D 247), Monuments and Commemoration (5D 183 and 254), and General Policy and Administration in French Equatorial Africa (Politique et administration générale). I found the richest material in dossier 5D 64, titled "Secret Societies" (*Sociétés secrètes*), which included fairly complete cases of investigations and trials on poisoning and witchcraft in Gabon.

But the French did not ship everything back to the metropole. Crucially, they left behind the huge archive that, across the entire colony, each district officer (*chef de circonscription*) produced about events, statistics, and daily life in their district. Now preserved and cataloged in the National Archives of Gabon in Libreville (ANG), these funds are more detailed than the syntheses the district officers regularly sent to the central colonial government in Libreville, and that were shipped to Paris and Aix-en-Provence after 1960. In the ANG, I consulted the following series in the Fonds Presidentiel (FP): administrators' diaries (*journaux de poste*) from 1924 to 1961, invaluable on the colonial perception of daily disturbances and the local atmosphere; the monthly and annual administrative reports on southern Gabon (Ngounié and Nyanga provinces); dossiers on native policy (*politique indigène*) from 1917 to 1960, rich with notes from police and infiltrators; dossiers on political affairs (*affaires politiques*) from 1904 to 1960; and dossiers on elections, prisons, police, native chiefs (*chefferie indigène*), and native petitions (*pétitions indigènes*). One of the richest funds for this book came from the series 1609 on the Organization of Native Justice (Organisation de la justice indigène). It comprises a significant—if uneven—series of judicial records from 1904 onward, abounding with transcripts on local investigations, interrogations of witnesses and convicts, witchcraft and tiger men trials, and conflicts over mystical attacks. In Libreville, another catalog, called "provincial archives" (ANG/*fonds provincial*), concerns the local documents of some districts that were sent in their entirety to Libreville after independence: I consulted those on Mitzic, Mimongo, Mouila, and Ndende.

The materials at the ANG, however, are characterized by internal unruliness: on paper, each dossier concerns a geographical or thematic issue. In practice, it contains a myriad of archives on various themes and issues. In a file, say, on political affairs in the district of Mouila between 1940 and 1950, one finds a haphazard collection of monthly reports by the district chief next to police notes, trial investigations, letters and petitions from Africans, and questionnaires on nutrition, epidemics, and fertility. During my three years of summer work at the Gabonese archives (1998–2002), I dug as broadly as possible in this rich material, organizing its treasures in thematic folders.

My archive on tiger-men murders in Gabon (chapter 6) shows how I built my own files from heterogeneous sources. First, I compiled judicial transcripts from the ANOM series 5d64, and the ANG/FP 1609 series on Organization of Native Justice (Organisation de la justice indigène). Other documents came from administrators' diaries in southern Gabon (ANG/FP 108), annual reports in the southern districts (*circonscriptions*), a report on a military tour in the district of Mekambo in 1924 (ANG/FP 112), handwritten transcripts of trials and the cross-examination of suspects and witnesses in several posts (ANG/FP 8, dossiers 303–4), monthly political and economic reports for the Ogooué maritime (ANG/FP 624), transcripts and papers kept in the dossier on Native Tribunals (Tribunaux indigènes, ANG 27), and prison rolls (ANG/FP 820). A couple of articles published in the *Bulletin de la Société de Recherches Congolaises*, along with documents in the Fonds Pouchet at the Holy Ghost Fathers' Archives in Chevilly-la-Rue (Dossiers 2D60–9a1 and 9a4) completed the file.

Missionary sources complement the official colonial ones. I spent several weeks at the archives of the largest Congregation in Gabon, the Fathers of the Holy Ghost (Pères de la Congrégation du St-Esprit), preserved in Chevilly-la-Rue, near Paris. The rich funds left by Father Pouchet (series 2D60), a missionary stationed in Gabon from 1935 to 1957, concern witchcraft, tiger-men, Gabonese Christians, and catechists. In addition, the Holy Ghost Fathers published an annual bulletin from 1889 onward, full of stories sent by missionaries in Africa, Asia, and the Americas, and destined to parishioners in Europe. Many of the anecdotes in the bulletin came from Gabon. Written as propaganda and often dramatized, these archives need critical reading. They nonetheless provide invaluable stories on daily routines and incidents at the missions, including evangelizing campaigns, the buying of young "slaves" by the fathers, events concerning pupils and schools, local rebellions, and the behavior of European traders and administrators. In Gabon, I also worked in the archives of the Sindara Catholic mission, generously provided by Father Zacharie Péron, and in some of the municipal archives of Mouila. The final portion of my written sources came from the local press: *Liaison*, the monthly review sponsored by the government for the *évolués* of French Equatorial Africa (Afrique Équatoriale Française, or AEF), where African authors published fascinating studies of local customs, generational conflicts, and aspirational stories from 1950 to the early 1960s; the historical journal *La Semaine de l'AEF*, founded in 1955 as a platform for the new African politicians, still running today, and some of the more recent titles in the Gabonese Press (*L'Union, Le Bûcheron, Le Nganga*, etc.), collected on site during my field research.

If this project starts in the mid-nineteenth century, the cornerstone of the book, emphatically, is the present. It is grounded in my time in the field, and people's current experiences with power and agency. From 1998 to 2012, I spent six summers in Gabon and one in Congo-Brazzaville doing field work. These moments were crucial to my understanding of mystical agency and the imaginaries central to the history of (post)colonial domination. I did participant observation, talking with healers, patients, informants, and various local actors, and transcribing information and conversations in notebooks, usually later at night. Not all of these interactions had to do with my research. On the contrary, I learned most in casual conversations with friends and acquaintances about daily life, and the many social, political, and personal grievances that they shared with me. I also worked many hours with colleagues and friends at the Université Marien Ngouabi in Brazzaville, and Université Omar Bongo Ondimba (OBO) in Libreville, including the students that took a graduate seminar with me in 2012. There, my learning was of a different nature, professional and cutting-edge, pushing me to absorb my colleagues' original, provocative, and insightful analyses. The most productive collaboration has been, and still is, with sociologists Joseph Tonda and Patrice Yengo. It has ended up in several publications and ongoing projects, and has nurtured my thinking about many issues tackled by this book. Last but not least, my education came from watching TV, listening to the radio, looking at advertisements and cartoons, and listening to the jokes and puns that people in Gabon delight in sharing. Boredom was a great teacher, too, bending my mind and body to the special rhythms and frustrations of daily life in Gabon.

A profoundly historical deity, Murhumi has been central to the lived experiences of the people in Mouila, we soon realized: the slave trade, the commerce in foreign commodities, and the power struggles of the colonial conquest.[5] Today, her rich lore works as a critical conservatory for *puissance*, a central component of power in modern Gabon. If in English *"puissance"* is an archaic term for power or prowess, here it encompasses long-standing beliefs in the capacity of people to harm and heal, to "see" spirits and ancestors and use their divine forces, to produce kin and allies, and to master the production of material goods. *Puissance* can also define the brainpower of "complex" people such as academics or politicians, and it can be economic, based on the resources of affluent persons. Its deep historicity means that, as a complex imaginary of power, *puissance* arose from long-term changes and reconfigurations: it now includes the technical expertise used by Westerners and French colonialists, what the Gabonese call the "science of the manifest" (*la science du visible*), while retaining aspects of "the science of the invisible," the local techniques, to harness power.

SIRENS

At the time of our visit, Murhumi agitated a great many controversies. The main lineage in the city, the Dibur-Simbu, claimed her as ancestor.[6] "[The] family owns the Mami Wata. Her name is Murhumi. She is the genie who belongs to the family, the Dibur-Simbu clan. She is the belly-womb of the family [*le ventre de la famille*] (the female ancestor of the family)."[7] Many generations ago, they said, Simbu, a beautiful and shrewd female, had founded Mouila; after her death, she had revealed herself to be the river spirit Murhumi. Some, however, expressed doubts about the capacity of the spirit to provide them with material goods and protection. Other inhabitants challenged Murhumi on political grounds, contesting the urban preeminence of the Dibur-Simbu and laughing the spirit off as a "fish" and a scam. During my subsequent trips to Mouila in 2007 and 2012, a shrine dedicated to Murhumi stood empty on a quiet plaza, the statue of the spirit missing (figure 1.1). Perhaps, people explained, the effigy had been stolen or destroyed, or perhaps a former prefect of the region kept it under lock. Meanwhile, municipal documents bore Murhumi's emblem—a black mermaid with a two-pronged fishtail (figure 1.2)—while other signs exhibited her as a white Mami Wata holding a book (figure 1.3).

Such traffic in images betrayed high insecurities in the vernacular imaginary of Murhumi and local *puissance*. Rare apparitions of the Siren herself struck people with fears of impaired vision, astonishment, and silence. During a foggy night, a young female informant told us, her stepbrother had encountered the Siren on the bridge over the river. Overpowered by the vision, he

1.1 Murhumi's empty shrine in the city of Mouila, Gabon, 2007.
Photograph by the author.

had recognized only her back, her fish tail, and the long hair around her silhouette. The shock left the young man unable to move for several minutes.[8]

A few days after our arrival in the city in 2002, a member of the municipal council asked us to follow him to the city hall's basement: leaning on the dusty wall of a small room, Murhumi glistened on a heavy board of precious wood, quietly raising her arms in distress (figure 1.4). Our guide explained that the ring around her tail signaled wealth. Her three tresses recalled the style of Punu ceremonial masks. Her raised elbow, however, signaled a "weakness in her kin."[9]

Murhumi's transfigurations and disappearances, this chapter argues, illuminate how Gabonese people imagined and harnessed power. In southern Gabon, agentive capacity rested on a transactional economy that exchanged material goods for immaterial agency and transmuted immaterial forces into tangible riches. In the eighteenth and nineteenth centuries, communities carried out such ritual exchanges with nature spirits. During the Atlantic trade, a period of intense economic competition, spirits helped clans and lineages to secure control over territories and commercial markets. The arrival of European firms in the nineteenth century undermined this political economy. In the twentieth century, colonialists entered the field of sacred agency as major

tlntic trade

1.2 A double-tailed siren as the city emblem of Mouila, 2012. Photograph by the author.

1.3 Murhumi as a Mami Wata holding a book, 2007. Photograph by the author.

1.4 Pierre Nzengui, bas-relief wooden statue of Murhumi, 1964. Photograph by the author.

experts and operators. By the 1960s, immobilized in a wooden statue and flimsy print media, Murhumi entered what I call a "crisis of symbolic uncertainty," characterized by major dilemmas about the role, the location, and the manifestation of sacred agency. Once managed through secret exchanges and invisibility, *puissance* depended now on manifest tools and representations. Once based on the capacity of the invisible spirit to produce material riches, puissance now rested increasingly on visible magic, in the forms of cash and human body parts. Once vested in the whims and elusive force of spirits, it was now handled by "white" men and ruthless "slaves," both notions I will clarify later in the chapter.

Exchange and Prosperity in the Eighteenth and Nineteenth Centuries

Economically, the south is the second poorest region in Gabon, dependent on extractive activities (lumber and mining) managed by foreign firms that little benefit local people. Almost 60 percent of the population lives in poverty, and only one household in five has access to potable water.[10] Yet in the mid-nineteenth century, the region had been among the richest and most populous of West Equatorial Africa. To reconstruct this history is vital for assessing the decline of local prosperity and, during the colonial era, the downfall of vernacular systems of production and exchange. But it is also crucial for understanding the early importance of the transactional tactics that people long exercised in the region. Central to this history was the role of nature spirits and the transactions that local people conducted with them to produce social and material riches (the second mostly as iron tools). The narrative will regularly center on the spirit Murhumi and the iPunu-speaking clan and subbranch that claimed her as an ancestor: the Bumweli and the Dibur-Simbu. After these groups arrived in Ngounié Valley in the late seventeenth century, they proved particularly skilled at using the nature spirit to claim sovereignty over farmland and, later, over rich commercial nodes. They later represented the most important part of the African population of Mouila.

When we visited Mouila for the first time in 2002, signs of economic stagnation were everywhere. A ghostly aura emanated from public buildings: erected during the brief interlude of the oil boom, they stood in empty plazas, weathered by dust and humidity. Downtown, a modest market offered food, plastic wares, and secondhand clothes. A few grocery and furniture stores manned by West African and Middle Eastern migrants clustered at a couple of crossroads. At lunchtime, the blazing sun forced the city to standstill. Only night-fall brought it back to life. Softly lighted by petrol lamps and coal fires, the sidewalks bustled with people who paused at the stalls to buy bread or cassava loaves for the evening meal. Young people chatted outdoors with friends, while older men congregated in bars for beer and music. TV screens flickered from living rooms where electricity worked.

The city was awash in cell phones, but until 2012, my third and last visit, it remained impossible to find an internet café and connect to the World Wide Web. Isolation and the plight of transportation provided endless topics of conversation. During two overland trips to Mouila in 2007 and 2012, I learned that an average truck took up to six hours to negotiate the first stretch of dirt roads from Libreville to Lambaréné, the capital of Ogooué Province. After spending the night in Lambaréné, travelers boarded a taxi or a truck to cover the last 330 kilometers to Mouila, a leg that could take up to seven hours.[11] The dense rainforest canopy of Chad Mountain, forty kilometers south of Lambaréné, hid highway bandits. Nervous passengers told me stories of a famous highway gang in the late 1990s, led by a young *métis* (the French and Gabonese term for people of mixed race) who ruthlessly robbed and killed passers-by. The road itself was dangerous, its crevices often running deeper than the height of the vehicles trying to pass through: "Politicians eat the money of the road, they eat all the subventions. They take the money and they don't suffer for it, they just do what they please with it. The rest of us, we are the "diminished" [*les diminués*], we are the oppressed [*les opprimés*]. . . . The road is what blocks everything."[12]

The contrast with the prosperity of the region at the end of the eighteenth century is striking. At that time, the "egalitarian uncooperative people" of Ngounié Valley benefited from a constant circulation of persons and riches.[13] Mixed farming provided subsistence food: men cultivated manioc, taro, plantains, and yams on the rich soil of the forest, and secondary crops on the thinner grasslands.[14] In the villages proper, women tended banana orchards and kitchen gardens. Game and forest products came from Babongo forest specialists (later named "pygmies" by explorers and colonialists), who exchanged them for crops and wares. Babongo allies also helped farmers to secure protection from the deities of land and rivers. Among clans and residential units (villages), intricate alliances and movement of people combined with a pronounced taste for competition and equality. In some locales, such attachment to autonomy and rivalry was so accentuated that villagers preferred to build a meetinghouse (*mbánjá*) for males in each family compound rather than a collective one for the entire village.[15] Virilocality and matrilineal descent fostered alliances and the circulation of individuals: wives moved to the houses of their husbands, but their children belonged to their (the wives') mothers' clan. Initiation societies encouraged cooperation across villages and districts. The most important of these associations were called Mwiri (Ghetsogho: *ya-Mwei*) for men; and Njembe for women. At the level of districts, individuals with special skills and insights served as therapeutic and judicial experts: they communicated with ancestors and spirits, healed illnesses and misfortunes, and took care of land resources by planting defensive charms to replenish barren grounds. In this fluid context, public authority followed the ebb and flow of big men and prominent families who competed for dependents, influence, and riches.[16]

The farming technique of slash and burn meant that villages had to move regularly to new grounds. The fertility of Ngounié Valley attracted significant migrations in the seventeenth and eighteenth centuries. The story of the powerful clan Bumweli, who came from the south and owned the water spirit Murhumi, shows how migrations occurred. The original ancestor of the group, Mweli, was a *fumu*, or great man, who lived in Niari Valley (Republic of Congo). The migration of the clan had followed an acute crisis of kinship alliance and transgression. Mweli's niece, a young woman named Simbu, eloped one day with a suitor named Ndombi, who had promised to give her some land controlled by his own clan, the Dibamba-Kadi.[17] Searching for the illegitimate couple, Mweli set out northward with his hunter-gatherers. He established a string of villages on the left side of the Ngounié River, and decided to rest for a while in one of them, named Bonda.[18] Meanwhile, he sent his pygmy scouts across the river to explore the right side of the stream and establish a temporary post at Mukuma. There, Mweli finally caught Simbu. The confrontation went well, and Mweli charged the young woman to occupy new land for the sake of the clan.[19] The details of these early foundations are important to know, as they contradict the later claims of the Dibur-Simbu that they were the first to settle in the locale. Simbu first transformed Mukuma into a proper village that she renamed Idumi. Pushing northward, she established colonies in places previously controlled by Apindji- and Ghetsogho-speaking clans.[20] Together with her husband, Ndombi, she gave birth to children who started two new matrilineages for the Bumweli: the Dibur-Simbu (children of Simbu) and the Bandombi (children of Ndombi).

At the time of the Mweli and of Simbu's migration, a clan (*kanda*) worked as a corporate unit of several matrilineages (*mabur,* or *divumu*) linked by a common origin story.[21] Mostly indifferent to territorial charts, clans crossed geographical distance and linguistic communities.[22] In the eighteenth century, however, a new idiom of ~~territorial seniority~~ recognized that "first-comer" clans, who had first settled in a locale with the help of forest specialists and nature spirits, "owned" the land. The idiom created discrete political divisions between "mother-villages" and "daughter-villages" that had formed later.[23] Owning a locale did not work in a merchant or capitalist sense, rather rights on land remained loose, collective, and decentralized. After a few years, the leaders of the senior clan often allowed junior villages to manage land duties such as dealing with newcomers and managing relations with forest specialists.[24] [→ Clans stopped moving and settled –]

The new idiom of territorial authority was anchored in the spiritual realm. Spirits (iPunu: *mughisi*; pl. *baghisi*), meanwhile, had to approve of, and collaborate with, villagers. *Mughisi* were attached to the sky, rivers, and land, although they could also move from place to place.[25] The spirit Tsumbu resided in the Blue Lake, upstream from the Ngounié River. A deep brook nearby was inhabited by a fairy named Mukani Mbabou.[26] Spirits resented human intrusion and would attack swimmers or fishermen who disturbed them.[27] "[*Baghisi*] inhabit rivers, mountains, caves, or the sky. Nobles and gracious, they hate dirtiness and strong odors."[28] If one encountered a spirit on firm land, one had to run away fast and throw something nauseating to stop the spirit in its tracks. To secure spirit protection over human settlements, villagers performed elaborate cults: "Their cult takes the form of a collective procession carrying cooked dishes. The attendants carefully bathe and wear white clothes. They put elaborate dishes on large tree leaves [and leave them by the spirit's lair] so they can quiet down the irritated [*mughisi*]."[29]

Once spirits accepted the collaboration with local clans, they helped them to assert genealogical identity and control over territories, and became incorporated in domestic politics. Although historians often draw a sharp distinction between spirits and ancestors (*dímo*), oral traditions often tell how one was confused with the other. The Dibur-Simbu often say that Murhumi became the new avatar of their ancestral mother Simbu, whose cadaver was transfigured into the water deity after she willfully sacrificed herself for her children.[30] Another Punu tale of origin collected in 1986 illustrates such flexible overlap of spiritual beings. Once upon a time, Ufura Sema, a barren woman who belonged to the Bandombi clan, had tended her plantation and planted pumpkin and gourd seeds. At harvest time, a spirit visited her in a dream. He ordered her to collect the calabashes in her field, except one that grew near a tree stump. The next day, Ufura cut the pumpkins, sparing the fruit designated by the spirit. A few nights later, the genie reappeared and asked Ufura to visit the field. There she heard a loud whistle coming out of the remaining calabash, followed by an explosion. In the pumpkin's debris, Ufura found a newborn, a gift of the genie, whom she adopted as her daughter. The baby grew into a healthy woman who bore many children and ensured many descendants to her mother. In recognition of the miracle, the matrilineage took the name of Dibur-Cuva (children of the calabash).[31]

Transacting Iron

In the Ngounié Valley, where Simbu and her children had settled, ironware and metal tools were the main form of material riches.[32] To obtain them, people needed to enter into a spiritual economy of transacting gifts and countergifts with nature spirits, crafting powerful formulas of exchange, at once economic, technical, social, and spiritual. Metal objects themselves reinforced this transactional cosmology; besides commerce, they facilitated social exchanges such as the payment of bride price, initiation fees, and judicial fines.

Trained metalworkers produced most of the metal locally. Inhabitants of southern Gabon had mastered iron technology as early as the second millennium BCE, and by 500–150 BCE, smelting pits were everywhere.[33] The technology was always submerged in spiritual intervention.[34] Among the Dibur-Simbu, ritual experts left raw iron ore for Murhumi on the riverbank. Under cover of night, she magically transformed the metal into finished tools.[35] The following description strongly associates the feat to the prosperous times before colonial rule:[36] "One leaves some charcoal and iron ore. The next day one finds machetes, tools, everything. This was before the coming of the Whites (*avant les Blancs*)."[37]

Because of the intervention of spirits in iron smelting, blacksmiths trained both as technicians and as potent spiritual experts.[38] They protected the forge with strict prohibitions, forbidding the presence of women and uninitiated youth. If a menstruating person touched the furnace, for instance, the blacksmith interrupted the work until he could perform a cleansing ceremony.[39]

In this economy, rituals and offerings enabled the spirit to perform iron technology for mankind, while humans sacrificed social wealth to obtain material goods. Indeed, the inaugural gift demanded by the spirit to furnish iron tools was the life of a distinguished member of the community. Communities also turned to sacrifice during times of extreme crisis. In the nineteenth century, for instance, under incessant attacks from Kele slavers, Ghetsogho-speaking communities resigned themselves to sacrificing their best. Senior families gave a prized female to ancestors and spirits, executing the young woman; elders then burnt her body to ashes, mixed the dust with ritual white clay (*pèmba*), and smeared the bodies of the warriors to make them invisible to the enemy.[40]

The episode insisted on how the magical medicine had rendered the warriors invisible. In local languages, to "see" was loaded with spiritual undertones—in iPunu, the verb for looking, *ulaba*, echoed with learning and knowing: *udjaba*.[41] While the gaze of the innocent and the uninitiated floated only on the surface of things, powerful *nganga* (experts) had "four eyes," one set for the world of the living, the other for "the night," the metaphor for the realm of spirits and ancestors. Spirits throve for secrecy. They needed invisibility and unpredictability to conduct their magical operations, tolerating only the expert vision of high initiates to produce riches. The mystical/material production of iron was also replete with visual trickery, deception, and competition between experts. In southern Gabon, farmers knew that they had stolen iron technology from indigenous forest specialists, the Babongo.[42] A Dibur-Simbu tale recorded the robbery in a mystical lexicon of deceit and visual fraud: One day, a group of Babongo men equipped with metal tools wandered near a lake to gather wild honey. One man inadvertently let his ax fall in the water. He saw the tool lying on the sand, quite close to the surface. Deceived by the vision, the hunter tried to retrieve his property and drowned. One after the other, tricked by the spirit of the lake, all his companions fell into the water and died, sacrificed by the spirit. As the story concluded, the Babongo were "finished" (*ils sont finis*), replaced by Punu blacksmiths.[43] Incapable of "seeing" the deep water, they had sunk in as ultimate offerings to the spirit.

In 1867, traveling near a large market by the Ngounié River, Paul Du Chaillu heard similar warnings about Fougamou, the blacksmith spirit that lived next to the nearby rapids. Fougamou had long worked with local experts to make iron tools, transforming the ore and charcoal they deposited on the riverbank into finished weapons and tools. One day, however, a man and his son could not fight a burning curiosity to see the spirit's magical smelting. After leaving gifts on the riverbank, the father hid in a hollow trunk, the son behind the boughs of a tree. After a while, Fougamou arrived with his son and began to work. Suddenly the son exclaimed, "Father, I smell the smell of people!" "Of course you smell people; for does not the iron come from the hands of humans?" replied the father. So they worked on until the son complained again of the pungent aroma of human beings. Then Fougamou looked round and saw the two men. Roaring with rage, he transformed the father into a termite hill and the son into a nest of black ants.[44] "Smelling" the trespassers was akin to seeing without eyes and penetrating what remained hidden to the ordinary gaze. Submerged in visual metaphors, the story spoke of secrecy indispensable to the magical transforming of iron ore in finished tools, opposing the innocent and toxic gaze of intruders to the pregnant invisibility of spirits and experts.

When Du Chaillu heard about Fougamou's wrath, however, new transactions in social and material wealth were taking place in the region, short-circuiting the role of spirits and blacksmiths in producing iron.[45] Indeed, selling slaves to Atlantic traders was now securing local communities' access to commodities and material riches. One version of Fougamou's story hinted at the shift, as it replaced the father and son with two slaves named Samba and Magotsi. The new commerce undermined the protective and productive role of experts and local deities, even if the mysterious origin of imported ironware added to their aura as extraordinary riches coming from the realm of mystical forces. Foreign traders could pass for magical experts in touch with faraway forces. Selling a person resembled the sacrifice that opened up the circulation of riches. But the social devastations of the slave trade soon evoked suspicions that destructive and unrestrained witchcraft (dogi) had been unleashed. Instead of elders conducting relatively rare sacrifices, witches were merely killing people over and over to facilitate undeserved profits.[46] Even the cheap, imported iron that flowed into west central Africa was a problem, putting forges out of business and undermining the regime of esoteric knowledge and complex transactions flowing between experts and spirits.[47] Once rare and holy, ironwares lost their central role in organizing social hierarchies.

The Atlantic Era

Yet during the era of the slave and legitimate trade, from the 1780s to the 1870s, the need for the territorial sanction of nature spirits endured, along with the relevance of the transactional formula that traded social wealth (people) for material riches (commodities). Some benefited from the new trade, their material wealth multiplying. New routes opened north of the Loango Kingdom, the former commercial power, and traders brought massive amounts of commodities in the form of sea salt, fish, iron machetes, knives, cloth, guns, mirrors, and cooking vessels that they exchanged for ivory, palm nuts, and captives.[48] Ambitious clans grouped in commercial clusters. On the upper stream of the Ngounié River, at the end of the road to the slaving port of Mayumba, a market emerged where the spirit Fougamou had crafted iron tools. In memory of the two slaves he had struck down, the market took the name of Samba-Magotsi. By the early nineteenth century, four large villages were supplying traders and their families with warehouses for commodities, barracks for slaves, and residences.[49] The prosperity of the locale soon attracted thieves and bandits. Kele-speaking newcomers settled on the left bank of the Ngounié and specialized in attacking river convoys to Samba-Magotsi. Later, Fang-speaking clans overtook the thieving business, displacing the Kele further upstream.

During the same period, the corporate unit of the clan served as a powerful tool of social and economic expansion, grounding the claims of local communities in territorial and sacred politics.[50] South of Samba-Magotsi, the powerful Dibur-Simbu and Bumweli became particularly adept at these tactics. Mukuma-Idumi, the village founded by Simbu, became a major commercial node on the Ngounié River. There, hundreds of families and firms traded in slaves with middlemen coming from the coast. As firstcomers, protected by the spirit Murhumi, the Dibur-Simbu controlled the river traffic and the routes to the Atlantic, adding economic to ideological preeminence.[51] Yet iron was now obtained with slaves, and water deities hardly appeared in the transactions anymore: "Ndinga [a Punu trader] said, 'We, the Bapunu, we prefer to get slaves.' The Mitsogho answered: 'We, too, are hungry for merchandises.' . . . Among the Mitsogho, there is nothing but slaves to exchange, so, you, the Bapinzi, if you have some merchandise, give it to me. And the Bapinzi took the merchandise and gave it to Ndinga. And Ndinga the Punu took the merchandise."[52]

New tactics of clan expansion used slaving and marriage to incorporate dependents. Slaves, by definition, had no other clan than their master's, and the masters could assert undisputed control over them as wives and offspring. Marrying female captives into rich households allowed rich men to accumulate offspring, and saved them from dealing with in-laws. In the early nineteenth century, matrimonial competition between clans became rampant, forcing weaker groups into matrimonial alliances and enslavement. A violent repertoire of "domestication" provided a double-entendre for enslaving and marrying: "This is how we encountered each other, the Mitsogho and the Bapinzi [Apindji]. We met for trading, for the commerce of commodities. It is in this context that we married the Bapinzi . . . The Eshira tribe [Gisir] was the one that liked to domesticate [domestiquer] others. The Eshira domesticated the

Bapinzi. The Bapinzi came to domesticate us, the Mitsogho. We, the Mitsogho, went to domesticate the Masango. Yes, and we also went to domesticate the Banzabi."[53]

Material riches seemed indispensable to survival itself, not simply social betterment. Despite the human cost of the trade, Mitsogho elders in the 1970s remembered enslaving kin as a process of civilization and humanization. Ironware and salt from the coast, they explained, had made them "true men" who could forgo the archaic technique of braising food over coals. Imported objects became so indispensable, they added, that they were willing to give some of their own kin into slavery in exchange.[54]

Ambitious clans could also marry spouses to their rivals, a process described as "eating" or "swallowing" (*dia*) the other clan. Since children belonged to their free mother's family, "bride-clans" soon outnumbered and controlled "husband-clans." The very name of the powerful matrilineage of the Dibur-Simbu gives a hint of this. In iPunu, *díbúrà* (pl. *màbúra*) means the branch of an original clan but also the children of a captive female.[55] Thus the figure of Simbu conjoined a noble woman, a spirit, and a slave. The Bandombi, for instance, the lesser lineage issued from Simbu's husband, managed to give many wives to their powerful in-laws, the Dibur-Simbu and the Bumweli. After a while, they obtained control over land located between the Dugundu and Ugeju Rivers, where they founded two villages, a process explained by today's informants: "Simbu and her pygmies built the villages of Luanga and Mutodu. They gave them to their in-laws, the Bandombi."[56] The volatile expansion of clans and material accumulation of the late eighteenth and early nineteenth centuries thus rested on domestic strategies and kinship alliances that used the slave trade to further expansion.

The End of Prosperity

From the 1870s onward, the transactional technology operated by spirits and experts disintegrated. By 1900, independent, indigenous long-distance trade in the Ngounié had ceased to exist. Colonial rule soon put social reproduction itself in danger of breaking down. The history of this demise, perhaps unique in Gabon, is the last part of this historical reconstruction: it is an important step to understand the transformation of local imaginaries about riches, spiritual expertise, and social transactions.

In the 1870s, European, Senegalese, and coastal Gabonese factory agents arrived en masse in southern Gabon. In 1875, 600 of them traded in Ogooué and Ngounié Valleys.[57] In contrast to independent Gabonese courtiers who worked in local markets by advancing capital and goods to partners and directly benefitting from commercial profits, they were waged employees.[58] Pushing inland, factory agents created a massive zone of turbulence in the region.

Instead of the caravans of old, the agents relied on steamboats that could carry tons of cargo inland on the Ogooué, Nyanga, and Ngounié Rivers, stopping at factories where huge crowds of customers waited for them to exchange rubber, ivory tusks, ebony wood, and beeswax for imported goods. These included cotton cloth from Manchester, red wool hats, pearls, tobacco, guns, gunpowder, rum and gin, crockery, and inexpensive perfume. Among the most desired items were those made of cheap metal: small bars of copper and lead, copper plates (*neptunes*), knives, machetes, scissors, and cooking pots.[59] In exchange for these products, in the 1870s, the British firm Hatton and Cookson alone shipped twenty thousand pounds of rubber from southern Gabon every month.[60] Foreign agents did not stop at the main river stations. They went in canoes to reach faraway customers along tributary streams and smaller lakes, directly competing with short-distance traders.[61]

Meanwhile, the French put increasing pressure on local and regional societies. In 1887, officers closed the slave warehouses at Cape Lopez and Mayumba operated by local kingdoms, and destroyed the salt factories that provided the main currency for smuggling captives from interior markets.[62] By 1890, they had dismantled the vast network of local traders, middlemen, and intermediaries that had prospered in the region since the late eighteenth century.[63] During the next decade, 1890–1900, the French government, eager to exploit conquered territories but short on funds, gave huge chunks of land to concessionary companies in exchange for exploiting local resources and collecting taxes. Privately owned by stockholders and charged to administer local populations, the companies enforced *corvée* (forced) labor and collected taxes in kind (rubber and ivory).

The system created immense zones where extractive violence reigned unchecked. In 1893, the Ngounié Valley was included in the huge concession (104,000 square kilometers) of the Société industrielle, commerciale et agricole du Haut Ogooué (SHO) in central Gabon.[64] Company agents started to operate on the ground in 1897.[65] Well funded and diligently organized, the SHO created numerous outposts staffed by commercial agents and African militias recruited in West Africa. Agents offered local customers generous credit lines, but when people paid the debts with local products, the agents undervalued the goods, effectively charging exorbitant prices. The militias stole goods from competing middlemen and confiscated their canoes. They extorted rubber from local communities by taking hostages, burning habitations and fields, and beating recalcitrant producers.[66]

Indigenous clans fought back, accentuating the economic and demographic downturn of the region. From 1903 to 1913, Ghetsogho-speaking and Punu-speaking clans rose against French outposts and concessionary companies, halting the depredations for a while. In late 1903, a Ghetsogho war leader named Bombe killed a couple of white managers of a small concessionary company, the Société de la Haute Ngounié, renowned for their cruel behavior. Soon the revolt spread down to Ngounié Valley, involving Pove-, Sango-, and Apindji-speaking clans.[67] In May 1904, a French officer and sixty black soldiers arrived in the seditious zone and established a military post where the city of Mouila would later stand. After a difficult campaign, the French finally captured Bombe in the summer of 1908. He died a few days later in the prison in Mouila, at the headquarters of the French army, but the rebellion continued undaunted. The French escalated their actions, building two new military stations (at Koulamoutou in 1912, and Mbigou in 1913). Punu-speaking clans, meanwhile, had risen in the southward triangle of Moabi, Ndende, and Tchibanga (1906–9). In 1907, the French troops had received instructions from Libreville to destroy rebel villages as well as fields and food.[68] By 1913, this scorched-earth tactic had destroyed the remnants of the riches and opulence of the past century. It had also crystallized powerful prejudices among the colonials against the South. For years to come, they blamed the "laziness," "nomadism," and "fetishism" of the locals.[69]

Prosperity continued to decline. World War I pushed workers in French-owned timber camps into the lakes region and along the Ogooué River.[70] Male absenteeism and a chronic deficit in births reduced many villages to naught. Even subsistence production dwindled, resulting in malnutrition and epidemics. During World War II (1939–45) half of the adult male population labored "for the administration," a euphemism for mandatory *corvée* on roads and in the plantations managed by state-sponsored Sociétés indigènes de prévoyance.[71] Those who refused were rounded up and sent to prison. In Sindara, the adult male population of 3,200 spent 1,260 days in jail in 1944 alone.[72]

In the aftermath of World War II, the Ngounié was on its knees. The toll of economic extraction, migrations, famines, and forced labor had broken social and biological reproduction. In many places, the population was barely half the size of what it had been in the nineteenth century. The rate of decline was staggering. In 1949, a discerning district officer in Mbigou reported that in the last fifteen years, the population of his district had declined by 60 percent.[73] In 1951, a report for the same district evaluated that the local Apindji had been reduced to one-thirtieth of their number in the nineteenth century, and that a third of the Mitsogho had vanished since 1946.[74] By 1960, the region had become an impoverished, marginalized backwater of independent Gabon.

Hatred and Exchange in a Colonial City

In this landscape of devastation, some people sought refuge in colonial outposts where markets and employment opportunities concentrated: Mouila and Fougamou on the Ngounié River and, further south, Ndende. In these nascent cities, social status and advancement depended on colonial institutions. Mouila remained a white town (*une ville de Blancs*), a bastion of French power since its origin as a military fort. In 1901, a Frenchman named Drille had built a small warehouse made of bamboo to trade with local clans.[75] In 1904, the colonial troops sent to crush local rebellions established their camp near Drille's residence: a fortified prison and barracks for officers rose as the first buildings *en dur* (in stone, bricks, and concrete). Suspicious of local communities, French officers demanded that all Gabonese who walked by the post "salute" it, or perhaps the flag in front of it.[76] The presence of foreign power was ubiquitous and severe, its roughness declining little until independence in 1960, and giving new shape to local imaginaries of power.

The French controlled commercial exchanges, metal goods, commodities, colonial currency, and local markets. They also wielded new forms of technological might and even a clear ascendency over nature spirits. Once the magical interference of a spirit slowed down a road construction site manned by forced laborers by covering the daily clearings with wild plants and bushes. But after a few days, a white officer set a trap on the road and caught the genie responsible for the deed, and work resumed.[77] Access to riches now mostly depended on colonial rulers, who acted as powerful experts. But it was unclear what they demanded in exchange, and the meaning of their transactions with the other world remained obscure. The French refused to enter into domestic and political alliances with indigenous clans. Their demands for taxes, labor, and submission were brutal, and they refused to compensate locals for them, emphasizing the nefarious side of their *puissance*.

In 1923, Mouila became the capital of Ngounié Province, further centralizing French colonial power in all its forms: disciplinary, economic, cultural, and biomedical. The residence of the governor of the province, the tribunal, the prison, schools, and medical dispensaries materialized the domination of the new rulers. Nonetheless, Gabonese migrants flocked to town, pushed by famines and the collapse of local economies. At first, few opportunities were available. Administrative jobs remained out of reach, as the French hired clerks from other parts of the colony, categorizing them as "foreigners" (*étrangers*). After a while, however, locals found cleaning and sentry jobs in the white residential district and administrative bureaus.[78] In 1950, two hundred of them worked for the administration.[79]

The concentration of services slowly fed the growth of the city. In 1938, a large and modern hospital replaced the old dispensary. Headed by a military physician, presumably French, the hospital was staffed by a handful of African doctors and nurses, and a larger team of hygiene agents and midwives.[80] That same year, a radio station opened in Mouila, and, in 1939, a small airport.[81] In 1940, the city rose to national and federal prominence: for six months it was the capital of the Free French Forces marching from Congo-Brazzaville against the Vichy-loyal government of Gabon led by Governor Pierre Masson.[82] In 1957, the decline of the historic mission of Saint-Martin-des-Apindjis, founded in 1880, prompted the Catholic Church to name Mouila the seat of the archbishop of southern Gabon.

Two secondary schools, one public and one Christian, opened, respectively, downtown and in Val Marie on the left side of the river.[83]

Despite their power over the city, the French remained a tiny minority. In 1951, only fifty-one "Europeans" lived in Mouila among about ten thousand black residents.[84] Most worked as administrators and officers. The rest were private *colons* who managed stores, transportation businesses, and plantations.[85] They wallowed in prejudice against locals. Civil servants often saw a position in the Ngounié as a form of relegation to the imperial margins, at the very least, an inglorious rung in one's career. They saw the province as a backward corner of Gabon, its population rampant with disobedience and full of concealed hatred. African residents, a political report explained, regarded the French with a mixture of "arrogance and pathological suspicion."[86] The opinion justified colonials' own contempt: "To be sure, we have never been confronted with races so impermeable and of such low intellectual level. We find here, I think, a confirmation of Darwin's theories. In over a hundred years, these races did not adapt, and they have remained opposed to our methods."[87]

Racial acrimony was particularly high among the increasing number of *petits blancs* (petty, or poor whites). Impoverished by the global economic recession of the 1950s, they disparaged the southern Gabonese as lazy, *amorphes* (amorphous, inactive), and uninterested in official events.[88] A few Catholic priests regularly appeared in colonial records for insulting or beating African parishioners.

In the economic slowdown after the war, racial frustration came out into the open. In Ndende, the second-largest city of Ngounié Province, the archives are full of reports on the bankruptcy, debts, tax evasion, and reckless behavior of petty whites. In 1955, for instance, two Frenchmen who earned a modest living as hunting guides kept fighting with each other and with local people.[89] The district officer arrested one of them, Ernault, for insulting an African guard named Athanase Doumboubadi. Doumboubadi had come to Ernault's residence to present a subpoena. Ernault, crushing the paper and throwing it away, shouted insults and violently pushed the guard, throwing his hat across the street.[90] He was later sentenced to a fine. In the smaller post of Lebamba, many whites lived in poverty, competing for a meager slice of economic profit. In 1956, two white "tramps" crashed the post. One of them, twenty-six year old Léon Teixeira de Mattos, was arrested for vagrancy and embezzlement.

The Gabonese mocked French territorials by naming their cruel or ridiculous streaks. In 1930, the colonial Rougemont earned the iPunu name Mitongou (Stick). His successor, Tastevin, was nicknamed Moudokou (the Thin Pole). In 1947, MacLatchy's sobriquet, Makonongou (the Elbow), derided his habit of walking with bent arms. In 1951, people called the territorial Da Costa Boulambata (the Slapper), and his district chief Malangui (the Drunkard).[91] The arrival of low-paid employees of the gold mining firm SOREDIA further damaged whatever respect colonialists enjoyed among local Africans. Political reports noted a new, "low-level," and persistent "hostility" against the French rising among the local *évolués* who worked in civil services.[92] After independence, white French expatriates retaliated by scorning the personnel of the new independent state.[93]

Throughout the twentieth century, colonialism had brought unprecedented devastation and decline to local people. Yet, even on the eve of independence, French domination seemed unshakable.

"Mupunu Ibamb": If You Do Not Seek the Company of the White, You Are Finished

Secretly, underneath the separation and hatred, some clans infiltrated colonial institutions to build power in the city. They collaborated with the French, engaged with the new ethnic grid of politics, and utilized spiritual anchors to claim territorial antiquity in town. By the 1920s, the newly minted "Punu" tribe and its senior clan, the Dibur-Simbu, emerged from these battles victorious over other clans. Their newfound dominance rested on modern *puissance*: a composite array of power tactics that wedded white hegemony to an older spiritual repertoire. The proverb "Mupunu Ibamb" encapsulated the move, playing on words. *Ibamba* (pl. *bibamba*) means a white person in iPunu, and resonates with the verb *wubambana* ("to get closer," "to seek protection"). The proverb above can thus translate as both "The Punu is white" and "The Punu seeks the protection [of white people]."[94]

The Punu were in some senses created by French misunderstandings of local dynamics and their remapping in terms of that misunderstanding. French administrators knew that clans existed but saw them as meaningless units compared to their own taxonomy of "tribes," ethnic groups, and "races" (French: *tribus, ethnies*, and *races*). They understood tribes to be mini-nations with a single body of authority, a single language, and a discreet territory.[95] When the template clashed with what they observed on the ground, French territorials blamed the disruptions of the slave trade and colonial warfare. By the 1910s, they set out to "reconstitute" *ethnies* of old by grouping inhabitants around a single vernacular language.[96] Around Mouila, they discerned ten major tribes: the Punu (pl. Bapunu), the Tsogho (pl. Mitsogho), the Eschira, the Apindji, the Massango, the Bakélé, the Vumu, the Eviya, the Lumbu, and the Fang, and fixed them on neat administrative maps (map 1.2). The template obscured the dynamic migrations, intermarriages, and alliances that had long characterized clan polities and residential units, forcing clans to map themselves on to the permanence and graphic existence of ethnic territories.[97]

Before the colonial conquest, Punu-speaking clans had remained concentrated around Idumi, south of Mouila, the original village and commercial center created by Mweli and his niece Simbu.[98] The West or right side of the Ngounié River, where Mouila would later stand, had been inhabited by Ghetsogho- and Apindji-speaking communities. Starting in the 1920s, colonial charts obliterated this historical presence, bringing the newly minted Punu as the "first settlers" of the area in and around Mouila, and displacing "Tsogho" and "Apindji" tribes on the left bank of the river.[99] The grid was in utter contradiction with the history of migrations in Ngounié Valley. In 1920, further reorganizing benefited the Punu, enthroning them as the main urban interlocutors of the French.[100] Colonial rulers divided the Mouila and its peri-urban district into four cantons, each led by an African *chef* (chief), each unit named after the largest ethnic group they contained.[101] The largest canton,

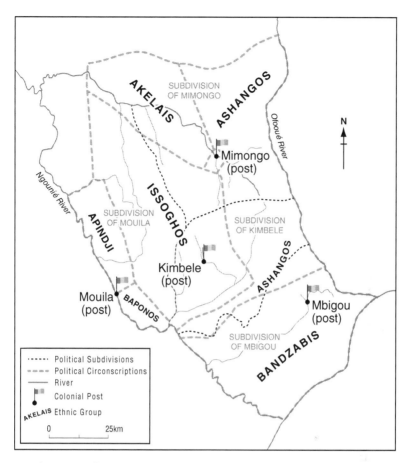

1.2 Ethnic map of Ngounié in 1916, based in an original map titled "Répartition des groupes ethniques" (Distribution of ethnic groups), hand-drawn and signed by the chef de circonscription de l'Ofooué Ngounié, Titault, 15 January 1916, ANG/FP 633.

under Punu leadership, included the city of Mouila. Three more (Vungu, Apindji, and Mitsogho) comprised the suburbs and the rural areas.[102]

Indigenous clans, Ghetsogho- and Apindji-speaking, did not fight the elevation of the Punu. Instead, they pursued escapist strategies that unintentionally furthered the rise of their Punu rivals. After their defeat in Bombe's war in 1913, rebel clans retreated from the area controlled by the French military. Apindji-speaking clans retreated on the right, or east, bank of the Ngounié River. Ghetsogho-speaking clans regrouped further away to the east of Kimbele, the rebellion's headquarters in the steep hills of the Chaillu Massif; they established *mpidi*, or forest encampments, where they could cultivate manioc and seek respite from colonial pressures.[103] But the French pushed them to the brink of extinction: militias impeded the mobility of farmers and destroyed *mpindi*, while taxes, *corvées*, and punishments depleted land and men. In 1947–48, the Mitsogho population barely reached 1,300 in the broader province, compared to the more than 3,700 Punu residents in Mouila alone.[104] Ignoring their role in the changes, the French interpreted the demographic vitality of the Punu as a sign of political strength. They described the dying tribes (Mitsogho and Apindji) as "awkward" and "full of savagery," ranking them well behind the more "resilient," "dynamic" and "interesting" Punu tribe.[105]

The few Tsogho and Apindji inhabitants who had stayed in Mouila became quickly absorbed in the growing sprawl of the city. I became aware of their history after developing a relationship with Mitsogho informants in Mouila in 2007. Invited to meet the *evovi* (judge) and village chief, Léon Ghetombo, and a group of Ghetsogho elders in the village of Divindet, in the outskirt of Mouila, I drove there one afternoon in 2007. The first encounter took time to warm up. The older men did not seem to care a bit about my questions, whether about the spirit Murhumi or the history of Mouila (figure 1.5). Out of despair, I confessed that so far I had only heard the story of Mouila from a Punu perspective. Although I was interested in the spirit Murhumi, I said, I had learned about the great rebel Bombe, the famous Tsogho warrior, and noticed that no monument celebrated his memory in the city. Suddenly, the ice thawed. With recollections of Bombe, a real exchange started, enlivened with questions, riddles, laughter, and admonitions.

The defeat of the Mitsogho, the elders told me, came in part at the hands of members of the Dibur-Simbu branch of the Punu-speaking clan who had infiltrated colonial institutions. They bullied the Mitsogho, chasing them from colonial sites of learning and power: "The Punu served the French. They slighted other ethnic groups. They used the *chicotte* [whip]. They stole the roads. The

1.5 Tsogho judge (*evovi*) and the council of elders, Divindet
(near Mouila), 2012. Photograph by the author.

Punu went to school, so they take everything [*ils s'accaparent*]. When the Mitsogho went to school, the Punu beat us. So we did not have access to school development. Those among us who could bear such bullying made it. Those who could not bear it returned to the village."[106]

The main battle occurred in the realm of mystical agency and spiritual empowerment. In the words of the Divindet elders, the Punu tribe had broken down the *puissance* of the Mitsogho. My interlocutors used a repertoire of blinded vision and deprived eyesight to explain how missionaries, colonials, and African converts (the Punu) had made them, mystically as much as socially, *lesser* members of the city: "The Catholics were the most dangerous. They wanted to go around [*contourner*] people and the tradition. They wished to close people's eyes in order to steal their *puissance* and bring it to Europe.... We are not poor, we are only 'lesser' [*moindres*], because we respect all the taboos."[107]

Sometime during the colonial period, *puissance* had become a core concept of power, a composite amalgam that included new and older forms of capacity. It included both the older ability of experts to transact protection and riches with nature spirits, and newer technologies by which people got access to material prosperity. With the term, the Gabonese also profoundly engaged

ιith the pantheon of the new God, combining indigenous skills in attacking
ωr healing individuals with the miracles of the Christian saints, and the nefarious strength of Satan. Older lexicons of agentive power survived. In iZèbi,
for example, magical talents were called *mavaande* and *bikooke*. *Lenzangue* or
ndoghe meant the ability to work in the night, while *mundoghe* was a simple
curse. People used *misaambe* to talk about the oral skill of managing debates,
and they called riches *mabwè*.[108] In contrast to this rich but circumscribed vocabulary, *puissance* was a catchall term, a flexible, generic concept straddling
indigenous and Western forms of power. In Mouila, mystical *puissance* and
social status remained inextricably linked.

In 2007, during my second visit to Divindet, my interlocutors also explained how the beautiful Simbu, the ancestral mother of the Dibur-Simbu
matrilineage, had played a central role in annihilating their *puissance*. During
the rebellions of the early twentieth century, Bombe had sought to form an
alliance against the French. He approached Nyonda Makita, the leader of
Punu resistance in the southern part of the Ngounié, around Ndende. The
two men agreed to collaborate, and decided to seal the coalition with a mari-
tal union. Bombe agreed to marry Makita's sister, a young woman named
Simbu. He brought her to Otenbo, the Tsogho settlement where Mouila
now stands, for the wedding. Many of her kin, calling themselves Mweli and
Dibur-Simbu, followed the young bride to her new residence. Sometime
after the wedding, however, Simbu betrayed her husband: she placed a cord
around his neck and "finished" his *puissance*. Now reduced to a slave and a
captive, the powerless Bombe was delivered to the French post, where, after
a few days of imprisonment, he died in unexplained circumstances. Thus my
informants pushed the later notion of *puissance* back into the early twentieth
century, replacing other vernacular terms for capacity and power in their historical memory.

Powerscapes and *Puissance*

Borrowing from African and European investments in the physical and mystical
dimension of the city, *puissance* worked as a core component of urban politics,
saturating the landscape with political, economic, and social agendas. "Powerscapes" is the name I give to such historical alignment of architectural and
immaterial forces in town.[109] The notion redirects attention to the ways in
which symbolic and spiritual power is wedded to physical space, encouraging
us to read the city in a different way.[110]

Beyond rationalized processes of inequality, marginalization, and social engineering in African cities, scholars have rarely looked at urban space as imbued with ideological and spiritual meanings.[111] Here I focus both on "rational" and "spiritual" tactics used by people to anchor ideological and mystical forces in the landscape. In the colonial context, the powerscapes that resulted from and produced these meanings often differed from racial residential patterns and the apparent logic of colonial domination.

At first sight, French monuments and infrastructures in Mouila served the agenda of colonial domination. The central cemetery built in the 1920s forced Africans to bury their dead in racially separated areas. The large hospital campus opened in the 1930s, and organized colonial biopower by gathering patients in hygienic wards, scrutinizing diseases, and applying biomedical science to cure them. Emptiness was full of meaning, too: the absence of any official trace of Bombe, the Tsogho rebel, spoke loudly, and only the stubborn stockiness of the prison walls, where he had met his defeat and death, met the gaze of urban residents.

Underneath colonial authority, however, the urban grid of the city helped the Dibur-Simbu to assert the antiquity of their presence, disqualifying other clans. Looking at the cemetery again, we can see that they made immediate use of colonial urbanity to anchor spirits and ancestral graves in areas saturated by French power. First, the Dibur-Simbu claimed that a large forest grove behind the colonial cemetery sheltered the graveyards of their ancestors. They called it Mouila Mangondu, "the Invisible Mouila," declaring "Mouila u labe—Mangondu u gholabe" (You will reach Mouila but you will never find Mangondu).[112] Second, they moored strategic sites with the aura of vernacular deities and in particular, their ancestor Murhumi: "Other people, they have their genies in the village, but not in the Ngounié River, or in Mouila.[113] According to their narrative, the water spirit had even allowed the Dibur-Simbu, as firstcomers, to welcome French colonialists in the land:

> When the French came, the Dibur-Simbu consulted Murhumi to know whether the white people should stay. In agreement with the villages on the other side of the Ngounié River, they collected the money of the Whites. They put the coins in the water as an offering to Murhumi. If she t[ook] it, it mean[t] that the Whites must go. . . . The next day, the money was still on the riverbank, near the government building. Therefore Murhumi approved of the Whites. The Dibur-Simbu from both sides of the river shared the money of the foreigners and allowed them to stay.[114]

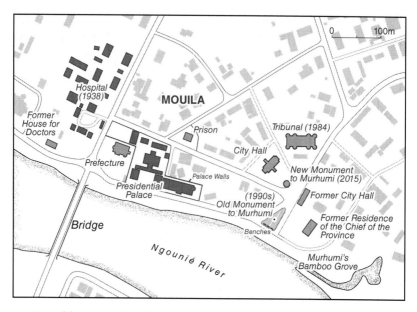

1.3 Map of downtown Mouila, 2018.

A small beach on the right side of the river served as Murhumi's traditional abode. Shaded by a bamboo grove, it stood right underneath the residence of the French governor of the province (*chef de region*), fastening Murhumi to colonial powerscapes [figure 1.6]. It also rested a few yards from the landing of the river ferry, associating the spirit with the safe crossing of the river. Thus settled in town, the spirit retained key elements of its previous functions: caring for its children, facilitating access to goods and wealth, and protecting travelers across the Ngounié River. For some time, it retained its extraordinary quality of invisibility and secrecy: living in town as a volatile and capricious spirit, and appearing to devotees in dreams or abrupt apparitions.

In this environment, ritual experts and clan elders continued to manage older forms of spiritual capacity. Young Élise's great-grandfather, Ndinga Mougoungou, was such a man.[115] He performed miracles, inscribing his ritual power on the city's powerscapes. Once he joined the two sides of the city across the river and changed the topography of the land: "Ndinga Mougoungou could swim underwater to talk to Murhumi. He was able, before the bridge was built, to cross the river seated on a mat.[116] Sometimes he stayed sitting on the mat on the water for a whole day, as if he was on firm ground. One

1.6 Photograph of the bamboo grove reputed to be Murhumi's den, 2012.
Photograph by the author.

day, he told the Dibur-Simbu: to show you that I am your chief, I will make
you witness how my urine can dig up a river. And indeed, this happened."[117]

Soon, however, white *puissance* undermined the efforts of Murhumi and
her allies to shape the powerscapes of the city.

Crises of Symbolic Uncertainty

One day in late 1959 or early 1960, Mrs. Tailleur, the wife of a French territorial administrator, spotted Murhumi in the river.[118] She alerted her husband,
who grabbed a camera and took a picture of the spirit. Inhabitants of Mouila
recalled the amazing vision: "Mrs. Tailleur saw her with binoculars; Mr. Tailleur saw her with a photograph." Astoundingly, the water spirit did not retaliate against the trespassers. Something else happened: the gaze of the camera
ended the power of the spirit. Breaking with older regimes of mystery and
concealment, the photograph made the water spirit unable to disappear at
will. The Tailleurs had converted Murhumi from a spirit to an image, something flat and something powerless. The incident opened a new era, one that
recognized white people as the new mediators with the spiritual world, a
realm they sought to expose in plain sight.

Visual instruments had long enabled the French to convert things and people in images. The deed reversed the formula that converted the secret agency of invisible spirits into metal tools. Here a metallic contraption fixated and disempowered invisible forces. In the 1960s, binoculars and cameras still evoked a register of colonial ambush.[119] Shooting landscapes and uneasy crowds had long furnished the French with leisure and a rite of domination. In 1930s Brazzaville, Madame Reste, the wife of the governor of Congo, liked to round up native children during photographic expeditions in Brazzaville. While the juvenile subjects waited, terrified, she disappeared under a black cloth and shouted directions at her assistant to "make the kids look natural."[120] In Gabon, a 1948 decree mandated that all persons over sixteen needed to carry an identity card with a picture, address, tax records, and employment information, entrapping Africans into a bureaucracy of paper.[121] The card also meant that all Gabonese had to procure and pay a photograph for the document. The rule benefited colonialists: in Ndende, a colonial bum named Fernand Maquelle made good money by taking identity photographs for African customers.[122]

A few months after the incident, working from the model taken by her husband, Mrs. Tailleur had cut out sheets of plywood to look like a Western mermaid. On 18 August 1960, the day of independence, she posted the silhouettes of "Murhumi" on the main avenues of Mouila. A few months later, the Tailleurs left the country. In a gesture interpreted by the Dibur-Simbu as a theft of *puissance*, they took the original photograph of the Siren with them. To retain an effigy of Murhumi, the municipal council decided to commission a young artist, Pierre Nzengui, to create a sculpture of Murhumi. Nzengui used Mrs. Tailleur's cutting to carve a beautiful bas-relief of the Siren in precious wood (figure 1.4). Completed in 1964, the statue was set up on a small stele built on the government plaza.[123] Now condemned to appear in public to all, initiates and noninitiates, kin and nonkin, the Siren experienced further duplication. Soon, the city adopted Murhumi as its official emblem. From municipal letterheads to commercial signs, hundreds of similes representing a mermaid diffused across town (see figures 1.2 and 1.3). By photographing the secret realm of the "night," the Tailleurs had started a new spiritual economy characterized by mass visibility, traffic in images, and a new permanence of presence.

The spirit's effigies were characterized by their two-dimensional nature. Even the statue sculpted by Nzengui looked more like a bas-relief than a traditional statue (iPunu: *itumbe, kosi*). Although unique, the wooden figure has come to occupy an intermediate zone between a powerless image and a power-object charged with *puissance*. The fact reflects the ambivalent status of pictures in West Equatorial Africa. In the Kongo kingdom, the effigies of Catholic saints worked as potent charms able to perform miracles.[124] Three hundred years later, however, the power of images became uneven and weak. In the Democratic Republic of the Congo, owners of Mami Wata paintings consider them as a kind of ex-voto, and a protection against evil.[125] In Brazzaville however, people consider the statues of saints carved in the likeness of local inhabitants to be powerless.[126] In Lambaréné, wandering in the empty buildings of the Catholic mission of Saint François Xavier in 2007, I stumbled over statues of catholic saints represented as Africans. Left to rot in the veranda of a peripheral building, none seems to attract much devotion or desire (figure 1.7).

These differential beliefs partly relate to the Gabonese perception that white people have higher spiritual powers. The remarkable indecision of Murhumi on paper is a case in point. On official letterhead, she is a black mermaid, but on commercial signs, she is white. Black, she symbolizes the endurance of old regimes of power but also the Gabonese's doubts in the ability of vernacular spirits to mediate access to riches. For local informants, the white "science of the manifest" (Fr.: *science du visible*) defeated the vernacular "science of the invisible" (Fr.: *science de l'invisible*).

The transformation of Murhumi from invisible and potent spirit into a flat, empty statue reflects how she has lost capacity to convert sacred and invisible forces into tangible objects and material riches. People wonder if Murhumi's statue is a simple symbol (a representation of the spirit with no intrinsic power), or if it is a charm charged with capacity. Murhumi's original agency worked at the interface between secrecy and materiality, immateriality and tangibility. As a blacksmith deity, the spirit created material assets out of incorporeal components. The technology was similar to a *travail symbolique* (symbolic labor) of endowing material objects or concrete situations with symbolic meanings. Social beings, as Lévi-Strauss and many others have argued, are constantly busy producing symbolic sense from the physical world in which they are immersed.[127] In precolonial Gabon, when blacksmith spirits shaped and worked the iron ore into a finished object, they added value, usability, and meaning to raw matter. The exchange needed to be mediated with regular offerings between experts and the spirit, and needed to be covered by secret knowledge and invisibility. In turn, offerings to the spirit, a person or other gifts, became dematerialized, sometimes transforming into protecting figures of the night. It is precisely at this point of mutability that the Tailleurs,

1.7 Wooden carved statue of a female saint abandoned on an outdoor terrace at the Catholic mission of Saint Francois Xavier in Lambaréné, 2007. Photograph by the author.

by ossifying Murhumi in photographic images, undermined her potency. Caught in visibility and permanence, the spirit lost the capacity to triangulate exchanges with vernacular experts, to create riches, and to add symbolic meaning to objects.

In this *crisis of symbolic uncertainty*, beliefs in Murhumi's productive capacity have become highly ambiguous. Among Mouila residents, her lifeless avatars now elicit mostly feelings of stolid absence and haunting emptiness. Meanwhile, white experts have hacked the transactional formula that used to secure riches and protection for the Dibur-Simbu.

A Bridge and a Shrine

This crisis of symbolic uncertainty reached a peak in 1976. That year, the opening of a bridge over the Ngounié River demonstrated that white people's *puissance* could invade the last remnant of the spirit's iron technology: the boundless open waters of the Ngounié River.

1.8 The bridge over the Ngounié River, 2012. Photograph by the author.

After independence in 1960, the municipal authorities had decided to better connect the two sides of Mouila, and upgrade the old ferry passage to a modern bridge. They commissioned a European firm to inspect the banks of the Ngounié and find a suitable site.[128] The engineers decided on a site located near the ferry route and the sacred den of the water spirit Murhumi.[129] The firm anchored six pairs of struts in the river floor, topping them with horizontal beams on which they laid a paved road with sidewalks, railings, and streetlights. The new bridge allowed hundreds of cars and people to cross the river day and night (figure 1.8). Murhumi ceased to appear in the Ngounié River.[130] The Dibur-Simbu blamed the mystic "polluting" of the water by the new bridge, along with some fish nets installed in the river by a white man. The old ferry went out of business, and the miraculous reed mat on which Ndinga Mougoungou used to float across the river survived only in the memory of Dibur-Simbu storytellers.

The assault on Murhumi, however, did not entirely contradict older vernacular technology. Indeed, by accelerating the mobility of people and riches and offering new access to manufactured goods, the bridge replicated the largesse and protective power of local water spirits. The Dibur-Simbu, moreover, could symbolically insert the triumph of the white mastery of iron into a historical continuum: that of the technological shifts that had seen hunter-gatherers, then Punu farmers, succeed one another as ritual specialists. The logic of the mythical sequence, and the substitution of experts, remained pregnant among modern informants. In 1986, a member of the Dikanda clan explained to historian Monique Koumba. "The pygmies are our whites, because they know so many things."[131]

The construction of the bridge, moreover, differed little from Murhumi's ritual formula of production. It relied on what Marcel Mauss defined as "technique," a practical application of knowledge that brings about expected outcomes, or an "efficacious action."[132] White people in Gabon did not necessarily understand the underlying principles of modern science and technology. Indeed, when, in the late nineteenth century, they had brought firearms, steel boats, and ferries, and later, bicycles and cars to West Equatorial Africa, the pragmatic recipes that they used with the devices were grounded in scientific causes that, for most, remained, inexplicable. Few grasped the deeper working of the material forces they mastered by proxy; the physics of electrical fields, magnetic waves, or photography remained a mystery for most. In the loopholes and gaps of white "mastery," local ideas about spiritual agency could anchor enduring explanatory power.

The true revolution introduced by white experts concerned the discernibility of sacred agency or, as people explain today, *la science du visible* (the science of the manifest). Where Murhumi worked in the shroud of the night, white engineers labored in plain sight. Where Murhumi provided tools that waned and wore out, the bridge stubbornly stands in the river, forever altering the urban landscape.

A few years after the completion of the bridge, the defeat of the spirit materialized in the design of her new municipal shrine. The architectural language of the monument, indeed, promised to ruthlessly expose the statue to the gaze of the public. At night, the wall where the statue should hang was bathed in the electric glow of the city lights and faces away from the river. Moreover, the shrine's concrete platform and the decor in white ceramic tiles resonated with the ornaments found on the nearby bridge. The protective cage around the shrine, in wrought iron, was painted in the same blue hue found on the bridge railings.

Yet, where the bridge successfully connected the two sides of Mouila, the shrine proved unable to revive Murhumi's *puissance*. Its rhetoric of detention, impaired vision, and powerlessness could only trap her effigy in maximal exposure. For this reason, perhaps, the Dibur-Simbu never dedicated the monument. The statue languished in her lonely basement in city hall, leaving the empty shrine to rust and wear down.[133] Murhumi had deserted her children, leaving behind a hidden statue and a lost photograph.

Sirens and Saints

Today, Murhumi survives only through her partial fusion with figures of foreign power: "Murhumi is white, she has the body of a woman, and her lower part looks like a skirt [*pagne*], not really like a fishtail. She raises her arm to comb her hair."[134] Surrounded by the markers of Western might, she has coalesced with a Mami Wata, a Siren, and the Virgin Mary, figures of motherly protection and nefarious harbingers of commodity desire.[135] Histories of religious hybridizing in Africa often start with separate and discreet bodies of belief that later combine and blend. But Murhumi emerged in fields of power already traversed by dynamics of mutual influence and cross-fertilizing. In West Equatorial Africa, people have long envisioned vernacular capacity as a substitute or complement for white power. Saints, spirits, witches, and mermaids worked together or alongside as providers of riches and misfortune.[136]

The accumulative metamorphosis of the water deity started early. On the coast, people called water spirits *imbwiri* (sing. *ombwiri*). Perhaps as soon as the seventeenth century, *imbwiri* began to fuse with white traders coming from the sea to bring precious commodities in exchange for slaves. Thus anthropomorphized, they filtered inland, sometimes through tales told by factory agents and missionaries. There, they confronted indigenous spirits, or *mughisi* (iPunu). *Mughisi* had no precise gender, nor anthropomorphic traits.[137] They came to plague a person during a time of sickness, prompting the patient to seek a diagnosis from a ritual specialist and to observe a period of initiation and apprenticeship. After this, the afflicted person became able to work with her spirit to divine, diagnose, and cure.[138] Some of these traits changed in the nineteenth century, when the Ngounié entered into intensive contacts with the Atlantic. In the 1880s, Trader Horn reported an anecdote that allows a glimpse into this process. During a trip to the Ogowe River, Horn noticed a white woman sitting by the rapids and drawing a sketch of the landscape on paper: "The natives thought she was trying to break the *ambwini* [*sic*]—putting the white god against the black. They were uneasy, they'd never seen a lady sketching. . . . I had to let the natives understand I thought it was the usual things for ladies to do."[139]

The posture of the lady, next to the water, demonstrated that she was herself a *mughisi*. For local observers, pens, paper, and guns went hand in hand with white people's ability to trade exotic riches and gaze through the secrets of the night. After the 1900s, the circulation of mass-produced advertisements and pictures showing figures of exotic *puissance* in the form of white mermaids, snake charmers, and women equipped with mechanic tools reinforced the sight of white women.[140]

In Gabon and West Equatorial Africa, Mami Watas embodied the passage to the Atlantic era and the transfiguration of the vernacular spirits who asked for people in exchange for material riches.[141] They never became subject of a cult regulated by initiates. Elusive and dangerous creatures from the underworld, they borrowed their modus operandi from the older pantheon of heroes, ancestors, and spirits, appearing to people in unpredictable visions and fugitive dreams.[142] By fusing with Mami Wata and sometimes with Mère Mambu, a rich, older and single female spirit, Murhumi captured the destructive and lethal aura of the predatory capitalist system. To see them was an omen of riches and power, and a promise of social death: in return for money, one must offer a person in sacrifice. Mami Wata barred her devotees from bearing children or having sexual relations. Mère Mambu worked with dangerous and powerful snakes, a symbol of sexual power and riches. After she copulated with them, they vomited money for her.[143] Although it is difficult to reconstruct a precise timeline for the fusion, Murhumi probably became "white" as early as the 1920s, when a missionary record described the "harmonious physiognomy," "white skin," and "long black hair" of the water spirits worshipped in Ngounié Valley.[144] The transfiguration manifested painful ruptures. Where Murhumi worked with initiated and powerful ritual experts, Mami Wata could be seen by anybody, including the uninitiated. Where Murhumi asserted the genealogical identity and divine origin of the Dibur-Simbu matrilineage, Mami Wata worked as a free-floating genie, impervious to social relations and aggregation.

Perhaps more unexpectedly, Murhumi's fusion with the Virgin Mary reinforced the ambivalent nature of the spirit. Entangled with Atlantic wealth and commerce, Catholic saints had a long history of mingling with local pantheons in Kongo and Angola. In the sixteenth and seventeenth centuries, they primarily served the political ambitions of the ruling elites.[145] In the nineteenth century, however, Catholic and Protestant missionaries associated them more closely with popular worship and material offerings. As Jan Vansina reported about the Kuba kingdom: "Missionaries were not charismatic ... they did not wander around the country to proclaim the faith to all and sundry with the help of translators. Rather, they acted like traveling businessmen representing corporations."[146] This certainly was true in southern Gabon. The five Catholic missions established between 1883 and 1900 explicitly deployed commodity appeal to attract converts.[147] In the late 1890s, the expedition that settled on the site of the mission Saint-Martin-des-Apindjis boasted thirty-five porters and numerous boxes of foodstuff, commodities, and medical goods. Nearby villagers paid the missionaries "incessant visits, burning with curiosity to look into the boxes, and to examine all the objects."[148] In 1907 in Sindara, Father André Raponda-Walker confided that the Mitsogho always welcomed him with the question "O kéa na sawtété gomi? To gnongéo motété." (Where will you establish a factory? We want to do commerce.)."[149] Soon however, the converts experienced what Joseph Tonda coined as a form of "material confusion" (*malentendu matériel*).[150] With little material or spiritual compensation to offer, European priests requested that Gabonese Christians relinquish social assets such as wives and children, and get rid of their therapeutic and genealogical charms. They deepened the locals' dread of losing spiritual and technological expertise, and facing aggravated forms of social decline.

Harnessed to nefarious dynamics of loss and deprivation, the Virgin Mary and Catholic saints also carried new visual styles. The missionaries lavishly distributed images of the Catholic saints and medals among their parishioners, and dedicated copious numbers of statues and portraits in vernacular chapels.[151] The plaster statues that they installed in southern Gabon belonged to the global style known as "Saint-Sulpician," a name coming from the main manufacturing center located near the Church of Saint-Sulpice in Paris. The production of these cheap effigies, characterized by pastel colors and a vapid realism, reached a peak in the second half of the nineteenth century, a high revival period for the Marian cult in France.[152] Hundreds of them flowed to Equatorial Africa. Their public display, in contrast with the secret rituals of specialists transacting with nature spirits, demonstrated white people's mastery of the "science of the visible." In 1899, the missionaries at the Sainte-Croix-des-Eshiras, thirty miles north of Mouila, blessed the statue of Saint Joseph in a village chapel, installed on the celebratory saint day.[153] Fifty-eight years later, in the northern city of Mitzic, the Fathers celebrated the dedication of a statue of the Virgin in front of a crowd of Gabonese parishioners extending over three kilometers. They brought the new statue in front of the church and sprinkled it with sacred water while mission girls and catechists sang the "Hymn to Glory." Gun salvos accompanied the entrance of the statue in the chapel.[154]

Catholic missionaries used the cult of the saints to directly compete with blacksmith deities.[155] To do so, they relied on the new devotion to Our Lady of Lourdes. In the French mountains of the Pyrénées in 1858, Mary had appeared several times to young shepherd Bernadette Soubirous in the grotto of Massiabelle, and asked the girl to dig in the ground and drink from a miraculous spring. Pope Pius IX authorized the cult of Our Lady of Lourdes in 1862, opening the door to an increasingly popular cult in France and beyond. Thousands of pilgrims, hoping for healing and salvation from the sacred water of the grotto, converged in Lourdes. In southern Gabon, Catholic missionaries busied themselves with the building of duplicate sanctuaries of Lourdes, such as at Sainte-Croix-des-Eshiras in 1897: "A little path goes from the cross to the grotto of Our Lady of Lourdes. . . . Our fountain springs from the rock and, on top of it, Father Hermès built a grotto with enormous blocks of rocks. On March 25, a pretty statue of Our Lady took possession of the grotto and, from afar, many Eshiras now come to see Maria in her house of stones. 'Here is what our eyes have seen, what our fathers would have desired to see and did not see!'"[156] The cult emulated nature spirits in their function as blacksmiths and protectors of prosperity. In Sindara, the main chapel was adorned with a copy of a famous pietà miraculously discovered in the city of Colmar in the Middle Ages, and a famous protector of rural harvest.[157] The fathers set out to build a grotto near a spring and dedicated it to "Our Lady of Lourdes." Every year on the celebratory saint day, they organized a mass procession of local villagers, and sprinkled the machetes, axes, and knives of the pilgrims with blessed water from the spring.[158]

In Mouila, the close association facilitated by missionaries between the Virgin Mary and Murhumi can be retrieved from the architecture of the shrine to the water spirit. The monument borrowed important elements of a large monument to Mary built in 1963 at the entrance of the Catholic mission grounds, on the left side of the Ngounié River (figure 1.9). Both included structures in concrete covered in white ceramic tiles, and white-and-blue motifs. In the central cemetery of Mouila, an imposing grave in concrete, shaped as a capital *M*, provides evidence that the cult of Mary, complete with her palette of white and blue hues, diffused among the ordinary citizens of the city (figure 1.10).

1.9 Memorial to Saint Mary, the mother of Jesus, Catholic mission in Mouila, 2012. Photograph by the author.

1.10 A white-and-blue grave with a bust of Mary, Mouila's cemetery, 2012. Photograph by the author.

1.11 The Virgin trampling the Serpent. From Henri Trilles, *Fleurs noires et âmes blanches* (Lille: Desclée, De Brouwer, 1914), 104.

Despite or because of these efforts, the Virgin Mary, worshipped in plaster statues and associated with water spirits, projected a double aura of salvation and curse, prosperity and loss. The devotional images of the saint that circulated on paper, blessed medals, and pamphlets confirmed her ominous traits. Sometimes vernacular catechisms represented the saint as trampling Satan in the shape of a serpent. An early collection of Gabonese novellas authored by Father Henri Trilles exhibited one such image (figure 1.11).[159] The ambivalent symbol lurking at Mary's feet resonated with the snakes of Mère Mambu and, more generally, with powerful metaphors of indigenous witchcraft.[160]

Reversing Sacrifice

In the summer of 2012, I visited Mouila for the third time. The shrine to Murhumi remained conspicuously empty. Yet the Dibur-Simbu were discussing the possibility of freeing the statue and putting her "on her feet" (*la mettre debout*). They hoped that politicians of local origin, *grands hommes* (great men) working in national circles, would help and heal oppositions to the project. As I was visiting that summer, they asked if I could support them in Libreville. A few yards from the old shrine, facing city hall, a new monument was already in construction (figure 1.12).[161]

1.12 New monument
to Murhumi under
construction, 2012.
Photograph by the
author.

Other, stranger rumors circulated. They warned that the Dibur-Simbu, in order to restore the *puissance* of the Siren, needed to "charge" the monument with "things" (*des choses*), a French euphemism for human body parts. The Gabonese call these crimes, often performed during electoral periods, "ritual murders" (*meurtres rituels*), in part because they seek to obtain human flesh and the magical force it contains.[162] For example, a wealthy *commanditaire* (patron) hires thugs to kill an anonymous victim and take his or her limbs and organs. The crime differs in considerable ways from the old economy of sacrifice. It targets body parts, not the life, of a remarkable member of a lineage. Performed by outsiders indifferent to clan obligations, ritual murders resemble the transactions of slave traders and nefarious witches. In the case of the new monument to Murhumi, a Dibur-Simbu elder tried to explain the sacrifice that, reputedly, was going to empower it: two kinds of supernatural beings existed, she said; and together they erase kin ties: the vampire, who "kills in the family," and the water genie, who decides who she will "take" (e.g., accept a sacrifice).[163] Yet the spiritual and material transactions of old, like the spirit itself, now survive as the dim memory of a bygone era.

Two shifts indeed have affected the economy of *puissance* in Mouila. From white colonialists and expatriate experts, the control of magical agency has shifted to a group of *puissant* Gabonese people. Also called "whites," these men and women are mostly unconcerned with lineage duties. When they need to strike hegemonic alliances with local experts, for electoral reasons, for instance, they deal with shady, mercenary specialists called *charlatans* and *escrocs* (crooks) in French. Working at the margins of older networks, *charlatans* use large sums of cash and ritual murder to mobilize the *puissance* of the other world. The second innovation lies at the heart of transacting gifts with the spiritual world: made of money and anonymous body parts, the offerings primarily serve the greedy interests of powerful "white" people. Like the French, they behave more like witches than elders and ritual specialists, and push *puissance* into the realm of transgressive exchange.

Today, a "white" person (*un blanc, une blanche*), is somebody who can mobilize the composite amalgam of power and agency that the Gabonese have come to call *puissance*. Whites are "complicated" (*compliqués*) people endowed with many talents and hidden powers. The appellation is a social and spiritual category rather than a racial one.[164] On the one hand, they recapitulate the capacity of ancestral healers and seers (*voyants*) and their talent of double sight.[165] On the other hand, they have civil functions, good salaries, and fruitful political connections. Since their *puissance* depends little on clan or family support anymore, whites are often perceived as enemies to lineage logics and family morals. When they fail to redistribute wealth and protection, a distinction appears with the colonialists of old: the public recalls former French rulers with nostalgia: "The Blacks do not have any love, contrary to the Whites who love and protect their kind," somebody told me in Mouila.[166] "Politicians have the vampire of the Whites. But contrary to the Whites, they kill their own kin like they would do to chickens. They punish the family."[167] For this reason, people also call the new politicians "slaves" (iPunu: *baviga*).[168] Slaves are people who dream of revenge and power, seeking to undermine the prosperity of the house that captured them, and to assert domination over their masters by initiating them to rituals that they control.[169]

The new whites need to strike alliances with local experts, and these men have thoroughly changed, too. Among the Dibur-Simbu, Dikakou Ngounass was the last representative of the older generation of specialists in charge of Murhumi. After his death in the late 1970s, his adoptive son, a suspicious character named Nzaou Dikakou, took over. Instead of dealing with the spirit itself, he focused on Murhumi's statue. Nzaou proclaimed himself the guardian of the bas-relief, still exhibited on the government plaza. He made "tourists" pay to see the statue. He washed it in ritual libations and collected the water to compose charms and remedies that he sold for very high fees. With the help of a local female associate, the mother of a powerful member of the Gabonese government, Nzaou also convinced the political elite to be "enthroned" (*intronisée*) in the local cemetery.[170] For another large fee, in cash, Nzaou guided the candidate to the graveyard, where his female accomplice forced the applicant to disrobe and crawl between her legs.[171]

Nzaou was not a true child of the Dibur-Simbu, since he was connected to the lineage through the paternal descent of his adoptive father, a genealogical position in direct contravention with the matrilineal order of clan loyalties.[172] Yet informants remembered Nzaou as a *charlatan* and a "sorcerer" (*sorcier*), showing that they believed in his ability to deal with spiritual agency. Nonetheless, based on money and individual aggrandizement, his magical techniques violated the moral sanctions of the past, bypassing the logic of gifts and countergifts between spirits and clans. The political initiation he managed with his accomplice, moreover, blurred the gendering of older initiation rites, in particular those commanded in the male society of Mwiri.[173]

Nzaou helped the ambitious elites that had risen in Mouila after World War II. Western-educated and often rich in cash, they used the new electoral system to compete for local seats. They also worked hand in hand with colonial authorities, who rejoiced in their "excellent cooperation" with elected Gabonese counselors, and patronized their liquor stores, bakeries, hotels, and bars.[174] They misread their rise, however, as a symptom of declining spiritual and religious beliefs in the larger population: "Religion [has] completely disappear[ed] to the benefit of political events, elections, national ceremonies and commemorations," reported an officer in 1959.[175] Unknown to them, the new political class was surfing on a new power complex, equally adept at using the older science of the invisible and the new science of the manifest. With self-made experts such as Nzaou, they neglected existing initiation societies, investing instead in international and esoteric associations such as the Freemasons, Njobi, and the Rosicrucians. Some had been imported in the 1920s by colonialists and had recruited Western-educated Gabonese into their ranks early on. Others, like Njobi, had reworked older spiritual legacies.[176] Instead of initiating young men and women into the collective history of clans, these esoteric societies reserved membership for influential and rich elites, asking the candidate to procure high fees or to be coopted by big men already established in national politics. Already in 1964, Pierre Nzengui had represented the coming of this new spiritual age. He had carved two keys in the upper corners of Murhumi's bas-relief, one oriented downward, one upward, representing "the scale of King Mérode," a Masonic sign for the finite and the infinite (figure 1.4).[177]

And yet the relation between Murhumi and her statue, an image that does not have real *puissance*, embodies the quandary that accompanies the rise of these new men, and that I have called a crisis of symbolic uncertainty.[178] In less than a hundred years, the imaginary of power that the Gabonese call *puissance* has become based on white technology and a logic of transgressive exchanges with the world of spirits and ancestors. The science of the manifest has displaced *la science de l'invisible*, based on secret knowledge, when no charm, only offerings to spirits, mediated the circulation of riches. Today, the inaugural sacrifice to the spirit has deteriorated into ritual crimes. White people and their various incarnations control the exchanges with the world of the night. The Siren absent, the rumor says, they want to "stuff" her statue with body parts to transform it into an active charm (iPunu: *ilongu, vandi*) that will serve their selfish purposes.[179]

TWO : The Double Life of Charms

This chapter turns to the history of the physical artifacts that the Gabonese compose for divination, therapy, and cursing. They call them *charmes* (charms), *fétiches* (fetishes), and *médicaments* (medicines), along with vernacular terms such as *biang* (Fang), *vandi* (iPunu), *imounda* (oMyènè), and *mbogha* (Ghetsogho). Today, "tradi-practitioners," Christian prophets, foreign specialists, *charlatans* (in French) and magicians—the latter name being reserved for white people—compete to offer their services to the Gabonese, who keep relying on such therapies, even if they often express serious doubts about the expertise and the motives of modern specialists. During the colonial period, white people and the Gabonese became partners in a mystical economy in which transactions in the agency and value of objects reinforced the power of charms and the procedures to activate them.

Before the arrival of the French, an original African formation that I call *therapeutic markets* had long existed in Equatorial Africa. Therapeutic markets capture the fact that objects charged with extraordinary agency could cross over general commodity networks and the confined realm of healing practices. Thus, contrary to conventional histories of exchange in precolonial Africa, which posit these as separate spheres, market and ritual transactions overlapped. Customers, traders, patients, healers, and specialists gave, used, and acquired medicinal ingredients and devices charged with sacred agency in a variety of places: in domestic and public areas, in local markets and fairs, in the shops of itinerant traders, in the compounds of ritual specialists, and in the reunions of kin and clansmen seeking to address various sorts of misfortune. Across these sites, even when behaving like commodities, charms preserved their agency. Instead of destroying them, the transactions of the colonial era reinforced these patterns.

Beyond Gabon, the chapter thus brings a new perspective to the "problem-idea" of the fetish.[1] Few scholars have been able to approach this history by looking at how charms behaved in Africa over a long period of time, and fewer still in the colony. From Marx to William Pietz and art historians, students of the fetish strapped the notion to centrifugal agendas and outward philosophies. The empirical reconstruction that I develop here calls into question many of the assumptions inherited from this Western tradition, in particular the opposition between matter and un-matter, and the conundrum of market versus magical value.

From the fifteenth century onward, countless foreign objects entered African ritual complexes, tempting local specialists and patients to use new therapeutic techniques. Scholars theorized this process as creolization, bricolage, and medical pluralism, but tended to cleave African objects into two separate narratives, one preoccupied with charms and fetishes, the other one with ordinary commodities.[2] When these spheres overlap, and charms circulate like merchandise, scholars often blame capitalistic pressures for "commodifying" local religious practices.[3] But this chapter demonstrates that charms in Equatorial Africa had long behaved in ways similar to ordinary goods, circulating widely in commercial markets without losing their capacious agency. Colonialism changed the pace and composition of these fluxes, but not their ability to cross over commercial, domestic, and ritual spheres.

Anybody spending time in Gabon will be struck by the copious and ubiquitous life of the therapeutic objects and "things" that people use every day, an experience perhaps unexpected in a country where material abundance is rare. The power-objects that I encountered at every turn of my inquiries struck me with their diversity. An early encounter with a healer made me aware of how one can work with different therapeutic traditions and use a vast arrangement of local charms and objects from faraway places. In July 1998, anthropologist John Cinnamon introduced me to a friend, a specialist named Florence Ngoma.[4] A pleasant and welcoming woman in her forties, Florence lived in a large house made of raw planks at Carrefour Iyayi, Libreville. In the courtyard stood a Bwiti temple adorned with a central pillar and images of Jesus Christ. A high initiate of the syncretic Bwiti cult, Florence also worked in the therapeutic tradition of another antiwitchcraft movement called Mademoiselle-Minbara.[5] Inside the house, John and I greeted a few patients, along with Florence's daughters, her grandmother, and a young boy named Geoffroy. We soon fell into a casual conversation about Bwiti and the virtues of *iboga*, the sacred hallucinatory drink made from the root of the *Tabernanthe iboga* tree and used by Bwiti initiates.

Twelve days later, I visited Florence again, this time with a small present for her shrine. Florence asked me if I wanted to be introduced to her *entités spirituelles* (spiritual entities). After I said yes, a young woman in her twenties, Florence's personal assistant, fitted us both with a white hat. Then she led us toward a room in the back of the house, where two large tables, heavily decorated with dolls, framed portraits, plastic flowers, and devotional objects, stood along the rear wall. We took off our shoes and entered the room. Florence's assistant had me turn around twice and kneel down in front of the left table, where a large image of Jesus Christ stood; the shrine, Florence said, was devoted to Mademoiselle-Minbara. Florence lowered her hand toward the floor as if collecting a blessing and then poured the benediction on my head. She made the sign of the cross, and her assistant rang a small bell. We repeated our gestures in front of the second shrine, which was topped by a large image of the Virgin Mary and a crucifix. This second altar, Florence explained, was named Force Tranquille (Quiet Force) or Tour des Saints (Tower of the Saints). I became intrigued by the dolls and figurines that crowded the shrines. Many were plastic toys mass-produced in Europe and Japan; a few others resembled Punu masks from southern Gabon. I asked about their role. Florence said that they were the pathways to her *entités spirituelles* (spiritual entities) and that she had baptized each doll with a special name.[6] Florence presented my gift to her entities, a small jar of Plénitude face cream from the cosmetic brand L'Oréal, and asked them to provide me with plenitude, longevity, and many blessings.

I had not chosen the present entirely by chance. In the national archives where I was working that summer, I had seen documents showing the central role of imported commodities in religious initiatives. Jean Emane Boncoeur, the founder of the Mademoiselle (Young Lady) movement to which Florence belonged, had made considerable use of Western objects in his struggle against Gabonese "fetishes." In 1952, Boncoeur had bought a flask of perfume and a small book from Monsieur Benoit, a French engineer. Then the spirit Mademoiselle, in the shape of a white woman, had visited him at night. Mademoiselle taught Boncoeur to recognize the men and women who owned bad fetishes and who tried to bewitch people. She gave him a cane carved in ebony and told him that it was called a *boussole* (compass) and that he could communicate with her by applying the stick to his ear.[7]

I encountered an even greater variety of fetishes, ingredients, and professionals at the Marché Mont Bouët, the largest open-air market in Libreville that sprawls over several blocks in the older part of the city. I asked a Gabonese friend, Maurice, a forty-year-old Myènè man whom I had met at the archives, to escort me on my first visit, in June 2000.[8] In a small boutique sheltered by concrete walls, a woman displayed products for traditional ceremonies, including the annual initiation of Gabonese boys and girls. Her stand offered baskets of cosmetic powders, in oblong cakes of white kaolin and red clay, bird feathers stuck in round dry sponges, and long tresses and squares of raffia fiber. She also sold gunpowder, calabashes, and cast-iron cooking pots (French: *marmites*; oMyènè: *mbumba*). I asked questions about these, but she was reluctant to answer, so we left her and ventured further into the market until we reached a large rectangular plaza covered in sand and surrounded by houses. The place is known as *stands à fétiches* (fetish-stalls): a multitude of open kiosks were aligned in regular, parallel rows, and displayed products on reed mats on small tables. Large umbrellas or makeshift roofs of plastic sheets protected the traders sitting behind the merchandise. The variety of their products was staggering. Some came from the forest: dry and fresh leaves, roots, various seeds, beans, and calabashes. The fauna of Gabon was also well represented, with animal skins, horns of antelope and buffalo (to be stuffed with magic ingredients), skulls of monkeys and antelopes, the jaws of small crocodiles, and, more rarely, dried hands of monkeys and gorillas. Handmade products included blankets, gunpowder, cooking pots, large double clapperless metal bells, and small wicker twigs bent in intricate knots.[9] Numerous bottles of potions and powders waited on shelves (figure 2.1). Everywhere, we saw baskets full of small, roughly carved anthropomorphic statues with an open cavity in the abdomen.

When I asked the sellers about the products, they answered that they did not know anything about them. Only experts and healers (*nganga*), they explained, could discern the power of the various ingredients. After a *nganga* gave a prescription to the patient, the person could purchase the ingredients at the market and give them to the *nganga* to make an appropriate medicine (French: *médicament*). (Indeed, during other visits to Mont-Bouët, I often saw Gabonese customers looking at various stalls while holding a piece of paper with a handwritten list of ingredients.) A young man named Mohamed, overhearing our queries to the sellers, invited us to the store of his father, a Nigerian trader established in Libreville since 1977. Comfortably seated in the opulent front room, we chatted with the young man. Most of his father's

2.1 A market stall at the Mont Bouët market, 2012.
Photograph by the author.

clients, Mohamed explained, did not come to the store to buy products. Instead, they placed a *commande* (order), and returned later to collect and pay for the purchase. Gesturing toward the store shelves, filled to capacity with perfume bottles, statues, red woolen blankets, and small bells, he added, "But here, what you see, it is nothing . . . here everything is raw [French: *brut*]. You need to consult a charlatan and get the products to work [French: *faire travailler les produits*]."[10] Then he showed us an example of a client's *commande* (custom order). He went to the rear of the store and came back with a small glass bottle filled with a red liquid in which floated a cross with silver ornaments. "One can order anything, even the heart of a man, dried up or fresh," he said. My friend Maurice boldly asked if we could get some vampire, the witch-substance contained in the belly of powerful people.[11] Mohamed did not flinch. He slipped again in the rear storage, coming back with what looked like a dried chunk of meat in a glass vial. Maurice examined the fetish and told me later that it was not high quality: a vampire must be "fresh" and recently collected from a corpse.[12]

The astounding diversity of market sellers' magical merchandise, and the fact that they refrain from specific prescriptions, provide an apt entry in the changes and continuities of the last century. Starting with the role and circulation of early charms in Equatorial Africa, we first explore how Westerners and the Gabonese struggled over the value of objects in the context of museum collections, therapeutic markets, and colonial warfare.

Early Charms

At the end of the nineteenth century, Gabonese specialists mediated the extraordinary agency of ancestors, spirits, and heroes by animating objects with medicines.[13] The use of charms has a very long history in Gabon and in the broader region: historical linguistics has documented it as early as the first millennium CE.[14] The proto-Bantu root for "experts" (*-ganga) and "charms" (*bwanga) stemmed from the same verb, *-gang-, "to tie up," and referred to the ability of specialists to secure various ingredients and forces in a material object. Social scientists and historians often translate this binding technique with the English verb "to compose." Named according to their form or function, charms allowed people to protect themselves, to muster influence over other people, to obtain riches, to divine the cause of afflictions, to cure, and to kill.[15]

The size and look of charms varied enormously. Some were small talismans worn on the body, others were large anthropomorphic statues hidden in ritual compounds.[16] Some could serve several functions. The capacity contained in the object was changing and evasive, in turn invisible and visible, tangible and intangible. It did not permanently attach to a particular site. It could vanish and disappear, but also materialize and travel between objects and persons, a pattern famously explained by Wyatt MacGaffey as the "personhood of objects" and "the objecthood of persons."[17] This is why I prefer to describe the capacious force contained in charms with the adjectives mystical, sacred, or divine (without any reference to a singular god) rather than "invisible" or "otherworldly."[18]

West Equatorial Africans did not follow any strict procedures or dogma in manufacturing charms. People saw them as devices endowed with predictable agency and, as Jan Vansina wrote, "No one worried excessively about the precise nature of their wonderful power."[19] They worked when the correct ingredients were correctly gathered, the correct words spoken, and, above all, when the medicine man and the customer or owner observed the correct ritual taboos.[20] Since the power of ingredients always derived from divine entities, medicines that used plants and other "natural substances" to cure illnesses were always also called "charms," and charms were also called "medicines."[21] Their lifespan was fairly short: specialists and clients constantly reworked and discarded charms according to the rise of new afflictions and the dictates of dreams and visions. Often, a person had a dream in which a spirit instructed him to compose a charm. If the new device worked, its reputation quickly spread and displaced older charms. Ancestral reliquaries made out of the bones of ancestors and bound up with various medicines in a bundle, a basket, or a box were not radically different from other charms (figure 2.2).[22] They too protected and cured the community, and served as means of divination.[23]

Wyatt MacGaffey coined the idea of "ritual stickiness" to describe the highly ritual ways in which such charms worked.[24] The fee that the patient gave to the healer, he wrote, did not work as a price but as a ritual gift for partaking in the sacred force present in the object. "In economic terms, . . . the successive gifting of an inalienable object, the *nkisi*-package, includ[es] the knowledge of those who know how to compose the charm, what songs to sing, and what rules to observe. . . . The first *nganga* of the *nkisi* passes on the gift to his successor for a fee." Whoever acquired the charms needed to observe specific ritual prescriptions, stepping into a "ritual clientage" headed and maintained, even from a distance, by the original expert.[25] The many derivatives that experts produced and circulated far and wide among patients, MacGaffey argued, remained dependent on the original.[26] But on the ground, the situation was often more fluid than "ritual stickiness" can capture. In West Equatorial Africa, indeed, the magical efficacy of most charms coexisted with their flexible, commodity-like circulation among ordinary customers. Moreover, their marketability probably preexisted the Atlantic trade. After the advent of that trade, and throughout the seventeenth and eighteenth centuries, people could acquire charms and their magical agency in marketplaces and along trading routes. One could purchase them for a fee or a price, away from any chain of ritual agency. They behaved, therefore, in ways not considerably different from commodities.[27] I will now examine this history more closely.

Rethinking the Fetish

But we first need to retrace the genealogy of the Western idea of African charms, or "fetishes." Indeed, historically, the western definition of the fetish opposes charms (unsalable, sacred objects) to ordinary commodities (saleable, duplicable objects). William Pietz showed that this notion emerged in the sixteenth century, on the coast of West Africa, in the midst of early commercial

2.2 Punu reliquary bundle, Lumbo, Africa, nineteenth-century Female figure above a packet closed by string; object connected with divination practices in Punu populations. Photograph by Patrick Gries/Valerie Torre. © Musée du Quai Branly—Jacques Chirac, Dist. RMN-Grand Palais/Art Resource, NY.

relations between Atlantic traders and their African partners. Euro-Brazilians became intrigued by the devotional objects owned by Africans on the Coast and called them *fetissos*. In the cradle of these early interactions, a fundamental contrast started to emerge, in the European mind, between merchandise that moved freely in the markets, and ritual objects that did not. Europeans described *fetissos* as devoid of market value and complained that, because of the taboos they enforced, they impeded their commerce with Africans.[28]

Yet it is precisely in the midst of these encounters that we find evidence contradicting the radical contrast researched by Pietz. The same travelers who crafted the idea of the *fetisso*, indeed, critiqued the "African priests" who earned profits by selling charms to clients and patients. This is how French trader Nicolas Villault, traveling in Sierra Leone in 1669, described the deals: "Their Fetiches [are] most often so filthy and vile that one would not wish to touch them. They all have some which they carry on them, certain ones are small ends of horns filled with ordure, other ones are little figures, animal heads, and a hundred other infamies which their priests sell them, saying that they found them under the fetish tree."[29]

Villault thus recognized that charms could enter into exchange at the same time he made the fetish priests responsible for the false valuation of valueless objects. His disgust and contempt for the "filthy and vile" objects in question, however, suggests an interesting source for the Western refusal to recognize the salability of charms: the fact that Europeans, not Africans, regarded fetishes as the things that they did not want to buy. From this moment of denial, the fact that local consumers exchanged charms as commodities became a blind spot in Euro-American theory. The Eurocentric idea of the fetish, meanwhile, continued to deny fetishes any aesthetic, cultural, or religious value.[30]

While they mocked objects and also local beliefs in their mystical agency, traders and travelers hardly characterized the commerce as a new or strange habit. Sales in *fetissos* did not seem to strike Europeans as a recent change linked to the expansion of Atlantic markets. Instead, their descriptions of the mercantile life of charms remained casual. Some observers recognized, meanwhile, how Africans combined ritual and economic worth in these objects. The capuchin monk Dionigi Carli explained in 1668 that the Kongolese called their national currency, the *zimbu* shells, the "children of God." According to Carli, *zimbu* monies carried two kinds of worth: "They [we]re valued so much that they [we]re worth more than any treasure. They [we]re exchanged for any all king of merchandise, and the richer and happier of man [was] the one who possesse[d] them in greatest number."[31] Other records, when read closely, abound with similar evidence. In the Kongo kingdom, European testimonials reported that the livelihood of healers depended on the fees they charged for healing services and on the sale of charms.

Although the price of these devices depended on the strength of the spiritual agency they contained, there is little evidence that they needed to be activated by performing ritual procedures or by recognizing a ritual clientage with the original expert.[32] A charm bought for money could work simply by being owned, carried around, or touched. The Kongolese often wore fetishes directly on the body. Women carried small statues and protective bracelets (*milungu*) to stay healthy. Little charms named *irikua* protected children from disease and witchcraft. Charms were also purchased to protect the foundations of houses, to kill thieves, or to preserve the crops from predators.[33] Similar patterns have been documented on the coast of Guinea in the early sixteenth century, where small pouches named *bolsas* (Portuguese: "purses"), and containing powerful substances, were widely available for a money price. White customers in Lisbon purchased them from African slaves sent to Portugal.[34]

In fact, the portability and marketability of early African charms differed little from the value attached by Europeans travelers to Christian sacra. Early Catholic priests in Africa routinely exchanged devotional objects for food or money. In 1668, traveling in the Kongolese hinterland, Carli obtained a hen from local farmers by making some rosaries with a ribbon of red silk.[35] Later, having used his last *zimbu* shells, the monk paid for food and shelter with holy objects. "With rosaries and beads," he wrote, "I maintained myself as well as I could."[36] Like Carli, European priests to the Kongo exchanged rosaries, blessed medals, *Agnus vitae*, crucifixes, and images of the saints for political and commercial bargains.[37] The Catholic Church itself had long endowed sacred objects with mercantile and divine worth. Since late antiquity, Christian relics and the bones of the saints had worked as self-contained, powerful charms that could be sold or exchanged for a price. After the crusaders had captured and brought relics to Europe, such as the remains of Saint Mark from Alexandria to Venice, the Church reasserted its identity and significance through carefully reconstructed narratives of their saintly origins.[38] Like charms in Equatorial Africa, the therapeutic agency of Christian relics depended on demonstrated efficacy rather than ritual formulas or chains of agency.

If we have an abundance of sources for the Atlantic trade (1600–1850), the commercial life of charms is harder to document prior to this period. A few early cases suggest that even powerful devices could be activated outside of sanctioned ritual bondage.[39] For instance, in the fourteenth century, in the middle Kwilu region (now in the Democratic Republic of the Congo) local leaders derived their authority from a charm of office that embodied a special relation with nature spirits. Later, leadership became increasingly vested in the charms themselves rather than in the support of spiritual entities: as a result, whoever managed to capture a charm of office became a legitimate chief.[40] Other evidence suggests that theft and crime, which are negative forms of exchange, did not cancel out the agency of a charm. Among the Orungu on the Gabonese coast, daring lords had long captured the relics of rival communities to weaken them and enhance their ambitions.[41] A final structural trait, probably present before the Atlantic trade, was the limited life span of charms.[42] Even sacred relics, the most potent of indigenous charms, declined in efficacy over the years. After a few generations, families and clans lost direct memory of ancestors and destroyed reliquaries, sometimes reburying the skulls and bones they contained. This technique is probably ancient.[43]

In summary, if charms and power objects usually worked in the context of ritual ceremonies and therapeutic compounds, their agency did not entirely depend on those contexts, or on the expertise of the *nganga* who first composed them. Instead, they could circulate in commercial markets and retain their efficacy. Europeans, blinded by their disdain for African artifacts, invented the notion of the fetish as an unsalable object in sustained contravention to the complex life of African charms and their own Christian objects.

Shifting Value in the Nineteenth Century

The Euro-American narrative that fetishes had no recognizable efficacy or aesthetic or commercial value, continued in the nineteenth century, as new Western appetites for African land and people moved explorers and colonialists back to the region. During one of his many trips to the Gabon Estuary, the French admiral Fleuriot de Langle exclaimed that he "would not have given 10 cents" for a goat's horn stuffed with medicine.[44]

But in the 1860s, a few traders and explorers ventured into buying native curios in Gabon. The reasons for the shift are difficult to explain with any certainty. At first, foreigners remained ambivalent about local objects. Franco-American explorer Paul Du Chaillu's opus, *Explorations and Adventures in Equatorial Africa* (1861), featured many negative comments on the "repulsive figures" of the idols owned and worshipped by local folks, yet the author had persistently tried to obtain a "fetish" among the Mpongwe, then the Orungu and Nkomi people, managing to acquire one such "idol" only near Lake An-engue.[45] The local king, he wrote, had agreed to sell it for a reasonable price because he had stolen it from his own slaves.[46] In 1879 or 1880, a similar mix of disgust and lust moved Trader Horn, a young British agent who worked for the trading firm Hatton and Cookson. Trader Horn derisively described a "rather hideous wooden God" he encountered on the Ogooué River, and how he decided to buy, for three bottles of gin and a few articles of trade, the "largest gorilla skull [he] ha[d] ever seen." The animal charm, he boasted, had great power in spirit land, and he could purchase it only because he had been initiated in the society of the Ipsoga.[47] Other visitors, meanwhile, were beginning to display a stronger taste for local artifacts. Emile Graux, a French trading agent who spent twelve years in Gabon from 1876 to 1888, shocked his family by bringing back a collection of "horrible," "ugly," and "cumber-some" objects from the colony: "I relentlessly hunted for everything native, all the old irons, all the old pots that I encounter in the smoke-filled huts of the Gabonese, the Bantu and the Pahouins. I had in my possession the most powerful fetishes."[48]

The shifting value of fetishes came in part from the emergence of a new form of collecting. In the 1870s, museum curators encouraged explorers and scientists to purchase art objects and sacra as ethnographic specimens.[49] Oskar Lenz, an Austrian geologist in the Gabon and Muni Estuary between 1874 and 1876, managed one of the first acquisitions on behalf of the Deutsche Gesellschaft zur Eforschung Äquatoriaafrikas. While traveling among Aduma, Sebe, and Ossyeba (Make) peoples, he obtained a reliquary statue adorned with brass strips.[50] The charm came without the reliquary bundle that it nor-mally topped. Ten years later, the Brazza mission to West Africa in 1883–85 purchased dozens of ethnographic specimens in the Haut-Ogooué, some com-plete with consecrated human remains.[51] Acquiring Gabonese charms soon in-volved massive exchanges in objects and capital. One of the most prolific field collectors was anthropologist Günther Tessman in Southern Cameroon. He sent hundreds of objects collected in southern Cameroon to the Lübeck mu-seum in Germany.[52]

In contrast to local therapeutic markets, foreign buyers exchanged Gabo-nese sacra for ethnographic and political reasons. The objects traversed vast distances to end up in museums and collections, acquiring new layers of value and significance. Racial exoticism and ethnic documentation animated the sales, while aesthetic prejudices remained strong until the 1930s.

The lust for African artifacts emerged later in the metropole, solidifying only after the turn of the twentieth century. Shortly before World War I, French art dealer Paul Guillaume promoted the artistic value of "negro art." His gallery in Paris soon opened a profitable market for African artifacts in the French capital and beyond, in which objects from Gabon figured prominently.[53] Around 1930, Guillaume's personal collection included fifteen statues of Fang *bieri*, a similar number of Kota reliquary boxes and figures, and a few Mpongwe masks.[54] The Western market in African art rested on a paradox: the aesthetic and commercial value of a piece depended on its "authenticity," itself predicated on the assurance that the item had had no commercial life in Africa itself but had only served in religious or ritual contexts.[55] An avatar of the idea of the fetish, the assurance reverses and sustains the early scorn for the aesthetic, religious, and commercial value of *fetissos* on the coast of Guinea.

Although many specialists of art and museum studies have discussed these transfers in Western museums, very few have worked on why and how charms could be acquired on the ground, in Africa. Why did some Gabonese expose and sell sacred objects? Although we will never know these motives with any certainty, a few hypotheses can be made. The power and capacity of some charms, first, could decline in time, and the genealogical protection of relics lose significance for local groups. Obtaining a hefty price for objects whose capacity had weakened, indeed, allowed clan elders to purchase powerful ingredients for composing new and better charms. Another factor came from the outsider status of European traders: local rulers and experts preferred to deal with transient partners who would soon leave and would not be likely to use the charms against them.[56] Last but not least, the long coexistence of commercial and magical value in therapeutic and magical objects, their circulation in and out of ritual networks, and their general availability along commercial routes helped local people to interpret the foreign demand from the perspective of habitual commerce in sacred objects, and to see them as extending, rather than upsetting, local regimes of power and value.

One of the earliest pieces of evidence of Gabonese specialists showing and selling charms to outsiders dates from the 1880s: Hans Gehne's photographs of two large reliquary boxes exposed circa 1913 in a Fang village in Southern Cameroon.[57] Ethnographers sent such images of charms to museums to obtain money to purchase the pieces. The cameraman usually asked that the artifacts be displayed outside their ritual compounds, in a place where he could

2.3 Two Fang relic vessels with bones and carved figures collected by Georg August Zenker in Southern Cameroon, late nineteenth or early twentieth century. From Felix von Luschan, "Zusammenhänge und Konvergenz," in *Mitteilungen der Anthropolgischen Gesellschaft in Wien*, vol. 48 (1918), 102.

use natural light for the photograph, and the background for authenticating the objects.

The photograph is not evidence that ritual specialists actually sold the reliquaries or were willing to do so. Indeed, traces of failed deals exist. According to Günther Tessman, Southern Cameroonians were reluctant to relinquish containers with ancestral relics.[58] Yet in 1897 the botanist Georg August Zenker, stationed in southern Gabon, wrote that such transactions did happen: "The chief's worries dissipated once I paid him generously and he promised to assist me in acquiring other objects. The container sewn in tree bark contained five crania of the chief's ancestors, along with some medicine including tin containers and one bark box filled with red wood and wrapped in leaves, two arrowheads. Paid 95 marks."[59] Zenker brought back several reliquaries containing bones and skulls to Berlin (figure 2.3).

By the end of the nineteenth century, a solid market for African artifacts existed among Europeans, reinforced by a growing aesthetic appreciation, and a fascination for the magic of primitive charms. The Gabonese increasingly accepted that local therapeutic markets extended to the demand of foreigners.

Transacting Objects under French Rule

The colonial era massively increased transfers in physical artifacts. Missionaries and administrators confiscated charms and demolished therapeutic compounds in the name of civilization, public order, and the Christian faith. Even larger campaigns swept the countryside as Gabonese movements blamed colonial misfortunes on the nefarious power of *nganga* and fetishes. The prophets who led these movements were pushed by spirits they encountered in dreams, and by specific objects of power given to them by white people. Armed with the Bible and white paraphernalia, they collected and destroyed charms and reliquaries owned by the families and communities that welcomed them. Art historian Louis Perrois estimates that, by the late 1940s, the craftsmanship in masks, charms, and reliquaries had virtually disappeared from Gabon. In the 1960s, foreign art dealers and antiquarians methodically emptied out the country: they removed all the remaining objects that they could find, taking advantage of the lack of protective legislation. After 1965, Perrois concludes, no ancient Gabonese art survived.[60]

Dramatic stories of annihilation, however, obscure complex and constructive processes. The flexible technologies that had long presided over the composition and circulation of charms helped local experts to replenish and recreate sacred complexes. In 1899 in Libreville, Catholic missionaries lamented how, after they confiscated sacra from their parishioners, local experts had soon renewed the fetishes.[61] And the preparing and selling of medicines endured and multiplied throughout colonial times. In 1955 in Mouila, *nganga* Moutsinga Diramba testified in court about a charm he had prepared for a villager, mixing palm oil with some "fetish." The client wished to punish the man responsible for murdering his child, and paid Moutsinga 1,000 French francs.[62] Foreign commodities and religious sacra continued to enter in the composing of fetishes. In 1957 in Ndendé, a ritual specialist composed a fetish by wrapping a chunk of wood in a sheet of paper covered in Arabic script, to help a client to divine the identity of the man who had killed his son.[63]

Ancient techniques survived colonial devastations, even if people used new and foreign materials. The Gabonese people continued to interpret the making of charms as transactions in material and immaterial power. Yet colonial attacks made them understand white domination as a veritable spiritual war, and suspect that the confiscated charms augmented the *puissance* of the whites. In the 1990s, an elderly Shamaye informant remembered French rule as a fraudulent exchange of spiritual and material capital: "White people found us in the village of Ndzokaloundza. I was already a grown-up. . . . With the arrival of the missionaries, things started to change. To receive baptism, you needed to accept to give the missionaries all your relics. . . . It is how, little by little, we entered the era of the whites, and gave up everything that belonged to us."[64]

In 2002, Mr. Diata, a local carver and healer in Mouila, put a similar, vehement interpretation of colonial depredations to me: "White people came and destroyed the power. They took all the power objects [*objets de puissance*] from black people. But it is good, it is very good that all these things [*choses*] were destroyed. It is what allowed you to defeat us. Now the medicines [*médicaments*] are serving the Whites. Now we are weak."[65]

Missionaries and administrators often kept the artifacts they forced local communities to relinquish. In the 1890s, Monsignor Jérome Adam confessed to such a theft:

> In the evangelized village, the day of baptism has come. . . . To demonstrate their good will, all the villagers wanted to sacrifice their fetishes, their amulets, their boxes full of skulls, their bracelets, their horns, their bundles, and even the old village sorcerer's magic tusk! . . . I took in the pile two bracelets decorated with small antelope horns that had the power to stop the rain. . . . Then the villagers brought the magic tusk in triumph and put it on the pile that we were about to throw in the river. But then (I must accuse myself of this), I laid hand on the famous magic tusk. All my colleagues agree that, now secure in my bedroom as a simple *souvenir*, it is better there than on the bottom of the river.[66]

Others sought to augment their ethnographic collections, fueling the suspicions of the Gabonese. In 1934, Monsignor Leroy, the new bishop of Gabon, asked the young Catholic missionary André Raponda-Walker to try and persuade his parishioners in Sindara to relinquish a *bieri* complete with ancestral bones and skulls, and to send it to him in Libreville.[67]

Remarkably, missionaries, like the Gabonese, envisioned evangelizing work as a form of material-cum-spiritual exchange. They left innumerable traces of this transactional imaginary in the archives. In 1910, Fang converts in Donghila asked the Catholic fathers to appoint a catechist to instruct them. In exchange, the priests demanded that local families build a chapel in the village and bring

all their fetishes to the mission.[68] The Catholic and Protestant archive celebrated these exchanges and the confiscations of local fetishes as "voluntary"
gestures from Gabonese who desired salvation and admission to the Church:

> One day . . . a good old man . . . came to whisper in my ear: "Father, I own
> a big fetish named Boniti [Bwiti?]. Please come and burn it, I want to put
> a medal around my neck." The idol was 1.8 foot high, its feet rested on two
> gorillas' heads, and the abdomen was filled with bones, skulls, small mon
> keys, insects' legs and the ashes of dead people, etc. The fire soon took care
> of the idol, as well as several others brought by neighbors to fuel the fire.[69]

Most of these anecdotes were apocryphal and written to encourage parish
audiences to support African missions. But not all. And enormous trauma
was involved in relinquishing genealogical and therapeutic charms. How did
a recent convert feel, for instance, when Monsignor Carrie, a Catholic priest
stationed in Mayumba in the 1870s, seized his family reliquary, opened it and
threw the skull into a nearby body of water?[70] In 1896, the annual Bulletin
of the Congregation of the Holy Spirit published a short notice that captured
the distress of a Gabonese ritual specialist after trusting a missionary with all
his fetishes and seeing the Father throw them into a fire: the specialist "shook
all over."[71]

By destroying indigenous charms and distributing blessed rosaries, medals, and other paraphernalia to Gabonese parishioners, missionaries anchored
locals' beliefs in the material agency they wanted to eradicate. Their transactions in objects and faith resembled, echoed, and doubled Gabonese people's
reliance on the capacity of sacred objects to mediate power.

Curing Witchcraft

In the 1940s, powerful indigenous movements followed in the footsteps of
colonial destructions. Gabonese prophets suffered visions that urged them to
fully abandon themselves to the teaching of the Gospel and the power of the
Christian cross, and to renounce the nefarious reign of fetishes and "witchcraft" (*sorcellerie*).[72] Witchcraft (proto-Bantu: **dogi*) is the nefarious and
malevolent use of extraordinary forces by greedy individuals (Fang: *beyem*).
It is opposed, in goals and effects, to the work of healers (*nganga*). But antiwitchcraft movements did not distinguish between these two modalities,
claiming that charms were responsible for the epidemics of jealousy, rancor, lies,
adultery, and other sins. The earliest of these initiatives was called Moulimfou.

2.4 Joseph Ndende and his assistants eradicate evil fetishes in the village of Ayol, Mitzic District. Photo courtesy of James Fernandez. From James Fernandez, *Bwiti: An Ethnography of the Religious Imagination in Africa* (Princeton, NJ: Princeton University Press, 1982), 230–31.

In 1948 near Mouila and Ndende, Moulimfou emissaries traveled from village to village, claiming to be working under a white man in Brazzaville.[73] They encouraged people to pay a small fee (ten to fifteen French francs) or offerings in kind (chickens, bananas, groundnuts) to be cleansed of evil magic. People needed to relinquish all the charms and fetishes they owned so they could be destroyed.[74] A few months later, similarly, Njobi swept the provinces of Nyanga, Adoumas, Ogooué, Ivindo, and Woleu-Ntem. Njobi leaders, or *prêtres* (priests), attacked the influence of healers and claimed that they could destroy hidden sorcerers.[75] Anyone could join the association by paying a small fee, by confessing his or her sins to the *prêtre*, and by revealing ownership of any *fétiche* (fetish).[76] Finally, around 1950 or 1952, the witch-cleansing movement Mademoiselle (Young Lady), led by Jean-Emane Boncoeur and Joseph Ndende, spread across northern and central Gabon (figure 2.4).[77]

Transactions in faith and objects were a central concern of these grass-roots initiatives. As they destroyed older charms, the prophets introduced new therapeutic and divinatory paraphernalia composed of Western imports. Emissaries of the Mademoiselle movement brought images of white women cut from French magazines to represent the white lady. Mass-produced consumer products featured prominently in the cleansing enclosures they built in the villages:

> The operator arrives in a village and gathers the inhabitants. He draws a small circle (sixty centimeters in diameter) that he delineates by planting eight to ten sticks (fifty centimeters high) connected by vines in their middle. In the center of the circle, he digs a hole and puts the image of Mademoiselle (a newspaper clip with the picture of a young white woman), surrounded by nine matches that symbolize the fire that will burn the witches. He arranges small pieces of glass over the eyes of the woman, and sprinkled them with water that he has brought with him. Then the man covers the whole device with dirt and crowns it with a stick that acts as a relay with the supernatural world. After this grand spectacle, there is a public confession. The villagers, following the command of the operator, bring their fetishes and amulets to be immediately destroyed. Finally, the public is sprinkled with so-called "magic water," or with powder, so they can be preserved from "bad fetishes." Of course, this protection is preceded by the payment of a small dime (*obole*). . . . Finally the fetish-man, who calls himself Monsignor, leaves for another village.[78]

By targeting older charms and pantheons, antiwitchcraft movements played a central role in spreading, in French, the derogatory repertoire of the *fétiche*. "Fétiches" became a popular term in Gabon to shun the charms of older pantheons, and for the suspicion that these objects may channel nefarious and anti-Christian witchcraft. In the endless cycle of discarding and creating capacious objects, local beliefs in the magic of charms, and Western faith in the agency of material things, mutually combined and grew together.

Travailler les Fétiches

So far this chapter has insisted on continuities in the use of charms and the colonial transactions that kept adding to their meaning and value. But important ruptures characterized the role of experts (*nganga*). Today, if the Gabonese believe that specialized expertise is indispensable to make and activate fetishes, they lament that the transmission of knowledge has weakened, and the relation between healer, patient, and charm had often become fraught.

In contemporary Gabon, the ability of an expert to activate the agency of objects is called *travailler les fétiches*.[79] The expression is a double entendre; it means both "to work with fetishes," and "to make the fetishes work." People describe *nganga*'s expertise as one of the "invisible" dimensions of the object, in contrast with its tangible, physical appearance. "True medicines," people say, "are the medicines that cannot be seen." In the 1960s, Ghetsogho speakers called invisible cures *maghanga*, contrasting with *mbogha*, the medicines that can be seen.[80] The transaction that takes place between patient and expert also belongs in the indiscernible nature of the charm.[81]

As we have already seen, only people who possessed an innate quality in the form of *evu/kundu*, a substance located in the body, could develop knowledge of the mystical realm.[82] In line with the "achieved leadership" paradigm of Equatorial Africa, this talent revealed itself in childhood and adolescence, or later, if a dream or a sudden illness affected the person: she or he then sought guidance from a knowledgeable specialist.[83] No special class or clergy dictated how to transfer expertise. At the end of the training period, the teacher blessed the apprentice to render his or her knowledge effective. A simple and personal ceremony, the blessing contrasted with another form of knowledge transmission, the collective rituals of initiation that involved many participants and several strata of revelation.

Training remains a central element in the reputation of healers and diviners. In 2000, I made a visit to the rural practice of Ta Mouketou, a relative of my friend Maurice and a healer practicing at Cap Esterias, west of Libreville.[84] After inviting us to sit in the therapeutic enclosure (figure 2.5), Ta Mouketou recounted how, as a child, he had a thirst for knowledge that pushed him to ask incessant questions of his grandfather, an herbalist of repute and a *guérisseur* (healer). When young Mouketou was old enough, he went in the fields alone to collect medicinal plants for the old man. Before the grandfather died, he was able to bless his grandson, officially recognizing him as a specialist. Ta Mouketou cured his patients by washing them with water in which special herbs have macerated. He also performed special massages and prepared fresh potions to drink.[85] Ta Mouketou also said that he was not a real *voyant* (seer) able to divine the identity of the malevolent person who sent misfortune to a patient; he defined himself only as an herbalist or apothecary (Fang: *mbelala*) who procures and sells medicinal ingredients.[86]

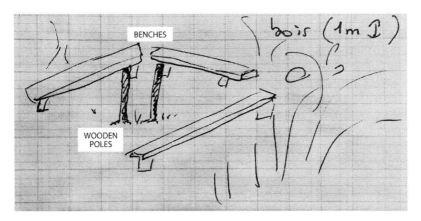

2.5 Ta Mouketou's therapeutic enclosure, 2000. Drawing by the author.

But the Gabonese often complain that experts fail to give blessings to their students, or stop transferring knowledge altogether.[87] The greed and selfishness of *nganga*, they claim, has undermined African *puissance*. I also often heard that white people "share" (*partagent*) their *puissance* with one another, and use it openly for the benefit of all.[88] In addition, charms and *puissance* cannot anymore be thought away from the white magic of the Church and the Holy Spirit. That the vernacular work of experts and local charms is imagined in constant relation with white people is also revealed in the lexical borrowing of *travail* and *travailler* (to work), a direct reference to the regime of production and knowledge brought about by former colonialists.

For the Gabonese public, the decline of African expertise is obvious in the proliferation of fake experts and pseudospecialists. One of my informants, a female *nganga* in Libreville called Mme Njoni, complained that most "charlatans" are only reselling ingredients and medicine, and do not know anything about composing charms or curing patients.[89] She used the word "charlatan," like many Gabonese, in a much less pejorative way than we do in English and French, as an equivalent for a lesser *nganga*, or a "pharmacist" (*pharmacien*), who cures with plants (like Ta Mouketou). Mme Marcelle, a specialist of the Njembe female initiation society, also lamented the decline of expertise: "Today anybody any proclaim himself a nganga, even if they have limited powers."[90]

In the 2000s, Patrice Nguéma-Ndong was perhaps the most famous of these dubious specialists. A self-professed expert in magic and healing, Nguéma-Ndong hosted a hugely popular radio-show, *C'est la vie* (That's Life), on radio Afrika No. 1. Listeners called the host to talk about their dreams and to ask questions about witchcraft, curses, and personal fortune.[91] Although Mme Njoni had cautioned me earlier that Nguéma-Ndong was probably uninitiated, he always warned callers against handling charms and medicine without the advice of an expert:

> It is not enough to invoke Jesus: you need a technique. Faith is not enough. Remember vampire movies: the cross can stop the vampires, but, for the arch-vampire, one needs more! . . . So you need [to consult] a tradi-practitioner. A *blindage* [armor] can stop any disease; it is a shield that insulates you completely. We, the warriors, we had a *botte secrète* [hidden technique], we don't tell about it. But nobody attacks me! The techniques always change. Like martial arts, they evolve constantly. Ten years ago, the techniques that could paralyze someone, now they are laughable. One cannot work and do black magic with nothing. You need things taken from the body, or some dirt, or to work with relatives.[92]

In the summer of 2000, I interviewed Nguéma-Ndong. At the beginning of our conversation, he said that he was not a *nganga*, although he came from a family famous for its *grands magiciens* (great magicians).[93] He had received a master's in English at the University of Indiana–Bloomington, and had come back to Gabon as a high-school teacher of English before being recruited as a journalist at Afrika No 1. For his activities in magic and healing, he worked with a mentor from West Africa, Papa Ndaye, whom he called "my father." Nguéma-Ndong thought, like many Gabonese, that West-African experts were more trustworthy than local *nganga*: "Many are dishonest. When a family consults about an issue for instance, one group pays 100,000 XFA to the nganga to give a diagnosis, then another faction gives him 200,000 XFA to change the answer. . . . So an outsider is a better option."

Like Nguéma-Ndong, modern Gabonese *nganga* use a wide array of techniques and ingredients to deal with misfortune and illness, and build a national rather than a local reputation. Their *travail* (labor) with fetishes borrows from a global library that included everything from Socrates to the Q'ran and the Bible. A rich assortment of *blindages* (shielding) protect them against witches: Jesus and the Holy Spirit, combat moves from martial arts, and talismans from global markets. Often connected to international esoteric societies such as the Freemasons, the Rosicrucians, or the Templars, they work alongside other *nganga* and *tradi-praticiens* (tradi-practitioners) versed in "traditional" diagnosis, divination, and cure.[94] A third group is made up of *charlatans* and herbalists, individuals who deal in the use of medicinal plants and commerce in magical ingredients. Last, but not least, prophets and pastors in Pentecostal churches perform divine healing for the faithful: heirs of the antiwitchcraft movements of the 1950s, they work with the Holy Spirit to destroy the remnants of ancient healing techniques and charms, which they damn as evil witchcraft.[95]

The Gabonese reserve the term *magiciens* (magicians) for white people and for the class of Gabonese "whites," powerful politicians and rich individuals with fearsome *puissance* and international connections. *Magiciens* rose at the confluence of the missionaries' sleights of hand and spectacles, the rise in mail-order markets in magical objects in the 1950s, and, finally, French rulers' vast and sinister accumulation in wealth, political privilege, and domination (in addition to their sustained stealing of local charms). Indeed, despite the proliferation of experts, ordinary people express a sharp sense of loss in expertise and *puissance*. We will see now how some of the analytical categories crafted during the colonial era compounded this issue.

Charlatans

Colonialists never recognized the legitimacy of local healers and diviners. They fought and mocked them as fetish-doctors (*féticheurs*), poisoners (*empoisonneurs*), and *charlatans* (crooks).[96] British colonies had witchcraft ordinances, but French law did not sanction witchcraft (*sorcellerie*) as a crime, nor did it recognize indigenous accusations against witches. Colonialists classified local cures and rituals as misdemeanors, "frauds" (*escroqueries*), deceits, and trickery.[97] Many of these terms experienced much use among the Gabonese, who actively borrowed and reworked them. In the 1950s, creole terms *féticheurs* and *charlatans* displaced vernacular lexicons, attaching new meanings to ritual expertise.

In French, *charlatan* comes from the Italian *cerratano*, a resident of Cerreto, a village near Spoleto in Umbria, where merchants sold drugs and medicines. The word also borrows from *ciarlare*, "to chat" or "to pitch."[98] It spread through southern France in the sixteenth century, naming the itinerant traders who sold drugs on open-air markets and occasionally performed surgery in public. The word soon became loaded with a negative meaning, that of impostors making profits from the credulity of the public. In colonial Gabon, the term named a fairly stable view among the French: that local experts were crooks who used tricks and sleights of hand (*tours de passe-passe*) to build false reputations and exploit local communities.[99] The perception was also grounded in the notion of the fetish developed during the Atlantic era, suggesting that Gabonese religions were nothing more than a hodgepodge of backward and meaningless superstitions.[100]

Catholic and Protestant missionaries agreed: few of them considered that Gabonese beliefs amounted to a coherent doctrine, or represented a significant threat to the Church. In order to downplay vernacular beliefs, most refrained from using the unitary figure of the Devil or witchcraft. Moreover, missionaries kept thinking that the superstitious errors of the Gabonese would soon disappear under the influence of Christianity.[101] This rationalizing discourse framed the evangelizing mission as a mere episode in the modernizing victory of the higher God, a God scientifically and technically stronger than local divinities. The attitude explains why missionaries used the "colonial sublime" in Gabon—or the effort to dazzle the natives with Western devices—with specific elements of the burlesque.[102] They loved to joke about Gabonese converts and perform prestidigitation to astonish them. Sometime in the 1880s, when his pupils asked Father Pouchet to give them a protective medicine against thunder, he made them swallow a solution of menthol, laughing heartily at the children's grimaces of pain and discomfort.[103] In 1904, an American doctor and associate of Protestant pastor Robert Hamill Nassau, at the Talagouga mission, used "parlor magic" to stupefy local kids: "He quite astonished my school children by swallowing and subsequently vomiting up a pen-knife, and by passing a threaded needle through the thigh of one of the boy. . . . The exhibition was a happy one in revealing to the natives how an evil-disposed sorcerer would be able to deceive them."[104]

The term *charlatan* disseminated late among the Gabonese, probably from the 1940s onward. It first left the confined realm of administrative reports when the term appeared in the 1944 penal code applied to black subjects of the colony (*code pénal indigène*), which codified practices of "witchcraft, sorcery and charlatanism" as misdemeanors.[105] Then the word probably spread to the larger public through courts and through Gabonese clerks and *évolués*.[106] By the 1960s, the archives show, it had achieved wide currency among Gabonese bureaucrats.[107]

The term *féticheur* was more negative. Administrators called African ritual experts *féticheurs* (fetish-doctors) and regarded them as the principal political obstacle to colonial influence.[108] After vanquishing armed resistance in the 1930s, however, they joined missionaries in considering *nganga* as harmless crooks and "charlatans." In the 1950s, their dismissal of African politics went so far as pushing administrators to label nascent political parties as "mono-fetish sects."[109] Meanwhile, the antiwitchcraft campaigns of the 1940s and 1950s loaded the term *féticheur* with a negative meaning and a distinctive commercial flavor.

In a fascinating contrast with the classic definition of cargo cults, in which native people, kept ignorant of the conditions of production and distribution of manufactured products, mistake them for magical items, Euro-Americans decried local *féticheurs* for transforming sacred charms and therapies into trivial commodities by selling them.[110] Among countless examples, this one illustrated the prejudice: "[The fetish-doctor] usually begins practice by exploiting some particular fetish in which he really believes and whose power he has proved. Finding the trade lucrative he invents other fetishes upon the same principle. . . . If some of his first fetishes should be successful and gain him a reputation, he may come to believe in his own power."[111]

Féticheur is documented in Gabonese usage at least since 1943.[112] Today, with *charlatan*, it retains the commercial meaning suggested by French usage, but the Gabonese public generally uses the words in a neutral or positive fashion, belying colonial efforts to draw a distinction between commercial and ritual markets. Africanized by the public, the two terms bridge the older figure of nineteenth-century experts with global markets in magic, and express the enduring permeability of the ritual and commercial spheres.

Médicaments and Therapeutic Markets

New commodities entered Gabon during the colonial period, traveling through the post and entering ritual usage through new and surprising ways. The colony indeed became a profitable market for a global commerce in magical objects procured by mail order. Like the foreign objects that arrived in West Equatorial Africa from the sixteenth century onward, magical devices easily entered the paraphernalia handled by *nganga* and ordinary persons. Unlike them, however, they significantly changed local therapeutic relations and usage.

The commerce became visible in Gabon in the 1950s. Sometime around 1951 or 1952, the police had caught a certain Ruchpaul in Paris, who, under the alias "Hindou Sankara," had widely advertised in Gabonese newspapers and in the mail.[113] He offered magic perfumes from India, known for their "talismanic qualities." At two thousand francs a bottle, these were expensive commodities. Customers with more modest means could order pendants with the signs of the Zodiac. Hindou Sankara promised to charge the jewels with incantations for a small additional fee.[114] By 1954, another French magician, Mme Arika, aka L'Astrale de Montmartre (The Star of Montmartre), had been caught mailing "radiating perfumes" and "sources of happiness to fall in love" to Gabonese customers. That same year, the police arrested two merchants in Nice, on the French Riviera, for sending fraudulent talismans to the colony.[115] Back in Gabon, French administrators noted that the advertising and selling of such paraphernalia had developed in the colony "on an extraordinary scale," and Gabonese charlatans had followed in the steps of mail-order crooks.[116]

The commercial success of global magical objects made them part of the local paraphernalia used for healing, harming, and protecting. Yet careless usage had catastrophic consequences.[117] In the late 1950s, in the town of Assok Ening in northern Gabon, anthropologist James Fernandez witnessed the death of a man who had ordered magical objects from France. The rumor was that a white spirit had struck the victim dumb. No one was able to cure him: the man could neither drink a medicinal potion, nor confess his deed to a priest.[118] Forty years later, in the 2000s, many of my informants talked about an illness called *maboulisme* (craziness); it befell people who had bought magic medals and talismans from French firms and used them without the necessary knowledge.[119]

Traditional *nganga*, in particular, often invoked incidents of *maboulisme* associated with free-circulating magical objects.[120] But such discourse, if it was normative and helped to support the status of reputable experts, did not necessarily describe practical situations of fetish use. In fact, anecdotes of magic gone wrong confirmed that the raw force of fetishes could strike unqualified or incautious people without any intercession. When I visited sellers of medicinal ingredients in Libreville, I noticed that my friend Maurice always took the precaution to point at the products with his index finger bent. This, he explained, prevented *la puissance* from waking up and attacking him.[121] In the twenty-first century, as in earlier centuries, charms possess a free-standing capacity that does not depend on ritual procedures—even if the latter do help to enforce its beneficial effects.

The enduring agency of magical objects signals an important parallel between Equatorial African and Western ritual complexes. The role of Gabonese experts, the capacious devices they use, and the relations they establish with patients display striking similarities with biomedical doctors or pharmacists in Euro-America. After arriving at a diagnosis, the *nganga* determines a prescription and composes an appropriate medicine. The power of the cure comes from the extraordinary forces of the night that activates the healing power of a charm or prescribed ritual. In contrast, the agency of Western medicine comes from what we call experimental science. But at the level of usage, procedures, and results, it seldom differs from that of Gabonese ones.

The Gabonese repertoire of the *médicament*, a popular word that came to be used alongside vernacular ones during the crucible of the colonial era, captures these complex histories in the region.[122] *Médicament* defines both portable medicines in the shape of objects that retain efficacy and capacity while circulating across different markets, the correct usage prescribed by an expert, and performative therapies such as curative baths, restorative massages, and initiation to a spirit. Like biomedical drugs, they come with a prescription or a therapeutic protocol. They also keep their power across commercial spheres. Their free-standing agency, however, means that a person can ignore the prescription and self-medicate, taking the risk of releasing the *médicament*'s effect in adverse ways. In this way *médicaments* are not dissimilar to biomedical drugs.

Today, the therapeutic scene in Gabon still enacts what John Janzen famously coined "medical pluralism," but with the strong market component elucidated in this chapter: patients pragmatically seek treatments in diverse places, at medical facilities, in churches, in the ritual compounds of reputable *nganga*, and in the shady workshops of marabouts and charlatans.[123] They buy and use *médicaments* and *fétiches* made with various ingredients, some "traditional," some pharmaceutical, some purchased from mail-order catalogs. These practices prolong an ancient historical process in which the healing agency of objects was based on the demonstrated efficacy of composite ingredients, and enhanced by circulation in the market; a process I have called the double-life of charms. Colonialism changed this landscape, multiplying negative transactions, thefts, and dispossession of power. Incessant attacks against the healers and experts who "worked the fetishes" encouraged the suspicion of the public and feelings of nostalgia for lost regulations and expertise. Yet colonialism did not fundamentally change the logic of local therapeutic markets. Today, individual healers like Florence, and ritual entrepreneurs like Patrice Nguéma Ndong, can choose from a renewed variety of tools, recipes, and ingredients at the market stalls or in their own therapeutic networks. In Gabon, the astounding array of objects of power, described at the beginning of the chapter, is a complex legacy of these pasts.

THREE : Carnal Fetishism

In today's Gabon, not a month passes without the public and the press lamenting another *crime rituel* (ritual crime), a killing in which thugs mutilate a victim to harvest his or her body parts, preferably the tongue, the eyes, and the genital organs. The Gabonese say that ritual experts compose the stolen substances into an expensive charm that they sell to a rich patron. Scholars who have analyzed similar body trafficking in other parts of Africa have brought attention to important factors such as the commodification and social devaluation of the person, the rise of global markets for transplants, and, more generally, the spread of biomedical views of the body.[1] I focus here instead on the flip side of these dynamics, the complex and powerful *reenchanting* of the body that they reveal. In Gabon, I argue, the process derived from the accretion of judicial, moral, and spiritual engagements between Africans and Europeans over the location of power.

At the end of the nineteenth century, indeed, both the French and the Gabonese believed that power was partly located in, enacted by, and symbolized by the physical body. From the 1880s onward, during the colonial conquest, these congruent imaginaries combined and clashed, making the human body an integral site of the struggles for dominance and autonomy. The Gabonese fought to maintain local techniques for composing powerful charms with corporeal substances. They also attacked white bodies, processing them as magical capital. The French insisted on the spectacular power of their presence in Gabon and the extraordinary agency of their own flesh. Yet they also attempted to desacralize black bodies and to construct African corpses as dead matter that should be disposed of in hygienic fashion. In these tense and intimate struggles, a rich cultural formation surfaced, a paradoxical and composite imaginary that I call carnal fetishism. Across the racial divide, carnal fetishism produced the body simultaneously as an organic entity and a sacred device of power, a political fetish charged with a crisis of meaning it could not resolve.[2]

In an empirical narrative of these productive arrangements, this chapter starts in the 1880s, when new policies to enforce segregated cemeteries revealed French colonialists' contradictory views of the body. It follows with a history of African imaginaries of corporeal power before and during colonialism. Under intense judicial repression, the making of ancestral relics declined, and the techniques of composing charms with human substances became detached from genealogical constraints, as specialists turned to anonymous body parts harvested in deregulated markets.

Hygiene and Magic: Colonial Cemeteries

When colonialists arrived in Gabon, they believed that the physical body partly held, enacted, and symbolized public power and personal capacity. Yet because they also trusted in the biomedical nature of the flesh, contradictions riddled their policies. Here the racial divide was central, and this section examines it in the historical site of death, as illuminated by state regulations and funerary rites.[3]

Since the mid-nineteenth century, the French had reported on native burials as examples of barbarism and racial inferiority. Vice admiral Fleuriot de Langle, an officer and writer stationed in the Gabon Estuary, disparaged the fact that people exposed their dead in rickety huts and open-air sheds.[4] Exploration stories and travelogues regaled their readers with scandalous stories of the Gabonese leaving slaves and sometimes even rulers to decay on the ground after death, and native families burying their relatives near them.[5] French funerary rites in the metropole were themselves changing dramatically. Since the French Revolution, secularist theories envisioned death as a form of organic failure and social deprivation, increasingly detached from the intimacy of family rituals.[6] Grand funerary ceremonies and public memorials insisted, paradoxically, on the symbolic significance of the dead.[7] In Africa, the French erected private tombs for some colonialists, and official funerary monuments to others, crystallizing important nodes of power in the spatial and temporal landscape of the colony.[8]

In the early twentieth century, colonialists remained haunted by stories and rumors about the native voracity for white bodies. Yet their perspective slowly shifted. Early tales of cannibalism depicted a violent situation of confrontation and conquest, with Africans killing and devouring the live flesh of foreigners. Rumors about African harvesting of white remains from graves talked about cultural and spiritual engagements with the colonized.[9] The

3.1 Tomb of Valentine Lantz, Talagouga Mission in Cape Lopez, ca. 1906/1920. Photographer unknown. Courtesy of Archives Défap-Service protestant de mission, Paris.

3.2 Tomb of Edouard Lantz, Talagouga Mission in Cape Lopez, ca. 1901/1905. Photographer unknown. Courtesy of Archives Défap-Service protestant de mission, Paris.

awareness that their corpses could be used for local purposes was a terrifying image of the colonial enterprise. Colonization, after all, might not be about imposing a policy of presence and progress for the natives. It might be about providing local people with material resources—the white body—for local goals. The fact testified to the stubborn vitality of African initiative and the uselessness of white action.

Europeans' fear was so great that they usually surrounded isolated white graves in Gabon with sturdy fences in wrought iron (figures 3.1 and 3.2). In the early twentieth century, they extended these defensive tactics to whole cemeteries. In 1910, for instance, the district officer at Sette-Cama asked the governor in Libreville for funds to construct fences around the European graveyard: "I do not want people to say that I did not take all possible means in order to avoid the profanation of tombs. . . . It is our duty to insure that Europeans buried here can rest in peace, and prevent additional attempts by natives from stealing European skulls or bones in order to organize fetishistic rituals."[10] In 1920, when the district chief of the Djouah region found the grave of a European man in the small village of Massinegala, he also immediately reported that the village chief, a man named Londa, had attempted to loot the place and gather bones in order to make a *médicament* (charm) against white people.[11]

Rumors and imageries are never disconnected from reality or from concrete practice: as social facts, they participate in both.[12] Gabonese experts had long incorporated the body parts of dead white foreigners into charms and medicines, although not on a massive scale nor regularly.[13] After conquest, white body parts were key ingredients in the making of magical charms. In part to prevent such desecration, French authorities in Gabon imposed funerary segregation and burial regulations in the 1880s, starting in the capital, Libreville, and later extending to the rest of the colony.[14] In 1910, the governor of the colony issued a general decree for the protection of white cemeteries across the entire territory.[15] In 1916, a new, elaborate *circulaire* from the governor-general of French Equatorial Africa mandated new separate cemeteries for white people and Africans.[16] This was partly based on hygienic concerns. It stipulated that the graveyards should be at least forty meters from residential buildings, and should lie away from any bodies of water to avoid contamination. It instructed district chiefs to post notifications of the construction across town, to conduct a *commodo et incommodo* (expediency) investigation, and to draw a map at the scale of 1:5000 and 1:1000 displaying the proposed location of the new cemeteries.[17] A handful of such maps survived in the archives, and one is recreated below (map 3.1):

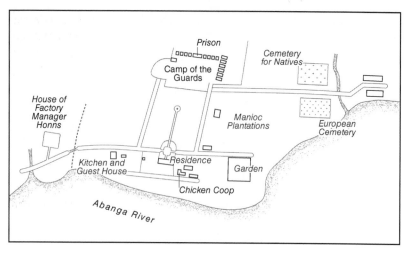

3.1 Layout of the cemetery in Afane, Abanga Post, 1917, from original map drawn and signed by the Chef de subdivision, 1 June 1916. ANG/FP 551.

The 1916 law diffused fairly rapidly but evenly across Gabon. Administrators started to create segregated cemeteries out of mixed ones, often using penal labor to displace graves in the new locales and to cover white tombs with slabs of stone and concrete.[18] They also took more control of local funerals: they mandated that officers record official declarations of death within twenty-four hours, and they required bereaved Gabonese families to obtain death certificates and burial permits (*permis d'inhumer*). These initiatives proved patchier in rural areas. In 1949 in Koula-Moutou (in central Gabon), the administrator lamented that burials "occurred in the most haphazard places, sometimes next to residential buildings," and invoked native "inertia" to explain why the town had not yet implemented the instructions of the 1916 *circulaire*. He set out to break ground for a new graveyard, one reserved for blacks and another for whites, one on each side of the river Bwénguidi. A permanent civil servant supervised burials, registering the declarations of death, and assigning burial sites.[19] Illustrating the macabre transfer of racial tactics into the realm of death, these initiatives also provide fascinating insights in the ways in which French colonialists attempted to racially bifurcate the meaning of human remains.

White legislators launched a massive assault on local regimes of power by undermining Gabonese funerary and burial rites, and by using biomedical *racial divide*

claims to strip the native body of symbolic significance.[20] The requirement that burials take place within a few days after death prevented families from exposing the deceased for several days or weeks. It also hampered them in organizing reconciliation ceremonies that usually took place in the family house, around the exposed body of the deceased.[21] The obligation to bury a person in an official cemetery weakened families' protection of the dead and the possibility of communicating with ancestors.[22] In 1923, a decree defined the making of ancestral charms as an act of "anthropophagy" and "trafficking in human flesh": seeking the "repression of anthropophagy," it labeled the collection of bones as the "violation of tombs and profanation of cadavers."[23] It set severe sanctions, including the death penalty, to punish offenders. It widened the scope of colonial misreading of African usages of the body: now, to perform a ritual autopsy, or to collect bones from a grave for making ancestral relics, could be construed as "cannibalizing" human remains and punished by death.

Devaluing the importance Culturally of the burial process and therefore the value of the native body.

Partly as a result, the making of relics in Gabon dramatically declined. Ritual autopsies survived only at the risk of considerable danger and important reconfigurations. In the classic procedure, ritual specialists (or, more rarely, slaves or outcasts when people feared mystical pollution from death) had searched a dead body for traces of witchcraft attacks, or for evidence that the person had used bodily power to attack others by witchcraft. Specifically, the operator had usually opened the abdominal cavity, and the lungs and heart, to search for internal wounds, lacerations, bleeding, and the presence of tumors and growths that documented such witch attacks or witch power. If a witch-substance was found, it could be removed to be destroyed, or to compose a charm. Now specialists conducted these operations in secret, and with new participants.[24]

Meanwhile, in the name of judicial prescriptions and biomedical science, colonialists did not hesitate to exhume African corpses to probe the cause of death.[25] In 1938, for instance, a local chief named Asogo Nze died suddenly in Minvoul, the capital of the Woleu-Ntem region in northern Gabon. Rumors accused a rival of having poisoned him. To settle the matter, the French director of the sanitary services commissioned a medical autopsy and sent Nze's viscera to Brazzaville for analysis. Such operations dramatically unsettled the intimate possibility, for the family and the community of the deceased, of conducting funerary rites that ensured social reproduction and genealogical continuity. First, biomedical autopsies often took place at a moment when

Segregation in conflicting laws imposed by European colonialists

local rules forbade any interaction with the dead, and allowed only initiates to proceed to the collecting of bones. Second, autopsies prevented relatives from keeping a safe watch over the deceased, and make sure that his or her organs would not be stolen for composing charms. Third, by removing the entrails of the dead for laboratory tests, colonial agents behaved as powerful competitors stealing and feeding on carnal resources. We do not know the results of the test performed on Nze's body, nor what happened after the official report came back, but the removal of Nze's organs by white sanitary agents positioned them as destructive insiders/outsiders.[26]

The regulation of burials and funerary rites in the colony made Frenchmen's attitudes explicit: anxieties about African assaults on their bodily remains, scorn of native customs regarding death and afterlife, and determination to biologize and medicalize black bodies. Concerted French attacks on techniques of corporeal power among the Gabonese, under the facade of preventing anthropophagy, considerably lessened Gabonese use of the body. We now turn to the history of these technologies.

The Sacred Capacity of the Gabonese Body

Historian Joseph Ambouroué-Avaro has described early Gabonese societies as "civilizations of the body."[27] Across the region, the social importance of a person was defined by her physical and intellectual talent, and by a mystical capacity that can be translated as "lifeforce" (Adyumba: *ngulu*; Fang: *ki, ngul*).[28] *Ngul* was encapsulated by the body, yet it extended far beyond a person's physical or biological abilities. Although the slave trade had weakened the value of the person, nineteenth-century Gabonese societies continued to rely on and celebrate the sacred potential of human flesh. Human substances were part of many medicines and charms. To charge a device with therapeutic or aggressive force and to bind fortune or misfortune to a particular individual, ritual specialists used bone fragments, nail clippings, hair, or items that had been in contact with a person: a piece of their clothing, soil from a place where the person had walked, or a bit of dirt from a fresh grave.

Although rituals and powers varied substantially across the region, the Gabonese in general believed that the entire person was suffused with marvelous social power and enchanted efficacy. To give birth to many offspring, to nurture social and religious networks, to build and transmit knowledge, to hunt and produce material wealth for one's relatives, or to act mystically upon the life and well-being of other persons, a multiskilled and all-powerful body mediated all of these actions.[29] The body was a fluid, composite, and potent entity, and this capacity (*ngul*) lived in several places inside it. In Gabon, a rich repertoire spoke of this reality. Besides their visible body, Fang-speaking people talked of *nsisim*, or the "body-of-the-shade," that left their house at night to perform occult deeds.[30] An innocent person's body-of-the-shade, in turn, could be harmed or captured by malevolent individuals.[31] In the Galoa language, the mystical body of witches was called *ognyèmba nyèmba* (lit. "the witch-body of the witch").[32] Mystical bodies survived after death and traveled to the world of ancestors. Yet they were not of a substance radically dissimilar to the body visible. Both served as conduits to the extraordinary forces of the world of ancestors and spirits. Bantu languages differentiated between a living person's body (Fang: *nyol*), the dead cadaver (Fang: *mbim*), and the person's body ritually prepared for burial (Fang: *kón*, e.g., "ancestor").[33] In this context, the material, social, and mystical capacity of a person could not be pinpointed to a precise or localized mechanism, nor could it be compartmentalized in clear and waterproof categories.

A convenient starting point for understanding how local societies saw the body as suffused with *ngul*, or force, is the ancient notion that most people had a witch-substance (Fang: *evus* or *evu*; Punu: *kundu*) located inside their body.[34] *Evu/kundu* also possessed a multiple nature: an organic and material substance, it nevertheless participated in the world of spirits and ancestors. In the nineteenth century, the Gabonese thought that this substance existed in every person and that its size and strength grew according to personal skills. In ordinary people, *evu/kundu* remained a latent, undeveloped talent, whereas powerful people could expand and shape it for their own benefit or for the public good.[35] Healers and leaders were reputed to have a capacious *evu/kundu* that they could use for protecting the community. Yet the substance was not an entirely personal attribute and was not permanently attached to an individual.[36] It could enter the body or leave it; it could survive the person's death and depart from the corpse in the form of small animals. Indeed, ritual specialists (*nganga*) often manufactured power by capturing these animals from tombs and graveyards, or by removing fragments of the witch-substance from the dead and incorporating them into a charm.

Evu/kundu had an aggressive, destructive aspect. It could prove harmful if not socialized by proper ritual, or if an individual used it only for egoistic and greedy purposes.[37] Although the substance provided the core component of healers' and leaders' ability to enact public authority and to ensure communal protection, one could always be tempted to use *evu/kundu* for antisocial attacks and revenge. Moreover, people believed that even the positive talents of healers and political leaders came from killing a relative and offering the sacrifice to ancestors or teachers to enable their *evu/kundu*.[38] At the other end of the social spectrum, a witch (Fang: *neem*; Galoa: *olovalovi*) was a common person who relied on his or her witch-substance to harm and kill. These antisocial, destructive individuals invisibly assaulted and fed on a person's body, mind, and social assets. The attacks made the victim fail in all his or her enterprises, or waste away with no obvious cause. Ritual specialists could diagnose the cause of such misfortune and illness, and find the responsible party. If the witch did not confess, the *nganga* submitted him or her to an ordeal, which often involved drinking a highly toxic substance. If the accused died, he was assumed to possess an antisocial *evu/kundu*.[39] In the rare case that a convicted witch was executed after the ordeal, the *nganga* either removed the witch-substance from the cadaver and processed it into a beneficial charm, or destroyed the corpse entirely to get rid of its nefarious power.[40]

The enchanted efficacy of the body was not impersonal; it was always connected to a particular individual. Yet it also had metonymic qualities. As Fang informants in Cameroon explained to Günther Tessman around 1900, people's mystical power remained in each part of their body after the organic death of a person, as long as her bones did not decay and disappear.[41] This was a belief crucial to the widespread cult of relics throughout the region.[42] During colonialism, Christian-inspired attempts to impose Western categories on local cosmologies obscured these notions.[43] Foreign observers often criticized Gabonese notions as stubbornly material, suggesting that Africans were incapable of conceiving immaterial, symbolic manifestations of authority and agency. In fact, Gabonese worldviews were far more symbolic than Western secular science or materialist philosophies. Local communities did not draw an impermeable divide between a physical/material reality and a mystical/immaterial one. Tangible things such as the body or therapeutic charms symbolized, signaled, embodied, and enacted superhuman forces. In turn, material realities could always transform into dematerialized ones and vice versa: the energy of an ancestor could be charged in therapeutic ingredients and act through a material charm. A witch-substance could change into a ghostly, immaterial "body-of-the-night" to attack victims in their sleep. Hence people's bodies and corporeal fragments did not differ ontologically from ritually empowered charms: both had the ability to circulate sacred forces.[44]

3.3 "Invocation of the fetishes among the Duma people," drawing by Edouard Riou, based on a sketch by Jacques de Brazza between Madiville-Lastoursville and Masuku-Franceville, around 1883, published in Pierre Savorgnan de Brazza. "Voyages dans l'Ouest Africain," in *Le Tour du Monde. Nouveau journal des voyages* 54, no. 1402 (1887), 329.

The human substances in the most powerful charms were the consecrated bones of remarkable ancestors. Relics (Fang: *bekón*; iPunu: *malumbi*) channeled the power of the dead and grounded the genealogical identity of clans, families, and initiation societies. Kept in shrines, where initiates regularly worshipped and questioned them, they protected the well-being of societies. Only higher initiates could fabricate them.[45] Several weeks or months after the death of a remarkable person, a small group of initiated men (or women, in the case of relics composed for female initiation societies) gathered near the grave at night. After exhuming the body, they collected a few bones from the skeleton, usually parts of the skull, tibias, and hands.[46] After cleaning and drying the remains, they adorned them with red powder from the *paduk* tree (*Pterocarpus soyauxii*). They placed the bones in a container, usually a wooden box or a bundle, also containing potent medicines. They topped the reliquary with a decoy figure carved in wood (figure 3.3).[47] Thus consecrated, the relics embodied the ancestor himself or herself, ensuring the protection of the community at large.[48]

The capacious power of flesh and bones was not absolute or unchanging. Instead, it was produced in a transactional relation between experts and kin, allies, ancestors, and spirits. One gave offerings (Mpongwe: *ntsago*; Ghetsogo: *eago*; Gisir: *dilagu*) to thank an ancestor for a favor. A patient paid the ritual specialist in order to activate the human substances composed in a therapeutic charm. During highly secretive occasions, initiates and experts cleansed the community's relics. Tessman witnessed such a ceremony in the early twentieth century, among a Fang community of southern Cameroon. After gathering in the shrine, male specialists removed craniums from reliquary boxes and cleansed them in basins filled with powerful medicines. They smeared the skulls with a red ointment, the blood of a sacrificed chicken mixed with *paduk* powder. The next day, the initiates sacrificed a sheep and shared the meat with the ancestors. Then they made demands of the craniums, protection over the community, or personal skills and cures.[49]

Considerable risk of loss and contagion were the other side of the transactional relation involved in harvesting and enabling human substances. At the time of death, a person's corporeal power experienced a moment of uncontrollable fluidity, when, with the rare exception of powerful *nganga*, the deceased could no longer control his or her overflowing force.[50] As initiates detached the person's forces in the form of body fragments, or as the magical capacity leaked from the corpse as sacred fluids, another dangerous period commenced. People knew that body parts and corpses could be stolen and recycled in criminal networks trafficking in bodily power.[51] As we've already seen in chapter 2, human sacrifice, a rare ritual, obeyed a logic of exchange.[52] The iKota verbs *ikaba* and *ihoutchiyè*, "to pass" and "to give," when used in the context of sacrifice, described the offering of a human life to ancestors and spirits.[53] Transactions could be destructive, and carnal technologies could end up in loss and theft. Witches killed for their sole benefit.

Disputes over bodily resources were more likely under some specific circumstances. Witches could appropriate the abundant power of the decaying corpse, especially during internecine conflicts. During the Atlantic era in particular, the sale of people into slavery came to be interpreted, at least in part, as transactions in human worth and bodily magic that benefited those who traded persons. Peter Geschiere finds that, long before the colonial conquest, in regions touched by the slave trade and commodity markets, basic notions of healing for the public good had been overrun by new fears of destructive witchcraft (in Cameroon: *ekong*, *nyongo*).[54] Powerful *nganga* and leaders across West Equatorial Africa often acquired new forms of material wealth

and magical capacity by "passing" a person to spirits or foreign slave traders. In times of warfare, the experts working for one faction could be seen as
criminal witches (Fang: *beyem*; Galoa: *olovalovi*) by those in opposite faction.
Sometimes, they could betray their own patrons.[55]

Body as Fetish, Body as Sign

In contrast with Gabonese philosophies of a fully capacious human body,
nineteenth-century French imaginaries had little faith in the enchanted power
of the flesh. But in Renaissance Europe, people had seen the body as an open,
fragmented, and cosmic entity that worked both as a metaphoric image of
the Church and as a sacred shelter for religious sacraments. The "grotesque
realism" of folk cultures, famously discussed by Mikhail Bakhtin, portrayed
flesh as universal and collective, an exaggerated macrocosm full of fertility
and brimming with abundance.[56] The human body lost much of its symbolic
power during the Enlightenment. In the nineteenth century, new medical and
scientific discourses helped to biologize the body, turning it into an organic
machine controlled by technical procedures.[57]

Emptied of cosmic excess, the body nevertheless continued to play a significant political role. During the French Revolution for instance, the fallen
bodies of monarchs informed public debates on the nature of modern authority. Even when democratic ideals delegitimized physical domination as
a legitimate source of authority, physical appearance and the spectacle of the
elite shaped popular imaginaries of public power.[58] In everyday life, the body
carried a person's social capital: learned postures, appearances, and behavior
(an unconscious training defined by Pierre Bourdieu as "habitus") continued to shape social hierarchies and gendered identities.[59] In the nineteenth
century, medical and biopolitical discourses increasingly described citizen-
ries as biological units or "populations" that could be counted, scrutinized,
and disciplined.[60]

At the time of the colonial conquest, therefore, Europeans paradoxically
viewed the body both as an organic entity animated by mechanical life, and
as a powerful symbol of social and political power, even if the relationship
between physical force and public authority had become one of increasing
metaphoric distance and mediation. The colonial conquest only deepened
these paradoxes, as well as the need to conceal them. In Gabon, the French
imagined the body as an abstract entity, in opposition to the (alleged) crude
and materialist perceptions of local communities. The view disincarnated

colonial rule and abstracted the physical brutality of conquest. A large majority of colonialists thought that the spectacle of civilized, ethical, and rational Frenchmen would, by example, inspire the Gabonese to change themselves, taking on the civilizing mission.[61] The metaphoric capacity of the white body worked as a *sign* of power, contrasting with the indigenous treatment of the human substances as *fetish*, an entity suffused with material agency. I call these colonial fictions of radiant authority a "politic of presence."

The archival record helps clarify the tenets of this imaginary of transformative spectacle.[62] In 1867, Paul Du Chaillu opined that the Gabonese, if left alone, would soon fall back into barbarism.[63] On the eve of World War I, local officers optimistically reported that local communities started to "feel the advantage of [French] presence" and would soon change their habits and customs by the virtue of example.[64] In 1931, Catholic sister Marie Germaine wrote that African intelligence functioned like a "photographic plate" onto which details slowly impressed themselves: Europeans should thus imprint their polite behavior on the Gabonese, who, by "aping" their white masters, would absorb the enlightening rays of civilization.[65] The metaphoric agenda of luminous presence also helped missionaries to attack Gabonese initiation societies and open up their esoteric secrets. Catholic priests rejoiced that this endeavor, like the mighty eye of God, would dispel the dark cloud of African ignorance. An iconic repertoire of radiating capacity circulated in the pamphlets and catechisms they printed and disseminated in the colony. *Le Messager du St Esprit*, the newsletter of Congregation of the Holy Ghost, the main Catholic institution in Gabon, featured an emblem of a dove surrounded by rays of light that hovered over the caption "Send your Spirit and you will renew the face of the Earth." The seal of the Holy Ghost Congregation displayed a similar but more sinister image in which the dove dives over a human heart pierced with a sharp sword and topped by flames (perhaps to eat it). The scene resonated with widespread Gabonese fears that missionaries stole black body parts for dark magic (figure 3.4).

The Catholic Church's discourse of disembodied "presence" contradicted the doctrine of the Eucharist and the miraculous power of saintly relics. During my field research in Gabon in 2002, I fell into a heated discussion with an unusually open-minded white missionary on the Church's failure to use the cult of relics in its evangelization of Gabon.[66] Full of naïve provocation, I listed the similarities between local cults of ancestors and aspects of the Christian tradition. Father Zacharie Péron listened patiently before observing that the death of Christ on the cross was not similar to pagan sacrifices but was the

3.4 Seal of the Congregation of the Holy Ghost Fathers, depicting the Immaculate Heart of Mary and the Holy Ghost, in an article "Congregation of the Holy Spirit," Wikipedia, https://en.wikipedia.org/wiki/Congregation_of_the_Holy_Spirit.

ultimate sacrifice that vanquished earlier economies of sacrifice. From then on, symbols and signs had replaced the pagan, material use of human victims. Communion, in which congregants consumed the host and the wine as the real flesh and blood of the Christian god, was materially different from pagan consumption.

Nevertheless, aware of the risk of such similarity, the Catholic hierarchy tried to enforce a separation between Christian objects and pagan fetishes. In 1952, on the one hundredth anniversary of the Congregation of the Holy Ghost Fathers, the bishop of Gabon published a "Pastoral Letter on Fetishism" that summarized the doctrinal position on this issue.[67] The letter forbade Gabonese Christians to use gris-gris, amulets, talismans, rings, or fetishes that worked "with the evil power of human sacrifice, poison, murder, revenge and ritual anthropophagy." Fetishes insulted God and assaulted domestic peace, the letter continued. In contrast, objects blessed by holy men promoted moral ends: "Christian crosses, medals and scapulars are first and foremost *signs* of our faith, and our love for the saints."[68] As Father Péron said to me in our conversation, these were disembodied signs and symbols rather than material fetishes.

Meanwhile, in the colony, the Gabonese could not miss blatant inconsistencies between the politic of radiant presence and the brutal reality of white domination. Warfare, forced labor, tax extraction, and the relentless lust of colonialists for native bodies and local resources were threatening the very survival of local societies. In utter contradiction to the benevolent agenda of the politic of presence, the French exercised "constant surveillance" over rural farmers, and enforced an "absolute obedience to orders."[69] In the early 1920s, many communities had become so weakened by colonial exactions that they reacted to the coming of troops by fleeing into seasonal camps (*mpindi*) or meeting the soldiers with complete "inertia."[70]

Historians have often recounted this history with a metanarrative of state disciplining, local resistance, and cultural transformation.[71] Few have noticed that in the eyes of local societies, colonialists often behaved as spiritual competitors for bodily resources. The following story provides a good example of rivalry and dispossession in the judicial realm.[72] On 14 January 1931, the French district officer in Mouila received the final order to execute a local convict, Maloundou Ma I Biatsi.[73] Restrained by ropes and guided to the execution ground, the prisoner was pushed to stand in front of the firing squad.[74] A group of African notables and witnesses, forcibly called to witness the execution, stood near the white officer. After reading the capital sentence, the Frenchman asked Maloundou through an interpreter whether he had any final requests. The condemned man listened to the interpreter and demanded that his belongings be given to his family, with the exception of two *pagnes* (loincloth) for a fellow convict. Then he begged for forgiveness and frantically enumerated the goods he would exchange for his life. Indifferent to the pleading, the officer lowered his arm and commanded fire. He then walked to Maloundou's dying body and shot him in the head in a final coup de grâce. The corpse was probably buried according to the law in official grounds at the station, depriving specialists' access to it and the witch-substance it might have contained.[75] In this feat of judicial and spiritual incapacitation, the criminal body had escaped local procedures of social healing and retribution. In the eyes of local elders, Maloundou's body had been punished but not disempowered. And colonialists clearly behaved as spiritual competitors.

In turn, the Gabonese physically attacked white people to retaliate for the theft of bodily power and other resources. In the early morning of 19 November 1917, Pierre Izac, a French trader, went on some errands, leaving his wife and a young black employee to tend the store. Two men of Fang origin, Ekoro Mabizoro and Ndongo Nzigue, entered the premises. They chased the boy into the nearby forest and attacked Mrs. Izac with a machete. They ordered her to lie down on the floor, struck her on the face, cut off her hands, killed her, and carried the lifeless corpse to the edge of the forest. Then they went back into the store to steal merchandise.[76]

Although the official investigation concluded that the killing of Mrs. Izac was not an open rebellion against colonial rule, it was hard for French colonialists to ignore its blatant political meanings. The severing of Mrs. Izac's hands mirrored the most publicized form of torture against natives in neighboring Congo, the target of an international campaign. The graphic cruelty of the attack replicated the violence of the colonial project, which failed to establish hegemony on little else than physical violence. By taking the carnal existence of the white woman seriously, the killers had upset the orderly distance of racial hierarchies, throwing them into deadly promiscuity. They had transformed Mrs. Izac's mortal body into a substance whose annihilation facilitated their access to imported commodities, inverting colonials' ongoing predation of African labor and resources.[77] In Gabon, colonial offerings of enlightening presence barely concealed the battles that raged over political oppression and material profits, and the device that buttressed these struggles, the human body.[78]

Hegemonic Transactions

In looting the Izac store, the police investigation recorded, Ekoro Mabizoro and Ndongo Nzigue took away 120 *pagnes* (pieces of imported fabric), nine bars of soap, four rolls of thread, seven small sacks of salt, a jar of fuel, a lantern, and an alarm clock.[79] The precision of the list written down by the district officer betrays something more than bureaucratic meticulousness. The swift murder and the painstaking inventory are the two sides, I think, of a moment of vertiginous recognition for colonialists: that the benevolent politics of presence, along with the fiction of hegemonic transactions, could be overturned in an instant. Political scientists have used the notion of hegemonic transactions to describe the ad hoc alliances established between colonizers and colonized as they negotiate power and authority in a volatile context.[80] Here I narrow down the idea of hegemonic transactions to describe the actual *deals* and *operating exchanges* that occurred on the ground. These transactions centered on material resources, among them the human body and its immense symbolic resources.

In the colony, the fiction was that the French could master and control the direction of interracial exchanges. White rulers, I argue, imagined domination, literally, as a dynamic structure made out of unequal flows of gifts, expenses, returns, earnings, acquisitions, losses and profits between themselves and the natives.[81] Some of these exchanges were material, others symbolic and ideological. Colonialism, for instance, was justified by the European effort to "regenerate the negro race" and to bring civilizational investments in Africa. The fiction was charged with heavy sexual and patriarchal metaphors, both vivid and banal. In 1899, colonial author P. Payeur-Didelot compared the explorations of Marquis de Compiègne in Gabon to "a fecund seed [*semence*] for the future of West Africa."[82] From the 1880s to the 1950s, hundreds more metaphors peppered the colonial archive, often discussing the need to manage the economy of Gabon as "a good father" (*un bon père de famille*) would his domestic household.[83]

Two short novels set in Gabon and Congo can serve as a rhetorical window into these fancies, and demonstrate the utter failure of colonial hegemony: *An Outpost of Progress*, published by Joseph Conrad in 1897 after this trip on a steamer up the Congo River in 1893, and *Un Coup de lune*, written by Georges Simenon in 1933 after a brief visit to Libreville. Conrad's novella details how European racism and insularity, combined with brutal material greed, dooms white domination.[84] The story starts when two factory managers, Kayerts and Carlier, arrive at an isolated station on the upper Congo River, three hundred miles away from any other European presence. Their only companion is Henry Price, an experienced African clerk from Sierra Leone, who "despises the two white men." Convinced of their superiority, Kayerts and Carlier become increasingly immersed in stupendously circular conversation, and grow more isolated from the Africans while leaving the care of the factory to the African clerk. The two men ignore a country that they see only as a large "void." In a crucial episode, they let Henry Price sell ten of the factory workers as slaves to passing African traders, in exchange for a considerable amount of ivory. After a few months, rendered mad by solitude and greediness, and unable to sustain the pretense of moral superiority, Kayerts and Carlier kill each other in a frenzy of narcissistic annihilation.

A few decades later, Georges Simenon's *Le Coup de lune* (A crazy spell) depicts the journey to Libreville of a young and inexperienced Frenchman, Joseph Timar.[85] Timar is imbued with moral principles and ideas of social justice, yet upon his arrival in the colony he is caught in a destructive passion for an older white woman, Adèle, the owner of a hotel. She embodies the decline of French moral values in the colony, and in general, the corrosion of social justice. The liaison between Adèle and Timar shows the impossible coexistence of metropolitan norms and colonial realities. Timar is a powerless outsider (*en dehors du jeu*). His moral nerve proves weak: he is outraged by the sight of colonialists beating and killing natives but fails to do anything about it.[86] Timar's moral decay is mirrored by his body's physical decline, suggestively weakened by criminal pleasure, lack of social discipline, and undeserved material benefits. Soon, his debt and traffic in bodies culminate in a morbid frenzy. In the face of Timar's mounting detachment, Adèle casually kills a black servant and bribes a local chief to accuse another black man of the crime. During the court hearing, Timar tries to testify to the truth, but he is unable to disrupt the colonial order and collapses into a mental breakdown and tropical illness. The book ends with two departures. Adèle leaves with indentured African workers for a plantation in the forest, and Timar is forcibly put on a boat back to France.

Using the individual body as a metaphor for the moral failure of white settlers, Conrad and Simenon locate destructive potential within the settlers. It is not so much racial proximity or the failure to escape the contagion of native bodies and culture that dooms colonialism, two versions of a colonial narrative classically documented by postcolonial scholars—"going native"— but white people's evil capacity to create a regime of destructive transactions and/or and narcissistic isolation.[87] Colonial hegemony is less threatened by the blurring of racial frontiers than by white people's inability to conduct moral, productive exchanges with Africans. In both novels, the heroes benefit from illegal and immoral exchanges and profits. Worst of all, they confuse people and commodities: Kayerts and Carlier trade human beings for ivory, and Adèle, the hotel manager, negotiates in cash for the life of a black man who will take on her crime and stand trial for her.

Against these deathly yearnings and failed interactions with Africans, the colonial imaginary was also full of redemptive solutions, culminating in the iteration of self-sacrifice. First and foremost patriotic, imperial propaganda celebrated the "battles, sacrifices and efforts" by which the French had established a colonial empire and helped France to regain its rank among the leading nations of the world.[88] In the empire itself, stories of selfless colonial lives featured missionaries, nuns, and colonials devoted to the betterment of the natives, isolated in the colony, and ultimately defeated by illness and death, a theme that contrasted with Conrad's and Simenon's novellas.[89] Incidentally, white sacrifice also tied Africans to a moral debt to invaders: the death of colonialists demanded appreciation and justified the conquest as moral venture. Native ingratitude was feared: in 1912, Jean Dybowski wrote that "[the moment] [Africans] think they are stronger than us, they will invert the proverb and cut the hand they used to kiss."[90] In tales of debt, caution, and blind revenge, the repertoire of transactions reigned supreme.

Albert Schweitzer, an Alsatian doctor who opened a pioneering hospital in the center of Gabon in 1913, was the most accomplished figure of self-sacrifice, in part because he overcame the moral contradictions embedded in colonialists' transactions with the Gabonese. It does not take much imagination to see in the legend of the "bush doctor" an image of self-sacrifice of almost Christlike dimensions, one that can be read as a redeeming resolution to the kind of anxieties Conrad and Simenon exposed in their novels. A Protestant minister, physician, and musicologist born in 1875 in Alsatia (the French martyr province ceded to Germany just a few years earlier), Schweitzer came to the little station of Lambaréné, on the Ogooué River, to organize a "native hospital."[91] The story was that Schweitzer had given up a brilliant career in Europe to tend to savages in the jungle. His organized, routinized, and bureaucratized heroism replaced the flamboyant adventures of explorers and missionaries in Africa. The daily miracles that the good doctor performed in his hospital conjured a tale of benevolent racial hierarchy greased by scientific expertise.

Aloof and intellectual, Schweitzer never really mixed with his African patients. His medical work, therefore, did not threaten his quintessential, iconic European status: Schweitzer's familiar sacrifice did not make him "go native." A Christlike figure recalling Mauss's paradigm of the self-sacrificing divinity, the life of the bush doctor proposed to colonial rulers an impossible triumph: to transform from a vampirizing master bent on its own demise into a benevolent, self-immolating, yet replenished God.[92]

Unlike Schweitzer, however, most Frenchmen in Gabon feared that their sacrifices, big and small, were meaningless. Most, too, knew that the privileges they enjoyed in the colony did not derive from self-immolation or benevolent gifts but their coercion of unwilling victims. The bifurcated meaning of the word "sacrifice" itself betrayed ambiguity, referring to a religious or moral gift bringing returns, and also to a profane act of waste and destruction. Hegemonic transactions in the colony, and the resulting accruing of power for white people, rested disproportionately on the squandering of black lives and bodies.

From Sacrifice to Body Parts

The Gabonese experienced colonialism as the relentless theft of magic *puissance*, bodily capacity, and economic and social resources.[93] They rumored that white priests stole dead bodies from the mission cemeteries, and held on to the genealogical charms they confiscated from Africans.[94] This seemed a behavior typical of witches greedy for human substances.[95] An elderly informant in the 1960s remembered colonial exactions: "The missionaries kept the relics. What are the relics? They are the bones. We only worshipped the bones. So we are one. This was a deceit. Old people were angry because the country fell, and we had no *puissance* left."[96]

Detached from kinship and older therapeutic technologies, a market of free-floating, anonymous human substances emerged in the colony. Forced by law to work in hiding, Gabonese experts receded into clandestine practices and appeared to work for their own agenda, or for that of powerful witches.[97] The transactions and exchanges that realized bodily power were slowly contaminated with criminal intentions and dark suspicions.

The legacy of these reconfigurations can be seen in the grave robberies and ritual murders that reign today in Gabon, fueling criminal markets in human substances. In the Mindoubé cemetery of Libreville between 2009 and 2012, Gabonese anthropologist Lionel Ikogou-Renamy was able to map out and analyze the frequency of grave robberies that people carried out to procure such substances. The profanations often come to public attention on All Saints' Day, when families congregate in cemeteries to clean the graves of relatives and to "spend time with the dead." Forced to bury their relatives in official grounds, their loss of control over the dead continues unabated. Mindoubé had opened in the 1950s as a segregated graveyard for native Gabonese. Surrounded by fences and supervised by a guard, the cemetery concentrated the dead away from the surveillance of the families. In the 1990s, for lack of public funds, it fell into significant disrepair, its surroundings progressively transforming into a dumping ground and the cemetery itself mutating into a veritable mine for grave robbers.[98]

During his research, Ikogou-Renamy documented approximately 150 incidents of desecration.[99] To collect the remains, the thieves usually come at night with tools and instruments. They use hammers and chisels to break graves, and a motor pump to flood the cavity. When the contents float to the surface (figures 3.5 and 3.6), the thieves collect the remains, along with some of the soil and clothes that have been in contact with the dead. They sell them to shady ritual experts for a high price.[100] The techniques used by the thieves directly relate to the profane mechanics of biomedicine and engineering; at the same time, they signal the thieves' beliefs in the sacred and magical power of human substances. Unburied from the grave and exchanged for hefty sums of money, the body also reenters a composite realm of economic and magical transactions with ritual experts and clients.

3.5 A desecrated tomb in the Mindoubé cemetery, Libreville, 2009. Photograph by Lionel Ikogou-Renamy.

3.6 Hole in a grave emptied by the technique of pump flooding, Mindoubé cemetery, Libreville, 2009. Photograph by Lionel Ikogou-Renamy.

Thugs, meanwhile, procure fresh organs for rich and influential patrons (*commanditaire*). When they kill a victim and cut off parts of the body to make a charm, they sanctify human flesh at the same time as they desecrate it.[101] Indeed, the public often describes the murder as a parody of meat processing and trading, insisting on the organic, animalized nature of the flesh.[102] They talk about the victim as "game" (*gibier*) and "meat" (*viande*), and the killing as "butchery" (French: *boucherie*) performed by "butchers" (*bouchers*) eager to "deliver" (*livrer*) the "body parts" (*pièces détachées*) to a patron.[103] The paradoxical dynamic of reenchantment/profanation has culminated recently in a newer technique: the assassins now keep their victim alive while they mutilate her, so they can harvest the organs at their maximum power.[104] Elicited by colonial assaults on the human body, a double matrix of "anonymizing" and "biologizing" carnal power has radically transformed the techniques for composing corporeal agency.

Colonial intrusions did not transform bones and human substances into neutral and inert commodities, nor did they leave indigenous imaginaries untouched. The ambiguous reenchantment and biologizing of the human body in the colony challenges conventional views that a linear pressure of market forces, a sweeping reification of human flesh, or the indomitable resilience of African ideas about magic are enough to explain the particular beliefs and bodily praxis detectable today in Gabon, Africa, and Europe. Instead, these ideas developed from complex struggles and agreements between Africans and Europeans over the agency of human substances and the technologies that could activate such capacity.

Among both the Gabonese and the French, these operations were haunted by the awareness of moral transgression and undeserved profits. Colonial efforts to reenchant white bodies and to biologize African ones ended in paradoxical formations in which the sacred capacity of human flesh and bones was increasingly predicated on their anonymous, carnal existence. I have called this modern, composite, and aggregate belief in the biomedical, political, and individual agency of the human body "carnal fetishism." Far from being confined to Africa, the notion can help us to understand some of the quandaries of global biomedicine and philosophies of the body.[105] The next chapter shifts the investigation over to the value of people and human substances.

FOUR : The Value of People

— French terms.

References to *l'argent* (money) saturate the personal interactions of the Gabonese, often surging in angry or blasé complaints: "In Gabon, today, it's just the money ... [imitating a greedy person]: 'Give me the money!'"[1] With most people experiencing dire economic scarcity, the sentence expresses a constant preoccupation with survival. But it also suggests that the Gabonese recognize that money is a central component of relationships in the family and in broader social networks. *Bouffer l'argent* (to eat money) warns that excessive spending in the family can threaten communal survival, a danger akin to cannibalism. One "eats" (kills) the family by "eating" (wasting) its collective assets. People also use *bouffer l'argent* to describe how politicians embezzle public funds and waste money in grand fashion.[2] Indeed, if accumulating liquid assets remains a foremost strategy of social betterment, it is bounded by moral prescriptions. The Gabonese shun the destructive appetite, the devastating avarice of people giving themselves over to the sterile consumption of riches, suggesting that witchcraft and political success are based on some individuals' inordinate thirst for moneyed wealth. And in doing so, they also talk about people, bodies, and money as commensurate valuables.

The recurring tragedy of ritual murders (Gabonese French: *crimes rituels*) offers a spectacular avenue into this intellectual and practical formation, and the role of money in mediating an exchange between human flesh and *puissance*. Such commerce is not confined to Gabon; similar incidents happen in many parts of Africa and have received considerable scholarly attention. By and large, scholars see the murders as resulting from the reification of the person and the commodifying of magic and religious rites.[3] From this perspective, ritual crimes are a legacy of the unbridled consumerism of the slave trade and colonialism. The paradigm is part of a long tradition in the social sciences and the humanities that posits that economic value is incompatible with social value, and tends to destroy it.[4]

This chapter proposes another narrative: it shows how the modern commensurability between money, people, and human substances comes from older regimes of transactional value. In nineteenth-century West Equatorial Africa, societies posited a relative worth between material goods (commodities), money, and the person: even though they considered human beings as the most precious of assets, they did not find these equivalences to be impossible or immoral. Then, during colonialism, each of these categories—a "person," a "commodity," and an "economic transaction"—came under intense scrutiny.[5] Colonized and colonizers debated which things could be exchanged and which could not, whether the value of people could be measured with money, and whether trade should occur between equal and separate partners.

While the French caricatured the Gabonese as materialists who considered people as mere commodities and confused social value with material greed, their own philosophies were riddled with deep paradoxes. Aggregating the Gabonese in tight social and economic clusters around colonial posts, for instance, Europeans often replicated indigenous ideas of "wealth in people." Meanwhile, they used a legal device called "blood money" or "blood price" in local courts, compensating physically injured victims with cash.

[margin annotations: "shifting of transaction" ; "Commoditizing the value of persons" ; "value of damage to a person"]

Blood Money

The French created countless ways of equating people with cash. Head taxes and labor wages converted social wealth and time into money. In the judicial realm, the device of "blood price" (French: *prix du sang*) pretended to imitate and improve "native customs" by paying a standard amount of cash to the party of the victim and cancelling native *lex talionis*, a punishment that corresponded in kind to the offense of the wrongdoer.

I became aware of blood money when, in the Gabonese archives, I stumbled across a note sent in 1944 by governor Pierre Vuillaume to all district officers in Gabon, complete with a table, instructing them to standardize the rates of *prix du sang* (blood price).[6] The note eerily expressed a central axiom of modern witchcraft and ritual crimes: the exchange of human substances for riches. The expression *prix du sang* itself was a powerful image, suggesting that a bodily fluid could be priced in money. Governor Vuillaume's note demanded that *prix du sang* should be reevaluated in regard to the monetary devaluations that had occurred during the war. He asked the district officers to suggest new rates in French francs for African victims coming to court with a claim.[7] Only two answers survived in the archives, both sent by administrators from the Ogooué-Ivindo province who proposed the tabulation in table 4.1.

The official *Journal of French Equatorial Africa* did not yield evidence of any law or decree that set up blood price or explained these rates.[8] Finally, in the archives of the colonial tribunals, I found haphazard references to the legal device.[9] The courts routinely sentenced convicted parties to pay the *prix du sang* to the victim or his/her relatives. Yet blood money was not a fine and did not work as penal retribution: it was not the court sentence per se. Instead, it was a cash compensation (*indemnité*) for the victim's death or loss of limbs (damages for pain and suffering).[10]

In 1910, the French government had organized justice in the French Federation of Equatorial Africa (FEA) by forming first- and second-degree tribunals in colonial centers. First-degree tribunals, also called *tribunaux indigènes* (native courts), dealt with minor conflicts. They were fully controlled by colonial rulers: a French judge headed the court, and two native assessors played only an advisory role. The same principles applied to second-degree tribunals, though they heard more serious cases. Finally, a high court (*chambre d'homologation*) in Brazzaville, the capital of French Equatorial Africa, was in charge of reviewing the most serious cases arbitrated by lower courts, especially those that had ended up in a sentence of life imprisonment and death.

Table 4.1 Colonial Table of Value in People

	Ogooué-Ivindo	Mékambo
Young child	300 FF[1]	200 FF
Teenager	500 FF	400 FF
Adult male, single	1,000 FF	800 FF
Adult male, married	1,000 FF	1,100 FF
Adult male, married, with child	1,200 FF	1,200 FF
Adult female, single	1,000 FF	600 FF
Adult female, married	1,000 FF	800 FF
Adult female, mother of young children	1,200 FF	1,000 FF

Source: Compiled from réponse à la circulaire du 20 mars 1944, Ogooué-Ivindo, 15 May 1944, signed Le Lidec; and réponse à la circulaire du 20 mars 1944, Mekambo, 3 May 1944, unsigned.
1. French francs.

rix au sang

The archival record left by these courts, although spotty, showed that native tribunals had levied compensation payments under various names since at least 1921. That year, a Nkomi chief named Graystock had been sentenced to three years in prison and 1,000 French francs in fines for forcing a man to undergo an ordeal by poison. In addition, the court had ordered him to pay 250 French francs to the victim as *dommages et intérêts* (incidental damages).[11] Four years later, in 1925, the high court in Brazzaville cancelled a cannibal case because the judge had failed to provide *prix du sang* for the victims.[12] I found other mentions of blood money in court records in 1933, 1941, 1943, and 1944.[13] Yet the judges used different definitions and, contradicting the governor's instructions, often confused *prix du sang*, a compensatory sum of money, with fines or retributions.[14]

Courts struggled to define what they called "native customs" (*coutumes indigènes*).[15] The French imagined that Africans were unable to understand any kind of punishment beyond direct and physical retaliation (physical torture, death and mutilation, or the selling of criminals into slavery) and that they failed to translate arbitrary facts into a universal legal framework.[16] To the colonial mind, the *prix du sang* converted older forms of African retribution into a measurable, predictable, and symbolic form of reparation in colonial currency, preserving native mores while civilizing them. A feat of abstract sublimation, it replaced physical and social loss with money. Yet, belying French efforts to draw hierarchies between commodities and noncommodities, *prix du sang* established a standard value for an individual person, pulling social exchanges into the economic sphere. And the French imposed *prix du sang* as a highly normative institution controlled by judicial courts.

But nothing remotely similar to blood money actually existed in local societies, especially not the replacing of a person or her limbs by a payment in cash. In slave trading, people exchanged a person for commodities and wealth, but many considered the trade as detrimental to social wealth and a quasicriminal act, like greedily bewitching an individual for profit. Instead, local practices of compensation sentenced the wrongdoer to social fines in kind or labor to be paid to the victims, or to substitute a live person for the victim.[17]

During the colonial period, the local courts' widespread use of blood money triggered three major processes. First, the use of cash in legal reparation spread at the grassroots level, fostering a new correspondence between physical damage, social worth, and money. At least in the legal parlance used in French, the carnal, physical substance could now serve as a metonym for a person.[18] Second, the French retained control of blood money transactions, anchoring equivalence between body and cash in the sphere of foreign political power and central authority. Third, the term *prix du sang* itself echoed, and perhaps furthered, the rising importance of *sang* (blood) in vernacular imaginaries.[19]

Whether and how the wider Gabonese public imagination appropriated the colonial invention of *prix du sang* remains an open question. As a legal device, *prix du sang* did not explicitly survive in the Gabonese penal code of 1963.[20] Yet the lore of ritual murders, with their strong emphasis on cashing in organs, suggests that some transfer did occur. Moreover, the notion spread in the anthropological literature, often uncritically.[21] A recent study of Fang communities in Gabon argues that when a nephew dies, the uncles can claim the *prix du sang* from the paternal family. For the author, the reparation meant the substitution of a man for a man: to call this *prix du sang* shows how colonial terms managed to color past indigenous realities.[22]

Wealth in People: Revisiting the Paradigm

How did local societies assess and create human value? Everyday descriptions of people as propertied capital, documented in the twentieth century, help us to enter in the longue durée history of the value of people in West Equatorial Africa. They signal the enduring importance of money in describing and facilitating social relations, and widespread views that people, bodies, and money were mutually fungible items.

During the twentieth century, the lexicon comparing persons with material possessions remained remarkably stable. In 1938, the Gabonese Fang intellectual and chief Léon Mba wrote that *bioum*, the various goods owned collectively by a family (commodities, poultry, cattle, plantations, etc.), did include people. While the husband was expected to provide his wife with a house and clear her plantations, she was considered to be part of his property.[23] In 1967 in southern Cameroon, a Fang Bëti man "owned" his children, as expressed by the adage "Mbela abela bod bésa" (The owner owns all of his people).[24] Likewise, Fang males "owned" their wives and offspring, while the wealthiest among them could also rely on *mintobo* (clients), on slaves, and on dependent groups they had defeated in war. The Bëti knew from infancy that one had "to pay for everything," including any kind of superiority.[25] In the 1980s, the Ndumu in Gabon called their children and descendants *vilà vi me*, a term that also meant "my goods," "my things."[26] In 1999, a study of succession among the Nzébi showed that a man's belongings (Nzébi: *mabwè*; French: *biens*) included material capital (money, houses, plantations, livestock), reproductive capital (children and wives), and symbolic capital (such as *bikôôko*, the magical skills of the deceased).[27] The repertoire used for social transactions reveals similar ideas about people being wealth. The French-Gabonese verbs *gaspiller* (to dilapidate/to waste) and *dépenser* (to spend), for instance, refer to the squandering of both social and material wealth.[28] *Gaspiller quelqu'un* (to "waste" somebody) means to kill someone and reverse the cycle of social reproduction.[29] Indeed, in extreme situations, elders can "spend" the kin who "squanders" assets, threatening the collective well-being of the family.[30] As an older initiate of the Mwiri initiation society told me in southern Gabon in 2002, "Mwiri swallows the one for whom we have to spend too much."[31]

Historians often hypothesize that these expressions result from the increasing commodification of the person during the slave trade. Indeed, between the sixteenth and the nineteenth century, an increasing portion of long-distance and regional trading concerned human beings.[32] Spanning several centuries, the changes resulting from the slave trade defy generalization. Historians of Equatorial Africa, however, agree that the status of the person progressively eroded. Thousands of firearms penetrated the region, as did imported commodities, and foreign traders used a compelling system of credit to pressure local societies to sell outsiders or defenseless persons into slavery.[33] Increasingly relying on prestige goods in the form of imported commodities to secure the loyalty of vassals and allies, local leaders could not resist the foreign traders' demands for captives in exchange for these prestige goods.[34] They also realized that they could aggregate households and dependents more rapidly than allowed by older strategies of social composition.[35] Along the Congo River, Bobangi traders brought these tactics to the extreme: they created huge "firms" composed of dozens, sometimes hundreds, of dependents by incorporating bargain-priced slaves from the river trade into their households, including easily controllable slave wives. The new system generated unprecedented social gaps between a minority of free entrepreneurs and a majority of servile workers.[36]

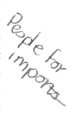

1500 - 1600s

People for imports

Yet, rather than inert material goods, people kept attaching a primordial value to human beings as ultimate riches. For Jan Vansina, "The spirit of capitalism [had] made no genuine inroads. Wealth remained what it had always been: a crucial avenue to authority and power."[37] Even after decades of trading in slaves and commodities, big men did not pursue material wealth for its own sake but to acquire dependents and assert influence over subordinates and allies. They did exchange less valuable individuals (prisoners of war, criminals, outsiders, low dependents) for commodities and currency, but then they rapidly reinvested these new trade items to attract social allies and dependents.[38] The scholarly theory of "wealth-in-people" captured the historical significance of this enduring ethic and reminded scholars that, in Africa, low population densities coupled with abundant land led societies to predominantly measure wealth in people and labor.[39] In an influential series of 1990s articles, Jane Guyer dispelled the quantitative connotation of the notion and offered subtle understandings of the ways in which West Equatorial African communities relied on human wealth.[40] Working on empirical material gathered in southern Cameroon, Guyer suggested that people sought to build human retinues of dependents, and that these strategies were not driven by simple quantitative or accumulative ideas. Instead, tactics of accumulation and growth were qualitative and compositional, considering the value of a person from the viewpoint of his or her skills and knowledge, and the outside alliances that he or she could foster. Likewise, the prestige of a leader was determined less by an abundance of people in his "house" than by the talent he exhibited in assembling a judicious array of personalities and talents, another form of wealth-in-people.[41]

Guyer's work breathed new life in Africa-centered models of social analysis. Yet it is possible that too rigid a distinction between material capital and the social worth of people obscures rather than illuminates the political economy of West Equatorial Africa. In the region, I suggest, the compositional quality of wealth acquisition did not always distinguish between people and things.[42]

To understand this, we need to start with the fact that local societies valued riches from the angle of their ultimate social potential. The worth and reputation of a powerful woman, for instance, was embedded in the connections, alliances, and losses that she could foster or undermine for the benefit of her clan. Such social and political exchanges, in turn, could be materialized and carried out by what Westerners qualify as simple "commodities." In this context, inanimate and animate (in the Western sense of the term) valuables could be exchanged for one another. Whether skills, persons, marked currencies, or commodities (raffia cloth or iron ore), all valuables could enter into transactions that continued to produce social accretion. Thus a clan or a person's social capital was made of commensurable reservoirs of valuables that were ready to be moved and exchanged, through commerce or alliances, for more productive assets.

In the 1880s, the relative commensurability between material and social wealth was visible in the fact that different spheres of exchange had permeable boundaries, as did the currencies used for social and commercial operations.[43] Although West Equatorial Africans did privilege specialized (or marked) currencies for social exchange (fines and marriage payments), evidence abounds that these monies constantly filtered through the realm of the commodity market, while unmarked ones penetrated social exchanges.[44] For instance, traders along the lower Congo River mostly used raffia cloth (*ntaa*) for social payment. But brass rod currency (*mitako*), goats, and fowls all also entered into the payment of fines and bride-wealth.[45] Further inland, the Tio people paid marriage payments in composite and convertible monies, acquired by the groom through various means. Once the bride's family accepted the payment, they would usually immobilize it for a time before recycling it in payments in the new unions of sons and nephews, and occasionally using it for more common transactions.[46] Indeed, among the Fang in Gabon, *bikie*, the iron rod money used for social payments, became in the nineteenth century the preferred currency for trading commodities.[47] The compound nature of social payments and the convertibility of currencies seem to have been widespread.[48]

The widespread principle of substitution and convertibility that regulated Equatorial Africans' relations with ancestors and spirits explained the oscillating and contextual value that they applied to both people and things. Substitution was a structural element of the sacrifice economy, and could still be documented in and around Gabon in the twentieth century, for instance, in the Fang Bëti's ritual of male initiation, the *So*.[49] During the *So*, the trials endured by the candidates stood in part as a form of expiation for the sins that had been perpetrated by higher initiates and the society at large: the boys' ordeal thus substituted for the punishment of adult men.[50] Other examples of substitution survived in the colonial archives, showing how exchanges in kin and goods could extinguish a crime debt.[51] In 1912, a complicated village feud unfolded in central Gabon. In the village of Makima, four inhabitants were killed during a skirmish. Fellow villagers pressured one of their relatives, a man named Pangangoy, to retaliate by executing four men in the village of Malingi. After Pangangoy refused to carry out the vengeance, the villagers took his two children and his wife away from him. They threatened to marry off Pangangoy's wife to Moboutsou, a man who, they claimed, was willing to avenge them. Under pressure, Pangangoy relented, agreeing to shoot a random traveler on the river nearby. But even after he did it (with a group of other men), the villagers decided that a single victim did not make up for the original offense. They asked Pangangoy to kill an additional person, or to pay a new marriage compensation for his bride in the form of two ivory tusks and one hundred copper plates (*neptunes*).[52]

The date of the feud shows that the commensurability between persons and goods had little to do with the pressure of economic capitalism. In 1912, little cash circulated in rural Gabon. Pangangoy's ordeal suggested the endurance of the old ethos of commensurable wealth that substituted, traded, and converted things into persons, persons into persons, and persons into things. Yet the fact that Pangangoy promptly resolved to kill a man to get back his wife and children introduces the role of sentiment and affection into the picture, often obscured by the academic formula of wealth-in-people. The strategic possibility of fungible valuables did not exclude the role of interpersonal feelings of attachment. The longue durée movability of riches in Gabon thus differed from a narrow-minded "materialism." In contrast with colonial prejudice, Equatorial Africans did not objectify people into inert "matter" and lifeless goods. Instead, they invested considerable social value in people at the same time they endowed objects with extensive social and symbolic capacity.[53]

Transactional Value

The relative commensurability between people and things in West Equatorial Africa accrued in dynamic processes that I call "transactional value."[54] In the nineteenth century, hardly any inert or immobile worth was permanently attached to assets and valuables. Instead, people regarded value as *realized* through exchanges. Capital, from this perspective, was "any resource productive of wealth in the future."[55]

[margin note: value comes from exchanges]

In nineteenth-century Gabon, people did not consider debt to be a limited financial obligation that could be fully cancelled by repayment. Rather, liabilities and dues between people constituted the very fabric of day-to-day social alliances and informed a wide range of exchanges, including trade, tribute, and marriage.[56] Receiving a gift or a loan of any sort enmeshed a person in liens of recognition and tribute with the giving party. The Fang pushed this ethos to an extreme with the potlatch-like custom of *bilabi*. *Bilabi* were large gift ceremonies during which rich Fang patrons gave lavish presents to their inferiors, competing among each other for ostentatious generosity. *Bilabi* thus served to destroy material assets, in particular those acquired through commerce, converting them into social wealth (respect for the generous donor). The ideal of generosity and capacity survives in today's Gabon: one's ability to "give," i.e. to capture the receiving party in a bond of obligation, remains the measure of social superiority. Conversely, poverty in material goods, hoard, or kin means that one is unable to mediate social wealth through gift giving.[57]

Hence wealth and worth were embedded in a practical ethic of realization through exchange, and existed only in relative and dynamic fashion. One pursued prosperity and influence through multiple acts of exchanging, accumulating, wasting, caring, investing, composing, or going into debt. All exchanges, including those labeled by the modern liberal language as "economic," were immersed in social meaning. This did not mean that riches were of equivalent value but that their relative worth could be measured against one another.

But one achieved success and wealth at the expense of other persons.[58] The Fang believed, for instance, that one could gain wealth and power only through assertive aggressiveness and maintain it with a strong *evu/kundu* (the witchcraft substance located in the body).[59] The stakes were high: a man felt that the economic security of his house depended entirely on his own success, a sentiment expressed by the precept "Mot ase a yiane tobo and djeng" (Each man should stay in his own house). Because other men felt and acted the same way, assets could also be lost, stolen, or captured, an ethos mirrored in the realm of spiritual warfare. Tellingly, the Fang considered witchcraft a form of thievery.[60] This economy was anything but "moral."[61]

Otangani: The People Who Count

Foreigners in West Equatorial Africa did not understand these local imaginaries or even suspect that they existed. In 1876, Fleuriot de Langle lamented, "Everywhere, life has little value."[62] Colonials and missionaries painted the Gabonese as cold-hearted slavers and die-hard materialists indifferent to the value of the person. They caricatured Gabon as a hellhole where tribesmen spent their time selling and eating one another.[63] Marriage provided endless terrain for their contempt.[64] Fathers and husbands were accused of selling their female kin to workers and white men so they could take advantage of the riches circulated by the new wage economy.[65] Women were suspected of lusting for money and commodities and, after prostituting themselves, of spreading venereal diseases through the general population: "Poor Joséphines! Unfortunate Sidonies! Pushed by a maddening lust towards fineries, they will, once they turn fifteen, get trapped in the Vice of the Civilized! Poor daughters of the Pongoués, Bengas and Fiottes, who could only be protected by virtue and labor, and who give in to depravation through laziness and frivolity!"[66]

And yet—again—the French often pursued practices strikingly similar to the indigenous habits they missed or misread and shunned. The Gabonese called colonialists Otangani, constructed from the Bantu verb -*tang* ("to count"), the name captured the material and social greed of foreigners and white people, along with their eagerness to scrutinize and capture indigenous wealth.[67]

One way that Europeans showed their social greed was to assemble dependents and workers. Starting in the mid-nineteenth century, traders, missionaries, administrators, and white *forestiers* (timber industrialists) gathered native clients, workers, and Christian converts around them. Traders and managers of factories (stores), for instance, lived in vast territories with no reliable means of communication with European outposts elsewhere in the colony.[68] Lacking personnel, they relied on a motley crew of regional guards, African clerks, and temporary hired hands to protect administrative and commercial outposts. These "auxiliaries" (*auxiliaires*) attracted a growing crowd of petty traders and other residents to the post.[69] Settlers who worked in the timber and mining industry, meanwhile, faced constant labor shortages, failing to attract Gabonese workers. They organized vast campaigns of recruitments throughout the colony, and established hundreds of migrants in labor camps and compounds near the mining sites.

The French often secured direct bondage through social aggregation and economic exploitation. Concessionary factory agents violently retaliated against indigenous workers and producers who were reluctant to gather products for them: they often rounded up their relatives and held them hostage until the workers did the work.[70] Governmental agents used similar tactics to gather taxes from the natives. In one incident in 1913 in Como Province, a district officer on tour took a young girl as hostage to force her family to pay their taxes. Although the governor of Gabon ordered them to release her, he explained that the administrator's initiative conformed to "Pahouin [Fang] customs."[71]

Taking hostages was also common among white traders. In 1922, an African agent of the commercial firm Société du Haut-Ogooué who had given credit advances of rubber to local producers, forced his employees to arrest nearby villagers. He instructed the hostages that he would release them if their families promptly brought cash and goods to pay their debts.[72] During the two World Wars, state authorities imposed mandatory *prestations* (forced labor) for porterage, cash crops, and rubber for the war effort.[73] Even after the official abolition of forced labor (1946), *prestations* did not stop. In 1948 in the district of Mbigou (Ngounié), for instance, the local administrator reported an annual amount of twenty thousand days of portage, an exorbitant amount that he had probably extorted from African chiefs.[74] Even outside of violent coercion, capitalist work arrangements changed social relations dramatically. Cut off from native communities, tens of thousands of men experienced new working schedules, combined with original forms of leisure and relative freedom from clan obligations. New occupational, spatial, and ethnic identities arose.[75]

Meanwhile, the project of "village regrouping" (*regroupement de villages*), which the French government implemented in the 1930s in the south of the colony and, in the 1950s in the north, forced villagers to move from their original land to larger settlements along colonial roads and outposts—one of the most traumatic initiatives of the colonial era.[76] Headed by municipal councils that powerfully relayed the intentions of the colonial authorities to local people, the new communities were soon wrecked by political infighting and social tensions between rival clans.

Last but not least, a significant part of colonial efforts to aggregate and control native populations came at the hands of Christian missionaries. Protestant ministers and Catholic priests aggregated their flocks by literally buying followers, thus furthering the practice of the pricing of persons. They primarily targeted young girls, whom Catholic fathers considered "enslaved" by parents eager to receive bride payment from the family of the betrothed.[77] The priests set out to substitute themselves for the spouse: they gave compensation in cash to the parents in order to "marry" the girls as brides of Christ, and bring them to the mission, thus saving their lives.[78] In Lambaréné in 1891, the fathers at the Saint-François-Xavier mission wrote, "Every time we have 50 francs we buy one of these little creatures and trust her to the nuns."[79] In 1897, the missionaries at Sainte-Anne in Libreville congratulated themselves on having that year "purchased back" (*racheté*) fifty female converts.[80] They frequently complained that the Protestants had more money for such purchases. In 1902, the priests at Lambaréné published the following tale about one of their pupils, a young girl named Joséphine, who had gone back to her family for vacation on the eve of her first communion.[81] Alas, a Protestant minister decided to visit her parents and give them presents. "Engrossed by such material advantages, a few nice *pagnes* and the friendship of the white man," the priest wrote, the parents forced their reluctant and desperate daughter to join the Protestant mission.[82] Missionaries also hinted that Europeans in town also acquired young African children with money.[83] In a case in 1922, two African guards (*capitas*) in Djambani presented a young Adouma abandoned by his master to the local district officer. The French administrator sent the boy to school and gave the *capitas* a small sum as reward.[84]

Imposing Christian Religion on Gabon + Her holidays buying holidays = increased commodity of persons

Missionaries failed to see that their behavior matched the practices they denounced, even though many were at the forefront of antislavery propaganda. The language for "purchasing back" young men and women, from the French verb *racheter*, played a pivotal role in this selective blindness. *Rachat* and *racheter* have another meaning in French; in a religious context, they mean to redeem a sinner.[85] For the priests, *racheter* thus converted a monetary transaction into a feat of moral redemption. They believed that they prevented the parents from selling their children in marriage as "commodities." The money of the priests, far from replicating slavery, elevated the subject of the deal from a gross commodity to an immaterial, aspiring Christian soul. In the process, money and goods acquired righteous social power: they freed the Gabonese from the barbaric bondage of materiality. From the viewpoint of local societies, however, the missionaries clearly acted like big men or slavers.[86] By using cash to compose a community of converts, they enforced a direct connection between colonial currencies and the value of a person.[87]

Today, the legacy of these transactions, and the ambiguous meaning of *otangani*, the nickname for "counting" foreigners in Gabon, survives in the behavior of expatriates and the gaze of the Gabonese.[88] In 2002, in southern Gabon, one of my contacts arranged a meeting with a ritual specialist, Mr. Diata.[89] Accompanied by Joseph Tonda, we arrived at Mr. Diata's house early in the afternoon and greeted our host. First, Mr. Diata put a display of carved masks for sale in front of us. After we made clear that we were not interested in buying masks but only wished to talk with him about "traditional beliefs," Mr. Diata started a coded performance meant to get money from us before he talked. Slowly putting his hand to his cheek, then to his leg, he lamented,

> —"I suffer, I am in pain."
> —[*embarrassed silence*]
> —[*talking to me*] "Are you French?"
> —"Yes, I am"
> —"Ah, Gabon and France, it's the same family."

After a while, Joseph Tonda discreetly gave him a 5,000 XAF bank note folded in four.[90] I told Mr. Diata I would pay after the interview, depending on what he told us. If the episode sounds awkwardly neocolonial, well, it was. A white French female in a position of economic power and social wealth, and a Gabonese sociologist, who the local imaginary described as a "white" and a "witch" (e.g., somebody who is "complicated," somebody who has occult wisdom), could hardly prompt a different exchange. Unlike Tonda, by choosing to pay after the discussion, I confirmed that I was an *otangani*, a greedy foreigner and a "person who counts."[91]

The Fetish Value of Money

The imaginaries of wealth-in-people that came together during colonialism changed the economic and social value of the person. We need now to focus on the *means* that made these transformations possible. French francs, a single, monopolistic, and state-backed currency, played a key role, displacing the credits and monies that the Gabonese had used before the coming of colonialism. The Gabonese had long assumed some commensurability between people and things that extended into the realm of money. The fungibility was complex and relative, realized in multilayered transactions. Under colonial rule, most people lost the ability to accrue any significant form of social and material wealth. The shortfall was linked to the obligation of trading and measuring worth with the new colonial currency.

Because it was difficult for them to obtain francs and control their value, the Gabonese saw them as a highly evasive currency that they needed *to buy* from the French.[92] By European and African design, francs—and later CFA francs (hereinafter XFA)—were invested with an abundance of symbolic, economic, political, and social functions. Like a fetish sated with autonomous meaning and agency, their "excessive" value accomplished more than met the eye, pushing the Gabonese to see modern money as a channel for power, but also for deprivation and powerlessness.[93] These perceptions slowly fused in the modern imaginary of *l'argent* (money), an economic tool, a powerful medical and magic capital, and an instrument of dispossession.

This shift has a colonial history. Before the 1870s, when the Gabonese used a rich variety of currencies and enjoyed considerable credit in regional and international networks, local rulers and traders remained in firm control of commercial exchanges, even when they used a combination of imported monies such as foreign coinage, brass wire, beads, cloth, and guns. Landowners deployed several tactics to secure abundant capital in coinage and goods and to prevent foreigners from getting economic monopolies.[94] First, they required huge advances in goods and monies from Atlantic traders who wished to establish factories.[95] Second, they retained jurisdiction over the convertibility and value of foreign and local monies. Gabonese blacksmiths could change the shape and weight of imported coins and metals.

Guided by local demand, they worked these materials into farming tools and valuables, or melted them back into their original form.[96] Until the late 1880s, Kwele-speaking blacksmiths in eastern Gabon smelted imported *mitako* (brass wire) and *mbonjos* (mass-produced iron monies shaped as an anchor to mimic indigenous money) to create a new metal currency called *mandjong*, whose value and convertibility was determined by local transactions.[97]

After the mid-1890s, this sovereignty deteriorated dramatically, not because of the competition of colonial currencies but because of French colonialists' systematic policy of money retention and scarcity.[98] In the name of the French government, largely absent from the ground, concessionary companies enforced taxes, mandatory labor, and the price of local products. In order to avoid competitive wages and high prices, they resisted the circulation of free-floating currencies in the territories they administered.[99] Concessionary agents paid workers with low-quality merchandise—rum, steel knives, copper bracelets, and *neptunes* (thin copper plates)—whose importation they monopolized and whose exchange value they determined. The Société du Haut-Ogooué, for instance, sold copper *neptunes* to Africans at a unitary value of two francs, but would buy them back (if locals wished to sell them) only for 1.25 francs.[100] Local societies were unable to use competitive monies and protect free markets, and their ability to govern the value of goods, labor, and the worth of people weakened.[101]

Monopolistic tactics also characterized the markets established by Protestant and Catholic mission stations in Gabon. They often printed "tickets" and "coupons" to control local exchanges.[102] In the 1880s, the Protestant ministers at Benita issued paper coupons to pay their Gabonese employees, "so that they are current as money, and are the only money in circulation at Benita" (figure 4.1).[103]

The coupons also served to pay the Gabonese female merchants who supplied foodstuff to Benita; they were the only currency accepted at the mission store. But the missionaries limited the number of coupons that any one woman could earn and use at the store, "in order that all may have an opportunity to procure at least a few of the goods the white ladies have to sell"—manufactured products such as oil lamps, soap, and textiles.[104] Paralleling the forceful monopolies imposed by concessionary companies, the coupons tightened the connection that Africans could draw between foreign monies, economic dependence, and the growing interference of Europeans in commercial exchanges.[105]

On the eve of World War I, pressed for revenue and aware of the disastrous economic state of the colony, the French government decided to circumvent concessionary companies by augmenting the circulation of French francs.

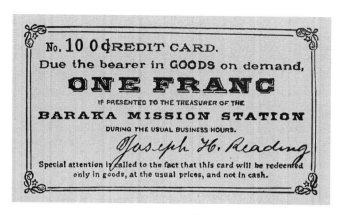

4.1 A money coupon used at the Protestant mission of Baraka, Gabon. From Joseph H. Reading, *The Ogowe Band: A Narrative of African Travel* (Philadelphia, PA: Reading, 1890), 248.

Economists hoped that local markets would expand and generate enough cash for the Gabonese to pay taxes in colonial coinage. Yet concessionary company agents resisted the initiative, so it had only a minor impact. Taxes also continued to bring high levels of insecurity on the ground, and a clear message of political submission. French administrators considered villages that defaulted as political "rebels," and retaliated with armed troops that often took hostages and burned plantations and habitations.[106] In 1922, for instance, the missionaries of the Catholic mission at Donghila in southern Gabon reported that tax collection and the constant harassment of colonial militias had brought widespread famine and an epidemic of flu among farmers, killing more than 10 percent of the parish residents that year.[107]

Cash remained a rare commodity across the colony into the 1940s, forcing farmers to pay taxes in rubber, palm oil, and ivory.[108] Worse still, the disruptions caused by taxes forced some families to give their children to wealthier households in exchange for food, leading to a revival of slave trading.[109] Under pressure, Gabonese families not only failed to acquire material riches but became increasingly unable to protect social wealth.

Political Matters

Throughout the colonial period (1880–1960), French francs continued to be a rare and "expensive" money whose purchasing power greatly exceeded its numeric or market worth. The accumulation of value and the multiple forms of capacity that the French and the Gabonese invested in colonial cash endowed it with fetish-like agency. The state and private colonialists paid wages in francs to Gabonese employees, and authorities pressed people to pay taxes in francs, clearly associating this agency with the white government's policies of monopoly and scarcity. Tellingly, the Gabonese understood the importance of this stately value: they refused to use newly introduced banknotes that could not be traced to the colonial government.[110] In Mouila in 1948, they declined to use newly printed bills worth five francs, because the number five did not appear on the note and they thought that they were fakes.[111]

The francs materialized the political connection between the Gabonese and the French, and indeed French domination. Gabonese "chiefs" (*chefs*), for instance, earned monthly wages paid in cash from collected taxes, and for which they needed to submit to extensive protocols of subordination.[112] Each one kept a *carnet* (notebook) with comments and grades written by the district officer that directly affected one's standing and the possibility of receiving additional bonuses.[113] In addition, local chiefs and informants received "political gifts" (*cadeaux politiques*) and allowances (*allocations*) in cash from the government.[114] In 1945, the district officer at Sindara rewarded some men for reporting on clandestine marijuana plantations, and catching escaped prisoners.[115] In turn, political gifts helped the chiefs to organize French national ceremonies such as the Fourteenth of July.[116] The custom remains alive in independent Gabon, where political candidates distribute cash and commodities to build electoral constituencies.[117]

Embedded in the political sovereignty of the state, the modern notion of *l'argent* progressively emerged in Gabon during the colonial period. The political significance of *l'argent,* and its ability to transform the status of people who owned or lacked it, extended to secondary objects of wealth and *puissance*. A brief history of the "tax token" (*jeton d'impôt*) illustrates this idea.[118] After collecting taxes from a person, the concessionary agent or the colonial officer in charge gave the person a token, a medal made out of cheap metal, perhaps with the stamp of the state. The token was to be worn around the neck and visible at all times. Failing to do this exposed the person to the risk of being arrested and harassed by colonial militias, and chained in public. *Jetons d'impôts* both symbolized and made tangible the authority of the French to levy taxes, and the racial segregation that befell the Gabonese. Only Gabonese taxpayers were forced to exhibit tax tokens, not Europeans. A tangible sign of economic and political obedience, the *jeton d'impôt* recalled the devices used by traders to mark and secure slaves in markets and caravans, marking the Gabonese as the captives of the colonial state. In 1911, a missionary reported,[119] "In the midst of famine, and in a country where rubber is almost exhausted, the government of the colony increased the head tax from 3 to 5 francs. . . . Taxes failing to come, the military administration started to track [the natives] day and night like wild beasts. *Tirailleurs* and managers arrested and chained every man who did not carry the tax plate, or, to borrow from native speech, 'the piece of tin can.'"[120]

In 1931, the colonial state trusted the distribution of tax tokens to African chiefs, providing them with the number of *jetons* equivalent to that of people recorded on tax rolls. The move transferred part of the moneyed power of the colonial state to Gabonese authorities.[121] Later, the administration stopped using tax tokens, although it is not clear when.[122] A striking legacy of the device survived in Gabonese and Congolese schools until the 1970s, showing the ability of colonial tokens and monies to remain empowered with political and racial agency. Teachers required pupils to speak and write in French, forbidding them to use native languages (*patois*). They punished delinquents by making them wear a *symbole* (symbol) around the neck, in the form of a small tin can filled with filth, rotten insects, and foul-smelling excrement. The humiliating device, whose contents transformed the child into a repulsive "savage," resembled the tax token hanging from the neck of Gabonese taxpayers. Though its name claimed only metaphorical power, the *symbole* was as a loaded, tangible charm whose agentive capacity *converted* its owner into someone of lesser social, racial, and political value.[123]

Mystical *Puissance*

Despite the multifarious power of colonial monies, older views about wealth and power remained palpable in the ways in which twentieth-century Gabonese continued to place a significant emphasis on rich people's redistributive and protective behavior, and their ostentatious generosity to inferiors.[124] Even an ordinary person was influential to the extent that he or she helped and provided for family, friends, and clients by composing, circulating, and reproducing various valuables—land, commodities, social alliances, debt, and cash. These tactics did not essentially differ from the ones that, in the nineteenth century, had allowed communities and individuals to think about material riches and people as commensurable assets. Yet colonial monies introduced subtle social solvents that upset local views about moral norms and the sacred value of the person.

The French themselves worried about the transformative power of their money. If they hoped that the Gabonese, by seeking money (in part by working for wages) in order to pay taxes, would acquire "a taste" for work and imported goods, they were also concerned about the divisive capacity of cash.[125] An administrator summarized this opinion in 1950 when he wrote that French francs had brought about endless speculation and a "complete immorality" in the colony.[126] The opinion found a significant echo among the Gabonese: they accused *l'argent* of helping young men and women to escape the authority of elders and to access economic and social autonomy without the help of their relatives. But as cash became indispensable to the survival of families, it also helped kin groups organize collective strategies to generate money for all. Some parents and husbands pushed young women to court wage earners, then channel their cash gifts back to the family, and sometimes to blackmail lovers into paying reparations for adultery.[127]

Today, siphoning off *l'argent* from outsiders has remained an important tactic.[128] Among the Mitsogho, a family can decide to consecrate a girl with a specific fetish called *pèmba a motètè* so she remains single and "attracts wealth" from lovers and pursuers: the money helps to feed and support her relatives.[129] A similar ritual exists among the Nzebi, among whom the woman who has been consecrated with fetishes is called a "man," to express the fact that she takes care of the family by being the provider of cash and that her womb has been "eaten" by the fetishes, that is, rendered barren.[130] Like the older sacrificial and transactional schemes discussed in chapter 2 (Simbu and Murhumi), the sacrificed person herself becomes a "fetish," a physical conduit for attracting and redistributing wealth. These practices exhibit the paradoxical capacity of *l'argent*, its double power to disrupt and confirm established social hierarchies while it destroys and nurtures social wealth. They also reinforce the perception that *l'argent* is a foreign, elusive, and dangerous means of acquiring wealth: controlled by others (lovers, rich men, the state), it can best be captured by sacrificing human assets.

The excessive power of colonial monies, and the new inequalities and hardships it introduced in Gabon, produced a paradoxical result: modern currencies now carry the magical *puissance* of a fetish. Coins, paper bills, and banknotes themselves have absorbed the *puissance* of the white state. While earlier currencies seldom entered therapeutic rituals, *l'argent* has acquired enormous mystical capacity. Old, white-colored five-franc coins (oMyènè: *disso*), a healer in Libreville explained, can be used as *médicaments* in curing patients.[131] A person can also charge a "lucky coin" (*pièce d'argent porte-bonheur*) with magical *puissance* and give it to somebody else, like the one offered by a dying mother to her young daughter in the early 2000s, and later stolen by an envious uncle.[132] Endless rumors circulate in Gabon about the banknotes that magical snakes vomit for the benefit of their witch owners, or the wads of bills that fill up magical suitcases overnight.[133] In return for these, however, one needs to sacrifice social wealth, either by renouncing having children or by killing a relative.

People, Value, Money

We started this chapter with ritual murders and an enigma: the fact that a price in money can express the value of a person and the magical capacity of her limbs. A historical inquiry has shown that the Gabonese, even before the Atlantic trade, had long transacted the value of people in "things" and vice versa, using economic transactions to realize the social and spiritual potential of both.

The narrative also identified subtler changes. During colonial rule, the French echoed Gabonese tactics of composing social assets by aggregating wealth-in-people and purchasing converts. Although they tried to enforce a moral separation between social and material wealth, their judicial policies contradicted these prescriptions. The institution of blood money opened new equivalences between corporeal injury, social worth, and cash compensation. The payment partly flattened and standardized the value of the person and his organs, allowing it to be measured in a currency produced and handled by a foreign authority.

Indeed, the main shift in the value of people in the twentieth century did not occur in the means that determined worth and wealth but in the declining control that the Gabonese experienced in nurturing such wealth. Introducing the French francs—a rare, unreliable, and expensive currency—colonialists helped to further three major transformations in the value of people: they put a significant portion of accumulative and reproductive means out of the control of Africans, they loaded currency with excess value and fetish-like qualities, and they made it impossible for Africans to dream of wealth outside the realm of white people.

FIVE : Cannibal Mirrors

Nineteenth-century Gabonese communities did not eat the flesh of human beings. Nor did they perform cannibalism as religious practice or revenge over the body of dead enemies.[1] Nevertheless, colonialists constructed cannibalism as central to the natives' "instincts" and "customs." They portrayed horrific scenes of black victims consumed by other Africans, and of the occasional cooking up of an unfortunate white man.[2] These cannibal stories left an immense paper trail traversed by vast oral arcs. Crucial to white imaginaries of domination, they also significantly influenced modern African idioms of eating and power.[3]

Modern scholars generally dismiss Western cannibal tales as misguided racializing fictions, while they tend to validate African stories of white cannibalism as effective social theory.[4] The view, however, proves only narrowly valid for the colonial period. Among Africans and Europeans alike, cannibalism conjured up fears of racial cohabitation and the impossible task of social reproduction. Among Europeans, cannibal fantasies not only dehumanized and racialized Africans, they also served to paint the impossibility of the colonial project. Among Africans, such stories had long expressed the mutual dangers of the Atlantic encounter, rumoring that foreign traders devoured slaves and processed them into cheese, canned meat, and gunpowder.[5] In the 1870s and 1880s, when the presence of missionaries and factory agents increased inland, Gabonese anecdotes started to describe the danger of dystopic contacts and social destruction.

This chapter focuses on white colonial fantasies: it shows how cannibalism served white colonialists to speculate about the danger of rule. In Equatorial Africa, "going native" often evoked being swallowed by a hungry black belly, or roasting over the primitive fire of unrestrained native desires. These dreams were quite political: the lore of human flesh eaten, devoured, or trafficked, articulated the tremendous appetites of colonial invaders and, facing them, the specter of unvanquished native hungers for revenge. In the nineteenth century, this imaginary merged with powerful European dreams about monkeys and the great apes. Their discovery in Gabon coincided with the publication of Charles Darwin's *Origin of Species* in 1859. In 1861, an obscure Franco-American explorer, Paul Du Chaillu, achieved fame by describing monster-like gorillas and human cannibals in the Gabonese rainforest; his *Explorations and Adventures in Equatorial Africa* sold ten thousand copies in its first two years in England alone.[6]

The political meaning of cannibals and apes extended to racial positioning in the colony. Here the racial imagination did not work according to a binary logic. Instead, Europeans mediated race through "middle figures," a notion I borrow from Nancy Hunt's rich conceptual lexicon.[7] In contrast with Hunt, however, I do not talk here about the African *évolués*, teachers, and midwives who negotiated and translated forms of colonial modernity. Instead, I mean the semifictional characters that white colonialists invented as intermediate mirrors between themselves and Africans: in Gabon, cannibals, apes, and monkeys provided some of the most important of these fictional "thirds."[8]

An engraving in Du Chaillu's *Country of the Dwarfs* (1872) vividly illustrates this form of triangular racial thinking (figure 5.1). The white explorer holds up a mirror to his friend King Quengeza, who admires the presents he has just received: a long coat, a stick, and a top hat made in London. Quengeza freezes in surprise at his reflection, as the mirror shows the features of a monkey.[9]

High cultural and biological instability characterized these colonial inventions, allowing colonialists to both impose racial identities in Gabon, and play with and transgress them. In their imagination, great apes could talk, mate, learn, and kill across race or species, mirroring colonialists' complex desire for both enforcing and blurring barriers. After all, a favorite pastime among colonialists was to "play" the native in tournaments of mimicry and usurpation, smearing their bodies with dark grease, or passing as ancestral spirits and kings in local communities.[10]

The first part of this chapter shows how colonial rulers used cannibal prejudices to hierarchize races and ethnic groups. It then moves to "tiger-men" murders in rural Gabon, and the institutional consequences, for the Gabonese and the French, of subsequent cannibal trials. The second part of the chapter centers on gorilla reveries and colonial interactions with the great apes. These brought fresh aspects to cannibal fantasies, voicing the pleasure of homoerotic impulses and the lure of a place where transgressive desires could be

5.1 Paul Du Chaillu and King Quengeza. From Paul Belloni
Du Chaillu, *The Country of the Dwarfs* (New York: Harper
and Brothers, 1872), frontispiece (discussed on 43–45). Artist
unknown; illustration signed C. R. S.

unleashed and pursued. The chapter ends with white cannibalism, and the gaze of the Gabonese upon Europeans' relentless quest for collecting, dismembering, and preserving animal and human specimens.

Cannibal Exotica

They are mere stomachs.
—Fernand Rouget, 1906

Foreign views of Africans as cannibals were complex: they came from several sources, served different agendas, and changed over time. Overall, however, these elements fused in a fairly stable cannibal imaginary, working in Gabon as an inescapable canon of colonial life. Whether seasoned or newly arrived, most colonialists invested in this idea and made it their own. Far from an abstract representation, it organized racist stereotypes and judicial codas that, in turn, underwrote decisions with enduring institutional and political consequences for the Gabonese.

"Seeing the cannibals" belonged to a century-old tradition started by Diego Álvarez Chança, the physician of Christopher Columbus. During the 1493 expedition to the Caribbean, seeing a few human remains collected by an officer on a beach, Chança invented the word "cannibal."[11] In the sixteenth century, travelers to the New World disseminated memoirs, pamphlets, and engravings that showed natives roasting human limbs and cooking them in caldrons—the so-called Tupinamba cannibals.[12] In 1641, Albert Eckhout's portrait of a "Tapuya woman" in 1641 (figure 5.2) quietly suggested that inhabitants of the New World practiced cannibalism as a routine activity, trading human meat for daily repasts.[13]

Du Chaillu's discovery of cannibals borrowed many aspects of this tradition. As he embarked on his expedition into inner Gabon, debates were raging in Western Europe and North America about the evolution of species and the origin of modern man. Charles Darwin's *On the Origin of Species by Means of Natural Selection* (1859) had appeared just a few months before Paul Du Chaillu's seminal text, and greatly influenced his writing. Du Chaillu approached local communities as possible remnants of "primeval men" who could prove to be an observable link with early humans (recently known through new archeological discoveries) and locate man's place among species (anthropogenesis).[14]

Following this scientific craze, and Du Chaillu's example, explorers reported on Gabonese cannibals as empirical figures.[15] They visited actual

5.2 Albert Eckhout,
*Tapuya Woman Holding
a Severed Hand and Car-
rying a Basket Containing
a Severed Foot*, 1641. Oil
on canvas, 272 × 165 cm.
Copenhagen, National-
museet. Photograph by
John Lee. Courtesy of
Nationalmuseet Denmark,
Copenhagen.

villages and interviewed native informants. Authors as different as Paul Du
Chaillu, Marquis de Compiègne, Savorgnan de Brazza, Albert de Chavannes,
Alfred Marche, P. Payeur-Didelot, Winwood Reade, Richard Burton, Mary
Kingsley, R. L. Garner, Günther Tessman, and Georg Schweinfurth wrote
hundreds of pages on cannibals in southern Cameroon and Gabon. "True
experience," however, was a strange construct that relied overwhelmingly on
indirect traces and oblique speculations. These works contained more deduc-
tive logic and racial preconceptions than direct observation. Indeed, we can
approach this early cannibal archive as a series of "dream-books" in which
scientific observations cannot be dissociated from rumors, projections, and
the enormous truth-value of narrative panache.[16]

Paul Du Chaillu was well prepared for his expedition in the Gabonese hinterland. In 1848, at the age of seventeen, Du Chaillu had left France to join his father, a factory owner, on the Gabon coast. He stayed there a few years, getting to know the country and the Mpongwe language. In 1852, after his father died, Du Chaillu decided to seek his fortune in the United States, where he studied natural history and made contact with several scientific and geographical societies.[17] Backed by modest grants from museums in Philadelphia and Boston, the young man returned to Gabon in 1855, and organized his first expedition in July 1856. Starting from Corisco Island and progressing along the Muni Estuary (then called the Tambouni River), his small caravan reached Fang country in August 1856, near what is now the frontier with Equatorial Guinea. Here Du Chaillu stumbled on the scene that would make him famous:

> The next morning we moved off for the Fang village, and now I had the opportunity to satisfy myself as to a matter I had cherished some doubts before, namely, the cannibal practices of these people. I was satisfied but too soon. As we entered the town, I perceived some bloody remains which looked to me to be human; but I passed on, still incredulous. Presently we passed a woman who solved all doubts. She bore with her a piece of the thigh of a human body, just as we should go to market and carry thence a roast or steak.[18]

Despite the empirical shock conveyed by Du Chaillu's frontal scene, the description suspiciously mirrored scenes from the Western cannibal library, in particular Eckhout's painting of 1641 (see figure 5.2). The explorer's second description of cannibal "carnage" emphasized the strange nature of his speculations. Brought inside a house by the chief of the village, he heard "great shouting" at a distance. Worried that he might have to witness another "infernal" scene, Du Chaillu hid inside a hut, from where he overheard the "noise" of "quarrels" and worse: "I was told by one of [the Fang] afterwards that they had been busy dividing the body of a dead man, and that there was not enough for all."[19] The retreating tactic occurred again, a few days later, in another Fang village: "A little boy of ten years had been accused of sorcery. . . . They took spears and knives, and actually cut the poor little fellow to pieces. I had been walking out, and returned just as the dreadful scene was over."[20]

Many prominent authors on Gabon embraced Du Chaillu's descriptive ploy. In 1876, for instance, French traveler Victor de Compiègne dismissed Du Chaillu's market scene as "fantastic," yet suggested that cannibalism existed among the Fang because they were related to the Niam Niam, the cannibal tribe made famous in 1874 by the German explorer August Georg Schwein-furth.[21] That same year, British ethnographer Richard Burton, stationed in a *dépôt*-factory on Lake Anengue, spent a single day in a Fang village on the Mbokwe River. In his published account, Burton laughed away Du Chaillu's claim that "joints of black brothers" and "smoked human flesh" hung in Fang villages. Yet on the basis of negative evidence, he hastened to confirm that local cannibalism existed: "I made careful inquiry about anthropophagy amongst the Fan and my account must differ greatly from M. du Chaillu. The reader, however, will remember that Mayyan is held by a comparatively civi-lized race, who have probably learned to conceal a custom so distasteful to all their neighbors black and white; in the remoter districts cannibalism may yet assume far more hideous proportions."[22]

Burton then spun fantasies on the sadistic inclinations of Africans: "The[ir] highest enjoyments," he wrote, "are connected with causing pain and inflict-ing death. . . . Prisoners are tortured with all the horrible barbarity of that wild beast which is happily extirpated, the North American Indian; and children may be seen greedily licking the blood from the ground."[23] Twenty years later, Mary Kingsley further tightened the cannibal trap around the Gabonese. In *Travels to West Africa* (1897), she used irony to tease the reader: "[The Fang] has no slave, no prisoners of war, no cemeteries, so you must draw your own conclusion. No, my friend, I will not tell you any cannibal stories."[24]

The oneiric quality of this early cannibal archive did not decline. On the contrary, it blossomed among French residents of Gabon during the colonial period, often borrowing the logic of association and embellishment proper to rumors and gossip.[25] In the first days of December 1903, in the south of the colony, Ghetsogho-speaking clans rebelled against the brutal depredations of the concessionary company Société du Haut-Ogooué. They attacked an out-post at Kimbele, killing two white men, a trading agent named Ourson, and a French sergeant named Sampic. Alarms and rumors buzzed among white residents. On December 5, news of the rebellion reached the nearby Catholic mission of Saint-Martin-des-Apindjis. Father Guyader wrote in his diary, "The savages quartered and ate the cadaver of the sergeant. His heart and brains pro-vided choice morsels for the killers. After that, they used his skull for drinking palm wine." On December 7, hearing that the rebels had kidnapped another manager, Guyader speculated whether the unfortunate prisoner had been "cut alive . . . by these barbarians."[26] Months later, he added, "We have been told that the Issogos of Kimbele have paraded the skulls of Mr. Ourson and Sampic all over the country."[27] Nineteen years later, a Joseph Blache attached exquisite details to the scene:

> The screaming gang overwhelmed the two men. What happened afterwards, I cannot describe. . . . . A factory employee had managed to escape and ran to alert the military post. But the garrison was too far away and, when the troops arrived, it was already too late. The Issoghos had captured the two men and conducted the most horrible tortures over the prisoners. The heads only were found: the rest of their bodies had been eaten![28]

Shortly after the attack, and many years later, colonial rumors thus added a wealth of details to a scene that no European had witnessed in person. Blache's description, published in France as the memoir of an ordinary *colon* (the term that French settlers and colonialists used for themselves), clearly played on sensationalistic strategies to find a large readership. Yet many similar speculations in the personal notes and administrative reports of French colonialists, and their incessant revivals in rumors, conversations, and reveries performed by incoming settlers, suggest that the cannibal imaginary was deeply anchored in white people's minds.[29]

Tiger-Men

After 1910, state authorities and district officers in Gabon became less interested in anthropogenesis and evolution, and more concerned with cannibalism as a legal transgression. In 1913–18, a wave of unexplained murders occurred in southern Gabon.[30] Colonialists knew very little about the incidents, but they heard villagers say that the assassins disguised themselves as "tigers" (*tigres*), the French misnomer for leopards (*Panthera pardus pardus*).[31] At first, administrators attributed the assaults to real leopards. But in 1916, a district officer named Hippolyte Charbonnier sent a ten-page report on "tiger-men" to the governor of Gabon. The report garnered wide attention and became a seminal text for investigations and prosecutions.[32] The report claimed that real men were responsible for the murders. They belonged to secret associations of "tiger-men" who killed victims to procure human flesh. The story corresponded to the local belief that witches can transform into an animal to kill a person. More murders occurred in the 1920s, and the district officer of Mekambo, a small outpost in the South, reported them in his diary in characteristic fashion:

- In the night of 26 to 27 of June, a young native of Sangha-Sangha race, employed by Lieutenant Cuivier, has his throat cut by the "tiger-man" while walking towards the kitchen, located at the extremity of the compound, to call on one of his friends.
- Second alert during the night of 27 to 28 of June: the sentinel, seeing a man crawling near the fence of the compound, fires and misses the suspect.
- During the night of the 28 to 29 of June, a "tiger-man" kidnaps a native near the CFHC factory.
- The same day, the "tiger man" eats a five-year-old girl in the village of Koto.
- That same day again, in the village of Cocofili, a "tiger-man" critically hurts a woman.[33]

The crimes slowed on the eve of World War II, reappearing sporadically after 1945, but they significantly transformed the white imaginary of African cannibalism.[34] The French now depicted cannibalism as serving the goals of a criminal organization, a bloodthirsty "African mafia" that terrorized the population.

Although borrowing from preexisting fears about African cannibals, Charbonnier's 1916 report was largely responsible for this change of view. Allegedly based on six months of research and multiple "interrogations" of Gabonese suspects, the text was succinct and straightforward, allowing for little doubt and offering advice for examining suspects. It drew an appalling picture of a terrorizing network of "secret societies" infesting Southern Gabon. A centralized organization had branched out into multiple divisions, each owning a fetish in the form of a cooking pot (*marmite*) called Maghêna (iPunu: leopard). To activate the *marmite*, the affiliates sacrificed a man and a woman. Then they needed to feed it regularly with human meat. Each new member also offered a person for entering the society. Charbonnier laced his essay with an impressive number of gory details about the cannibal feasts organized by the tiger-men. To prepare their banquets, he wrote, the tiger-men slit the throat of the victims and poured their warm blood into the pot. Then they mixed it with crushed leaves and drank it.[35] The meal consisted of parts of the victim's cooked corpses. The affiliates cut the soft organs—the tongue, heart, liver, lungs, and spleen of each dead body—before scraping the flesh of the forearms. They put the meat in the cauldron, cooked it, and feasted on it. The depiction of the banquet resonated with the visual repertoire of the witches' Sabbath and other Christian folklore (figure 5.3).[36]

5.3 Witches around a cauldron, woodcut. From Abraham Saur, *Ein kurtze treuwe Warnung Anzeige ind Underricht* (1582). Reproduced in Charles Zika, *The Appearance of Witchcraft. Print and Visual Culture in Sixteenth-Century Europe*, London and New York: Routledge, 2007, 75.

Curiously, Charbonnier's report also included elements of modern bureaucratic thinking. The tight hierarchy of leopard societies arranged in branches, subbranches, groups, and *marmites* was very implausible in a region with virtually no centralized institutions. But it sounded like French ideas about criminal societies and how they adopted nation-states' efficient networks. A more surprising influence was probably detective stories, a genre recently all the rage in the West: the public was fascinated that a single individual, armed with rational and scientific methods, could conduct an *enquête* (investigation) and solve mysterious crimes.[37] Charbonnier asserted that tiger-men could recognize each other from their "gaze" (French: *regard*). During an *enquête*, he boasted, he had arrested six men after scrutinizing their faces and finding "something quite particular."[38]

The possibility of discovering a web of tiger-men by following elusive "clues" and sparse confessions appealed to the French district officers, who were puzzled by the frequent attacks against villagers, uncertain whether they came from wild beasts or isolated criminals. As soon as the governor of Gabon circulated Charbonnier's report among them, they started arresting people. Because they believed that each criminal was part of a large clandestine cannibal network, the confession of an initial suspect often triggered a series of round-ups and prosecutions.

Local communities suffered terrible consequences. The slightest clues prompted officers to arrest and convict many villagers. Like Du Chaillu and Burton, the police read cannibal instincts from fleeting visual data and dubious acoustic evidence: following Charbonnier's cues, they read suspects' silences as evidence, and used projections and collective fantasies to fill evidentiary gaps. In 1917, for instance, a district chief reported the weird look on a suspect's face: "The gaze of his eyes immediately struck me. Is this a consistent characteristic [of tiger-men]? Charbonnier seems to say so. Or is it an effect of fear?"[39] Georges Le Testu, a district officer in southern Gabon, recalled that Charbonnier's report had encouraged him to arrest twelve men in the year 1915. A few years later, his colleague, Victor Aymard, pronounced seventy-four death sentences connected to tiger-men affairs.[40]

The tiger-men crisis solidified diverse French cannibal fantasies into new certitudes. It seemed to prove that, under the facade of the docile African, a true savage survived, ready to unleash murderous instincts. It also confirmed that African politics were hopelessly dysfunctional, driven by fetishistic superstitions and a rule of terror by predatory elites. Tiger-men trials *also* revealed the porosity of French barriers between material and immaterial agency: despite their rationalizing constructions, they wrote as fact that drinking pulverized bones and brain matter could contaminate a person's will, and that the Maghêna fetish pushed ordinary people to rush over to freshly killed victims and eat their flesh.

Erotica

Colonialists' most archaic fear in Gabon was obliteration: being swallowed by the wilderness of the forest, tropical diseases, or the unstoppable hunger of local cannibals.[41] Reducing French cannibal imaginary to digestive anxieties, however, would miss a large part of the picture. As the tiger-men crisis demonstrated, white cannibal fears spoke also of political doom. Colonialists perceived Gabon as a volatile field where objects and commodities, persons and bodies, constantly merged into one another. This instability, in turn, threatened social and moral limits, endangering the dominant position of white people and the development of the natives, who were constantly doomed by their cannibal instincts. White rulers seldom put these concerns into explicitly political language: instead, they voiced them in inarticulate forms and motifs. One of the most powerful of these obsessive tropes fused cannibal destruction with sex and the abject. Because it combined anxieties about reversed reproduction with motifs of erotic desire, I call it "cannibal erotica."

White cannibal reveries closely followed Western theories of disease and medicine. In the mid-nineteenth century, imperial writers construed cannibalism as a form of miasma contagion, fearing that they could become cannibals themselves. Du Chaillu wrote how "the neighboring tribes [stood] about me in such crowds that often I [was] half-suffocated with the stench which their unclean bodies [gave] out." Contagion also came through vision: "I could not bear to stay for the cutting of the body. . . . It made me sick all over."[42] Europeans, moreover, got "ill" from the repulsive (*repoussantes*) flavors of local food, and to become ill among cannibals was to risk becoming prey.[43] One day, a sickly Du Chaillu reflected that his hosts might take advantage of the situation and "be seized by a passionate desire to taste of me."[44] The fear signaled a haunting possibility: a reversal of position from eater to eaten.[45]

After Louis Pasteur (1859), Robert Koch (1882), and Edwin Klebs (1883) discovered microbes, colonial fears adjusted to germ theory and the traumatic images it carried: germs worked as a foreign yet innermost part of the self. Like the carnal intimacy of cannibalism, they entered the body and ate it up from inside.[46] In the colony, the threat was collective and considerable. Europeans blamed tropical infections on the "diseased environments" of Africa and the maladies collectively carried by local communities, envisioning them as an intimate component of the colonial relation.[47] Seeking to expel the threat, colonialists used the figure of the cannibal abject.

Anne McClintock has been the first to demonstrate the historical significance of the psychoanalytical theory of the abject in a colonial context.[48] The abject is something an individual tries to expel from the inner self even as it continues to haunt the person. Looking at nineteenth-century industrial and imperial England, McClintock showed that Victorians classified anything that lacked market value or remained outside mainstream ideals and exchanges as "abject." The term particularly attached to filth and dirt, relegated as the traces of female unwaged domestic labor, and the residues left by the work of the poor. Yet these vestiges kept haunting the Victorian imagination, working as the constitutive limits of bourgeois society.

In Gabon, the colonialists derided the populations that most fiercely resisted colonial domination as filthy cannibals: the French shunned the Shekiani, the

Fang, and the Issakis as defiled (French: *malpropres*) man-eaters.[49] They also expressed revulsion at the African taste "for abominable cuisines, for carcasses, and for the spoiled guts of hippopotamus," merging dirt, devouring, and death in a spectacle of ultimate pollution.[50] Gabonese cannibals, they wrote, delighted in ingesting the flesh of people who had died of disease; they immersed dead bodies in water to accelerate their putrefaction.[51] They also shattered the limbs of captives and forced them, still alive, to stay in water until their flesh softened. Then they butchered the victims for cannibal feasts. But soon they themselves developed hideous (*répugnantes*) diseases, a trope associated in Western thinking with illicit sex and fears of contagion.[52] A hideous orgy signaled the complete breakdown of Western laws of separation.

Missionaries, of all people, published the most extreme iterations of the cannibal abject in Gabon, mostly in the 1920s and 1930s. In sadistic and voyeuristic tales that explored the limits of the moral and physical person, their cannibal descriptions borrowed from Christian motifs such as the death of Christ, the persecution and torment of Christian martyrs, and the redeeming sacrifice of the Eucharist. They also unleashed powerful longings for exploring bodily interiors and tasting African flesh, erotically and otherwise. Here is how in 1922, Fernand Grébert, a prolific Protestant pastor stationed in Samkita, on the Ogooué River, narrated a Gabonese cannibal banquet that he claimed he had witnessed:

> People cut the head of the prisoner. Elders claimed it and boiled it in their cooking-pot, after roasting the hair over the fire. They stuffed the ears and the mouth with spices to season them. Lips were a choice morsel because of the taste of pepper and tobacco. The most respected elder received the eyes. He made them burst between his teeth with delight, holding his head back; after this, the emptied skull hung in front of the guard hut or on the roof.[53]

A flurry of convulsions and tremors enlivened the obscene story authored, a few years later, by the catholic bishop of Gabon, Mgr. Le Roy:

> Suddenly, at a given signal, the unfortunate's head falls under the saber of the executioner and rolls on the ground, the body still struggling in hideous convulsions. Blood inundates the ground, and immediately the assistants hurl themselves onto the body, they cut the flesh in small strips, that they cook and eat. For the gourmets, the fingers are highly regarded and they suck them with delight; but the heart is particularly sought for, as the place of courage that one assimilates by devouring it.[54]

The Latin root of the word obscene, "inauspicious," means something sacred that needs to remain hidden. The erotic appeal of these missionary tales for imperial minds, I argue, derived from the staging of a double violation of the body by African cannibals and by the voyeur writer: first as the sacred seat of the social person, and second as lustful flesh opened and tormented.[55] In turn, the cannibal obscene profoundly troubled colonial positioning. Making authors and readers swirl from voyeur to victim, and from prey to perpetrator, they exposed deep colonial yearnings for the reversal of domination. In a volume of short stories published in 1912 about his evangelizing work in Gabon, Father Henri Trilles recollected his young, homoerotic cannibal reveries about Africa: "We were heroes, then, in our dreams! At night, what a delicious shudder one felt when escaping from horrible savages thanks to a cold-blooded and audacious exploit. They were adorned with feathers, tattooed all-over in flamboyant colors and dancing around the fire where you would be skewed or roasted. Only that! But . . . it was only a dream!"[56]

Fantasies of Self-Destruction

Worried about the steep decline of the Gabonese population during the conquest, the French blamed the locals' atavistic, quasiorganic instinct of self-devouring.[57] In human societies, social and biological reproduction depends on marriage, child rearing, and the securing of various social alliances.[58]

Cannibalism was the radical opposite of reproduction: by destroying kin and outsiders, the community lost members and dwindled. Moreover, in the act of destruction, man-eaters became something less than human. In blaming the decline of the Gabonese population on cannibalism, the French biopoliticized African history and evolution and, conversely, the remedies proposed by colonial intervention.

FORMULA OF REPRODUCTION AND CANNIBALISM

Biological reproduction	$1+1=3$
Social reproduction	$1+1=2^+$
Cannibalism	$1+1=1$

Natural historians and ethnogeneticists argued that environmental determinism and the laws of evolution, popularized in France by racist authors Arthur de Gobineau, Gustave Le Bon and Georges Vacher de la Pouge, explained that Gabonese societies had barely risen from the animal realm.[59] In 1899, Le Bon transferred Darwin's notion of the "primitive horde" to early human communities. He argued that, after wandering alone and fighting like animals, early men had aggregated in small communal "herds" (*troupeaux*): "The first inspiration that came to our savage ancestors, facing the attacks of ferocious beasts and of their own species, was to create an original force with a few of their spare numbers [and to live] in small groups, each of them led by a robust male."[60]

Following Le Bon, colonial writers divided Equatorial Africans— sometimes described as a veritable "refuse of humanity"—between "peoples of the savannas" and "peoples of the forest."[61] They deemed the people of the savannas *races agricoles* (agriculturalist races), more civilized because of their mastery of farming. Peoples of the forest, or *races anthropophages* (cannibal races), instead, relied on cannibalism to compensate for their lack of agriculture.[62] In 1925, Mgr. Le Roy believed that "the children of the woods and steppes" would quickly enslave or eat an isolated man.[63] In 1930, Georges Bruel, the former director of the French Bureau of Geographical Services in Brazzaville, wrote that Bantu agriculturalists had overcome the pygmies of the rainforest by eating the males and mating with the females.[64] The words were for animals, not humans.

For these authors, African politics and religion did not rise above the level of gross biological eradication. They denied cannibalism any symbolic or spiritual meanings: in Gabon, anthropophagy was simply an organic "taste" for human flesh.[65] Even funeral ceremonies, missionary Robert H. Nassau wrote, provided the natives with a pretext to feast (on the body of the dead).[66]

First, cannibalism was the mark of Africans' failed evolution as a human species. Second, European authors argued that lethal cannibal instincts polluted the intimacy of domestic life and reproduction. In 1912, a novella published by Catholic missionary Henri Trilles recounted the tragic fate of Noélie, a young Gabonese Christian who had disobeyed her heathen spouse to follow the calling of her faith.[67] Trilles described how, in retaliation, the husband submitted Noélie to a horrific death: he buried her alive so cannibal ants would slowly devour her. After the crime, he suffered agonies of leprosy and pox, twice losing his fertility. Repugnant skin diseases have long been associated with deviant sexuality in the West: indeed, shadowing the novella with the transgression of incest, Trilles also calls Noélie *une enfant* (a girl).[68] But the cannibal imprint is what dominates the tale. The invasion of the victim's body by hungry insects suggests the husband's feral lust for unbounded sexual power, and Trilles' own fascination with the sadistic consumption of a black female body.

In a third and final biopolitical creation, imperial authors tied together the dysfunctions of intimate life with those of public power in the totalizing figure of "cannibal slavery." They wrote that the "two flowers of Barbary" (man-eating and man-selling) were at the core of African politics, poisoning the future of the colony.[69] This first appeared in an anecdote reported by Du Chaillu, when upon his arrival in a Fang village, the chief allegedly hastened to bring him a female slave for dinner.[70] The scene recalled a famous exploration genre (the natives giving a woman to the white man for sexual consumption), but substituted the promise of erotic relations with the destructive reality of cannibalism.

Many a text described the slaves as cannibal leftovers.[71] In 1931, Catholic nun Marie Germaine used the term "human refuse" to describe the captives sheltered at the mission, whom she derided as full of "stupor" and "bestiality."[72] They endangered the purity of local races. As "human meat," they also blurred the boundary between people and commodities, and between humans and animals. Colonialists remained convinced that tribes who did not own slaves or who did not participate in the slave trade were in fact secretly "fattening" dependents and prisoners to eat them. In a dizzying circle of biological determinism, the metaphoric meat and social refuse of the captive had turned into food for the natives.

Colonialists projected their own appetites and behaviors onto slaves, literally blaming the victims. Moreover, by reducing slavery, a complex social, economic, and political institution, into a singular act of consumption, they biologized and trivialized the symbolic life of vernacular societies, painting it as hopelessly material and literal.

The Fang as Ur-Cannibals

We now go back to the group that suffered most of the man-eating prejudice in Gabon, the Fang people. The *locus classicus* of cannibalism, the Fang were the site of colonialists' hopes for a partner race in the region, serving as colonial thirds and offering an inverted image of European invaders. The fantasy said little about the real Fang, although they suffered enormous prejudice at its hands, but it revealed a great deal about the French, their triangular fantasies, and moral worries in the colony.

Unique in the colonial literature, the Fang elicited a strange mix of horror and admiration. "Notwithstanding their repulsive habit," Du Chaillu wrote, "the Fan [sic] have left an impression upon me of being the most promising people in all West Africa. They treated me with unvarying hospitality and kindness, and they seem to have more of that kind of stamina which enables a rude people to receive a strange civilization than any other tribes I know of in

Africa."[73] The opinion rested on another powerful imaginary of colonialism, the contrast between "degenerate tribes" of the coast and the "noble savages" of the hinterland.

Yet early on, Western observers deplored the "Fang invasions" of Gabon: they accused them of "absorbing" the tribes they encountered in their sweeping race to the coast. In 1876, Marquis de Compiègne wrote, "Twenty years ago, we noticed a few Fang encampments near the French colony. . . . Since then, more tribes have come in extremely rapid waves and swept everything in their path."[74] In French stories, the incursions soon adopted the traits of a cannibalistic ramp-up. In 1912, Trilles explained that no other tribes could coexist with the Fang: "They would be purely and simply eaten up."[75] Accusing the Fang to cannibalize Gabon, colonial rulers projected their own absorption of local societies. The Fang mirrored colonial destruction: in the looking glass of cannibal politics, an intelligent, quasi-Caucasian race was swallowing native societies.

The French described the westward penetration of the fierce tribe, however, as that of a brave, intelligent and untainted nation (the only people in Gabon to win such a name): the Fang readily mirrored the eastward conquest of the French.[76] No author articulated the parallel in explicit language; only racial comparisons between Fang and Europeans suggested it. Citing high mesocephalic features and unusual mastery of iron smelting, Charles Seligman believed that the Fang derived from "Hamitic ascendency."[77] Another writer argued that they descended from ancient "Francs" who had migrated to Africa from Germany.[78] Even missionaries lauded the Fang's patriarchal lines of descent: in a region where most groups exhibited matrilineal rules, this made them a truly "chosen people" that had migrated from an old Christian Egypto-Hamitic cluster, perhaps under the pressure of Islam.[79]

Like other cannibal fantasies, European dreams about the Fang created a complex system of racial and political triangulation, helping white people find an imaginary place in the colony, and express awareness, guilt, and fears about the conquest. The transference was also remarkable for painting political domination in biological and organic terms. Ape reveries would express this process even more clearly.

The Monkey/Ape Transference

The monkeys and great apes of the Gabonese rainforest, like the human cannibals imagined by the French, served as colonial thirds, another figure by which Europeans positioned themselves racially, culturally, and morally in relation to Africans. European empirical observations, informed by the theory of evolution after 1859, were the groundwork for placing gorillas and chimpanzees as intermediaries between themselves and the natives, and for defining the biological and racial grid of the colony. Although scientific in some sense, these observations were irrational and obsessive. Born of guilt and fear, they also added fresh terrors and fancies to the colonialists' cannibal imaginary.

During his 1856 expedition, a few days before encountering the Fang for the first time, Paul Du Chaillu came face to face with Western gorillas (*Gorilla gorilla*).[80] The animal was still unknown in Europe. Du Chaillu became obsessed with gorillas: his successive travelogues devoted a considerable number of pages to them. This discovery, added to that of the cannibal Fangs, secured him great fame in Europe and in America. A couple of Europeans had witnessed gorillas before him and sent specimens to Europe and the United States in the 1840s. Yet the shipments were of poor quality, allowing Du Chaillu to be the first to publish a detailed description of the beast in the wild, and to provide well-preserved carcasses to Richard Owen, the head of the Natural History Collections at the British Museum.[81]

Du Chaillu's discovery gained huge international visibility. Soon, scientists established that the difference between gorillas and humans was unbridgeable, an argument duly reported in *Explorations and Adventures in Equatorial Africa* (1861).[82] Forty years later, zoologists proved that the two species ("hominids" and "anthropoid apes") descended from two separate branches of a common ancestor. Yet the gorilla continued to haunt the Western imagination.[83] Du Chaillu himself played on the proximity of the primate with humans. The first gorilla he encountered reminded him "of nothing but some hellish dream creature—a being of that hideous order, half-man half-beast."[84]

Later imperial writers used primates to reflect about biological and racial hierarchies, hailing the Gabonese gorilla as "the King of the African Forests" or "His African Majesty."[85] In 1875, Compiègne described the ruler of the Okota people as "a very small man, with very small eyes set deep in the sockets: his face is one of a monkey, but a very nasty monkey."[86] Schweinfurth likened the profile of Bongo women to those of "dancing baboons." Payeur-Didelot talked of meeting, among the Gabonese, "as many bestial and simian faces as pleasant and attractive ones."[87] Even Günther Tessman, the author of a detailed and perceptive sum on the Fang (1907), occasionally slipped into the comparison: "After looking around, with the absent face of apes . . . [the old healer] kneeled down, clenched his fists together in front of his—I was almost about to say his muzzle—and finally performed a sort of belly dancing; in brief, one would have believed oneself being transported in a herd of chimpanzees."[88]

Perhaps the most lasting comparison between apes and Africans concerned Gabon's hunter-gatherers, sometimes called in French *pygmées* (pygmies) and *négrilles* (literally "small negroes" in French). Léon Poutrin, an authority on races, found that "the convex space between the nose and the lips among [the *négrilles*] protuberated like a kind of muzzle."[89] In 1933, Georges Montandon reported two striking "simoïd" features in the pygmy race: their receding chin and the convexity of the upper lip.[90] The features, he added, demonstrated that Africans had regressed to a simian stage and that the laws of evolution could be reversed.

The idea of the merging between apes and black people borrowed heavily from cannibal imaginary.[91] Explorer Richard Burton recounted that a gorilla had severely crippled a huntsman: the beast "seized his wrist with his hind foot, and dragged his hand into his mouth, as he would have done a bunch of plantains." In 1929, Henri Trilles told how a great male had sprung to a Fang hunter and "devoured his hands, his face, and tore the skin from his feet."[92] White people themselves feared becoming easy prey. Joseph H. Reading recalled a fright at a family picnic:

> The picnicers were . . . engaged in quiet conversation, when a rustling was heard in the bushes and looking up, there stood a native African, pure and simple—a chimpanzee! He was a fine fellow, standing nearly three feet in height, and surveyed the pale-faced party with a puzzled look. To the frightened girls he appeared the size of a giant big enough to swallow them all, and they screamed in a manner befitting the occasion.[93]

Reading's direct comparison to an ape dehumanized the "native African" and humanized the chimpanzee: in the vignette, the girls' cannibal fear recalled other feelings, of guilt this time, when Europeans tasted monkey meat or shunned Africans for doing so.[94] Du Chaillu's first mention of the gorilla was soaked in such cannibal transgression. After his men shot a male, he wrote, "They immediately began to quarrel about the apportionment of the meat, for they really eat this creature."[95] The explorer usually refused to partake in the meal, unless famine threatened the camp, which happened at least once: "I found that the fellows had killed a monkey, which roughly roasted on the coals, tasted delicious, though I think, under average circumstances, the human look of the animal would have turned me from it."[96] Yet Europeans could not entirely conceal other carnal passions. In the 1890s, British explorer Mary Kingsley expressed a feat of ambivalent desire for a gorilla she endowed with the pronoun "he," like a person: "The old male rose to his full height (it struck me at the time this was a matter of ten feet at least, but for scientific purposes allowance must be made for a lady's emotions)."[97]

Europeans seldom expressed explicit feelings of sexual attraction or a sense of kinship toward human Africans, but they did not experience such inhibition with apes. They often wrote that the primates were more human and intelligent than the natives.[98] Du Chaillu thought that his monkey pet, the white-faced "Joe," contrasted nicely "with all these negro faces," and provided him with welcome company.[99] In 1867, he hoped to bring Peter, a young chimpanzee, to London, "as he [was] grow[ing] very intelligent," a fate he clearly thought none of his African companions could fulfill.[100] Payeur-Didelot called apes "our Gabonese brother(s)," and declared that they were smarter than local people.[101] In the 1920s, Gabrielle Vassal, the wife of an administrator in the French Congo, confided that she was struck by the difference in the learning ability of a young chimpanzee and a little Congolese girl. After she gave them some chocolate, she said, "The monkey took the object, sniffed it several times, brought it to its mouth, and finally, (seeing me doing it) energetically chew on it. The child looked at the black marble, turned it, and started to cry. I showed her that it was good to eat. All this was in vain: dumbly looking at me, she cried louder."[102]

It took another channel for Europeans to work out their yearnings and dread about sharing kinship with the natives. The mythical language of the archaic father, mediated by gorillas and African humans, helped them to articulate the ambivalent emotion.

Archaic Fathers in the Land of Desire

The archaic father, a powerful figure of maleness and destructive kinship, merged European reveries about sexual and political domination. In the Western folklore, numerous stories describe rebellious sons killing a murderous father to found civilization: Cronus devouring his sons, Prometheus tricking Zeus, and David confronting Goliath. In 1913, Sigmund Freud theorized the scenario in *Totem and Taboo*, arguing that Western civilization was born after the sons internalized the guilt of parricide.[103] In Gabon, few colonialists read Freud, but, in their relations with gorillas and Africans, many used the figure of the destructive father to justify the violence of colonialism. In one version, the French saw themselves as Promethean sons confronting archaic savages and wild gorillas. Here the killing and containment of the native enemy was a labor of civilization.

Positioning the French as Promethean sons and the gorillas as archaic fathers, this scenario unfolded in the primal scene of white men encountering gorillas. Narrated many times in colonial travelogues and memoirs, the encounter unfolded as oedipal tragedy, the writer adopting the viewpoint of a child numbed by the sight of giants.[104] Du Chaillu's first description of a great male, for instance, portrayed a gorilla "nearly six feet high with immense body, huge chest, and great muscular arms."[105] In another episode, he compared the male he had just shot to "Goliath, the giant."[106] In later colonial texts, the great apes of Gabon appeared as colossal patriarchs endowed with lethal strength: "One does not make faces [grimaces] to [male gorilla] with impunity: he would think one is mocking his spouse [sa dame] and would come to you in a fighting position . . . you will be lacerated and crushed."[107]

Western authors advised colonialists to shoot the great males at the last minute and with a single bullet, a prescription that opened acute moments of terror and violence: "If you miss the fellow, he won't miss you."[108] One story blamed such failure on an African hunter, who paid for the mistake by being crushed by the manly beast in an elaborate scene of symbolic emasculation. One day, hearing the cries of an isolated huntsman, Du Chaillu wrote, he rushed to see a mortally wounded man: the gorilla had charged him, "frightfully lacerating his abdomen, and with this single blow laying bare part of the intestines. As he sank, bleeding, to the ground, the monster seized the gun . . . and in his rage almost flattened the barrel in his jaws" (figure 5.4).[109]

At least another illustration of the scene appeared after 1861, in the form of a stuffed gorilla staged in the menacing pose (figure 5.5). This suggested the wide circulation of the story.

In contrast to the helpless terror of African victims in the anecdote, imperial texts boasted about the heroic mastery of white men. As Promethean sons and bearers of civilization, they coldly waited for charging gorillas and shot them with a poise that contrasted with the fearful agitation of their black companions (figure 5.6).[110]

In a second genre of gorilla stories, the French, burdened with guilt and doom, envisioned themselves as the destructive patriarchs of a dying colony. They projected the figure of the archaic Father onto themselves, revealing in blurry tones the deleterious consequences of their coming to Gabon. Here the primal scene was the murder of a mother gorilla.

5.4 Hunter killed by a gorilla. From Paul Belloni Du Chaillu, *Adventures in the Great Forest of Equatorial Africa and the Country of the Dwarfs* (New York: Harper, 1890), 243. Artist unknown.

Contrary to the shooting of male gorillas, the murder of female and baby apes filled white men with immense guilt: "We were walking along in silence when I heard a cry, and presently saw before me a female gorilla, with a tiny baby gorilla hanging to her breast and sucking. The mother was stroking the little one, and looking fondly down at it; and the scene was so pretty and touching that I held my fire, and considered—like a soft-hearted fellow—whether I had not better leave them in peace."[111]

Euro-American traders, explorers, and missionaries often adopted orphaned baby apes, becoming male mothers tending surrogate children. Du Chaillu nursed several chimpanzees. The first was Tommy, a young monkey whose mother he had killed: "He had a great affection for me, and used to follow me about. When I sat down, he was not content til he had climbed upon me, and hid his head in my breast. He was extremely fond of being petted and fondled, and would sit by the hour while any one stroked his head or back."[112] Du Chaillu also tried to domesticate baby gorillas. The craving to do so overpowered him to the point of muteness: laying hands on his first alive young gorilla, he "[could not] describe the emotions with which [he] saw the struggling little brute

5.5 Photograph sheet from the Appleton Cabinet at Amherst, with the follow-ing text on the back: "Here the stuffed skin and skeleton of the African Gorilla, presented by Rev. Wm. Walker, of Gaboon West Africa." Date unknown. Courtesy of Amherst College Archives and Special Collections.

5.6 Du Chaillu: "Death of the Gorilla." From Paul Belloni Du Chaillu, *Explorations and Adventures in Equatorial Africa: With Accounts of the Manners and Customs of the People, and of the Chace* [sic] *of the Gorilla, Crocodile Leopard, Elephant, Hippopotamus, and Other Animals* (London: John Murray, 1861), 434. Note how the central, vertical pose of Du Chaillu, slightly bent on his gun and gazing quietly at the gorilla, contrasts with the agitated behavior of African hunters.

dragged into the village. All the hardships [he] had endured in Africa were rewarded in that moment."[113]

One engraving, probably dating from the 1870s, illustrates both the cruelty of these captures and the proximity that Europeans imagined between apes and Africans. It showed Du Chaillu coming to meet a young gorilla led by African hunters with a fork attached to his neck, a device similar to the ones that secured slaves. In the picture, diffused in the press, the young gorilla fully looks like a man: he is touching the neck device with his arms, as if trying to free himself, walking upright on long legs, and looking at Du Chaillu with a human expression.[114] The explorer walks to meet the captive with both arms stretched as if to embrace him.

Male sentiment and love for young apes was both unbounded and ambiguous.[115] In tales of petting, nurturing, and teaching their young gorillas, white men veered from playing the roles of ruthless hunters and Promethean sons to those of tender mothers and companions. Meanwhile, the gorillas shifted from ferocious fathers to orphaned children and helpless babies. Fleuriot de

Langle adopted two young gorillas during his visit to Gabon and became very attached to one of them: he baptized him Jacques and brought him on board the ship when leaving the region. Jacques would watch the admiral writing. As soon as he set his pen on the table, the young gorilla jumped into his arms and pressed himself on his chest. At the pinnacle of happiness, Fleuriot wrote, the animal fixed its gaze on the admiral's eyes and refused to leave, as if it cuddled its mother's breast.[116] One of the most extraordinary of these pet stories had a Mr. Woodward bringing condensed milk to a baby gorilla. "Nurs[ing] him tenderly as a human babe, [he] allowed him to sleep in [his] own bed, as it moaned when put away by itself."[117] The pet, it turned out, was a she—a potential daughter-cum-incestuous "third" that could merge a host of typical colonial emotions: attraction, affection, aggression, repression, and guilt.

All of this nurturing occurred in a colony where European texts celebrated the role of the "fecund seed" brought to the land by explorers and colonials, and where colonial domination was described in affective terms. Here indeed, a minister of French colonies recalled that "no severe *disaffection* existed among the populaces who still trusted the "benevolent action" of the French, while a director of agricultural affairs compared colonial work to the domestic care of a "good *pater familias*" (*un bon père de famille*). The attachment between European men and their gorilla pets remind us of the extensive, protean role that affective sentiments, paternal care, sexual satisfaction, and pleasure played more largely in colonial politics.

But the French also portrayed themselves in gorilla stories as archaic fathers bringing desolation to the colony. At times paternal figures, at other times murderous fathers and parricidal sons, they fancied their civilizing mission in impossibly contradictory terms.[118] Perhaps the most disquieting example of the ease with which colonials experienced and initiated these permutations rested in the complete indifference with which they severed kinship ties with their young pets. After their death, they seamlessly transferred the docile companions from motherly domestic space to the male preserve of the laboratory. There, plunging them into alcohol or arsenic, they rebirthed them as scientific specimens.[119] In the 1860s, Compiègne and Alfred Marche had adopted a baby gorilla named Anatole. The young ape was in constant need of being caressed and cuddled. He soon began to sleep in a baby crib. Compiègne confided his growing attachment to Anatole, "whose society proved a significant distraction and pleasure in the midst of our many worries and miseries." After a few months, the young gorilla fell sick with consumption. Compiègne described with emotion the agony and death of his animal companion. Yet as soon as it was over, the author, his naturalist's instinct back, hastened to put Anatole's remains in alcohol.[120]

The occurrence was not exceptional: it reflected the increasing mania, among Euro-American visitors to Gabon, to collect, dismember, and preserve animal and human specimens. Historians of science and literary critics have explored these activities in Western laboratories and museums, but they have left unexplored their local meanings in Africa.[121] In Gabon, local people witnessed colonialists' unrelenting demand for ape and monkey body parts, and the strange manipulations that they performed on these samples. The production of specimens became an important site of engagement and conflict between foreigners and native people.

Indeed, local hunters made good business out of furnishing foreigners with animal remains. One of the first documented cases, in 1847, concerned a gorilla carcass that Gabonese men sold to R. B. N. Walker, an agent of the British firm Hatton and Cookson. Walker stowed the specimen in spirits, along with two boiled skeletons of large grey animals, and the rum-preserved brains, intestines, and body parts of other specimens, and sent the booty to naturalists in the United Kingdom.[122] Scientific pursuits and the quest for international fame cohabitated with material profit. In the 1870s, Augustus Collodon confided that after killing two gorillas, he immediately cut off their heads and "put them in pickle," to sell them for ten pounds apiece at his base camp.[123] By the 1880s, the Gabonese knew the weird routines of Euro-American hunters and visitors so well known that Robert Nassau, amateur naturalist and missionary, noticed that "the natives [have] learned that we, white people, want skins and they will now lay flat a carcass with some care."[124]

After a gorilla slaughter, native huntsmen removed the skin and disemboweled the animal before cutting it up and sharing the meat.[125] Then white explorers started their strange cuisines, often under the curious gaze of village onlookers.[126] Twice in his memoirs, Du Chaillu explained how he spent most of his nights laboring as taxidermist, toiling with the chemical compounds carried in his caravan (ten pounds of arsenic), and observed by fascinated villagers.[127]

Reverend Nassau, a Protestant missionary in Gabon, wrote one of the most detailed descriptions of specimen preparation.[128] In 1878, he prepared the corpse of a recently deceased young male gorilla for his medical correspondent in Philadelphia, Dr. Thomas G. Morton: he immersed the animal in a twenty-gallon cask of rum and made two small incisions in the skin so the liquor might bathe all the organs.[129] Two years later, Morton asked Nassau to find him another gorilla's brain: the soft tissues of the first carcass had decomposed and proven unfit for dissection. The missionary succeeded only in 1890, when he obtained the "still warm" body of a young gorilla that had been shot nearby. Nassau's first effort at sawing the cranium, however, ended in failure: working with a carpenter backsaw and a chisel, he wounded the brain. A few days later, Fang traders sold him two young live gorillas. Back at the mission, Nassau noticed that one of the captives was starting to waste away and seized the opportunity:

> I put him out of his misery and worked on the brain at midnight, by torch light. I worked very carefully with a chisel and no mallet, and loosened the brain without injuring the membranes. I took off the top of the skull. Being afraid to work down the base of the skull, . . . I sawed away the face and jaws as to make the mass small enough to enter the jar. . . . On arrival at my house three days later, I decanted the chloride of zinc and substituted rum and subsequently alcohol. This jar I carefully carried with me on my furlough to America in May 1891.[130]

This kind of cruelty and detachment perhaps went unpunished, but not unnoticed. For the Gabonese who witnessed white people dismembering apes and cooking their remains in chemical liquors, scientific toils looked like unabashed witchcraft—in fact, just like rival experts and usurpers composing corporeal agency in charms.

Hunger and Interspecies Sex

Like the adoptive parents who turned, in the laboratory, into murderous fathers, Europeans could forcefully reclaim the pleasure of violent domination. In the colony, they played games of minstrelsy that faked the role of African intermediaries. In Europe, scientists used apes for bloody and frightening experiments of sexual potency and interspecies grafting.

In Gabon, Du Chaillu enjoyed writing that the natives feared his magical ability: "My men knew as well as myself how important it was that I should maintain the reputation of being invulnerable; and it was universally believed that the arrows of the Ashangos glanced from my body without hurting me."[131] He also suggested that he could turn at will into a leopard and a gorilla, two sacred animals of the rainforest. The first had long been an emblem of public power and leadership in West Equatorial Africa, and people sometimes thought that witches and rulers could change into the wild beast to attack enemies.[132] Likewise, they viewed gorillas as quasihuman beings full of strength and power: on hearing the rumors about Du Chaillu turning into a wild beast, the Gabonese would have feared his witch-power.[133] Similarly, in the 1920s, Augustus Collodon, aka "Congo Jake" narrated an episode in nearby Congo in which he escaped from the "clutches of cannibals" by pretending he was a "leopard-man."[134]

During the high tide of the colonial period, practicality served as another pretext for mimicry: some colonials greased their faces to appear as a "negro" so they could hunt big game. Unlike explorers, colonialists organized such pastimes for pleasure and mischief, dressing up for a bit of fun that, neverthe-less, put colonial usurpation in plain sight: in 1952, the white residents of the Niari Valley in the Congo gathered in the small city of Madingou, at a farm owned by Mrs. and Mr. Des Isles, for a "Carnival of Colonialists." Garbed as a "magnificent village chief," Mr. Des Isles welcomed the many guests disguised as Africans.[135]

The lure of going native, even temporarily, and the complex attraction that Europeans felt for apes-Africans and their sexual-patriarchal power, some-times surged in the desire to assimilate parts of native body substances.[136] Working the fantasy, writers and scientists injected the public with cases of imperial mutation and ape enhancement, a cross-cultural and international genre circulating from Africa to the metropole and back.[137] In "The Adventure of the Creeping Man" (1923), Arthur Conan Doyle told the story of an aging scholar, Professor Presbury, who is engaged to a younger woman.[138] Anxious to satisfy his bride's sexual demands, Presbury inoculates himself with a drug manufactured from langur monkeys. Although the treatment gives him re-newed energy, the professor slowly acquires bestial traits until, in a frighten-ing episode, he turns into a wild ape.

Reputable scientists in the real world, meanwhile, experimented with in-terspecies therapeutic grafts. In France, Serge Voronoff, a celebrated surgeon, performed fifty-one transplants of monkeys' testis to humans from 1920 to 1923. The procedure, he claimed, fought "premature aging" and "exhaustion" in older men.[139] Voronoff believed that capillary vessels could nourish the mon-keys' bits grafted into the "vaginal tunic" of a male patient's scrotum, which would then secrete rejuvenating hormones. In 1924, his best-selling book *Forty-Three Grafts From Monkey to Man* boasted that the procedure amelio-rated sexual and intellectual faculties in 88 percent of his patients (figure 5.7).

Science discredited Voronoff's theories in the 1950s. But in the 1920s, the graft experiment was only one of the many sites where colonial desires for ex-

SERGE VORONOFF

Quarante-trois Greffes
du Singe à l'Homme

AVEC 88 PLANCHES DANS LE TEXTE

PARIS
LIBRAIRIE OCTAVE DOIN
GASTON DOIN, ÉDITEUR
8, PLACE DE L'ODÉON

1924

Tous droits réservés

5.7 Cover of Serge Voronoff's *Quarante trois greffes du singe à l'homme* (Paris: Librairie Octave Doin, 1924).

tracting force, virility, and power from Africa blossomed. Guilt, remorse, and the fear of racial transmutation often tainted these yearnings. In the colony, however, people deployed them in practical operations that occurred under the gaze of Africans, fueling local knowledge about white cannibalism and colonial witch-power.

Colonial Cuisine

For all of Europeans' scandalized opinions about Gabonese cannibalism, they failed to understand that their own actions looked like cannibal transgressions to outsiders. They relentlessly demanded and stole human remains, whether amateur anthropologists collecting skulls and bones in African graveyards, or explorers dismembering apes and preserving their body parts.

Du Chaillu alone collected more than ninety-three indigenous human skulls in Gabon.[140] In one village, he went to the burial ground to lift a skull, a hand, and part of an arm.[141] In another village, visiting a royal cemetery where bodies decayed right on the ground, he "seized a skull and rapidly decamped."[142] He also kept trying to measure the height and features of locals. One day, in the pygmy village of Niembouai, where he had provoked a panicked flight, Du Chaillu caught a woman by her leg and asked her where the villagers buried their dead. The bewildered captive remained silent. Later, when he returned to the village, the frightened women "sa[id] that he [was] a leopard coming to eat them." He nevertheless succeeded in taking the morphological measurement of five of them, "who," he mocked, "were so scared that they covered their faces with their hands."[143] In 1879, explorer Alfred Marche narrated similarly morbid exploits in central Gabon: after he found human skulls in a small wood, he said, "we hid them at the bottom of our bags to bring them back clandestinely to our lodgings. The blacks were not to see us collecting and carrying human remains away; not that there was any danger in these parts, but if the reputation of grave-diggers had preceded us, it could have brought some nasty business upon us."[144] Marche's collections of bones, like those of Du Chaillu before him and many afterward, could not fail to resonate with local fears about the loss of ancestral relics and corporeal power.

The French damned Africans as less human for their supposed inability to transcend the grossest of instincts and to reach a disincarnated level of social interaction. And they entirely failed to see that the cuisine they performed in their taxidermy workshops and the thefts they perpetrated in native burial grounds demonstrated that they were the ones worshipping the material magic of body parts, and seeking to sate their cannibal cravings.

SIX : Eating

In 2002, a strange anecdote circulated through Libreville: the wife of a prominent local politician, looking into her brand-new freezer (imported from abroad) to fetch something for dinner, had found frozen human organs and realized, in a flash, that her husband participated in the traffic in *pièces détachées*, or body parts.[1] She went mad. Despite its atypical elements, the story belongs to the contemporary lore of ritual murders performed by rich and powerful Gabonese to secure charms charged with corporeal power. When people discover a ritual murder, they usually find a cadaver outdoors, in an isolated spot. The murderers and the *commanditaire* (the patron who commissions the crime) remain in the shadows and seldom face prosecution. Under the lid of the ill-fated freezer, the unfortunate wife, instead, immediately knew who the responsible party was, while her discovery hinted of cannibalism in the realm of family dining. What the maddened spouse had seen was not only the proof of her husband's foul deed but, nestled deep in the household provisions, evidence that her family's prosperity rested on a horrible crime. In the hypermodern space of the freezer, the labor of reproduction had turned into intimate felony—the container, the good wife, and the frozen flesh binding together domesticity and global consumption, social mobility and murder. Seen from this angle, the Gabonese lore of *pièces détachées* exposes, I argue, the closing of the gap between the Western cannibal imaginary and African ideas on eating as power.

These breaches had moved and breathed since the nineteenth century, widening in places and sealing up in others. At the time of the conquest, Europeans understood anthropophagy as humans literally eating human flesh: cannibalism was material or it was not. In contrast, equatorial Africans' views of eating, regardless of the substance, belonged to a complex idiom of social aggregation, political consummation, and *symbolic* destruction. The dark side of this ethos of eating-as-power described witches killing people by mystically eating them (iKota: *idja moto*; Galoa: *nya mutu*); a witch assaulted a person's body, life force, and social energy.[2] In this case, the attacker needed to be related to the victim, and to possess a powerful witch-substance. Though the attack was mystical and invisible, its effects were tangible and real: the victim's life wasted away, and his or her social initiatives became hopelessly unsuccessful. The more positive side of eating-as-power understood a person's witch-substance (*evu/kundu*) and life force (*ngul*) to be potent tools for securing material power and distributing it for the benefit of others. From this perspective, to "eat" was symbolic, and it meant to give birth, to harvest and prepare food, to nurture and transmit knowledge, and to create social and religious networks—in short, to facilitate the flow of resources through a multiskilled and all-powerful body.[3]

In the freezer story of 2002, this productive Gabonese ethos of eating had congealed into oblivion, the figurative mode itself replaced by a trivial feat of frozen flesh and dead matter. The scene can tempt us to jump to the theory that colonialism showed the way, exploiting African bodies for banquets of economic exploitation, social crushing, and political fetishism. While not wrong, the idea does not go far enough to disentangle how colonial agents redefined the very terms in which we, English-speaking outsiders, mean, and what *they*, the Gabonese, meant by "cannibalism," *ventre* (belly-womb), or "ritual cuisine." In the long twentieth century, Europeans and Africans fought deadly wars over these ideas. Despite the immense complexity of the cluster of meanings carried by each one of these terms, never, perhaps, was a battle for words and ideas so weighted with concrete outcomes.

Gabonese and European imaginaries of eating did coincide at places. Such resemblance encouraged significant transfers, borrowings, expansion, and shrinking of meaning. Although today eating-as-power remains an immense machinery of agency and capacity, and a central imaginary of social disasters and cures in Gabon, its meaning has significantly shrunk, now connoting destruction and the literal ingestion of flesh.

This chapter recovers some of the battlefields where these changes took place: the belly-womb (*le ventre*), cooking pots, blood-sucking vampires, and the Eucharist. It is not possible to retrieve a linear chronology of these transfers and alterations, or any clear shifting or aggregating moment. We can only follow the imaginary of eating-as-power nimbly and lightly, in the clusters of practical situations, conflicts with colonials, discourses, and rumors where it absorbed new meanings. Colonial obsessions with African cannibalism, especially after the French passed a Decree on the Repression of Anthropophagy in 1923, narrowed "eating" from symbolic meanings to univocally harmful functions. Gabonese adopted biological and medical understandings of the human body. A series of cannibal trials between 1904 and 1955, along with a rich array of African oral and textual archives, will provide glimpses of the frontlines where cannibal imaginaries clashed and transformed.

The Belly-Womb

At the end of the nineteenth century in West Equatorial Africa, *eating* was a rich and multilayered idiom of empowerment and agency, operating in both harmful and productive ways.[4] To eat a person usually meant to kill her (iKota: *idja*, "to eat," and *iboma*, "to kill"), but it always involved an element of mystical and immaterial power, also subsumed by verbs derived from the proto-Bantu root for bewitching (*-dog-*).[5] Eating had less to do with organic and literal hunger than with a complex machinery of power, mediated by a body in turn social and individual, physical and metaphoric, and able to expand as a social unit by incorporating dependents.[6] Indeed, eating also expressed core ideas on the social recomposing of groups, particularly kin networks. To eat a rival clan, for instance, meant to deploy matrimonial strategies to aggregate it: because of matrilineal lines of descent, a clan that regularly gave wives to another clan ended up absorbing it.

Eating-as-power was always ambivalent: the witchcraft substance (*evu/ kundu*) that some individuals possessed could serve either harmful or healing purposes, both connoted by the verb "to eat" (iPunu: *dji*; Mpongwe: *nya*; Fang: *dzagh*; iKota: *idja*). When using their skills for the collective good, these individuals facilitated the flow of wealth by absorbing and regurgitating goods (marriage payments), people (wives and in-laws) and alliances (dependents and allies).[7] Eating, therefore, meant the possibility of accruing and redistributing wealth for the benefit of the community, following the ideal of the big man's generosity toward kin and dependents. Yet powerful men and women could also retain assets and destroy others' lives to nourish the witch-substance that made them powerful.

Culinary terms also named the ability of a woman's multiskilled body to nurture life and force. Ewondo speakers believed that a pregnant woman "cooked a baby in her womb." The Fang Bëti in Cameroon said that women "humanized" raw food products by cooking them.[8] The same groups related these two female activities—processing food in earthen pots and cooking a child in the womb. Conversely, many Gabonese communities associated raw food with wilderness and witchcraft: raw eggs, in particular, had the reputation of feeding the *evu* (witch-substance) of nightly witches.[9]

The stomach and the female womb combined in Gabonese symbolism. In English, I merge these organs of multilayered power in the notion of "belly-womb," understood as a single device of power. Across Gabon, ritual specialists composed charms by putting medicine in an opening generally (but not always) carved in the abdominal region of anthropomorphic statues; these magic substances charged the object with the healing forces and aggressive capacity of spirits or ancestors. Judicial ordeals forced the suspect to ingest poison (oMyènè: *mbundu*): if he or she regurgitated it, he or she was innocent. If the poison stayed in the person's body and killed him or her, it revealed guilt.[10]

Early evidence is immensely useful in understanding the dynamic flexibility of local ideas about eating-as-power and the location of the witch-substance: the early ethos of eating did not coincide entirely with physically ingesting a person's flesh, nor was the witch-substance equivalent to the stomach or liver.[11] The witch-substance itself (*evu/kundu*) was often seen as located in the stomach or the abdomen, but this was far from always being the case. As chapter 3 already documented, the Gabonese thought that *evu/kundu* could migrate in and out from the body of the person. It did not have a singular nature and appearance. By 1900, Karl Laman had transcribed the notes of his Kongo-speaking pupils, detailing their composite visions of the witch-substance: "The *kundu* appears as a blood-filled gland or a tumor somewhere in the body, usually in the stomach. When a dead *ndoki* is cut up, it is to secure his *kundu*. It is possible to have several of these glands, located in various parts of the body. . . . The *kundu* gland can be located in the throat and is then called *nkaku* (barrier)."[12]

Another story collected by Laman featured a great *ndoki* (witch) who owned four *kundu* glands, three in the chest and one in the throat.[13] The substance, moreover, could move and change place. During his sojourn among the Fang in 1890–1906, Günther Tessman described the *evu* substance as wandering in various parts of the body, sometimes placing itself in the brain, and in women, in the vagina or uterus.[14]

One of the major changes wrought by colonialism was to make these complex elements overlap and merge in the destructive figure of the cannibal belly-womb, or *ventre* (English: "abdomen," "stomach," "womb," "belly"), a French term widely used by the Gabonese in the 2000s. Better than its English equivalent, *le ventre* retains some of the multilayered meanings of vernacular repetoires for digestive, sexual, and social functions. Yet, people now mostly understand *le ventre* as a digestive organ and the place for harmful witchcraft: they use the slang French *bouffer* (to grub, to eat voraciously) to refer to the antisocial greed of the powerful.[15] To eat is no longer to process and regurgitate wealth for the benefit of others but simply to swallow and destroy assets for individual purposes. The witch-substance *evu/kundu* has come to reside only in the abdomen: people describe it as a fleshy growth in the belly. Again, this was not the norm in the nineteenth century.

Cauldrons and *Marmites*

A modest but pivotal element of the modern cannibal lore in Gabon, the *marmite* or cooking pot, shows how new metaphors of eating-as-power emerged at the intersection of European and Gabonese imaginaries. Gabonese understandings of cooking pots as material objects and social units influenced French colonialists' ideas about African cannibalism. In turn, the French inflected local idioms with the evil connotation of witches' banquets and devilish cuisines.

In nineteenth-century Equatorial Africa, cooking pots worked as the interface of domestic and ritual reproduction. To prepare food, farmers of the rainforest had long used earthen vessels (iPunu: *ikéngu*, plur. *bikengu*), usually made by female potters. Similar pots helped healers and herbalists to "cook" medicines and charms.

The diffusion of iron smelting in Equatorial Africa (2000 BCE) made metal utensils available in the domestic economy. Because male blacksmiths monopolized the procedures, the gender production of cooking utensils changed, asserting a new male dominance over the domestic economy.[16] Local societies gave different names to the pots according to the material of which they were made: in Fang an earthen vessel is called *vyekh*, and a metal one, *enyin*.[17]

From the seventeenth century onward, metal objects made up a considerable portion of the commodities imported in Gabon. The slave trade connected social wealth and social death to metal utensils imported from the Atlantic Ocean. Because they remained rare, the Gabonese used these objects as special currencies for social exchanges such as bride payment. This in turn encouraged people to sell slaves to obtain luxury metal items. An ambivalent cycle developed, in which the rich sold people for prestige objects that, in turn, could serve to attract new members to the community. Metal pots (oMyènè: *mbumba*) started to symbolize the cooking of evil witchcraft to procure material and human wealth.

In addition, the metal vessels entered into the new economy of firearms: broken and discarded utensils could serve as shrapnel for trade muskets. In the 1860s, Louis-Alphonse-Victor du Pont de Compiègne documented how Bakele men stuffed the muzzles of their weapons with such pieces of iron, and wrote about a young girl who had been shot by "two little pieces of *marmite* that had crossed her thigh."[18] Today, a reminiscence of the role of *marmite* in warfare animates the Gabonese lore of "magic guns" (French: *fusils nocturnes*; iPunu: *kumbule*), the name of talismans that one can use to harm another person.[19] These ideas found a strong echo in the European imaginary of witchcraft. Aware of the particular role of metal receptacles in the slave trade, European merchants must also have recalled the Western folklore of metal cauldrons and witches' brews.

An early description of a healer concocting medicine shows the interplay of African and Western imaginaries, suggesting how foreigners interpreted native cooking pots as cauldrons for "stewing ghosts" and eating flesh: "At [the nganga's] feet lay the roll of mysterious medicines by whose magic he unlocks the doors of futurity and there, over the mystic fire seethes the enchanted caldron out of which will arise at his command the visions of coming events and the rising vapor, as it ascends in his presence, will spread out before his prophetic eyes. . . . Occasionally he lifts the lid from the pot and takes a peep at the stewed ghost inside."[20]

In the 1920s, as we have seen in chapter 5, the French reemployed the repertoire of the witches' cauldron, or *marmite*, during the crisis of "tiger-men" murders. They explained that Gabonese tiger-men united around a *marmite* that they used as fetish, cannibal utensil, and rallying name for their gang.[21] After the 1940s, however, colonial administrators stopped using the word *marmites* to talk about secret associations of criminals, preferring the term of *sociétés secrètes*.[22] But the Gabonese had picked up the colonial lexicon. Today, one can say of other people that "they belong to the same *marmite*" to hint that they are witches.[23] In 2002, an informant in Mouila (southern Gabon) told me how witches congregated in a mystical tree around a *marmite* (iPunu: *mbidji* or *douengou*).[24] In the 1990s, anthropologist Kajsa Elkhom Friedman confirmed the pervasive use of *marmite* in witches' stories collected in Brazzaville, the capital of Congo. People said that female witches handed down to their daughters a *marmite de nuit* (nocturnal pot), in the form of an innocuous-looking earthenware utensil. In one story, a family believed itself to be cursed by a "nocturnal pot." The magic utensil, marching backward and forward across the compound like a person, had caused series of untimely deaths within the matrilineage. Called to help, a healer found the pot buried in the ground along with horrific items—bits of the flesh of those who had been eaten, a finger, and part of the harvest that had disappeared.[25]

It is extremely difficult to determine how people borrowed these images from Europeans, and how they spread them from one locale to the next. The frequency and large reach of cannibal investigations and tiger-men murders in southern and central Gabon, however, could have hardly left conversations untouched. The African clerks who translated and transcribed the interrogations of witnesses could disseminate intriguing details to their friends and relatives. The proximity between the rich African ideas of cooking pots and the vast European lexicon of witches' vessels opened many avenues for informal comparisons and influences. The stories about the witches' cooking pot in Mouila and the *marmite de nuit* in Brazzaville suggest that such circulation indeed happened.

Cannibals on Trial

The French moved quickly to bring alleged Gabonese cannibals to trial. In the early twentieth century, a period of intense colonial turmoil and disasters, they swiftly interpreted local conflicts and crimes as cannibal feasts driven by insatiable native hunger for human flesh. The judicial archives, despite their incompleteness and bias, are a trove of the history of eating-as-power: there, questions, responses, and speculations from various parties came together and started influencing each other, if only in partial and unbalanced ways.

Between 1904 and 1955, archival deposits preserved 126 criminal affairs dealing with cannibalism, or an average or two to three cases a year.[26] Only a few survived as complete dossiers including the full investigative report, the cross-examination of witness, the transcription of the court hearing, and the sentence. Even these comprehensive files present multiple challenges to historical analysis. Transcribed in French, the documents come from a context of asymmetrical power, misunderstanding, and oppression, in which they imposed a fairly rigid, foreign structure on local suspects and witnesses. No other version of each event exists, foreclosing any possibility of cross-examination and making the texts difficult to interpret. This archive mostly documents French reactions to local acts that might or might not have had something to do with eating people. Yet, with some imagination and an eye for nuance, we can see important patterns in the life and imaginary of the Gabonese as well: shifts in the role of elders and their ability to protect the young, and key alterations in local understandings of eating-as-power.

Indeed, cannibal trials often dealt with suspects harming young kin by "eating" them, or by forcing them to participate in cannibal covenants. They point to dire social stress endured by local societies under colonialism: for our purposes, they also show important reversals in the ability of adults to protect and circulate social assets, or wealth-in-people.[27] In 1924–25 in the village of Mocabi (Nyanga Province), the colonial authorities accused four men and a woman of killing a young girl and eating her cadaver.[28] The four accomplices included a couple, a local chief named Mongongo Migallo, and his wife. The victim was their own niece, a girl named Oulabo Ouroundiga. The murderers had allegedly cut off her head, skinned it, and boiled her body.

In addition, Mongongo Migallo had forced a young boy, his nephew, to participate in the cannibal deed. He had also requested that the boy sacrifice one of his siblings and bring him to the accomplices. The boy refused, and later told the court:

> They fell on me and tried to kill me. Chief Mougongo stopped them and said: "Don't kill him, he will give you a raffia square [for his life]." [The accomplice] forced my mouth open and poured some of the girl's brew, squeezing my nose to making me swallow it. I fell on the ground. My whole body swelled, and for several days, I was unable to stand up. Finally, [two of the accomplices] came to fetch me and brought me back to the village on a *tipoye* [colonial name for a chair or stretcher carried by porters]. Upon my arrival, I confessed the facts to several people. It took me a long time to recover. [29]

Before delving further in the case, it is important to mention a case that occurred thirty years later, near Fougamou on the Ngounié River; many of the patterns of the 1920s endured late in the colonial period. In Fougamou in 1955, the local police arrested four people for eating the flesh of a young man in a cannibal banquet.[30] The case appeared to be grounded in a complex family feud. A husband and wife had invited two men to feast with them on the boy, who happened to be the brother of one of the guests. The principal witness, a seventeen-year-old man named Bouvedi Jacques, had participated in the meal against his will and described the scene in great detail: the matron had put a large cooking pot next to a fire, and prepared four portions of cooked meat on large banana leaves. The husband served the dish, inviting the guests to mix it with cooked bananas.

Both cases, therefore, included a collective cannibal meal performed by adults with two victims: the youngster killed and cooked, and the young relative forced to participate in the crime. In both cases, adults transgressed the labor of family reproduction and ignored generational classification.[31] In contrast with earlier human sacrifices organized by elders and high initiates to protect the community in cases of extreme danger, the new cases pictured a profane repast in which everybody ate together without any distinction of age or position. Both banquets were overwhelmed by coarse materiality. In the first case (in Mocabi in 1925), the murderers cut and skinned the girl's head and forced a steaming brew down the throat of their young accomplice. In the second (in Fougamou in 1955), the meal prepared by a matron in a cooking pot disguised the crime as a trivial forest picnic. In both cases, European investigation largely contrived the profusion of carnal details and mundane actions: in tune with white cannibal imagination of the time, it denied the symbolic and abstract dimension of the criminals' acts. Yet there might be something else.

The crimes displayed a rich and multivalent repertoire of domestic cuisine, staging the cannibal banquet as an illicit reversal of homely cooking (oMyènè: *namba*). The witnesses insisted on detailing cooking pots, plates made of leaves, knives, vegetables, and starch food. Such a meal, in everyday life, would exemplify the adult task of nurturing one's extended kin. In Mocabi and Fougamou, the transgression was in the slain human flesh hidden in the pot, or in the innocuous-looking stew cooling on banana leaves. In addition, both the Mocabi and Fougamou cases included elements that resonated with the technique of "cooking" charms, composing therapeutic charms or genealogical devices with sacred human substances. In Mocabi (1925), the cutting, skinning, and boiling of the young victim's head recalled the processing of ancestral bones for composing relics. Moreover, healers and medicinal substances prominently featured in the transcripts. Near the scene, the police found a basket containing medicines individually wrapped in raffia and fragments of human bones and a skull. They discovered a small wooden chest (*une petite malle en bois*) hidden on top of a ceiling beam in the house of one of the convicts, holding various charms and ingredients: a piece of leopard fur (an emblem of leadership in the region), another bit of fur from a cat with a small bell attached to it, a small tin box full of ashes and suspended by a long twine, a *fétiche* painted in white, and a piece of raffia fabric containing fragments of human bones. The suspect claimed that the chest did not belong to him: a *nganga* had left it after healing his uncle. As to the *moulibi* basket, he simply used it to hide money whenever he had some.[32]

The Fougamou (1955) affair presented similar patterns. Upon being forced to consume the brewed flesh of the victim, the extreme physical symptoms of the young boy replicated the reaction to a strong *médicament* (medicine): he fell on the ground while his whole body swelled. The principal suspect in the case was a *féticheur* with a large clientele. His most recent patient, he explained, a woman from a nearby village, had come to consult him about pain in the back and abdomen. He had crushed some bark taken from five different sorts of trees before mixing it with water and gunpowder. After applying the mixture on the patient's sore parts, he said that her condition would improve in seven or eight months. The woman paid him one hundred French francs and a rooster.[33]

In both cases, these elements suggest that it is possible that the French mistook the preparation of charms for a cannibal banquet, relying too much on the testimony of a young "victim" who was perhaps resentful of older relatives.

Mistaken Cuisines

Local poetics of power likened the composing of charms to a form of cuisine: elders and heads of clans "ate" and "regurgitated" resources to nurture households and families, and ritual specialists "cooked" medicines and human substances in charms and relics. The first process mostly concerned social wealth, the second spiritual health. In the iKota language, for instance, *kolamba mi koua limba* means to prepare the bones in a ritual way.[34] The verb *kolamba* means to ritually process a person or a charm, and it can be literally compared to cooking. In the 1960s, according to Joseph Tonda, one phase of the initiation of young men consisted in "stuffing" the initiate with food but also with all sorts of advice, teachings, recommendations, and warnings about taboos. For a whole month, the elders gave all sorts of medicines (iKota: *malé*) to each initiate to transform (or "cook," *kolamba*) him into a strong, resilient, powerful, and charismatic individual.

During colonial rule, European observers thought that the native people who exhumed corpses or manipulated bones were moved by a monstrous impulse to eat them in such ceremonies. The comparison between an early twentieth-century initiation ceremony among the Fang of Southern Cameroon, and the report on tiger-men associations written by French administrator Hippolyte Charbonnier in 1916, can illuminate how colonialism could assign new deadly interpretations to local rituals. During initiation, elders allowed young adults to ritually care for ancestral relics for the first time. The ceremony repeated the initial processing ("cooking") of the bones by their elders. Tessman left us acute observations of such a scene among Fang-speaking communities in southern Cameroon. Before completing the initiation trials, adult leaders prepared a special compound by digging up two pits in the ground, lining them with banana leaves, and filling them with water mixed with medicines. Then they took the sacred relics out of their containers and displayed them on the ground. They guided the young men to this compound, where the initiates saw the ancestors lying next to the ritual basins. Elders cleaned the craniums in the first basin, then smeared them with a special ointment made out of the blood of a sacrificed chicken mixed with red *paduk* powder and rubbed the young initiates with the same mixture. They then had them drink water from one of the basins. After this, the boys repeated the ceremonial gestures of the elders: they cleansed the craniums in the second medicinal basin and smeared them anew with blood and cosmetic powder. The next day, the elders sacrificed a sheep and shared the meat with the initiates before all participants formulated demands to the skulls.[35]

Charbonnier's indictment of tiger-men, written in 1916, is a nightmare vision of Tessman's report.[36] The washing of the craniums turns into scenes of cooking flesh in pots (the reliquary boxes and the basins), with the consecrated bones changing into human stew. Charbonnier also seemed to have taken the initiates' drinking of medicinal water for the ingesting of warm blood, and mixed the sacrificial chicken with a human offering.[37] A couple of later investigations confirmed the impact and frequency of these misunderstandings. One night in 1928, a French administrator stumbled over a group of men dancing around a cadaver. At the sight of the white man, the men fled into the forest, leaving ritual objects behind. The administrator concluded that he had surprised a tiger-men trance before the criminals feasted on the corpse of their victim.[38] In 1938, near Lambaréné, a man named Ossima Nang quarreled with his wife while escorting her to their plantations. In the heat of the fight, he pierced her neck with a knife. Alerted by screaming, villagers arrived at the scene and arrested the husband. During the testimonies, witnesses revealed that Ossima suffered from debilitating headaches for which he had consulted the local *nganga*. The French administrator immediately jumped to the conclusion that two men had premeditated to kill the wife to use her skull in a *médicament* (medicine) to get rich.[39] Colonial prejudice thus led to terrible consequences, the indictment and sometimes the death of people caught in acts that resonated with French cannibal obsessions.

Colonial interference also came from mistranslations. Native interpreters, in the presence of the white officer of the court, interrogated witnesses in the vernacular before typing up the dialogue in French.[40] A case in Southern Gabon in 1920 suggests that the procedure could inadvertently criminalize the polysemantic expressions used by the interlocutors. One day in 1920, near Lambaréné, Kombila, a ten- to twelve-year-old boy had brought a piece of "meat" (*un morceau de viande*) to a man named Dinga. According to Dinga, Kombila had asked the man "to give him somebody in exchange" (*lui donner quelqu'un en échange*).[41] The local court portrayed young Kombila as an unwilling accomplice of a "tiger-men" society and sentenced him to five years of prison. Yet high uncertainties marred the words that the protagonists used in their official testimonies: the exchange between Kombila and Dinga allowed for alternative meanings. "Meat" in iPunu, the language of the suspects, translates either as *nyama* (animal meat) or *du-nyuru* (human flesh or body), although we do not know what word Dinga and Kombila used. Neither do we know Kombila's vernacular terms, nor his intent when he asked Dinga "to give" him somebody. The translator could have translated the word "something" as the indeterminate personal pronoun "somebody" (*mutu*). Likewise, to give is *–vèga* or *–pégi* in iPunu. Although both verbs can express the act of killing or giving a person in sacrifice, they can also signify a more innocuous behavior.[42]

In early twentieth-century vernacular languages in Gabon, no specific word conveyed the idea of ingesting human flesh as food. The rich and ambivalent repertoire of eating (iPunu: *-ji*) and killing (iPunu: *-boke*) could not be reduced to the specific Western theory of cannibalism among the savages: a habitual diet of human food.[43] Instead of "cannibals," the label that French courts applied to suspects, the Gabonese would have probably used a terminology associated with "witches" (proto-Bantu: *bandoki*; Fang: *beyem*, sing. *nem*), individuals moved by destructive drives and the will to hurt, who were able to attack the organic and spiritual life of a victim through various means. Yet the resemblance between the French imaginary of anthropophagy and the Gabonese idiom of eating-as-power helped to birth a judicial reality that charged indigenous metaphors and events with more negative and lethal meanings.

The 1923 Law on Anthropophagy

In 1923, during the peak of tiger-men murders in Gabon, the French minister of the colonies passed a Decree on the Repression of Anthropophagy (Décret sur la répression de l'anthropophagie) in French West and Equatorial Africa. Article 1 prescribed that a native person who had committed a crime "for the purpose of anthropophagy" should be punished by death.[44] Enforcement of the law devastated Gabonese communities: by a conservative estimate, French tribunals pronounced at the very least 150 death sentences on these grounds.[45] The law also had major consequences on the making and keeping of ancestors' relics.

A tragic affair in Djouah Province provides a glimpse into the disruptions prompted by the new decree. On 28 February 1930, Charles Meiss, a French district officer in charge of a small subdivision, overheard one of his guards (*planton*) accuse a fellow villager, a man called Nze Mane, of poisoning his wife. Meiss immediately set out to arrest and interrogate him. After Nze Mane confessed and accused another man, Eyeghenzork, of using poison, the police searched Eyeghenzork's compound. They failed to find evidence until a militiaman discovered a skull hidden in the courtyard. On 2 March, Meiss pronounced the death sentence for Eyeghenzork and Nze Mane on the grounds that they had poisoned people and eaten their cadavers. Two days later, he organized their execution.[46] The incident was only one of many resulting in innumerable sentences and death penalties for the Gabonese.

The decree also redefined the cult of relics as a "violation of tombs" and a "profanation of cadavers," a crime punished by six months to two years in prison.[47] The mere possession of ancestral charms exposed people to denunciations from neighbors and rivals, and severe sentences. French administrators seldom believed elders when they claimed that the bones they kept belonged to their ancestors. In 1941, in Estuary Province, a court sentenced a man named N'Dong M'Ba, the chief of a Fang village, to prison for keeping the skulls of his own father and grandfather. His pleading that he had inherited the family relics from his paternal uncle fell on deaf ears.[48]

The French also read the *absence* of human remains as evidence of cannibalism. In early 1942, Djibo, a canton chief in Djouah Province, complained to the local district officer that a member of his jurisdiction, a man named Boueza, had failed to alert him about his wife's death and had hastily buried her during the chief's absence. Djibo added that he had brought a few men to Boupinga's grave and tried, in vain, to dig up and find the corpse. "What do you think

Boueza did with it?" the colonial officer asked the chief. "He must have eaten it," Djibo answered, proceeding to accuse Boueza's second wife, his nephew, and another man as accomplices in the crime.[49] On such fleeting evidence, the officer arrested the suspects named by the chief and charged them with murder and anthropophagy. Acknowledging the absence of the body and indeed of evidence, he sentenced Boueza and another convict to five and three years of prison, respectively, for exhuming Boupinga and "eating part of her corpse."[50]

Last but not least, the 1923 decree established a new correlation between cannibalism and trafficking in body parts. Article 2 provided that "any native guilty of anthropophagy, or guilty of a free donation or moneyed transaction in human flesh [*trafic de chair humaine à titre onéreux ou gratuit*], should be punished by up to ten years of imprisonment." The article targeted the composition and circulation of relics. Aligning with the French imaginary of African self-destruction (cannibalism and the slave trade), it merged French prejudice about the natives' blurring of barriers (confusing human flesh for food, the social person for the body, relatives for commodities) with their greed for material profit (selling one's relatives in slavery for money). Detaching the cult of relics from the realm of domestic rites and family privacy, and transferring it to that of money, material wealth, and capitalistic impulses, colonialists fueled the discourse of marketing magic and trafficking in body parts which is so prevalent in contemporary Gabon. Relentlessly decried by the public and interpreted as a recent phenomenon, such trafficking actually started a century ago in colonial discourse.

The Bleeding Heart of Jesus Christ

In incorporating and reworking some of colonialists' lore about the witches' Sabbath and evil cauldrons, the Gabonese could borrow from the Catholic doctrine of the Eucharist, or the transubstantiation of Christ's flesh and blood in the host and the wine.[51] Blood figured heavily in the visual repertoire of colonial missions. The Fathers of the Holy Ghost (Pères du St-Esprit) had been the main congregation in Gabon since the 1860s, and images of their emblem circulated widely: a bleeding heart pierced with a knife, and surrounded by thorns. The image resembled the Sacred Heart of Jesus, then extremely popular in France (figure 6.1).

Biblical references in local languages to the Devil, blood, witchery, and evil cannibalism are easily discernible in the 1950s Gabonese texts on Prince Evus

6.1 Picture of the Sacred Heart of Jesus, France, nineteenth century.

and the *vampireux* that we will analyze next.[52] These references persist today. In 2002, the notable who talked to me in Mouila about the associations of witches called *marmites* further explained that they congregated around *tables de nuit* (night-tables) or *tabernacles* (in French) that sat invisibly atop large mango trees.[53] "Table" here means more than a piece of furniture: it is a sacred place for evil meals and collective feasting. It recalls and reverses the communion table, a fixture of colonial churches and chapels, and the "banquet of Eternal life" enjoyed by the faithful after the Last Judgment. The flip side of the Christian altar, it is the evil instrument of witches and satanic covenants.[54]

Only white missionaries in Gabon could accept the idea that eating a body and drinking blood could be both a physical and a symbolic ritual, and that the act could build community among the faithful. Yet they came from a church that explained the transubstantiation of Christ as a symbol of faith rather than the material incarnation of the agency of God.[55] They saw the Gabonese idiom of eating-as-power as the polar opposite: as literal cannibalism, bloody crimes, and human sacrifices outside of any legitimate moral order. By painting the Gabonese as worshippers of hopeless matter, the Church helped to impoverish African imaginaries of eating-as-power and make them more materialistic. Downplaying the role of Christ's flesh and blood in their own communion rites, missionaries let the Gabonese relate to the theme in their own terms.[56]

Indeed, Gabonese Christians actually followed the distinction between the Eucharist and cannibalism, closely associating cannibalizing flesh and shedding blood with the Antichrist and the Devil. The white Pentecostal and Revival congregations that arrived in Gabon in the 1940s played an important role in this process: they condemned former healing rituals, fusing them into the unitary metaphor of the Devil.[57] In referring to *evu/kundu*, or shunning the activities of traditional healers and charlatans, contemporary Gabonese often use the French expression Le Très Mauvais Coeur du Diable (the Very Bad Heart of the Devil) or *taper le diable* (lit. "to knock up on the Devil").[58] Overlapping with the vampire, the witch-substance is now an attribute of the Devil and of human superwitches who not only use bones and body parts but also the blood of victims for their deeds.

Vampires and Blood

In the 1950s, the Gabonese started to use the French noun *vampire* (vampire) to talk in new positive and negative ways about eating-as-power, mostly in dramatic circumstances. The vampire, however, was not a person, but *evu/kundu*, the witch-substance for individual power and agency.[59] Today, the term appears constantly in daily conversations, rumors, and news. It also works as an adjective and an adverb: "to surge as vampire" (*sortir en vampire*) means that the witch-substance gets out of the malevolent individual's body and flies into the night to strike a victim. A *vampireux* is somebody who has a powerful witch-substance, or a vampire. But people also use vampire in friendly conversations, showing that the word keeps the positive meaning of talent, intelligence, and special skills. During an email exchange I had with two academic friends at the Université Omar Bongo Onbimba in 2009, one of them exclaimed, "Can you guys hold your vampire a bit, please! You're writing so fast, I can't keep up with you."[60]

The history of the vampire in Gabon seems at first sight to echo other blood-drinking characters, especially the *bazimamoto*, *mumiani*, and *batambula* made famous by Luise White in East and Central Africa. As White convincingly argues, people debated vampires to express colonial situations of disempowerment and exploitation.[61] She refrains from connecting them to ancient notions of blood and wrongdoing in the region, to avoid reducing their meaning or imposing a univocal, foreign historical chronology. In Gabon, in contrast, vampire stories almost never applied to predatory outsiders or Europeans; although soaked in colonial legacy, they talk about the complex transformations of African mystical agency. We need to analyze them in dialogue with older forms of individual power.

Although the vampire was an equivalent of *evu/kundu*, it carried images and meanings from European folklore that combined and clashed with the Gabonese imaginaries of extraordinary agency and evil witchcraft, changing them in the process. Blood became more present, along with echoes from the Christian Devil. In fact, the vampire served to strongly associate the witch-substance with Satan as a cannibalistic—rather than what we would call vampiric—unitary figure. These ideas spread in transfer sites such as colonial ethnographies, trials of tiger-men and cannibals, debates in Catholic missions, and biomedical practices.

Amateur ethnographies served as an early site for the repertoire of the vampire describing Gabonese realities. Colonialists came from a world obsessed by blood-sucking monsters since the success of John William Polidori's novel *The Vampyr* (1819) and Bram Stocker's bestseller *Dracula* (1897).[62] They regularly compared Gabonese beliefs in spirits and witches to the evil character of the vampire. Fleuriot de Langle was the first to mention the word in his account of his travels in the Estuary in 1876, in a passing comparison between white people and vampires.[63]

The vampire blossomed mostly in the missionary literature, in which white authors attempted to describe the ability of the witch-substance to leave one's body and fly in the shape of a wind, a flame, or a bird.[64] In 1901, Victor Largeau claimed that the Gabonese believed that, to attack victims, a witch could transform into an owl, commonly named "the bird of the witches" (Fang: *onon be yem*).[65] In 1936, pastor Henri Lavignotte was the first to liken the owl to a blood-sucking bat (vampire): he wrote that *evus*, the witch-substance, fed on the fresh blood that it drank directly from the heart of the victim.[66]

Yet blood (iPunu: *malungu*; Fang: *meki*) played only a minor role in actual precolonial Gabonese rituals. The sacrifice of small animals (chicken and goats) sometimes involved shedding blood on charms and relics. Blood brotherhood, a fairly rare social and economic alliance between two men, was sealed by the symbolic exchange of their blood after a superficial cutting of the skin.[67] Few myths and oral traditions put any emphasis on the vital liquid:

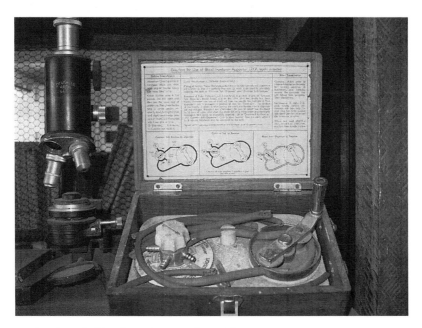

6.2 Machine for blood transfusion, Albert Schweitzer Estate, Lambaréné, 2007. Photograph by author.

the witch-substance and the power of bones and hard substances played a more prominent role in local imaginaries of eating-as-power. European descriptions of local rituals, however, projected inherited knowledge and ethnocentrism in order to wrongly insist on the importance of blood shedding in Gabonese religious practices.

Biomedical practices colored these cultural mistakes. After Louis Pasteur and Robert Koch, blood became more important to the Western imaginary of germs, illness, and contamination. Colonial doctors tested new medical findings in African dispensaries and hospitals, and, in the 1900s, introduced the new, still unsafe practice of transfusion.[68] In Gabon, Dr. Schweitzer kept a device for transfusion in his "native" bush hospital at Lambaréné (figure 6.2).[69] The witnessing of the procedures and the ability of Europeans to manipulate the passing of blood between individuals probably had a great impact on local people.

Last but not least, cannibal and tiger-men trials borrowed heavily from the European lore of bloody sacrifice, witch covenants, and vampires. In the confessions they extracted from suspects, administrators seemed to have paid inordinate attention to bloodshed and drinking. As chapter 5 already documented, the influential report on tiger-men written by Hippolyte Charbonnier in 1916 painted lengthy scenes of the murderers collecting the blood of their victims in *marmites* and drinking it.[70]

Yet these images transferred only sparsely and partially to Gabonese writings about evil actions and the witch-substance: the term vampire cannot be found in available African sources until the very late years of colonial rule.[71] Two remarkable texts from the 1950s are some of the earliest written mentions of blood and vampires by Gabonese literati. Yet if they abundantly describe cannibal banquets, blood drinking, and the killing of victims by *vampireux* (vampire-like figure), the texts do not do so with any coherence. Pierre Bekale, a Fang civil servant, wrote one of these texts in 1959. Titled "Le Mal ou la sorcellerie noire" (On Evil and black witchcraft), it draws a close connection between Satan, witch-substance (*evus*), and blood but never once mentions the term vampire.[72] The other text, also from the 1950s, uses the term *vampireux* but seldom brings up blood.[73]

Bekale's essay blames "Prince Evus" and his secret society Ngwel (Fang: witchcraft) as the orchestrator of all evil on earth. According to the essay, the prince regularly convenes the affiliates to a great banquet to feast on human "innocents."[74] They pierce the heart of their victims with a knife and collect the blood in luxury vases that they send underground to be processed and bottled. Meanwhile, professional butchers cut and prepare the flesh before giving it to "culinary teams" who cook and serve it at the "hotel." Many of Bekale's images resonate with tiger-men and cannibals court hearings and their abundant descriptions of victims knifed, butchered, and cooked, along with the murderers preserving the blood of victims in vases and bottles. Yet, if Bekale insists that Prince Evus's mouth and teeth "[are] always red from the blood he feeds on," the word vampire itself is absent. A creative interpretation of the Old Testament combined with Fang ideas about malevolent witchcraft, Prince Evus looks like the crawling animals that the Fang often compare to *evu/kundu*: "Evus is a spiritual monster looking like a bat, with hair like those of a person and eyes like those of an owl, and the rest of the body similar to a crab or a spider."[75]

During the same period, an anonymous Gabonese author wrote a twenty-five-page essay on witches and the Devil in Gabon.[76] Handwritten and unsigned, the text names the Devil a *vampireux* (vampire), but only refers to blood once: the *vampireux*, it explains, uses the blood of the victim to make a charm in the form of "an invisible animal."[77] The rest of the text features scenes of cannibal carnage and flesh cooking similar to that of Bekale's: the *vampireux* Devil is not a bloodsucker but a cannibal feasting on the cooked flesh of innocents. Like Bekale, the anonymous author seemed to have reworked the notion of *evu/kundu* by creatively juggling Christian ideas of the Devil, European metaphors of spiritual craft and witch-banquets, and Western images of blood-sucking vampires and the shedding of blood.[78] Together, their texts signal a transition into composite imaginaries of blood, cuisine, cannibals, vampires, and Evil.

Writing about vampires, early Gabonese authors strongly associated them with the figure of the Devil, the use of the witch-substance for evil deeds, and scenes of cannibal banquets that borrowed heavily from Western and Christian literature. A subtle change appeared as well: the possibility that cannibal acts took place in modern kitchens and pantries, the sculleries and cookery of European cuisine improving the swift cooking and preserving of human meat.

Cooking Bones, Tearing Flesh

The main shift in Gabonese imaginaries about carnal agency and eating-as-power concerned bodily ingredients for power: in contrast with the ways in which specialists ritually "cooked" ancestral bones in relics, ritual murderers now harvest raw organs to make a charm. The hard substances of remarkable ancestors have turned into the soft, raw flesh of anonymous victims. Displacing the older viscosity of ritual expertise and kin prescriptions between elders and initiates, money now quickly circulates between accomplices serving the nefarious agenda of a few individuals indifferent to the fate of ordinary Gabonese. That agenda is to use the corporeal power of anonymous and unrelated people to craft charms that secure riches and influence for the few. Although raw flesh had a long association with witchcraft in Equatorial Africa, since the 1920s it has played an increasing role in actual crimes.

In the nineteenth century, West Equatorial Africans believed that raw animal products and unprocessed food were the preferred food of witches.[79] They also distinguished between the polite, domestic activity of eating cooked meals and the wild devouring (iPunu; *-dji*, "to eat;" *-uvuna*, "to devour") of raw flesh. Tearing up and consuming fresh meat occurred in the forest, the domain of wild beasts, dangerous spiritual entities, criminal delinquents, and witches.[80] Wild animal predators of the bush furnished rich metaphors for talking about the transgressive appetite of human witches. In late nineteenth-century Congo, Kongo pupils' notebooks published by Karl

Laman explained, "The witches eat swiftly. . . . They cut up their victim like an animal."[81]

From the 1920s onward, cannibal cases regularly came to court featuring stories of people attacking other people in the wild, then tearing and eating their raw flesh. In 1920, near Mouila, the district officer arrested four men for killing and eating a man. The witnesses, four farmers, declared that they had come to an abandoned village to harvest palm nuts. In the evening, as they gathered around a fire, unknown men attacked them. While they fled, the bandits seized one of the four, named Mangari. The next day, the farmers looked for their missing companion and found his cadaver in the nearby forest, missing the head and the right arm. The arrested suspects confessed that they had brought the victim to the forest, slit his throat, beheaded him, and cut off his arm. Each of them had taken a chunk of the "meat" before returning to their village. One added that he had eaten the fingers and left the bones because they were too tough.[82]

In 1924, a man named Bouala confessed in detail to murdering his nephew Loundou, an excellent worker and hunter who refused to share the products of his labor with his uncle. With the help of accomplices, Bouala said, he caught Loundou in the forest, on his way to work. They seized the young man by the shoulders while holding his legs; the boy fell on the ground screaming. The murderers cut his throat with a machete and detached his head from the trunk. They gathered the blood in a gourd, and carried the cadaver into the forest. There, they opened Loundou's chest and tore his heart out before cutting off two fingers, the genitals, and a chunk of the heart. Then they scalped the head, opened the skull, and took the brain. The accomplices, he said, planned to use the organs for composing a *médicament*.[83] But the crime, with ordinary people harvesting soft organs and limbs from a freshly murdered victim, was a huge departure from the ritual experts' regulated art of composing medicine with hard human substances (bones, hair, nails) from long-dead ancestors.

Throughout the colonial period, judicial trials and confessions were full of murderers butchering cadavers to collect the flesh, sexual organs, the heart, and the fingers of the victims, sometimes eating them raw, sometimes mixing them with palm wine to drink them.[84] The frequency and depth of the details suggests that the transcripts and the confessions were not entirely fabricated or influenced by European misconceptions: something else was happening, the power of what the Gabonese now call nocturnal meat (*viande de nuit*), and wild witches progressively overwhelming the realm of eating-as-power.

The transformation of eating-as-power in the last century can be further historicized by looking at the major independent cult in Gabon today, Bwiti, and the relentless cannibal accusations it has attracted since the colonial period.

Bwiti arose in central and northern Gabon in the 1920s; the movement fused Christian rituals with local healing and initiation cults, and proposed new forms of revelation and atonement that helped to diagnose and cure the ills of the colonial era. The movement was mixed-gender and decentralized, with congregants grouped in independent local chapels or temples (*banzie*, "those of the chapel"). When the need arose, new and old initiates congregated in the chapel to seek revelation and healing from their ancestors by drinking a hallucinatory mixture made from the grated root of a small tree, the *eboga*.[85] French authorities and missionaries immediately singled out Bwiti chapels as a religious and political threat. Contrary to other Gabonese healing movements, such as Mademoiselle, Bwiti alone institutionalized in permanent communities and chapels, reaching urban as well as rural residents, and educated as well as uneducated people. The French soon cast cannibal suspicions on it: it is probably not a coincidence that the 1923 decree against anthropophagy was passed at the time Bwiti was becoming a powerful and visible presence in Gabon.

Bwiti borrowed important elements from Christianity. During a ceremony, for instance, when the initiates received the *eboga* root, they often knelt in front of the chapel's leader in a gesture that recalls the rite of the Eucharist.[86] Recently, André Mary suggested another parallel between Bwiti and god eating, in the myth of the *eboga* drink. Many versions exist, but the basic scenario tells how, one day, a widowed pygmy woman named Benzoghe went to a fishing party, and found a skeleton in the river. The skeleton led her to a cave full of bones (the country of the dead): these ancestors told her how to grate and drink the bark of a small tree near the entrance of the cave—the *eboga*. In return, Benzoghe offered the ancestors fresh fish from the river, and later, bananas and sugarcane. Later, intrigued by her wanderings, Benzoghe's brother-in-law followed her. The ancestors in the cave initiated him, too, but when they asked him for an offering, he gave them Benzoghe, his own relative. In one powerful version of the story, Benzoghe's own family strangled her, quartered her body, and voraciously ate it.[87]

Mary reads the killing as exemplifying the historical shift between the ancient regime of human sacrifice (when elders shed the blood of young women on ancestral bones) and modern ritual crimes (when vampire figures suck the blood from within the victim's body).[88] I differ from this reading on several counts. Precolonial forms of human sacrifice did not involve shedding the victim's blood on bones, nor do contemporary ritual crimes involve sucking the blood from the victim's body. Most importantly, instead of the story of a ritual murder, I see a myth in which the raw, unmediated flesh of a woman, selfishly ingested by her kin, replaced the civilized food and regulated transactions and offerings between ancestors and humans.[89]

Bwiti members became suspicious to the French because of the ways in which they reworked the cult of ancestral relics, already a matter of misunderstanding and concern for colonialists. To consecrate a chapel (*mbanja*), Bwiti experts buried the bones (Fang: *byeri*) of a remarkable ancestor near the central pillar of the building. This led the colonial authorities to suspect that Bwiti members desecrated tombs, or even killed a victim to obtain the remains. On January 4, 1941, the police raided a Bwiti dance in Nkok, a suburb of Libreville, and seized the skulls set out during the earlier ceremony. Later that day, a member of the chapel broke into the house of one of the police guards in a desperate attempt to recover the relics. He was arrested on the spot. Although he testified in court that he had inherited the *byeri* from his father, the judge sentenced him to six months in prison and five years of exile (*interdiction de séjour*), on the grounds that he had robbed a grave to obtain human remains.[90]

Perhaps the most famous case of colonial cannibal and Bwiti accusations occurred in the 1930s when the police accused a young Fang notable of Libreville of complicity in the poisoning of a European commercial agent named Dupuis, who had died in the hospital after a brief period of agony.[91] Léon Mba, later the first president of independent Gabon (1960–67), had been educated at the Catholic mission, and tutored in politics at the League for Human Rights (1918) and a local branch of the Freemasons. In 1926, the governor of Gabon appointed him a native chief of a Fang neighborhood in Libreville. Soon afterward, Mba's attendance at influential Bwiti chapels raised the suspicion of the colonial administration. In January 1932, a court charged him for embezzling public revenues, and soon afterward the police accused him in the poisoning case.[92] That case highlighted typical French concerns that, behind the façade of a refined *évolué*, Mba retained the primitive instincts of a cannibal Fang.[93] During the same period, rumors circulated in Libreville that Mba was connected to the recent discovery of female remains in an open-air market. People gossiped that Mba, along with members of the Bwiti movement, had dismembered the victim and sold her body parts, mirroring the French suspicion that African spiritual movements and religious associations hid bloody rites of human sacrifice and an insatiable thirst for material profit.[94]

The religious and political resonances of stories of ritual murders continued to increase after independence. They reached a new level after a seminal case in 1988 implicating Théophile Mba Ntem, the Fang "Butcher" of Owendo (a suburb of Libreville). In 1987, Mba Ntem led a Bwiti temple that belonged to a broader network of chapels called Mvoe Ening (Fang: Quiet Life).[95] In December 1987, Ono Ndong André, a young English teacher from the town of Oyem in the north, approached him to be initiated and to seek help in addressing his wife's adultery. Mba Ntem advised him to chase the wife and their three children from his house, accusing them of being witches. Ono Ndong followed the advice, but kept his three-year-old son, Herbert, with him. He traveled back to Libreville several times to consult Mba Ntem and to participate in Bwiti ceremonies. On 13 April 1988, Ono Ndong's brother, concerned that his brother had not shown up at his job, discovered his decomposed cadaver in a brook in Owendo. When interrogated by the police, little Herbert testified that he had seen men come to the house and kidnap his father. He formally identified Mba Ntem and his brother-in-law, Mve Owono, as the perpetrators.

After he was placed under arrest, Mba Ntem declared that he had indeed killed Ono Ndong. The crime had taken place at the temple, where he had given *iboga* to Ono Ndong, then tied him with rope. Accomplices from the chapel played the sacred harp and entered into trance, he said, then he struck the victim in the ribs with a knife he called "his surgical instrument" (*couteau de chirurgie*) and proceeded to cut Ono Ndong's tongue, genitals, lungs, heart, and intestines. The accomplices "consumed" (*consommèrent*) the body parts raw, garnished with a fresh cucumber.[96] The press article recounted another, more detailed version of the crime: Mba Ntem made his wife, Abogo-Owono Florence, prepare an opulent feast with the meat harvested from Ono Ndong's body, and share it with the "tribe" of accomplices. After the banquet, in this version, Mba Ntem cut and kept the victim's hair for fetishistic purposes, and placed a small piece of the tongue and flesh in a flask of commercial perfume, Bien Être (Happiness). The newspaper quoted him declaring that, every time he wished to obtain something from a person, he would taste the perfume, and wear it to his appointment.[97]

Many elements of these stories voiced older colonial suspicions in partial and spectacular fashion. Journalists reported that the residents of Owendo feared Mba Ntem and his clique of assassin–fetish-men (*assassins-féticheurs*) as "killer leopards" (*panthères tueuses*), mirroring old French fears that secret societies preyed on Gabonese communities and fomented the destruction of the country. Modern technology (surgical instruments) and mass-produced commodities (bottles of perfume) featured prominently in the crime. A legacy of the colonial period, the primal cannibal scene of eating the victim's flesh raw or cooking it for a communal banquet played a central role in the story and in the sentencing of Mba Ntem. Many other elements are not colonial legacies and do not signal changes in local imaginaries of power. Nonetheless, this affair and its narration suggest that, for the Gabonese public, the complex, reproductive transactions of eating-as-power were giving way to the destructive power of *le ventre*, and an apocalypse of social collapse.

Literality

Ritual crimes and the traffic in *pièces détachées* have been a reality of the Gabonese public scene since the 1980s: this chapter has shown that similar crises of criminal dismembering and eating took place early in the colonial period, embedded in the encounter between vernacular myths of spiritual agency and corporeal empowerment, and colonial cannibal fantasies. The Gabonese today do not speak of these incidents the same way they did a hundred years ago. Now they gossip of vampires, of the Very Bad Heart of the Devil, of *marmites* and freezers, and of human organs cut and frozen in the pantries of rich and powerful families. These repertoires bear the mark of colonial imaginaries that, in the early twentieth century, combined with local ideas and started shifting the ethos of eating-as-power from cooking the bones of ancestors to tearing the flesh of young relatives. In the 1950s, these dynamics solidified in new sets of beliefs, *le ventre*, as a digestive and lethal organ, *le vampire* as the Devil and witch-substance, the Western space of modern kitchens and appliances as laboratories for cannibal feasts, blood and raw flesh as the new target of selfish witches.

In the spring of 2012, Gabonese ritual crimes suddenly became an international sensation when a French TV channel, Canal Plus, aired a special show ("Organs of Power") about ritual crimes in Gabon.[98] The Gabonese government protested loudly and denied the charges, later taking timid action to better investigate ritual murders. It has also tried to replace the term "ritual murders" (*meurtres rituels*) with "blood crimes" (*crimes de sang*), a colloquial Gabonese expression for violent assaults leading to the death of the victim. If the government was eager to fight an overly exoticized, derogative image of the country abroad, it is ironic that it did so by centering its initiative on blood, one of the main French misnomers of indigenous agency, full of cannibals, vampires, and colonial baggage.

Yet the main transformation in the imaginary of eating-as-power, from the nineteenth century onward, is not the rise of blood, vampires, money, or even soft organs. It is, ultimately, *a turn to literality*, a dreadful process that, during colonialism, desymbolized and criminalized the earlier, enormously complex imaginary of eating-as-power, now subsumed in the French verb *manger* (to eat). We have seen in chapter four that the French and the Gabonese came to think of human flesh both as a mechanical, organic entity and as a sacred and potent ingredient of power, and that today, the Gabonese describe actual murders as profane technologies of meat processing and trading. Because of this, the imaginary of *manger* is torn by an impossible reconciliation between materiality and immateriality, symbolism and literality.

In Gabon, the lack of polarization between invisible acts and physical effects, and vice versa, was what unsettled colonialists most. In the end, the French criminalized eating in accordance with rationalist conceptions of material proof: the courts relied on "physical evidence," either in the form of a mutilated corpse, the discovery of relics and ritual substances supposedly acquired through cannibalism and desecration, or vivid eyewitness stories and confessions.[99] In doing so, they pushed African imaginaries toward univocal materialism. To some extent, ritual murders now partially exhibit what colonialists have derisively claimed to be true of the Gabonese: the impotence to produce symbolic action or transcendent meaning.

Conclusion

In a society torn by racial categories but also pushed together by them, power flows along unusual channels. On this, most colonial scholars agree. Yet the tools to recover the working of colonial domination remain highly contested. After subaltern and postcolonial studies, we have learned to doubt whether colonialism was fundamentally transformative for Africa. Our main framework, the paradigm of the colonial encounter, assumes that asymmetries of power rested in part on colonial actors' cultural and historical differences, and that emic or indigenous knowledge survived the trials of oppression.

This book has taken a different route to the past. Colonialism, it argues, extensively reconfigured African societies, and the mental and moral worlds of all agents on the ground, including their relations with the realm of spiritual entities and forces. But it also suggests that we need to surpass the racial and cultural dichotomies inherited from imperialism. Despite considerable differences, Europeans and Africans worked in part with conversant and congruent imaginaries, including in the realm of power, reproduction, and misfortune.

In the colony, as in other societies, complex field of forces shaped cultural production and innovation. Imaginaries furnished people with understandings and knowledge, scenarios for acting, and moral and emotional feelings. Colonialism threw many of these frameworks into lasting disarray and realignment. The Gabonese lost authority on land, on nature spirits, on youngsters, and on women. The technologies that had helped them to produce riches and secure social reproduction were increasingly failing. At the same time, Europeans living in Gabon knew that colonial rule betrayed their own moral compasses and political principles. Across the racial divide, people acted beneath the surface of implicit norms and standards: transgression and deviation opened important, mutual channels where Africans and Europeans constructed and transacted power.

Transactions, Transgression, Congruence

Colonial actors saw power and capacity as relational realities they produced in active transactions, if sometimes indirectly and involuntarily. Together, they also imagined the labor of political power and social reproduction (marriage, alliances, and the nurturing of kin) as forms of exchange. The concept of transaction helps to capture a number of historical possibilities for people to accumulate status, rework identities, and extract different forms of value and power.

French transactional imaginaries served specific colonial needs: they justified the civilizing mission, for instance, as "offering" civilization to Africans against some forms of political submission and economic compensation. Often, colonialists projected these transactions along triangular or triadic scenarios, especially when negotiating racial identities and positions of power vis-à-vis Africans. Their pragmatic view of technological production involved a formula of investing expertise and materials to produce new things. They also dreamed of self-sacrifice for the higher cause of national preeminence. The flip side of the fantasy fed a fearful awareness of colonial transgressions: the toxic consequences of narcissistic insulation, undeserved profits, and racial brutality.

The Gabonese, meanwhile, had long imagined their dealings with spirits and ancestors as a circulation of offerings and sacrifice. Therapeutic procedures involved transactions as a core component, while witchcraft was akin to stealing life and social assets. The metaphor of "eating" described the labor of composing power and distributing wealth. Under colonial rule, these transactional imaginaries did not fundamentally change, though people saw their outcomes as becoming more harmful.

If imaginaries resembled one another, people did not necessarily share them. Cannibalism, for instance, was a congruent imaginary among the French and the Gabonese, but both groups had different ways of expressing it: colonialists dreamed of abject, self-devouring black man-eaters, and Africans dreaded the attacks of wild witches tearing the flesh and drinking the blood of youngsters. The fact that imaginaries could be similar and conversant did not mean that they could combine, nor that colonial agents endorsed or assented to them. Sharing would have meant that Africans and Europeans spoke a common language and were ready to create single sets of imaginaries across the racial barrier. This happened only exceptionally, and in the later part of the colonial era. In the rare instances when imaginaries overlapped across races, people often rejected the fact as repulsive and abhorrent. The French

CONCLUSION 195

reacted to the perception that Africans resembled them by constructing differences (racial ideologies), projecting inner guilt on Africans (the cannibal abject), and suffering the moral transgression of these maneuvers. The Gabonese proved more adept at using similarities to dream of kinship and affiliation. But their attempts were riddled with fears about betrayal and intimate destruction. In Southern Gabon, the Punu welcomed white people but later saw them vanquish the ancestral spirit who had allowed them to settle in the land.

vanquished hope

Indeed, on all sides, transgression and awareness of it characterized the colonial experience and its violent dislocations. Fears increased about intimate outsiders attacking social reproduction and survival.[1] Many secrets corroded the power that French colonialists exercised in Gabon. They were hidden not only from the Gabonese but also from rulers themselves: too shameful for words, they left only occasional traces in dreams, fictions, and affectionate relations.[2] On the other side of the racial divide, transgression was a central experience among the Gabonese; it explained the attacks of witches, the nefarious power of old charms, and the dreadful crimes against youngsters. These ideas should not be confused with indigenous counterknowledge or counterfantasies.[3] Resistance here was directed against one's own knowledge of moral failure and illicit acts.[4]

Historicizing Witchcraft

This book argues that history can unearth some of the most vivid obsessions and modes of power of modern witchcraft in Africa. In Gabon, it has also mapped out the slow emergence of the repertoires and vocabularies that brought together, under the umbrella of "witchcraft" and *sorcellerie* (sorcery), indigenous ideas about mystical agency, prosperity, and misfortune. It has also tracked how those indigenous ideas sustained long-lasting engagements with Christianity, biomedical knowledge, and colonial action.[5]

A history of witchcraft during the colonial period shows that Africans were not alone in believing in the fetish agency of objects and the power of "invisible agents."[6] During the same time, Europeans held beliefs of a similar kind. In the colony, moreover, mutual strategies to reenchant the political significance and magical agency of the human body suggest that, to approach the history of body and power in the contemporary world, we need to go beyond the scholarly horizon of biopolitics and the commodification of the flesh.[7] In Gabon, colonial policies and ritual crimes composed body parts as sacred devices with mystical forms of agency and value.[8] Ritual crimes did not derive from the resurgence of old animistic beliefs in the animacy and potency of organs. Nor did they express the victory of a rampant commodification of the body. Instead, they were connected to a complex history of mystical investments initiated, in large part, by colonialists. The French and the Gabonese together imagined the body and its parts *both* as a mechanical, organic device and as a recipient of mystical and social power/value. These tactics occurred along the possibility of *exchanging* people and objects across ritual and commodity markets; the alienability of these assets *enhancing* their mystical and/or organic agency. The same can be said of fetishes, a site for cross-racial attacks and investments that were at once economic, aesthetic, and magical.

[Handwritten margin notes: *Conversant imaginaries? Exchange + enhance the human body transactions Use as a commodity.*]

We can now recapitulate the main Gabonese imaginaries that rose from the crucible of colonial rule.

Puissance

Missionaries took away our *gris-gris* statuettes: they sold them in France, Italy and elsewhere, to decorate their museums.... Our ancestors now tell us to keep our secrets, so we can preserve the little *puissance* that remains, because this *puissance* will one day find again its true master.
—*Le Patriote*, 1976

Today, the Gabonese's main imaginary of power is called *puissance*. *Puissance* captures the idea of individual power and charisma, and a mode of action that is based on the ownership of a witch-substance located in one's body. *Puissance* is a French term, but it encompasses long-standing beliefs in the capacity of people to harm and heal, to "see" spirits and ancestors and use their divine forces, to produce kin and allies, and to master the production of material goods. However, it now also evokes the cannibal power of the stomach and abdomen as digestive and destructive, rather than nurturing, forms of agency. In the past, the killing of a relative was enough to feed the witch-substance of powerful *nganga* and chiefs. Today, *puissance* is still based on transacting with spirits and ancestors, but these exchanges are steeped in transgression: ritual murders have replaced the initial sacrifice of a relative, and the making of charms, instead of using the hard substances of remarkable people, is based on the soft flesh of anonymous victims. In the 1950s, moreover, imaginaries of the witch-substance increasingly merged with the cannibal greed and selfishness of the Devil and vampires.

Puissance still circulates today from spirits and ancestors into charms and medicines. But the new might of white technology and magic is now vital to accumulate and enact it. As the Gabonese aptly say nowadays, the science of the manifest has replaced the science of the invisible. Global characters (God, the Devil, Mami Wata, and the Virgin Mary) have joined ancestors and spirits, blurring the power of these older entities. The mystery and indiscernibility of ancestors and spirits is in disarray: their new, problematic existence in the form of images, monuments, and statues has made them enter into what I call a *crisis of symbolic uncertainty*. The expertise of ritual specialists has declined. Now, international societies and esoteric networks, open only to the rich and the affluent, accumulate *puissance* for highly unfair and selfish purposes. They do not use secrecy and invisibility to protect the integrity of ritual exchanges anymore, but something else that people call "occult." In large part, the members of these societies behave like the successors of colonialists, stealing charms and power from the Gabonese.

L'Argent

During funerals, the powerful and affluent members of the bereaved families can show off their riches, especially fresh money (*l'argent frais*).
—*Echo de Missamba*, 2012

Today, *l'argent* (money) defines a currency with fetish-like qualities, that facilitates most of the social, political, and religious transactions performed by the Gabonese. It is the elusive, scarce, and powerful medium that allows people to harvest body substances for illicit magic, to establish and modify domestic and family relations. It is also the engine of witchcraft attacks, and the fuel of political warfare.

Rather than a symptom of social and material commodification, *l'argent* partly arose as a resolution to, and a product of, the unusual rarity and excessive power of colonial currency. French authorities monopolized the circulation and value of French francs (and later the XFA), depriving the Gabonese of any control over what was now the main means for circulating and accumulating wealth. Moreover, colonialists imagined the franc as a vehicle of social agency that would encourage Africans to accept wage labor, submission to the state, and new forms of capitalistic wealth. With the "blood price" (*prix du sang*), a moneyed compensation for physical damages to a person, the French introduced a new commensurability between the social and organic value of the person and a price in francs. Thus the value of the new money always exceeded its commercial or economic denomination, displaying an excess of elusive potentialities.

Manger

Acting under orders from the "master," the three young women turned into mosquitos, so they could bite and pump the blood of people, and fill with it the gas tank of his mystical airplane.
—Murielle Ndong, *L'Union*, 2016

Modern Gabonese talk of the witch-substance as the Very Bad Heart of the Devil, and describe the bloody meetings of secret "marmites" (covenants), in which witches cook the butchered "meat" of their victims in modern *cuisines* (kitchens), then sit around invisible "tables" and "tabernacles" to enjoy their cannibal feasts. The vivid scenes allude to the influence of Christian lore and other Western folk knowledge about evil. The cannibal obsessions of the French also contributed to the shift in local imaginaries of "eating-as-power." The belly-womb of powerful leaders and *nganga* has merged in a digestive and destructive organ, called *le ventre*, a machine of power that swallows and digests *l'argent frais* (fresh money) and *la chair fraîche* (fresh or raw flesh).

Before 1900, eating-as-power used to be a symbolic, all-encompassing imaginary for social and political action. It included processing and redistributing riches. After the conquest, colonialists univocally reduced eating to transgressive cannibalism and material destruction. Under relentless attacks from colonialists over the worshipping of ancestors, the Gabonese switched the main procedure of eating-as-power from cooking the bones of ancestors into relics, to relying on the enchanted and organic power of the raw flesh of anonymous victims.

Colonial Kinship

The Bongo regime stole our country, our freedom, our land, and our riches: we will not allow them to take our children, our blood, and our bodies.
—Jean Ndouanis, blog, 2015)

The colonial regime forced a new, intractable intervention of white people upon the Gabonese in the realm of spiritual transactions and the production of riches. The intrusion of insiders/outsiders tainted social reproduction itself with wondrous and nefarious power. Figures of white power, such as the Virgin Mary and Mami Wata, expressed a dreadful intrusion into the domestic politics of the Gabonese. French cannibal fantasies, in turn, ruminated on the awareness and consequences of this situation. In powerful narratives of paternal love and lustful devouring, they staged the devastating longings of white people for Africans.

Colonialists and the Gabonese alike interpreted the colonial presence and the future of domination with a double-layered metaphor: kinship and usurpation. They often discussed the trope indirectly: the French hid attraction and aggression toward the colonized under cannibal fantasies, a metaphor of reversed kinship and reproduction. The Gabonese used the substances of dead colonialists as powerful ingredients in their medicines, and called "white" the social descendants of colonialists who invaded the land and stole magic and *puissance* from them. The kind of kinship I am talking about is different from the "affective liaisons" that could exist between colonialists and colonized, and from the uneasy ties that bound people of mixed descent in the colonies.[9] This kinship, instead, was intellectual rather than emotional, political rather than biological. In the colony, and also today, relations of power mobilized powerful domestic and sexual metaphors of intimate strangers.[10] Often narrated inside out, and concealed by layers of denial, they still exposed a repertoire of affiliation and kinship between Africans and Europeans.

Beyond Africa: Concepts and Definitions

Besides a better understanding of colonial and postcolonial history south of the Sahara, this book has aimed to offer tentative propositions for changing the ways in which we analyze how people produce power and agency.

The first of these tools concerns transactions in power. So far, I have been discussing transactions mostly ethnographically, as local categories and imaginaries.[11] Here I extend the analysis to other societies and contexts. We know since Michel Foucault that power is produced by all and is multidirectional. To this idea, I add that its economy and mode of action are *transactional*, and defined by deals occurring between historical agents. Pierre Bourdieu likened knowledge, social distinction, and power to forms of "capital" owned and desired by people.[12] The notion of transactions follows the analysis to a point, but it displaces the gaze on the moment of exchange and negotiation, when people reach, enact, and modify such capital. It thus always explains power in action.

Transactions could be forced, deferred, indirect, and depriving. Regardless of race, class, gender, or culture, however, they brought people together, as individuals or groups, in single units of action and imagination, allowing power to emerge and circulate. Transactional moments of power themselves created domination, enacting it and making it fluctuate along with people's everyday negotiations. In short, domination itself resulted from accumulations and sequences of myriads of transactions, large and small, innerving a social field. Individual and collective, they were also shaped by institutions, and by broader patterns and cycles.

In societies made of various segments and groups arranged in hierarchies of power, *congruent and conversant imaginaries* also contribute to producing power and new social realities. Beyond the existence of emic, genuine cultures, I have underlined the role of compatible imaginaries in the colony, and the awareness of it among historical actors otherwise separated by segregating ideologies (race). I extend here Cornelius Castoriadis's notion of imaginaries as a component of institutions, bringing it to colonial domination, and to racially and historically diverse societies. But the role of commensurable imaginaries is not true only in colonial Gabon; it also appears in societies that pursued colonial domination, including modern European nations, and in those that never engaged in colonialism and were never colonized.

Social scientists have often excised *transgression* and the awareness of illicit action from political and cultural analysis. To understand how power and domination work, it is important that we pay better attention to the darker side of people's imaginaries, moral orders, and decisions. People constantly break their own norms and principles, often encouraged by the political system in which they live, and by historical incidents. Their inchoate recognition of such trespassing, I have shown, can be so powerful and lasting as to weave crucial hegemonic processes between classes, groups, and people otherwise separated by ideologies or power structures.

There are no such things as pure commodities or fetishes, and this book proposes that we get rid of the distinction entirely. Anthropologists and historians of value and exchange continue to discuss commodities and noncommodities as empirical realities. Even those scholars who successfully forge a theoretical continuum between these categories take the separation as conceptual horizon.[13] Instead, fetishes can become commodities, but not by losing their specific quality: they can be both fetishes *and* commodities at the same time, retaining their value and agency while entering markets. Likewise, people can invest special social and sentimental value in ordinary commodities while selling or purchasing them.

A theory of *carnal fetishism* helps us to understand how global, modern views of the human body can seamlessly join the enchanted, personal, and sacred value of the flesh to its organic nature. Complementing the theory of biopower and biopolitics, carnal fetishism shows that our views of the human body are steeped in enchanted credence *that is not antagonistic to medical and biological knowledge.* Beyond Africa, in Western hospitals and laboratories, organ transplants retain their sacred aura, and in funerary rites, the body of loved ones is hardly ever reduced to inert matter. Yet we trust in the physical and material nature of our flesh, making it, indeed, the very foundation of our fetishistic yearnings. Nor is the accumulative and complex value of the person and her body always erased by being exchanged for commodities and currencies. Even if we find them repugnant, economic transactions in people (and body parts) can nevertheless realize or confirm the social and spiritual potential of the traded person, or her flesh.[14]

Finally, we have found that *race* often works through triangular oppositions and placements rather than binary ones. This was true in Gabon, where colonialists invented semifictional figures, or colonial "thirds" (apes, gorillas, pygmies, cannibals, degenerate tribes, and hypersexualized women). These characters served as references, intermediates, and mirrors to both white people and Africans, in order for the former to define—in their own racial or civilizational terms—their position in the colony. The hypothesis is probably verifiable in many other contexts, and offers a dynamic tool to understand the relational creation of social identities.

After the Colony

Since the 1980s, the search for African perspectives and emic theories has renewed and refreshed the ways in which we, outsiders and foreigners, write African history.[15] The present book wonders, however, what we miss by sketching the edges of the African continent as so unforgivably detached from our own.

If Europe and the West are immersed in colonial legacies, also are the countries that directly suffered from it. Before the conquest, however, Europeans and Africans worked with compatible and conversant imaginaries, drives, and ideas, belying the separations and prejudices of colonial doctrines. This is a fact that, with the legacies of colonialism, needs to be confronted in order to

NOTES

Introduction

1 Paul Belloni Du Chaillu, *Recent Remarkable Discoveries in Central Africa* (Philadelphia, PA: Barclay, 1867), 63 and 71; and Appendix 1 in Paul Du Chaillu, *A Journey to Ashango-Land and Further Penetration into Equatorial* Africa (New York, D. Appleton, 1867), 439–60. See also testimony by Alfred Marche on stealing three human skulls in northern Gabon in *Trois voyages dans l'Afrique occidentale: Sénégal—Gambie—Casamance—Gabon—Ogooué*, 2nd ed. (Paris: Librairie Hachette et Cie, 1882), 109.

2 On preserving chimpanzees' heads, see Augustus C. Collodon, *Congo Jake: The Story of My Adventurous Life* (London: Sampson Low, Marston, 1932), 200. R. B. N. Walker, an agent of the British trading firm Hatton and Cookson, was the first to send a gorilla specimen to the United Kingdom in 1847. The carcass traveled along with two boiled skeletons and the brains, intestines, and body parts of other animals from the rainforest. Richard Francis Burton, *Two Trips to Gorilla Land and the Cataracts of the Congo*, vol. 1 (London: Sampson Low, Marston, 1876), 238. Jeremy Rich, *Missing Links: The African and American Worlds of R. L. Garner, Primate Collector* (Athens: University of Georgia Press, 2012).

3 Jan Vansina, *Paths in the Rainforest: Toward a History of Political Tradition in Equatorial Africa* (Madison, University of Wisconsin Press, 1990), 96–97.

4 Among scholars of Equatorial Africa, the verb "to compose," better than "to build" or "to manufacture," defines the elaborate practices observed by ritual experts to bring together composite ingredients to make a charm.

5 "Les 'honorables' qui siègent actuellement au palais Léon Mba ne doivent leur salut qu'à la livraison des organes que leur ont procuré pygmés, ngangas, marabouts et autres charcutiers d'organismes humains." "Cette affaire-là: Des 'Honorables' et des 'pièces détachées,'" unsigned editorial, *Misamu*, no. 252 (14–28 May 2002): 3.

6 Conversation with Denis Mugoma, his granddaughter Giovanna, and Michelle Musavu, Libreville, 7 July 2012. All names have been changed.

7 I use the English terms "witchcraft" and "sorcery" indifferently to reflect contemporary African usages in French (*sorcellerie*). On a similar theoretic '

stand, see Peter Geschiere, *The Modernity of Witchcraft: Politics and the Occult in Postcolonial Africa* (Charlottesville: University Press of Virginia, 1997), 12–14. Geschiere also aptly observed that academic distinctions should not mask the terms' fluidity and people's struggles over them, as they are in practice never self-evident (Peter Geschiere, personal communication, August 2003).

8 In the late 1990s and early 2000s, Peter Geschiere, Stephen Ellis, and Gerrie ter Haar brought spiritual forces and witchcraft into what Michael Schatzberg called the "parameters of the political" in Africa, pressing academics to "recognize the growing relation between religion and politics." Michael Schatzberg, *Political Legitimacy in Middle Africa: Father, Family, Food* (Bloomington: Indiana University Press, 2001), 70–110; Geschiere, *Modernity of Witchcraft*; Stephen Ellis and Gerrie ter Haar, *Worlds of Power: Religious Thought and Political Practice in Africa* (New York: Oxford University Press, 2004).

9 Achille Mbembe, *La naissance du maquis dans le Sud-Cameroun (1920–1960): Histoire des usages de la raison en colonie* (Paris: Karthala, 1996), 11. George C. Bond and Diane M. Ciekawy, *Witchcraft Dialogues: Anthropological and Philosophical Exchanges* (Athens: Ohio University Press, 2001).

10 Joseph Tonda, *Le Souverain moderne: Le Corps du pouvoir en Afrique centrale (Congo, Gabon)* (Paris: Karthala, 2005), 173. Geschiere, *Modernity of Witchcraft*, 17.

11 Nicole Eggers theorizes *puissance* in Eastern Congo in her PhD dissertation, "Kitawala in the Congo: Politics, Religion, Health and Healing in 20th Century Central Africa," (University of Wisconsin, 2013), and in a recent article, "Mukombozi and the Monganga: The Violence of Healing in a Kitawalist Uprising in 1944," *Africa*, no. 85 (2015): 417–36.

12 For a detailed and historicized theory of agency, see Mustapha Emirbayer and Ann Mische, "What Is Agency?," *American Journal of Sociology* 103, no. 4 (January 1998): 962–1023. On agency as the master trope of the new US social history on the enslaved, read the important reflection of Walter Johnson, "On Agency," *Journal of Social History* 37, no. 1 (autumn 2003): 113–24.

13 Paul Missioumbou, "Héritage, contradictions et changements socio-culturels chez les Nzébi: Contribution à l'analyse de la crise de l'institution familiale au Gabon" (Master's thesis, Université Omar Bongo Onbimba (hereinafter UOB), Libreville, 1999), 91–94. People in today's Gabon speak over forty-two languages, and none has a decided preeminence. All belong to classes A, B, and C of the Guthrie classification of Western Bantu languages. Malcolm Guthrie, *Comparative Bantu*, 4 vols. (Farnham, UK: Gregg Press, 1967–71).

14 Guy Donald Adjoï Obengui, "Njobi et pouvoir politique chez les Mbede" (Master's thesis, UOB, Libreville, 2008).

15 Note circulaire sur le Rappel des dispositions de principe qui définissent les rapports de l'autorité locale avec les indigènes, Lieutenant-Gouverneur du Gabon aux Commandants des circonscriptions militaires, Libreville, 9 February 1912, Archives of the district of Mitzic, quoted by James Fernandez, *Bwiti: An Ethnography of the Religious Imagination in Africa* (Princeton, NJ: Princeton University

Press, 1981), 611n99. On the importance of invisible agents as "freedom" and "fate," "state" and "law," or "love" and "hate" in Europe and North America, see David M. Gordon, *Invisible Agents: Spirits in a Central African History* (Athens: Ohio University Press, 2012).

16 Gordon, *Invisible Agents*, 2012. But as Gordon and Wyatt MacGaffey show, European societies also understood power partly in magical terms. Wyatt MacGaffey, "Changing Representations in Central African History," *Journal of African History* 46, no. 2 (2005): 189–207.

17 Similarly, white missionaries believed in the invisible and efficient agency of the host, blessed water, and wine. On the material and affective concreteness of the religious experience, see Birgit Meyer, "Mediation and Immediacy: Sensational Forms, Semiotic Ideologies and the Question of the Medium," *Social Anthropology*, no. 19 (2011): 23–39.

18 Emile Durkheim, *Elementary Forms of the Religious Life* (New York: Free Press, [1915] 1965). For a critique of the sacred-profane dichotomy, see Jack Goody, *Death, Property, and the Ancestors: A Study of the Mortuary Customs of the Lodagaa of West Africa* (London: Tavistock, 1962), 41.

19 Brian Larkin, *Signal and Noise: Media, Infrastructure, and Urban Culture in* Nigeria (Durham, NC: Duke University Press, 2008). On the relation between magic and technology, see Alfred Gell, "Technology and Magic," *Anthropology Today* 4, no. 2 (1988): 6–9.

20 On magic and commodification of the body, see Isak Niehaus, "Coins for Blood and Blood for Coins: From Sacrifice to Ritual Murder in the South African Lowveld," *Etnofoor* 13, no. 2 (2000): 31–54. On the traffic of organs for medical transplants, see Nancy Scheper-Hughes, "The Global Traffic in Human Organs," *Current Anthropology* 41, no. 2 (April 2000): 191–224. On moral economies and capitalistic ethics, see Bruce Berman and John Lonsdale, *Unhappy Valley: Conflict in Kenya and Africa* (London, James Currey, 1992); and Parker Shipton, *Mortgaging the Ancestors: Ideologies of Attachment in Africa* (New Haven, CT: Yale University Press, 2009).

21 For a powerful indictment of "othering" others, see Lila Abu-Lughod, "Writing against Culture," in *Anthropology and Theory: Issues in Epistemology*, ed. Henrietta Moore and Todd Sanders, 2nd ed. (Chichester, UK: John Wiley & Sons, 2014), particularly 393–96.

22 The concept of "imaginary" remains a newcomer in the English scholarly literature although it has appeared more frequently since the early 2000s. Luise White, for instance, uses it in passing in *Speaking with Vampires: Rumor and History in Colonial Africa* (Berkeley: University of California Press, 2000), 50–51. For a recent definition, see Lucy A. Suchman, *Human-Machine Reconfigurations: Plans and Situated Actions*, 2nd ed. (Cambridge: Cambridge University Press, 2007), 1n1.

23 The subaltern studies were instrumental in this turn. Ranajit Guha, *A Subaltern Studies Reader, 1986–1995* (Minneapolis: University of Minnesota Press, 1997). On African history, see Steven Feierman, "Colonizers, Scholars, and Invisible

Histories," in *Beyond the Linguistic Turn: New Directions in the Study of Society and Culture*, edited by Victoria E. Bonnell and Lynn Hunt (Berkeley: University of California Press, 1999), 182.

24 Jane I. Guyer and Samuel M. Eno Belinga, "Wealth in People as Wealth in Knowledge: Accumulation and Composition in Equatorial Africa," *Journal of African History* 36, no. 1 (1995): 91–120; Phyllis Martin, *Leisure and Society in Colonial Brazzaville* (Cambridge: Cambridge University Press, 1995); Florence Bernault, *Démocraties ambigües en Afrique centrale: Congo-Brazzaville, Gabon, 1940–1965* (Paris, Karthala, 1996); Didier Gondola, *Villes miroirs: Migrations et identités urbaines à Brazzaville et Kinshasa, 1930–1970* (Paris: L'Harmattan, 1997); Christopher Gray, *Colonial Rule and Crisis in Equatorial Africa. Southern Gabon, ca. 1850–1940*, Rochester (Rochester, NY.: University of Rochester Press, 2002); Tamara Giles-Vernick, *Cutting the Vines of the Past: Environmental Histories of the Central African Rainforest* (Charlottesville: University of Virginia Press, 2002); Rachel Jean-Baptiste, *Conjugal Rights: Marriage, Sexuality, and Urban Life Colonial Libreville, Gabon, 1849–1960* (Athens: Ohio University Press, 2014).

25 Nancy Rose Hunt's groundbreaking study of the Belgian Congo demonstrated how a new lexicon of power and fertility emerged from the "debris" of colonial and African practical discourse. This lexicon, she showed, was syncretic, creolized, and mutating. It was also often inarticulate and concealed in unexpected places. Nancy Rose Hunt, *A Colonial Lexicon of Birth Ritual, Medicalization, and Mobility in the Congo* (Durham, NC: Duke University Press, 1999), 11 and 12. Ann Laura Stoler takes the point into the realm of emotions and sentiments, that the colonized and colonizers' "affective liaisons" forced colonial hierarchies to be constantly (re)constructed through law and the vagaries of interracial social intimacy. Ann Laura Stoler, *Carnal Knowledge and Imperial Power: Race and the Intimate in Colonial Rule* (Berkeley: University of California Press, 2002), 12–13.

26 For instance, Thomas Spear, "Neo-Traditionalism and the Limits of Invention in British Colonial Africa," *Journal of African History* 44, no. 1 (2003): 26, writes that "colonial agents . . . shared few if any understandings with their African subjects." The most consistent effort to disentangle the history of slavery and African Diaspora from black ethnocentrism has come from Paul Gilroy, *The Black Atlantic: Modernity and Double Consciousness.* (Cambridge, MA: Harvard University Press, 1993); and Paul Gilroy, *Against Race: Imagining Political Culture beyond the Color Line* (Cambridge, MA: Harvard University Press, 2000).

27 Vansina, *Paths in the Rainforests*, 247. James Fernandez coined the notion of "creative misinterpretations" in 1982 (against "inculturation" and acculturation) to describe how colonizers and colonized elaborated new meanings out of mutual misguided representations; Fernandez, *Bwiti*, 284. Steven Feierman rethought the term as "working misunderstandings" in his *Peasant Intellectuals: Anthropology and History in Tanzania* (Madison: University of Wisconsin Press, 1990). Frederick Cooper elaborated on the idea of "negotiation" in his programmatic

article "Conflict and Connection: Rethinking Colonial African History," *American Historical Review* 99, no. 5 (December 1994): 1516–45. On hybridity and bricolage, see Frederick Cooper and Ann Laura Stoler, eds., *Tensions of Empire: Colonial Cultures in a Bourgeois World* (Berkeley: University of California Press, 1997); and Hunt, *A Colonial Lexicon*.

28 See the classic (but misleading) opposition between British indirect rule and French ideas of "assimilation" in African colonies. Frederick Cooper, *Citizenship between Empire and Nation: Remaking France and French Africa, 1945–1960*. (Princeton, NJ: Princeton University Press, 2014).

29 A point addressed in Anna Lowenhaupt Tsing, *Friction: An Ethnography of Global Connection* (Princeton, NJ: Princeton University Press, 2005), 88. I am using a "soft" definition of congruent here, as commensurable historical formations, not the mathematical idea of identical or coinciding figures.

30 Cornelius Castoriadis, *L'Institution imaginaire de la société*, 4th ed., revised and corrected (Paris: Seuil, 1975); translated into English as *The Imaginary Institution of Society* (Cambridge: Polity, 1987). Castoriadis defined imaginary against the mechanistic Marxist theory of false consciousness and alienation, Freud's emphasis on the individual psyche, and finally "imagination" in the sense of individual, delusory thoughts. Jean-François Bayart first applied the idea to contemporary Africa; Jean-François Bayart, *L'État en Afrique: La Politique du ventre* (Paris: Fayart, 1989). Ann Stoler uses imaginaries as common sense, or "what was unwritten but everybody knew about." Ann Laura Stoler, *Along the Archival Grain: Epistemic Anxieties and Colonial Common Sense* (Princeton, NJ: Princeton University Press, 2009), 3.

31 Imaginary somewhat overlaps with "collective experience" or "imagination." But few historians define these notions precisely. Benedict Anderson coined the famous idea of "national imaginings" and "imagined communities" but never elaborated on the terms "imaginings" and "imagined." Benedict Anderson, *Imagined Communities: Reflection on the Origin and Spread of Nationalism*, rev. ed. (London: Verso, [1983] 1991), 7–9. Ann Laura Stoler talks of "the psychic space of empire" but does not define it. Stoler, *Along the Archival Grain*, 25. Even the systematic effort of Susanne Zantop to unearth German colonial "fantasies" and "political unconscious" leaves both notions under-explained. Susanne Zantop, *Colonial Fantasies: Conquest, Family and Nation in Precolonial Germany, 1770–1870* (Durham, NC: Duke University Press, 1997), 1–6.

32 Arjun Appadurai, *Modernity at Large: Cultural Dimensions of Globalization* (Minneapolis: University of Minnesota Press, 1996), 7–8, contrasts imaginaries (impersonal) with fantasies (personal), but I take a more flexible approach to fantasies, considering them to be both personal and collective. Imaginaries are not emotions, or sentiments, even if they include them. Nancy Rose Hunt, *A Nervous State: Violence, Remedies, and Reveries in Colonial Congo* (Durham, NC: Duke University Press, 2016).

33 On this idea, see Jean Comaroff and John Comaroff, *Of Revelation and Revolution*, 2 vols. (Chicago, IL: University of Chicago Press, 1991 and 1997), 1:195 and

1:244–46. On the politics of difference applied to the native body, see Megan Vaughan, *Curing Their Ills: Colonial Power and African Illness* (Cambridge: Polity Press, 1991).

34 In the vernacular, locals had recourse to many other identities based on linguistic, cultural, and clan-based names: a man could use his given name and also refer to the name of his clan for identification. He could also use the term *mutu* to talk about a person in general.

35 On deconstructing the categories of "Europeans," "whites," and "Africans," see Berman and Lonsdale, *Unhappy Valley*; and John Lonsdale: "Kenya: Home Country and African Frontier, in *Settlers and Expatriates: Britons over the Seas*, edited by Robert Bickers (Oxford: Oxford University Press, 2010), 74–111.

36 Jean-François Bayart and Romain Bertrand coined the idea of *transactions hégémoniques* (hegemonic transactions) to study cultural formations and power alliances between colonial actors. Jean-François Bayart and Romain Bertrand, "De quel 'legs colonial' parle-t-on?," *Esprit* 12, no. 330 (2006): 154–60. In Africa, Bruce Kapferer used "transaction," first in an empirical study of relations between workers and managers in a factory in Zambia, and second, in a collected volume on theories of social change and exchange. Bruce Kapferer, *Strategy and Transaction in an African Factory: African Workers and Indian Management in a Zambian Town* (Manchester, UK: Manchester University Press, 1972); and Bruce Kapferer, introduction to *Transaction and Meaning: Directions in the Anthropology of Exchange and Symbolic Behavior* (Philadelphia, PA: Institute for the Study of Human Issues, 1976). Jonathan Parry and Maurice Bloch, in their illuminating collection on money and exchange, use the term "transactional orders" to talk about the cultural meanings of systems of exchange, but they mostly restrict the term to the economic realm. *Money and the Morality of Exchange* edited by Jonathan Parry and Maurice Bloch (Cambridge, Cambridge University Press, 1989), 23–30.

37 Better than "exchange," "transaction" broadly applies at the level of individuals and groups, and beyond financial and economic deals. Moreover, transaction skirts around the immense anthropological literature on exchange, gifts, and reciprocity that would detract from the main argument of this book.

38 Anthropologist Fredrik Barth coined the concept of transaction (and transactionalism) to explain cultural changes through individual bargaining and maximizing profits, in part as a critique of structural functionalism. Fredrik Barth, "On the Study of Social Change," *American Anthropologist*, no. 69 (1967): 661–69. On the psychoanalytical school of transactional analysis, see Eric Berne, *Games People Play* (New York: Grove Press, 1964).

39 Frederick Cooper demonstrated how Africans' intimate experience of wage labor, subsistence rights, and leisure encouraged them to craft a new language of labor that featured prominently in negotiations about independence. Frederick Cooper, *Decolonization and African Society: The Labor Question in French and British Africa* (Cambridge: Cambridge University Press, 1996). See also Greg Mann's study of the shared "political language" of sacrifice and debt that helped

Frenchmen and West African veterans to dialogue about political rights and citizenship. Gregory Mann, *Native Sons: West African Veterans and France in the Twentieth Century* (Durham, NC: Duke University Press, 2006), 4–6.

40 Jan Vansina, *Being Colonized: The Kuba Experience in Rural Congo, 1880–1960* (Madison: University of Wisconsin Press, 2010), 303–10.

41 For a description of a "transfer of office" in 1987 Cameroon, see Achille Mbembe, "Provisional Notes on the Postcolony," *Africa*, 1992, p. 26.

42 Marcel Mauss reads the sacrifice as a process of exchange that brings about simultaneous sacralization and desacralization. Thanks to the destruction of the intermediary (the victim), two worlds interpenetrate and yet remain distinct. Henri Hubert and Marcel Mauss, *Sacrifice. Its Nature and Function*, London, Cohen & West, 1964, pp. 91–100.

43 In the proposed example, the missionaries believed that they were "paying" the charms by offering the Christian salvation to the Gabonese. The broader principle derived from the "zero sum game," the belief that people cannot create new things without destroying or subtracting others. Robert Harms demonstrated that this economic and spiritual ethos was ingrained among the inhabitants of the Congo Basin in the eighteenth and nineteenth centuries, and differed from the capitalistic idea that riches can expand indefinitely. I argue that the French in Gabon, when it came to domination, subscribe to similar, pre-capitalistic ideas. Robert W. Harms, *River of Wealth, River of Sorrow: The Central Zaire Basin in the Era of the Slave and Ivory Trade, 1500–1891*. New Haven: Yale University Press, 1981.

44 In his initial set of propositions, Antonio Gramsci defined hegemony as "the spontaneous consent given by the great masses of the population to the general direction imposed on social life by the dominant fundamental group." Antonio Gramsci, *Selections from the Prison Notebooks of Antonio Gramsci*, ed. and trans. Quintin Hoare and Geoffrey Nowell Smith (New York, International, 1971), 12. Dagmar Engels and Shula Marks, eds., *Contesting Colonial Hegemony: State and Society in Africa and India* (London, British Academic Press, 1994). Only Steve Feierman found that "a substratum of agreement existed between the colonized and the colonizers on the worth of basic institutions and on the distribution of social benefits." Feierman, *Peasant Intellectuals*, 18–19. This is close to what Jean and John Comaroff theorize in *Of Revelation*, 2:27. Jonathan Glassman reminds us that consent is not equivalent to consensus: hegemony lies in the questions asked, not their content. Jonathan Glassman, *Feasts and Riot: Revelry, Rebellion, and Popular Consciousness on the Swahili Coast, 1856–1888* (Portsmouth, NH: Heinemann, 1996), 18.

45 Guha, *Subaltern Studies Reader*, xix. See also Nicholas B. Dirks, introduction to *Colonialism and Culture*, edited by Nicholas B. Dirks (Ann Arbor: University of Michigan Press, 1992), 7–9.

46 Hunt, *Colonial Lexicon*, 11–12, provides a detailed discussion of "middles" as leading translators, readers, and writers of colonial syncretism. She compares them to the "central midwives of colonial mutations." Others insisted on the

counterhegemonic initiatives of Africans. Pier Larson, "Capacities and Modes of Thinking: Intellectual Engagements and Subaltern Hegemony in the Early History of Malagasy Christianity," *American Historical Review* 102, no. 4 (1997): 969–1002. On "research for hegemonic power" (*recherche hégémonique*), see also Jean-François Bayart, *L'État au Cameroun* (Paris, Karthala, 1979).

47 Ann Stoler and Luise White have insisted on the polysemantic stories and irreconcilable narratives that constitute (post)colonial power formations. Ann Laura Stoler, "In Cold Blood: Hierarchies of Credibility and the Politics of Colonial Narratives," *Representations*, no. 37 (1992): 151–89; and Luise White, *The Assassination of Herbert Chipeto: Texts and Politics in Zimbabwe* (Bloomington, Indiana University Press, 2003).

48 In contrast, the anthropological concept of "symbolic systems" hardly leaves space for useless or self-destructive ideas. The same applies to Gananath Obeyesekere's concept of "ritualized scenario"; Gananath Obeyesekere, *The Work of Culture: Symbolic Transformation in Psychoanalysis and Anthropology* (Chicago, IL: Chicago University Press, 1990).

49 Ferme's "underneath of things" describes how Sierra Leoneans believe in agentive forces that activate the visible world beneath the surface of discourse, objects, and social relations, and how people practice everyday tactics of concealment. She argues that some of these concealed meanings were made of sedimented memories of historical violence (the slave-trade, wars, and wealth extraction). Mariane C. Ferme, *The Underneath of Things: Violence, History, and the Everyday in Sierra Leone* (Berkeley: University of California Press, 2001). For another study on embodied memories of violence, see Rosalind Shaw, *Memories of the Slave Trade: Ritual and the Historical Imagination in Sierra Leone* (Chicago, IL: University of Chicago Press, 2002).

50 I borrow the term from Robert Young, *Colonial Desire: Hybridity in Theory, Culture, and Race* (London: Routledge, 1995), 98.

51 For studies that do look into the criminal and the transgressive, see Zantop, *Colonial Fantasies*; White, *Speaking with Vampires*; and Hunt, *Colonial Lexicon*. I also agree with, but try to go beyond, Michael Taussig's idea of the "colonial mirror" in his study of red rubber exploitation in the Amazonian rainforest. For Taussig, colonialists imputed their own barbarity to the "savages" they wished to colonize, and sustained a culture of terror that they pretended to enact through mimesis. Michael Taussig, *Shamanism, Colonialism, and the Wild Man: A Study in Terror and Healing* (Chicago, IL: University of Chicago Press, 1986).

52 "La Défense magique," manuscript signed by Jérôme Adam (future bishop of Gabon), n. d., Archives de la Congrégation du Saint-Esprit (Holy Ghost Fathers' Archives) (hereafter Archives CSSP), 271-Dos. B-IV.

53 On colonizers' feelings of guilt and usurpation, see Albert Memmi, *Portrait du colonisé: Précédé du portrait du colonisateur* (Paris: Buchet/Chastel, 1957); translated into English as *The Colonizer and the Colonized* (Boston, MA: Beacon Press, 1967). See also Aimé Césaire, *Discourse on Colonialism* (New York, Monthly Review Press,

2000) (first published in French as *Discours sur le colonialisme* [Paris: Présence africaine, 1955]).

54 Lettre du chef de la subdivision de Mouila au lieutenant-gouverneur du Gabon, no. 25, 14 February 1922; and audience du tribunal indigène de la subdivision de Mouila en matière répressive, 4 November 1920, Archives nationales du Gabon, Fonds présidentiel (National Archives of Gabon, Presidential Fund)(hereafter ANG/FP) 1609.

55 On the West Equatorial tradition and its moving character, see Vansina, *Paths*, 249–63.

56 Fernandez, *Bwiti*, 4 and 12.

57 Vansina, *Paths*, 74–81.

58 Guyer and Belinga, "Wealth in People."

59 Among scholars of Equatorial Africa, the verb "compose," better than "to build" "make," or "manufacture," defines how ritual experts bring together composite ingredients in a charm to charge it with efficacy and power.

60 Bantu terms for "experts" (*ganga*; plur. *banganga*) and for "charms" (proto-Bantu *bwanga*) stem from the proto-Bantu verb *-gang-*, "to tie up." Vansina, *Paths*, 298.

61 After slave trading was abolished by Great Britain (1807) and France (1818), the rise of new industrial factories in Europe demanded large quantities of cash crops and exotic products.

62 Nicolas Meteghe-Nnah, *Histoire du Gabon: Des origines à l'aube du XXIe siècle* (Paris: L'Harmattan, 2006), 106; Gray, *Colonial Rule*, 144–46; and Catherine Coquery-Vidrovitch, *Le Congo au temps des grandes compagnies concessionnaires* (Paris: La Haye, Mouton, 1972), 380 sqq.

63 See chapter 6. Bwiti became by the 1950s the dominant Gabonese religious institution after Christianity. For details, see André Mary, *Le Défi du syncrétisme: Le Travail symbolique de la religion d'Eboga, Gabon* (Paris: Éditions de l'École des Hautes Études en Sciences Sociales, 1999).

64 On the history of this French lexicon and its repurposing by the Gabonese, see Florence Bernault, "Witchcraft and the Colonial Life of the Fetish," in *Spirits in Politics: Uncertainties of Power and Healing in African Societies*, ed. Barbara Meier and Arne S. Steinforth (Frankfurt am Main: Campus Publishers, 2013), 53–74.

65 In the 1930s, the colony extended over approximately 250,000 square kilometers, or 100,000 square miles, roughly the same surface as modern Gabon.

66 The French administration encouraged a fairly successful cocoa plantation economy in the north of the colony among Fang farmers. Gilles Sautter, *De l'Atlantique au fleuve Congo: Une géographie du sous-peuplement: République du Congo, République gabonaise* (Paris: La Haye, Mouton et Cie, 1966). Mining products such as diamonds and gold also brought significant revenues, but they were entirely in the hands of French settlers. Considerable reserves in manganese (1944) and oil (1950) started to be exploited after 1960. Today the production of crude oil (onshore and ultradeep offshore) has been slowly declining from 18 million barrels in 1997 to an average of 12 million since 2002. Gabon is the

third producer of manganese worldwide, and has significant reserves of uranium and diamond. Gabrielle Hecht, *Radiance of France: Nuclear Power and National Identity after World War II* (Boston, MA: MIT Press, 1998). Data retrieved from Alexander Simoes (lead developer), The Observatory of Economic Complexity, The MIT Media Lab Macro Connections group available at http://atlas.media .mit.edu/profile/country/gab/, accessed 27 March 2014.

67 The Gabonese, like most subjects of the French empire, received substantial economic and political privileges after 1945. Bernault, *Démocraties ambiguës.*

68 François Ngolet, "Ideological Manipulations and Political Longevity: The Power of Omar Bongo in Gabon since 1967," *African Studies Review* 43, no. 2 (2000): 55–71.

69 In 2010, the gross national income per inhabitant was $7,760. It increased to $10,040 in 2012. These variations mirror the world price of crude oil (81 percent of Gabon's exports in dollar value in 2013) rather than any real increase in the wealth or disposable income of the population. Data retrieved from World Bank Group, http://siteresources.worldbank.org/datastatistics/resources/gnipc.pdf, and from http://data.worldbank.org/country/gabon, accessed 27 March 2014. In 2014, 47 percent of the Gabonese population was employed in rural activities and farming. According to the World Bank, almost 33 percent of the Gabonese population in 2005 fell under the poverty threshold ($1.25 a day). Data retrieved from World Bank Group, http://data.worldbank.org/country/gabon, accessed 4 April 2014, and from World Bank Group, http://data.worldbank.org/topic /agriculture-and-rural-development, accessed 27 March 2014. The measurement of poverty ratios is notoriously inaccurate and varies enormously according to the criteria used by researchers.

70 "Ce sont des peuples qui fonctionnent à l'idéologique. Les conflits se déroulent à ce niveau-là, et c'est ça que l'on cherche à conquérir." Personal communication, Anaclé Bissiélo, Libreville, 14 June 2002.

71 Although the Gabonese have recourse to biomedicine and doctors when they can afford to do so, few entirely disentangle life's incidents and promises from mystical causes. Many occasionally consult healers and diviners to diagnose illnesses, interpret dreams, or wrestle with and understand unusual series of afflictions and hardships. Only a minority, in my experience, feel that they can entirely neglect the care of ancestors, the Holy Spirit, or other numinous protective entities.

72 A "nightly gun" (French *fusil nocturne*; Fang *eluma*) is the term for a witchcraft attack.

73 Joseph Tonda theorized this constellation as the "Modern Sovereign." Tonda, *Le souverain moderne.*

74 In the eighteenth century, cosmopolitan African families living on the Gabon Estuary and the coast established a tradition of international training, career building, and networking in the Atlantic world. Phyllis Martin, *The External Trade of the Loango Coast, 1576–1870: The Effects of Changing Commercial Relations on the*

Vili Kingdom of Loango (Oxford: Clarendon Press, 1972); David K. Patterson, *The Northern Gabon Coast to 1875* (Oxford: Clarendon Press, 1975). For Cabinda, south of Gabon, see also Phyllis Martin, "Family Strategies in Nineteenth-Century Cabinda," *Journal of African History* 28, no. 1 (1987): 65–86.

75 The only exception concerned the rulers of the Gabon Estuary, who signed a treaty with the French in 1839. In the 1950s, their descendants obtained financial compensation from the French for the occupation of their land. Elikia M'Bokolo, *Noirs et blancs en Afrique équatoriale: Les Sociétés côtières et la pénétration française, vers 1820–1874* (Paris: Editions de l'Ecole des Hautes Études en Sciences Sociales, 1981).

76 Mary Motley, *Devils in Waiting* (London: Longmans, 1959), 42.

77 Jean-Baptiste, *Conjugal Rights.*

78 The best account of a *forestier*'s life in colonial Gabon is the biography of Jean Michonnet transcribed by Christian Dedet, *La Mémoire du fleuve: L'Afrique aventureuse de Jean Michonet* (Paris: Éditions Phébus, 1984).

79 Bernault, *Démocraties ambiguës*; Jeremy Rich, *A Workman Is Worthy of His Meat: Food and Colonialism in the Gabon Estuary* (Lincoln, University of Nebraska Press, 2007).

80 Max Gluckman famously argued that a single society can contain several cultures, and that anthropologists should study colonial societies as wholes. Max Gluckman, "Analysis of a Social Situation in Modern Zululand," *Bantu Studies* 40, no. 1 (1940): 1–30.

81 Luise White, *Unpopular Sovereignty: Rhodesian Independence and African Decolonization* (Chicago, IL: University of Chicago Press, 2015), 4.

82 Bernault, *Démocraties ambiguës*, 40, 46, and 54.

83 Michael Adas, *Machines as the Measure of Men: Science, Technology, and Ideologies of Western Dominance* (Ithaca, NY: Cornell University Press, 1989). Many defined Republican ideals in stark opposition to African polities. Alice Conklin, *A Mission to Civilize: The Republican Idea of Empire in France and West Africa, 1895–1930* (Stanford, CA: Stanford University Press, 1997).

84 Gustave Le Bon, *La Psychologie des foules*, 1895; translated as *The Crowd: A Study of the Popular Mind* (New York: Penguin Books, [1896] 1977). See also his *L'Homme et les sociétés—Leurs origines et leur histoire* (Paris: J. Rothschild, 1881); and *Lois psychologiques de l'évolution des peuples* (Paris: Félix Alcan, 1895).

85 Judith Butler, *The Psychic Life of Power* (Stanford, CA: Stanford University Press, 1997), 28.

86 Affaire Léon Bekale, lettres de demande de libération de prison, 1930, ANG/FP 571. On fears of witchcraft performed by relatives and insiders, see Peter Geschiere, *Witchcraft, Intimacy, and Trust: Africa in Comparison* (Chicago, IL: University of Chicago Press, 2013).

87 Florence Bernault, "Suitcases and the Poetics of Oddities: Writing History from Disorderly Archives," *History in Africa* 42 (2015): 269–77.

88 Paul Du Chaillu, *Lost in the Jungle. Narrated for Young People* (New York: Harper and Brothers, 1875), 133. An earlier version of the engraving can be found in Paul

Du Chaillu, *Explorations and Adventures in Equatorial Africa: With Accounts of the Manners and Customs of the People, and the Chace [sic] of the Gorilla, Crocodile, Leopard, Elephant, Hippopotamus, and Other Animals* (London: John Murray, 1861), 297.

89   One needs to confirm these interpretations by cross-reading other colonial texts and sources of the time.

90   Psychoanalysts define a "primal scene" as one exposing a child to his or her parents' sexual relations. The child witnesses or fantasizes the scene, and generally interprets it as an act of violence performed by the father. In the case of the gorilla hunt, both meanings apply: French colonialists often imagined the conquest as a violent act of raping Africa. Jean Laplanche and Jean-Bertrand Pontalis, *Vocabulaire de la psychanalyse*, 5th ed. (Paris: PUF, 2007), 432–33.

91   "Le Père Jacques et la légende de la main du drapeau du P. D. G," typescript, n.s. Archives CSSP, Fonds Pouchet 2D 60–9-a-4. Official explanations, instead, argued that the hand referred to Bongo's promise that he would leave office with his hands "white" (pure of any crime), and that the nine ropes represented the provinces of the Gabonese nation. See, for instance, the unsigned article "Bongo-PDG 46 ans: Signification de l'emblème du parti 'ouvrons un secret,'" posted on the website Gabon.libre on 8 March 2013, www.gabonlibre.com/bongo-pdg-46 -ans-Signification-de-l-embleme-du-parti-ouvrons-un-secret_a20070.html, accessed 10 October 2015.

92   On imperial Europe, see Anne McClintock, *Imperial Leather: Race, Gender, and Sexuality in the Colonial Contest* (New York, Routledge, 1995); and Zantop, *Colonial Fantasies*. Only a handful of scholars have applied psychoanalytical interpretations in the colonial terrain: Johannes Fabian, *Out of Our Minds: Reason and Madness in the Exploration of Central Africa* (Berkeley: University of California Press, 2000); Stoler, *Along the Archival Grain*; and Warwick Anderson, Deborah Jenson, and Richard Keller, eds., *Unconscious Dominions: Psychoanalysis, Colonial Trauma, and Global Sovereignties* (Durham, NC: Duke University Press, 2011). Fewer still have done so to approach the experience of the colonized: besides Ferme, *Underneath of Things*, see Hunt, *Colonial Lexicon*; White, *Speaking with Vampires*; and Achille Mbembe, *On the Postcolony* (Berkeley: University of California Press, 2001).

93   Freud defines "projection" as a defense mechanism that attributes to another person some qualities, affects, and desires that the subject refuses to or cannot recognize as his or her own. Laplanche and Pontalis, "Projection," *Vocabulaire*, 343–50.

94   I borrow the expression from Esther Rashkin, *Unspeakable Secrets and the Psychoanalysis of Culture* (Albany, NY: SUNY Press, 2008), 19. A clinician and literary analyst, Rashkin warns that historians must respect the accidental and irreducible originality of the individual psyche. She also provides a useful history of the "vexed' relationship between psychoanalysis and cultural studies. On

psychoanalysis as a "mobile technology" of colonialism, see Anderson, Jenson, and Keller, *Unconscious Dominions*, 1–18.

95 Achille Mbembe, "La colonie, son petit secret et sa part maudite," *Politique africaine*, no. 102 (June 2006): 101–27.

CHAPTER 1 ⁂ A Siren and a Photograph

1 I also decided against Eastern Gabon; as the native place of President Omar Bongo, the region has received considerable investments from the state, a scientific university in Franceville, and the *Transgabonais* railway to Libreville. My fieldwork in Mouila also benefited from Christopher Gray's masterful study *Colonial Rule and Crisis in Equatorial Africa: Southern Gabon ca. 1850–1940* (Rochester, NY: University of Rochester, 2002).

2 Florence Bernault, *Démocraties ambiguës en Afrique centrale: Congo-Brazzaville, Gabon, 1940–1965* (Paris: Karthala, 1996), 34, 63–64.

3 Classic books on the Bwiti movement include James W. Fernandez, *Bwiti: An Ethnography of the Religious Imagination in Africa* (Princeton, NJ: Princeton University Press, 1981); André Mary, *Le Défi du syncrétisme: Le Travail symbolique de la religion d'Eboga, Gabon* (Paris: Éditions de l'École des Hautes Études en Sciences Sociales, 1999); and Julien Bonhomme, *Le Miroir et le crâne: Parcours initiatique du Bwete Misoko (Gabon)* (Paris: CNRS: Fondation de la maison des sciences de l'homme, 2006).

4 By using the hyphenated term "belly-womb," I try to give justice to the multilayered meaning of the French term *ventre* used by informants when they talk about Murhumi as the female ancestor whose womb gave birth to their matrilineage (in iPunu, *divumu*). On the historical emergence of *divumu*, see Jan Vansina, *Paths in the Rainforests: Toward a History of Political Tradition in Equatorial Africa* (Madison: University of Wisconsin Press, 1990), 153. See this volume's chapter 6 for a detailed study of the notion of *ventre*.

5 I borrow the expression from Jean Allman and John Parker, *Tongnaab: The History of a West African God* (Bloomington: Indiana University Press, 2005), 6 and 104.

6 "Dibur-Simbu" literally means "the children of Simbu."

7 Interview with Élise Combila, June 2, 2002, Mouila. Names of informants, unless otherwise noted, have been anonymized.

8 Interview with Élise Combila, Mouila, June 1, 2002. The witness was Élise's sister's boyfriend.

9 One cannot hold somebody by the elbow. Male members of the Mwiri association used the expression of "hitting the elbow" (*taper le coude*) for "to curse someone." Interview with Mr. Anatole Nguimbi, Mouila, June 4, 2002.

10 The national average for the poverty rate was 32.7 percent. Ministère de l'économie du commerce, de l'industrie et du tourisme, *Annuaire statistique du Gabon, 2004–2008*, 53. Since 2015, the World Bank does not give local statistics

on water and poverty in Gabon. According to field research conducted by a team of political scientists at the University of Michigan-Ann Arbor, almost 74% of citizens in Gabon reported going without enough water at least occasionally. Cora Walker and Catherine Logan, "Africa is failing to close the gap on providing water and sanitation," *The Conversation*, article online, June 9, 2016. Accessed October 12, 2018: https://theconversation.com/africa-is-failing-to-close-the-gap -on-providing-water-and-sanitation-58820.

11 In 2012, the government paved the road between the two cities and improved the traveling time a great deal. In the rest of the country, the lack of paved road is proverbial. In 2004, the total length of roads in Gabon was 9,170 kilometers (937 kilometers paved; 8,233 kilometers unpaved). Data retrieved from the Central Intelligence Agency's The World Factbook, Gabon, 2012: www.cia.gov/library /publications/the-world-factbook, accessed September 13, 2013.

12 Conversation with Catherine Ignanga, fellow passenger, road from Lambaréné to Mouila, 30 June 2007.

13 Monique Koumba-Mamfoumbi, "Les Punu du Gabon des origines à 1899" (PhD thesis, Université of Paris 1-Sorbonne, 1987); Vansina, *Paths*, 271–72. "Egalitarian uncooperative people" comes from James W. Fernandez, "Christian Acculturation and Fang Witchcraft," *Cahiers d'études africaines* 2, no. 6 (1961): 244–70.

14 During the dry season, each household spent several weeks to clear and plant a large field in the forest. Men cut trees and cleared brushes before burning the field to accumulate ashes. After the first rains, women planted roots, seeds, and banana and manioc offshoots using a short knife or a planting stick.

15 Koumba-Mamfoumbi, "Les Punu," 5, 86–87, and 198.

16 Rich families incorporated slaves and pawns in their households. Gray, *Colonial Rule and Crisis*, 41–43. A few larger districts did develop the institution of a district leader.

17 José Hervé Manghady, "Le Commerce inter-ethnique au Gabon: Le Cas des Nzébi et des Punu du sud Ngounié dans la seconde moitié du XIXe siècle" (master's thesis, Université Omar Bongo Onbimba (hereinafter UOB), Libreville, 1997. Koumba-Mamfoumbi, "Les Punu," 79.

18 Koumba-Mamfoumbi, "Les Punu," 81 and 82 (map).

19 Koumba-Mamfoumbi, "Les Punu," 81–83.

20 Gabonese historians have argued that the first occupants of the riverbank in the vicinity of Mouila were Massango hunters and pygmies. But the myth recalls that when Simbu and her children arrived near what is now the site of Mouila, she encountered the house of a Mitsogho couple with their children. The two families fused and formed the Dibur-Simbu clan. Monique Koumba, "Contribution à l'histoire de Mouila des origines à 1971" (master's thesis, UOB, Libreville, 1984), 22; and Koumba-Mamfoumbi, "Les Punu," 141–42. Other historical research suggests that the Gisir-speaking clan of GiTandu lived on the right bank of Ngounié, and Apindji-speaking communities on the left bank. See Christian Mamfoumbi, "L'Évolution des sociétés secrètes chez les Gisir du Gabon" (master's thesis, UOB,

Libreville, 1981); and Eric Gilles Dibady Mandendi, "Stations missionaires et postes administratifs dans la Ngounié nord (1850–1959)" (master's thesis, UOB, Libreville, 1991), 44 (map).

21 The clan provided individuals with affiliation to a larger group of people who recognized a single ancestor, here an ancestral mother. Nicolas Metegue N'Nah, *Mariage morganatique et intégration sociale chez les peuples matrilinéaires du Gabon précolonial: L'Exemple punu* (Libreville: Éditions des Annales de la Faculté des Lettres et Sciences Humaines, 2005), 166. See also Gray, *Colonial Rule*.

22 Today, for instance, the Bumweli has members in the Punu, Gisira, Nzabi, and Balumbu ethnic groups, a fact recognized through names and food taboos. Only specialists and clan leaders knew the full extension of their clan, and could rework kinship to fit circumstances and the demands of the time. In southern Gabon, some clans allowed endogamy, and some did not. Pierre-Philippe Rey, *Colonialisme, néo-colonialisme et transition au capitalisme: Exemple de la Comilog au Congo-Brazzaville* (Paris: F. Maspero, 1971), 111; and Gray, *Colonial Rule*, 29–30.

23 Jan Vansina, "Peoples of the Forest," in *History of Central Africa*, edited by David Birmingham and Phyllis Martin (New York: London and New York, 1983), 1:91.

24 Rey, *Colonialisme*, 151 sqq. See also Gray, *Colonial Rule*, 14–15; and Vansina, *Paths*, 274.

25 Vansina, *Paths*, 95.

26 Interview with Mr. Diata, Mouila, 3 June 2002.

27 André Raponda-Walker and Père Tastevin, "Le Culte des génies au Gabon," printed text, s.d., 60–75, Archives de la Congrégation du Saint-Esprit (hereinafter Archives CSSP), Fonds Pouchet 2D 60–9a3. See also André Raponda-Walker, *Au pays des Isoghos: Simple récit de voyage* (Libreville: Fondation -Walker, 1994), 19.

28 Père Macé, "Fétiches et pratiques superstitieuses du Gabon, dactyl," 1923, Archives CSSP, Fonds Pouchet 2D 60 9-a3. Koumba-Mamfoumbi, "Les Punu," 188.

29 Père Macé, "Fétiches."

30 Interview with Mémé Prudence, Mouila, 2 July 2007.

31 Story collected and quoted by Koumba-Mamfoumbi, "Les Punu," 149. The author translates the vernacular word for "spirit" (*mughisi*) with the French *génie*.

32 Colleen E. Kriger, *Pride of Men: Ironworking in 19th-Century West Central Africa* (Portsmouth, NJ: Heinemann, 1999), 11–12. In the 2010s, Punu historians recall that the technique came from the Nzebi, who themselves received it from the Tsengi, Tsangi, and Wumbu. The Punu, they say, sent apprentices to Tsengi workshops in order to learn the smelting craft. Interviews, Mouila, July 2012.

33 For earliest dates, see Kriger, *Pride of Men*, 36; and for later dates, see Vansina, *Paths*, 58–60.

34 The blacksmith and his team first had to produce high-quality charcoal. They gathered a large quantity of wood that they fired cautiously in a heap, covering the mound with soil to slow the combustion. Once it cooled, they combined the fuel with iron ore in a pit (*dìkúbà*) layered with clay. Blowing air in the smoldering

mound with clay pipes and skin bellows, they increased the temperature to melt-
ing point. Koumba-Mamfoumbi, "Les Punu," 237–38. A very similar description is available for the Tsengi group (Nzabi), in F. Delisle, "La Fabrication du
fer dans le Haut-Ogooué observée par Léon Guiral, membre de la mission de
l'Ouest africain," *Revue d'ethnologie* (1884): 469–70. See also Georges Dupré, *Un
Ordre et sa destruction* (Paris: Editions de l'ORSTOM, 1982), 101.

35 Nature spirits frequently intervened in smelting iron in Equatorial Africa. Con-
versely, blacksmiths worked as intercessors with nature spirits. Kairn Klieman,
*"Pygmies Were Our Compass": Bantu and Batwa in the History of West Central
Africa, Early Times to c. 1900 C.E.* (Portsmouth, NH: Heinemann, 2003), 199.
Wyatt MacGaffey, *Religion and Society in Central Africa* (Chicago, IL: University
of Chicago Press, 1986), 68.

36 Interview with Father Zacharie Péron, Sindara, 5 June 2002; interviews with Raphael Tsande, Mouila, June 6, 2002, and Pierre Carrousel, Mouila, 9 June 2002.

37 Interview with Mr. Diata, Mouila, June 3, 2002. See also interview with Pierre
Carrousel, Mouila, 9 June 2002: "Murhumi was a blacksmith genie [*génie forg-
eron*]. Men who belonged to Punu clans, or who were coopted by them, left raw
iron and charcoal by the river, next to an old machete. The next day, they found
the new tools they had asked for."

38 For examples among the Mitsogho, see Otto Gollnhofer and Roger Sillans, *La
Mémoire d'un peuple: Ethno-histoire des Mitsogho, ethnie du Gabon central* (Paris:
Présence africaine, 1997), 78. Günther Tessman detailed the charms (*bian akua*,
plural *abub akua*) used by Fang ritual experts during smelting operations. Günther
Tessman, *Die Pangwe: Völkerkundliche Monographie Eines Westafrikanischen
Negerstammes; Ergebnisse Der Lübecker Pangwe-Expedition, 1907–1909 und Früherer
Forschungen, 1904–1907.* Berlin: E. Wasmuth, A.-G., 1913; partial translation in
Fang, edited by Christine Falgayrettes-Leveau and Philippe Laburthe-Tolra
(Paris: Musée Dapper, 1991), 207–8 of the French translation.

39 Kriger, *Pride of Men.*

40 This example of extreme crisis shows that ritual killings occurred only in the case
of dangerous protocols and chancy outcomes, such as smelting iron. Gollnhofer
and Sillans, *La Mémoire*, 195 and 199–201. Despite a detailed description of iron
smelting, Dupré does not mention the need for a ritual sacrifice; Dupré, *Un
ordre*, 100–105; nor does Kriger, *Pride of Men.* Only Philippe Laburthe-Tolra
signals the use of "medicines" (*médicaments*) for smelting iron among the
Fang-Beti: Philippe Laburthe-Tolra, *Les Seigneurs de la forêt: Essai sur le passé
historique, l'organisation sociale et les normes éthiques des anciens Bëti du Cameroun*
(Paris: Publications de la Sorbonne, 1981), 271.

41 In the past, young apprentices refrained from asking questions of their teachers.
Instead, they learned their trade by looking at the masters and snatching
knowledge from them. Conversation with Jean-Émile Mbot, Monique Koumba-
Mamfoumbi, and Joseph Tonda, Libreville, 13 June 2002.

42 Klieman, *"Pygmies Were Our Compass."*

43 Interview with Mr. Diata, Mouila, June 3, 2002.

44 Paul Du Chaillu, *A Journey to Ashango-Land: And Further Penetration into Equatorial Africa* (New York: D. Appleton, 1867), 107.

45 André Raponda-Walker and Roger Sillans, *Rites et croyances des peuples du Gabon: Essai sur les pratiques religieuses d'autrefois et d'aujourd'hui* (Paris: Présence africaine, 1983), 110.

46 The returns profited witch-individuals, rather than the whole community. Mac-Gaffey, *Religion and Society*, 62. Locally produced iron survived in part to provide marked currencies necessary for social payments and blacksmiths reworked imported metals to feed this demand. See Georges Dupré, "The History of a Monetary Object of the Kwele," in *Money Matters: Instability, Values, and Social Payments in the Modern History of West African Communities*, edited by Jane Guyer (Portsmouth, NH: Heinemann, 1995), 77–100.

47 Kriger, *Pride of Men*. Du Chaillu, *Journey to Ashango-Land*, 107.

48 Gray, *Colonial Rule*, 27–29; Phyllis Martin, *The External Trade of the Loango Coast, 1576–1870: The Effects of Changing Commercial Relations on the Vili Kingdom of Loango* (Oxford: Clarendon Press, 1972); Hubert Deschamps, *Traditions orales et archives au Gabon Contribution à l'ethno-histoire* (Paris: Berger-Levrault, 1962), 47; and Koumba-Mamfoumbi, "Les Punu," 225–36.

49 Eviya-speaking residents inhabited two of the villages, and Vili and Nkomi traders from the coast, the other ones. Gray, *Colonial Rule*, 47–48, 57, and 134–35.

50 Vansina, "Peoples of the Forest," 81.

51 The Bujala clan supervised the left bank of the Ngounié River. Joachim Buléon, quoted in Gray, *Colonial Rule*, 65n60. See also Gray, *Colonial Rule*, 51–52, 75, and 82.

52 Gollnhofer and Sillans, *La Mémoire*, 207 and 205–11.

53 Quote from a local informant in Gollnhofer and Sillans, *La Mémoire*, 203–4.

54 Gollnhofer and Sillans, *La Mémoire*, 205–6 and 209–11.

55 The descendent of a free person is called a *muisi*. Micheline Koumba, "Le Dibur-Simbu et la naissance du Mwil Bapunu" (bachelor's thesis, UOB, Libreville, 1985).

56 Informant Simon Mapangou-Mabika, text no. 13, in Koumba-Mamfoumbi, "Les Punu," 313–16.

57 Vansina, *Paths*, 234.

58 A few local men entered these networks unwillingly, often after being violently torn away from their families and community. See the story of Thomas Ondo, a former Ghetsogho-speaking slave who later became a trader for the British firm Hatton and Cookson and later for the French firm Daumas. Raponda-Walker, *Au pays des Isoghos*, 11–12.

59 Louis-Alphonse-Victor du Pont de Compiègne, *L'Afrique équatoriale: Okanda, Bangouens, Osyéba* (Paris: Plon, 1875), 225 and 231.

60 Rubber was the main export. Agents were only marginally interested in palm oil, camwood, kola nuts (exported to West Africa), and beeswax. Compiègne, *Afrique équatoriale*, 219 and 232–36.

61 The practice was still alive in the 1930s. Rapport annuel du Gabon 1932, quoted in Sautter, *De l'Atlantique au fleuve Congo: Une géographie du sous-peuplement. République du Congo: République gabonaise* (Paris: La Haye, Mouton, 1966), 733.

62 Koumba-Mamfoumbi, "Les Punu," 249.

63 In 1900, 224 European trading posts operated in Gabon. Hatton and Cookson of Liverpool supervised 78 of them, John Holt of Manchester, 59, and Adolph Woerman, of Hamburg, 20. Elikia M'Bokolo, *Noirs et Blancs en Afrique équatoriale: Les sociétés côtières et la pénétration française (vers 1820–1874)* (Paris: Editions de l'Ecole des Hautes Études en Sciences Sociales, 1981), 186–87.

64 The west corner of the SHO concession, the largest of its kind in French Equatorial Africa, sat in the Ngounié Valley. Nicolas Meteghe-Nnah, *Histoire du Gabon: Des origines à l'aube du XXIe siècle* (Paris: L'Harmattan, 2006), 106. Catherine Coquery-Vidrovitch, *Le Congo au temps des grandes compagnies concessionnaires, 1898–1930* (Paris: Mouton, 1972), 44. David Gardinier, *Historical Dictionary of Gabon*, 2nd ed. (Metuchen, NJ: Scarecrow Press, 1994), 116.

65 The concession was to last until 1925. Two smaller companies obtained concessions along the coast, the Compagnie Coloniale du Fernan Vaz and, along the Nyanga river, the Compagnie Française du Congo Occidental (CFCO). Gray, *Colonial Rule*, 143.

66 Gray, *Colonial Rule*, 145–48.

67 Maurice Eugène Denis, *Histoire militaire de l'Afrique équatoriale française* (Paris: Imprimerie nationale, 1931), 86–106.

68 Nicolas Meteghe N'Nah, *L'Implantation coloniale au Gabon: Résistance d'un peuple* (Paris: L'Harmattan, 1981), 84–88. Coquery-Vidrovitch, *Le Congo*, 198–99. Christopher Gray, "Territoriality, Ethnicity and Colonial Rule in Southern Gabon, 1850–1960" (PhD thesis, Indiana University, Bloomington 1995), 290–320.

69 Rapport politique du 4ème trimestre 1929, Ngounié, unsigned, ANG/FP 99, Tournée Ndende–Mouila.

70 Gray, *Colonial Rule*, 153–56; and Christopher Gray and François Ngolet, "Lambaréné, Okoumé and the Transformation of Labor along the Middle Ogooué (Gabon), 1870–1945," *Journal of African History* 40, no. 1 (1999): 87–107.

71 Sociétés indigènes de prévoyance provided local farmers with seeds and capital, but, as they were organized by the colonial state, that also scrutinized local agriculture.

72 Rapport politique semestriel de la subdivision de Sindara, n.s., 13 January 1945, ANG/FP 35.

73 Chef de district de Mbigou, rapport politique de 1949, ANG/FP 344.

74 Rapport politique de la Ngounié pour 1951, 14–15, ANG/FP 94.

75 Calendrier historique de Mouila, Archives CSSP 2D60.2a5. Nicolas Metegue N'Nah, *Histoire du Gabon: Des Origines à l'aube du XXIe siècle* (Paris: L'Harmattan, 2006), 111.

76 Calendrier historique de Mouila, Archives CSSP 2D60.2a5.

77 Interview with Mr. Fulgence Mboukou, Mouila, 2 June 2002.

78 In 1948, the tribunal examined one hundred penal cases and forty-four civil ones. The *état-civil* services delivered 298 birth, marriage, and death certificates. Rapport politique du chef de district de Mouila, 1st semester 1948, unsigned, ANG/FP 52.

79 Rapport politique de la Ngounié pour 1951, 5–15, ANG/FP 94.

80 Interview with Raphael Tsande, Mouila, 1 July 2012. Rapport politique de la Ngounié pour 1951, n. d. unsigned, 6, ANG/FP 94.

81 Planes allowed the city's postal service to distribute the mail twice a week. Rapport politique du chef de district de Mouila, 1er semestre 1948, unsigned, ANG/FP 52. Calendrier historique de Mouila, Archives CSSP, Fonds Pouchet 2D60–2A5.

82 A secondary east-west network connected the city to Lebamba, Koulamou-tou, Lastourville, and Franceville and the port of Mayumba on the Atlantic coast. Forced workers completed the section of the road between Sindara and Fougamou in 1927, and the road between Fougamou and Mouila in 1937–38. In 1948, wage workers completed the northern section to Ndjolé, and the southern section to Ndendé and Dolisie in Congo-Brazzaville. Gray, *Colonial Rule*, 172–76; and Roland Pourtier, *Le Gabon* (Paris: L'Harmattan, 1989), 2:45 and 2:218–28. Metegue N'Nah, *Histoire du Gabon*, 130–34.

83 Rapport politique du district de Mouila de 1959, n.s., n.d., 84, ANG/FP 346.

84 Another forty-three Europeans lived in the Ngounié Province. Rapport politique de la Ngounié pour 1951, 5–15, ANG/FP 94.

85 In the rural hinterland of Mouila, a few French lumber firms, of a modest size, employed African workers. In 1948, the SHO boasted a workforce of thirty-nine black employees, while none of its competitors had more than fifteen. Rapport politique du premier semestre 1948 de Mouila, n.s., n.d, ANG/FP 52.

86 Rapport politique Mbigou 1953, signed Serre, 54–55. Serre added that, in all of Equatorial Africa, "I never saw a region where racial hatred was greater."

87 Rapport politique annuel de la Ngounié, 1950, signed F. Soulier, ANG/FP 101.

88 Rapport politique de la Ngounié 1951, Mouila, unsigned, ANG/FP 418.

89 Fiche d'activité de Ndendé, no. 8/CF, October 1956, ANG/Fond provincial Ndendé.

90 Lettre du chef de district Mr. Blin à Mr. Ernault, 31 March 1955, no. 240, procès-verbal, signed Mr. Blin, n.d., Dossier 27, Justice 1953–1960, ANG/Fond provincial Ndendé.

91 Calendrier historique de Mouila, with help from Raphael Tsande, 4 July 2007, Archives CSSP 2D60.2a5.

92 Rapport politique de la Ngounié 1956, Mouila, signed Langle. ANG/FP 346. *Evolués* was the French name for Western-educated Africans who worked in clerical jobs.

93 Fiche d'activité de Lébamba, 26 November to 31 December 1962, no. 30/CF, signed Mboumba-Maganga, ANG/Fonds Provincial Ndendé, 14.

94 Interview with Raphaël Tsande, Mouila, 4 June 2002.

95 The process culminated in the early 1950s, when historian Hubert Deschamps and ethnographer Marcel Soret produced tribal maps of Ngounié Province. Deschamps, *Traditions orales*, 17–20, and 19 (map).

96 Gray, *Colonial Rule*, 171.

97 See also ethnic map in Deschamps, *Traditions orales*, 19.

98 Downstream, meanwhile, Eviya clans and Vili traders controlled the Samba Magotsi market.

99 In the 1940s, the French lumped together the African residents of Ngounié Province in what they called five "super" ethnic groupings. The first and most important one, around the city of Mouila, fused the Punu, Eschira (Gisira), Sango, and Vungu inhabitants. The second grouped the Tsangi and Nzabi. The third lumped together the Mitsogho and the Apindji. The Bakele made up the fourth group. Further south, a fifth grouping was created for the Vungu of Divenié. Rapport politique de la Ngounié pour 1951, s.n., s.d., 14–15, ANG/FP 94. The demographic censuses for the other "tribes" were: Apindji 1,416; Vungu 4,196; and Banjabi (Nzabi) 5,764. Rapport politique du chef de district de Mouila, 1er semestre 1948, n.s., ANG/FP 52.

100 The French might have known that the Punu had little territorial legitimacy in Mouila, and used them to further weaken the influence of the Ghetsogho clans who had rebelled against them. Although Punu-speaking clans had also stood in arms under Makita Nyonda's leadership, this had occurred further south, around Ndendé.

101 The French also created the tribal units of the Eschira (Gisira), Massango, Bakélé (Kele), Vumu, Eviya, Lumbu, and Fang in southern Gabon. But they considered that these were too small or too recently arrived in the region to warrant their own canton chief. Calendrier historique de Mouila, Archives CSSP, Fonds Pouchet 2D60–2A5. See also Gray, *Colonial Rule*, 204. Beneath the cantons, the French delineated smaller units that they called *tribus* (tribes), whose name corresponded roughly to existing local clans: for instance, one of the Punu canton included the Boumouelle (Bumwele), Dibamba and Bouyala (Bujala) *tribus*. The *tribus* created by the French relied on appointed chiefs and spatial boundaries rather than cognitive or genealogical knowledge.

102 Of the seven additional cantons created by the French between Mouila and the city of Ndende further south, three were headed by Punu chiefs, while the Bavoungou (Vungu), Apindji, Mitsogho, and Massango (Sango) had only one canton each.

103 Gray, *Colonial Rule*, 149–50.

104 Rapport du chef de district de Mouila au chef de la région de la Ngounié, no. 165, 9 May 1947, ANG, Archives provinciales Ndendé box 15; and rapport politique de la Ngounié pour 1951, 5–15, ANG/FP 94.

105 Rapport politique de la Ngounié pour 1951, 14–15, ANG/FP 94.

106 Interview with Léon Ghetombo, village Divindet, Mouila, 2 July 2007. The *chicotte* refers to the whip used by colonial troops, agents, and administrators in Central Africa to beat the natives.

107 Interview with Léon Ghetombo, village Divindet, Mouila, 2 July 2007. I returned to talk with the elders in the summer of 2012.

108 Paul Missioumbou, "Héritage, contradictions et changements socio-culturels chez les Nzébi: Contribution à l'analyse de la crise de l'institution familiale au Gabon" (Master's thesis, UOB, Libreville, 1999), 32, 94 and 101.

109 Ariadne Vromen, Katharine Gelber, and Anika Gauja, *Powerscape: Contemporary Australian Politics* (Sydney, Australia: Allen & Unwin, 2009). The volume eschews surprisingly little analysis of power in physical or spatial terms.

110 I used this approach to make sense of the urbanistic, mystical, and ideological effects of the 2006 monument to Savorgnan de Brazza in the Congo. Florence Bernault, "Colonial Bones: The 2006 Burial of Savorgnan De Brazza," *African Affairs* 109 (July 2010): 367–90.

111 For instance, Allen M. Howard and Richard M. Shain, eds., *The Spatial Factor in African History: The Relationship of the Social, Material, and Perceptual* (Leiden: Brill, 2005); and Simon Bekker and Laurent Fourchard, eds., *Governing Cities in Africa: Politics and Policies* (Cape Town, South Africa: HSRC Press, 2013). More recently, urban studies have "turned" to infrastructures and "mobility." John Urry, *Mobilities* (Cambridge, UK: Polity, 2007); Brian Larkin, "The Politics and Poetics of Infrastructure," *Annual Review of Anthropology* 42 (2013): 327–43.

112 Interview with Anaclé Bissiélo, Libreville, 14 June 2002.

113 Interview with Mémé Prudence, Mouila, 2 July 2007. Other informants contest the Punu claims of firstcomers in Mouila. Interview with Pierre Carrousel, Mouila, 9 June 2002: "The last to arrive in the region were the Punu, so they needed a myth. The first inhabitants were the pygmies, the Mitsoghos. . . . Where do you see Punu villages? There are none. Dikouka, three kilometers from Mouila, is populated by Mitsoghos, Moualo and Apindjis. Moualo is home to Apinji inhabitants. . . . The Punu never venture in the forest, they stay in valleys, and do not navigate on rivers. They are not men of the river, and they have been settled in town by the whites. This is where the name of the city comes from: 'Mwil'Bapunu: Mouila, the city of the Punu.'"

114 Interview with Mémé Prudence, Mouila, 2 July 2007.

115 Interview with Honoré Maganga, Anna Maganga, and Élise Combila, Mouila, 3 June 2002.

116 Interview with Élise Combila, Mouila, 1 June 2002.

117 Interview with Raphael Tsande, Mouila, 4 June 2002.

118 Information varies on the couple that took Murhumi's picture. An assistant to the mayor of Mouila described Tailleur in 2002 as the "prefect" of the region. Interview with Mr. Anatole Nguimbi, Mouila, 4 June 2002. Another informant,

Raphael Tsande, remembered that the picture of Murhumi was taken in 1961 by a Mr. Gandon, special agent for the public treasury. A list of governors and prefects published by Roland Pourtier in his book establishes that a certain H. Tailleur served as governor (or prefect) of Ngounié Province from 1957 to 1960. Pourtier, *Le Gabon*, 2:29.

119 A few Africans owned cameras, and some had opened photographic studios for African clientele. Christaud M. Geary, "Photographic Practice in Africa and Its Implications for the Use of Historical Photographs as Contextual Evidence," in *Fotografia e storia dell'Africa*, ed. Alessandro Triulzi (Napoli: I.U.O., 1995), 107.

120 Mary Motley, *Devils in Waiting* (London: Longmans, 1959), 49.

121 Arrêté portant institution d'une carte d'identité dans le Territoire du Gabon, 3 July 1948, no. 905bis/APS. Archives CSSP, Fonds Pouchet 2D 60. 1b5.

122 Fiche d'activité de Ndendé, No 8/CF, October 1956, ANG/Fond provincial Ndendé.

123 Interview with Pierre Nzengui, Libreville, 2012. The first stele (*stèle*) featured a small niche and a zinc roof to shelter Murhumi from the tropical rains. Oriented toward the Ngounié, it allowed the Siren to look at her original element. I did not find any visual evidence of this early monument.

124 Linda Heywood and John Thornton, *Central Africans, Atlantic Creoles, and the Making of the Foundation of the Americas, 1585–1660* (New York: Cambridge University Press, 2007), 66.

125 Bogumil Jewsiewicki, "Painting in Zaire: From the Invention of the West to the Representation of Social Self," in *Africa Explores: 20th Century African Art*, edited by Susan Vogel (New York: Center for African Art, 1991), 130.

126 Jean-Pierre Missié, "Signification et influence des enseignes à caractère religieux dans le domaine commercial à Brazzaville," *Annales de l'Université Marien Ngouabi* 8, no. 1 (2007): 60. Earlier on, in the 1940s, among the Nzabi in Congo-Brazzaville, the leaders of the antiwitchcraft cult La Mère (French: Mother) used magazine portraits of white women to show the tutelary figure of their spirit. Georges Dupré, *Les Naissances d'une société: Espace et historicité chez les Beembé du Congo* (Paris: Éditions de l'ORSTOM, 1985), 375–80.

127 Claude Lévi-Strauss, *The Savage Mind* (Chicago, IL: University of Chicago Press, 1966).

128 According to Fulgence Mboukou, the bridge was built in the mid-1970s by a Dutch firm. Interview with Mr. Fulgence Mboukou, Mouila, 3 June 2002. Other informants remember Yugoslavian workers. In July 2012, Michelle Musavu pointed to convincing evidence that the bridge had been built by the German firm Diekorf Wiedman. Interview with Michelle Musavu, Libreville, 10 July 2012.

129 Despite my best efforts, I was not able to find hard evidence of the construction project.

130 Interview with Mr. Diata, Mouila, 3 June 2002. Other informants mentioned that the spirit felt neglected after the death of Dikakou, the powerful *nganga* and

leader of the matrilineage. Interview with Anna Maganga and Élise Combila, Mouila, 1 June 2002.

131 "Les pygmés sont nos blancs, parce qu'ils connaissent beaucoup de choses." Koumba-Mamfoumbi, "Les Punu," 120.

132 Marcel Mauss, "Techniques of the Body," *Economy and Society* 2, no. 1 (1973), 70–88.

133 In the early 1980s, indeed, the statue carved by Pierre Nzengui disappeared from the public stele where it had been displayed. The monument had been displaced to allow the construction of the city hall, but nobody seemed to be sure where the statue had been brought to rest. In 1989, a female elder of the Dibur-Simbu matrilineage saw in a dream that the prefect of Ngounié Province, a Fang man, had locked the bas-relief in the new *préfecture*. She confronted the official until he relinquished the statue and gave it back to city hall. Preserved in the dusty basement room where we found it in 2002, the statue remained "imprisoned," as the Dibur-Simbu lamented. Interview with Mémé Prudence, 2 July 2007.

134 Interview with Mémé Prudence, Mouila, 2 July 2007. Interview with Raphael Tsande, Mouila, 4 June 2002.

135 Today, the word *Sirène* (Siren) is the most frequent one used by people in French to talk about the water spirit.

136 This included studies of modern witchcraft that pin vernacular practices against Christian ones. For instance, Peter Geschiere, *The Modernity of Witchcraft: Politics and the Occult in Postcolonial Africa* (Charlottesville: University Press of Virginia, 1997); and Adam Ashforth, *Witchcraft, Violence, and Democracy in South Africa* (Chicago, IL: University of Chicago Press, 2005). See also Allman and Parker, *Tongnaab*.

137 The name of the spirit Murhumi, without the prefix *mu-*, probably comes from the Bantu root *-dúm-*, which means "male," "husband," "brother," or "maternal uncle." Jan Vansina, personal communication, 12 April 2007. *Bantu Lexical Reconstruction* available at the Online Database, Bantu Lexical Reconstructions 3, Africa Museum, http://www.africamuseum.be/collections/browsecollections/humansciences/blr/any_lexicon_dictionary.

138 Nicolas Metegue N'Nah, "Imaginaire populaire, croyances et établissement de la domination coloniale au Gabon au XIXe siècle," *Annales de la Faculté des Lettres, Arts et Sciences Humaines,* Université d'Abomey-Calavi, Bénin, no. 8 (December 2002): 79–92. Among the Mitsogho, a woman possessed by genies (*mighesi*) consults a diviner to understand the cause of her physical troubles. If she is possessed by a genie, she can become an adept of its cult, and after a few years, serve as a higher initiate (*mbamba*) of the Ombudi association, where she learns divining and curing skills. Gollnhofer and Sillans, *La Mémoire*, 97–99.

139 Trader Horn and Ethelreda Lewis, *Trader Horn: Being the Life and Works of Alfred Aloysius Horn* (New York: Simon and Schuster, 1927), 216.

140 Henry Drewal, "Mami Wata and Santa Marta: Imag(in)ing Selves and Others," in *Images and Empire: Visuality in Colonial and Postcolonial Africa*, edited by Paul

Landau and Deborah Kaspin (Berkeley: University of California Press, 2002), 193–211. Gray, *Colonial Rule*, 140.

141 Stephen Ellis and Gerrie ter Haar, *Worlds of Power. Religious Thought and Political Practice in Africa* (New York: Oxford University Press, 2004), 122.

142 T. K. Biaya, "La Mort et ses métamorphoses au Congo-Zaire," *Cahiers africains*, no. 31–32 (1998): 101–4. For the lore of Mami Wata in the broader region of Gabon and Congo, see Joseph Tonda, *La Guérison divine en Afrique centrale (Congo, Gabon)* (Paris: Karthala, 2002), 73–98; and Dupré, *Un Ordre*, 383. For rich studies of Mami Wata in Congo-Kinshasa and in Africa, see Bogumil Jewsiewicki, *Mami Wata: La Peinture Urbaine au Congo* (Paris: Gallimard, 2003), and Drewal, "Mami Wata."

143 Biaya, "La Mort et ses métaphores." See also Joseph Tonda, *Le souverain moderne: Le Corps du pouvoir en Afrique centrale (Congo, Gabon)* (Paris: Karthala, 2005), 188–93. Tonda thinks that the rumors about money, sex, and the serpent appeared in Equatorial Africa in the 1990s, but I think that they have a deeper antiquity, especially since (as Tonda himself signals) images of the serpent as the Devil had been diffused by official churches since the mid-nineteenth century.

144 Macé, "Fétiches." See also Pierre Daney, "Sur les croyances des indigènes de la circonscription de Sindara (Gabon: A.E.F.)," *Revue anthropologique*, no. 34 (1924): 272–82, quoted in Raponda-Walker and Sillans, *Rites et croyances*, 23 and 260–61. These authors warned, however, that the Gabonese seldom represented water spirits in images, but believed in the actions (*essence, puissance*) of the spirits themselves. They suggested that the descriptions collected by Europeans were in fact scams invented by ritual experts to distract them from the real meanings of the spirits.

145 A vigorous Marian cult, for instance, diffused in the Kongo kingdom in the early sixteenth century, and addressed the dangers associated with mercantile forms of wealth coming from the sea. Heywood and Thornton, *Central Africans*, 171. John K. Thornton, *The Kongolese Saint Anthony: Dona Beatriz Kimpa Vita and the Antonian Movement, 1684–1706* (Cambridge: Cambridge University Press, 1998), 114–17. In the 1600s, Mary made several apparitions in San Salvador, the capital of Kongo. John Thornton, *Africa and Africans in the Making of the Atlantic World, 1400–1800*, 2nd ed. (Cambridge: Cambridge University Press, 1998), 258. For the eighteenth century, see Filip De Boeck, "Borderland Breccia: The Mutant Hero in the Historical Imagination of a Central African Diamond Frontier," *Journal of Colonialism and Colonial History* 1, no. 2 (winter 2000).

146 Jan Vansina, *Being Colonized: The Kuba Experience in Rural Congo, 1880–1960* (Madison: University of Wisconsin Press, 2010), 273. Achille Mbembe, "La prolifération du divin en Afrique sub-Saharienne," in *Les politiques de Dieu*, edited by Gilles Kepel (Paris: Karthala, 1993), 11.

147 Chérubin Délicat, "Recherches sur la Mission Catholique du Saint Esprit de Mayumba de 1888 à 1960" (bachelor's thesis, UOB, Libreville, 1983). Sainte Croix des Eshiras was trusted to a Gabonese catechist, Léon Mboumba, in 1925.

Rapport politique du premier semestre 1947, district de Fougamou, 25 July 1947, ANG/FP 35 (rapports politiques Fougamou). Monique Koumba-Mamfoumbi, "La Mission Saint Martin des Apindji (1900–1954); Étude de cas sur l'histoire de l'évangélisation du Gabon" (master's thesis, UOB, Libreville, 1983). For the Saint Etienne Mission in Mouila, see Francis Ambrière, *Afrique centrale: Les républiques d'expression française.* Les Guides bleus (Paris: Hachette, 1962), 173. Protestant missions arrived earlier, in the late 1840s, but did not use the saints. David K. Patterson, *The Northern Gabon Coast to 1875* (Oxford: Clarendon Press, 1975), 115–20.

148 Koumba-Mamfoumbi, "Les Punu," 29. In southern Gabon in the early 1890s, a report from the Catholic mission at Bata noted that local villagers were willing to entertain close relations with the mission if no factories existed in the vicinity. *Bulletin* CSSP, tome 18, no. 121, report on Communauté St-Dominique à Bata, 1894–1896, 502.

149 Raponda-Walker, *Au pays des Isoghos*, 20. See also a report from the Catholic mission at Okano: "Our ministry is difficult . . . our primitive people don't understand yet the goal of the coming of the *minissé*. They imagine that the coming of the father or the catechist in their village meant the exemption form taxes, caravans, forced labor. Deceived in their expectations, they keep repeating: 'You do not bring us anything, you forbid us everything that our fathers liked and did, polygamy, fetishes . . . what are you good for?'" Okano, Notre-Dame-des-Victoires, June 1922, *Bulletin* CSSP, vol. 30, no. 382, 705.

150 Tonda, *Le Souverain moderne*, 127–56.

151 There are few studies on the cult of saints in contemporary Gabon, but for Congo-Brazzaville and Congo-Kinshasa, see Phyllis M. Martin, *Catholic Women of Congo-Brazzaville: Mothers and Sisters in Troubled Times* (Bloomington: Indiana University Press, 2009). Jean-Luc Vellut, "Quelle profondeur historique pour l'image de la Vierge Marie au Congo?," *Canadian Journal of African Studies* 33, no. 2 (1999): 530–47. The Marian fervor is attested today by the recent apparitions at Kibeho (Rwanda 1981) and in Kinshasa (1985, 1989, and 1995). Isodore Ndaywel à Nziem, "Du Zaïre au Congo: La Vierge du Désarmement et la guerre de libération," *Canadian Journal of African Studies* 33, no. 2 (1999): 500–29.

152 At that time, the Catholic Church ranged itself firmly on the side of the legitimist and conservative parties in France that had fought against popular revolutions and the Paris Commune (1871). Churches such as the Basilica of the Sacred Heart in Montmartre (Paris), also called Basilica of the National Vow, devoted to the Virgin Mary, were erected in order to atone for France's "sins" and to redeem the horrors of the Commune. The Saint-Sulpician style for devotional statues reached a first apex in the 1870s, and a second one in 1905 after the separation of the state and the church.

153 L. Lejeune, "Station St François à Lambaréné dans l'Ogooué," Annales CSSP 1899, 55–57.

154 Jean Roger Mba, "Élévation de la statue de la Vierge à Mitzic," *Semaine de l'AEF*, no. 234, 23 February 1957, 5. See a similar feast for the dedication of a statue to Our Lady of Lourdes at the Loango mission in Martin, *Catholic Women*, 59.

155 Ndaywel è Nziem observes the same spreading Marian grottos in the Belgian Congo: Ndaywel è Nziem, "Du Zaire au Congo," 503.

156 "Mission des Eshiras," *Bulletin* CSSP, tome 18, 1896–1897, 515–16.

157 The original pietà was discovered in the city of Colmar (Alsatia) in 1491 as a miraculous statue in the trunk of an old oak tree. At Sindara, a local Gabonese sculptor, Mr. Tom, created a similar statue of the Virgin holding in her left hand a *tsibitsi*, a little rodent that feeds on plantations. The visual message was supposed to teach the Gabonese to choose between good and evil, and to convert so God would bless their plantations. History summarized in "Les Trois Epis: Pourquoi?," *Newsletter Notre Dame de l'Equateur, Trois Epis-Sindara*, no. 15 (2000) and no. 16 (2002), author's archives. Interview with Père Zacharie, the senior priest at Sindara, Mouila, 6 June 2002.

158 The saint's day was on either February 11 or August 15 (the celebration of the Ascension of Mary). Conversation with Père Zacharie, Mouila, 6 June 2002. *Newsletter Notre Dame de l'Equateur, Trois Epis-Sindara*, no. 10 (1998). The bridging of water spirits and the Virgin has also been studied through the diffusion of the Bwiti cult. According to Richard Garner, "Every buiti consists of a rudely carved figure of the human form, formerly male, later bisexual and still more recently, quite often female. This modification is probably due to missionary innovations, especially of the catholic missions in which the image of the Virgin are frequently made conspicuous, and a few of the most recent patterns I have seen have an image of a child as accessory." Richard Lynch Garner, "Buiti," Box 1, folder "Buiti," National Anthropological Archives, Smithsonian Institution. I thank Jeremy Rich for sending me a copy of this text.

159 Henri Trilles, *Fleurs noires et âmes blanches* (Lille: Desclée, De Brouwer, 1914), 104–5.

160 See also the carving in Belgium in 1891 of a statue representing Mary as the "Queen of Congo," crushing the head of a snake under her feet. Ndaywel è Nziem, "Du Congo au Zaire," 503.

161 It was finally inaugurated in the summer of 2014. I could not attend the ceremony. "Mugumi, le génie protecteur de Mouila, réapparait 24 ans après sa disparition," n.s., in *Gabon Matin*, 8 May 2014, 10.

162 Interview with Joseph-Vincent Dinga, prefect of Ngounié Province, Mouila, 3 June 2002. A member of the Varama ethnic group, he belonged to the communities (in particular, the Vungu-, Gisir-, and Apindji-speaking clans) that withdrew from the region after the colonial conquest and the mounting hegemony of Punu-speaking clans in the region.

163 According to Mémé Prudence, to be in contact with or to take care of Murhumi, one has to have "the vampire." Only those endowed with superior power can approach the spirit without being harmed. Mémé Prudence was a member of a female initiation association (Njembe). Interview with Mémé Prudence, Mouila, 2 July 2007.

164 In 1968, a pioneer article by Wyatt MacGaffey documented how modern BaKongo in the Congo-Kinshasa reflected on "whites" and "blacks" as spiritual rather than racial categories. Although BaKongo had a prolonged and com-

plex experience of the "modern" world, and had long given up on considering ordinary Europeans as supernatural beings, they continued to suspect inquisitive Europeans such as anthropologists to be dead people returned from Mputu (old Kongo name for Portugal, and hence for Europe). In times of crises, such knowledgeable whites could even pass as witches who engaged in the occult commerce in people. Wyatt MacGaffey, "Kongo and the King of the Americans," *Journal of Modern African Studies* 6, no. 2 (1968): 171–81.

165 Interview with Mémé Prudence, Mouila, 1 July 2012. On double vision and people with "four eyes," see Geschiere, *Modernity of Witchcraft*.

166 Interview with Mr. Anatole Nguimbi, Mouila, 4 June 2002.

167 Interview with Mémé Prudence, Mouila, 2 July 2007.

168 *Muviga* defines a slave who is integrated to a lineage. Pierre-Philippe Rey, "Articulation des modes de dépendance et des modes de reproduction dans deux sociétés lignagères (Punu et Kunyi du Congo-Brazzaville)," *Cahiers d'études africaines* 9, no. 35 (1969): 415–40.

169 Meteghe-N'Nah, *Histoire du Gabon*, 40n54. On the enduring figure of the slave in Equatorial Africa, see Bernault, "Colonial Bones," 367–90.

170 My informants explained, "The minister embodied himself in his mother who became a fetish." Interviews with Raphaël Tsande, Mouila, 4 June 2002, and with Mémé Prudence, Mouila, 2 July 2007. On Mwiri, see Gray, *Colonial Rule*.

171 Interview with Pierre Carrousel, Mouila, 5 July 2007.

172 A true child of the matrilineage is born from one of its female members. Despite the rules of matrilinearity, however, children who rose to prominence in their father's clan could also become full-fledged members of it. Interview with Honoré Maganga, Libreville, 26 June 2007.

173 Another one of these new ritual specialists, a certain "fetish-man" named Pambou, exercised in the city of Ndendé. Political delegations, including the deputy of Fougamou, Léon Mboumba, came to consult him from Libreville. Fiche d'activités de Septembre 1961, District de Ndendé, no. 53/CF, 1, ANG/FP 13.

174 Rapport politique de la Ngounié 1953, signed J. Titaux, 31 January, 1954, 26, ANG/FP 101. See rapport politique de Ndendé, Ngounié for 1953, 12, ANG/FP 418: "Yembit Paul has little influence on the population. His main concern is to create a clientele by intervening on the behalf of voters who come ask him to solve a myriad of personal business issues. . . . He seems to want to stay in good terms with the administration, to which he owes important privileges such as owning a high-end quality gun, and managing a liquor store (*débit de boissons*)."

175 Fiche d'activités du district de Mouila, 1958–1959, ANG/FP 125.

176 In 2002, people murmured that Omar Bongo was the highest initiate of Njobi, and an expert in roping politicians into the secret association in order to enforce their loyalty.

177 King Mérode, he added, had a vision of two angels, one ascending and one descending, that taught him that "what is up is the same as what it is down." Interview with Mr. Anatole Nguimbi, Mouila, 4 June 2002.

178 They used the same iPunu term, *monima*, "image." Interview with Mémé Prudence, Mouila, 1 July 2012.

179 A female elder explained that after the Tailleurs shot Murhumi's picture, female specialists took a big chunk of wood, sawed it, and made the vampire. Interview with Mémé Prudence, Mouila, 1 July 2012. "Vampire" here means the witch-substance owned by powerful people. We will examine witch-substance in chapter 4, and vampires in chapter 6.

CHAPTER 2 ⁝ The Double Life of Charms

1 William Pietz, "The Problem of the Fetish: I," RES: *Anthropology and Aesthetics*, no. 9 (spring 1985): 5–17.

2 John Janzen and William Arkinstall, *The Quest for Therapy in Lower Zaire* (Berkeley: University of California Press, 1978); John Thornton, *The Kongolese Saint Anthony: Dona Beatriz Kimpa Vita and the Antonian Movement, 1684–1706* (Cambridge: Cambridge University Press, 1998); and Nancy Rose Hunt, *A Colonial Lexicon of Birth Ritual, Medicalization, and Mobility in the Congo* (Durham, N.C.: Duke University Press, 1999).

3 For instance, Jean Comaroff and John Comaroff, "Occult Economies and the Violence of Abstraction: Notes from the South African Postcolony," *American Ethnologist* 26, no. 2 (May 1999): 279–303. On consumer culture and new technologies of the self in Africa, see Timothy Burke, *Lifebuoy Men, Lux Women* (Durham, N.C.: Duke University Press, 1996); and Lynn Thomas, "The Modern Girl and Racial Respectability in 1930s South Africa," *Journal of African History* 47, no. 3 (2006): 461–90.

4 John Cinnamon works on the Fang people and on spiritual movements in Gabon. John Cinnamon, "Ambivalent Power: Anti-Sorcery and Occult Subjugation in Late Colonial Gabon," *Journal of Colonialism and Colonial History* 3, no. 3 (2002): n.p.

5 Florence was the niece of the famous Fang *guérisseur* Papa Minko, one of the leaders of the witchcraft-cleansing Mademoiselle-Minbara movement in central Gabon. Names of informants, unless otherwise noted, have been anonymized. On Mademoiselle, see Cinnamon, "Ambivalent Power"; and Joseph Tonda, *La Guérison divine en Afrique centrale (Congo, Gabon)* (Paris: Karthala, 2003), 63–98. On Bwiti, see James Fernandez, *Bwiti: An Ethnography of the Religious Imagination in Africa* (Princeton, N.J.: Princeton University Press, 1981).

6 Florence had named one of the dolls Sardonix, after her semiprecious protective stone, a *sardoine* (orange chalcedony). Two other dolls responded to Force Tranquille (Quiet Force) and Confiance (Trust). Fieldwork, Libreville, 29 July 1998. A few years later, I sadly learned of Florence's untimely death.

7 Circulaire du gouverneur du Gabon Yves Digo aux chefs de région et de district, no. 634 bis/AP, 12 July 1956, ANG Mitzic 2D J III-9–2.

8 Fieldwork, Libreville, 19 June 2000.

9 On clapperless bells as emblem of power in the region, see Jan Vansina, *Paths in the Rainforest: Toward a History of Political Tradition in Equatorial Africa* (Madison: University of Wisconsin Press, 1990), 151. On the signification of knots as tying sacred forces, Wyatt MacGaffey, *Kongo Political Culture: The Conceptual Challenge of the Particular* (Bloomington: Indiana University Press, 2000), 82.

10 Fieldwork, Libreville, 19 June 2000. I explain the term "charlatan," here an equivalent of "healer," later in this chapter.

11 See chapters 3 and 6 for details on the witch-substance, and the label vampire.

12 Fieldwork, Libreville, 19 June 2000.

13 Wyatt MacGaffey, "Aesthetics and Politics of Violence in Central Africa," *Journal of African Cultural Studies* 13, no. 1 (June 2000): 64. The extraordinary agency of spirits and ancestors was potent and dangerous, and could be used for positive aims such as healing, or for destructive purposes such as cursing or killing. Peter Geschiere, *The Modernity of Witchcraft: Politics and the Occult in Postcolonial Africa* (Charlottesville: University Press of Virginia, 1997), 11. Ingredients depended on the device's expected action, but they almost always included dried plants, resins, clays, and small pieces of fabric and animal parts. Evidence in the nineteenth century suggests that some components held a metaphorical quality. For instance, the presence of resin could recall and activate a lightning flash against enemies to burn them. Karl E. Laman, *The Kongo* (Uppsala, Sweden: Almqvist & Wiksell, 1953), 1:83–84.

14 This stability suggests that early composing techniques remained fairly unchanged over time. Early written records authored by European visitors to the region are skewed, however, by an abundance of descriptions for the southernmost part of West Equatorial Africa: the Kongo kingdom, Loango and Angola. No such evidence exists before the seventeenth century for Gabon, especially in the interior.

15 For instance, Fang speakers called a horn (*nlakh*), an animal horn filled with medicine.

16 Most charms and talismans contained various medicines mixed together and put in a container, small or large—a bag, a sack, or a basket (oMyènè: *epambo*) secured with twines or strings. Others were stuffed inside anthropomorphic statues, and sealed with resin, clay, or metal. André Raponda-Walker, *Notes d'histoire du Gabon, Suivi de Toponymie de l'Estuaire Libreville et Toponymie du Fernan Vaz Port Gentil* (1960; Libreville: Éditions Raponda-Walker, 1996), 59; and André Raponda-Walker and Roger Sillans, *Rites et croyances des peuples du Gabon: Essai sur les pratiques religieuses d'autrefois et d'aujourd'hui* (Paris: Présence africaine, 1983), 77–96.

17 MacGaffey, *Kongo*, chapters 5 and 8.

18 See similar argument in Vansina, *Paths*, 74.

19 Vansina, *Paths*, 96.

20 Vansina, *Paths*, 96.

21 **-té*, derived from "tree." Vansina also lists the proto-Bantu **-pengo* for "omen," "religious statues/charms," and **-kíndá* for "village charm." Vansina, *Paths*, 273, 298.

22 Vansina, *Paths*. MacGaffey, *Kongo*, 79. Louis Perrois, *Arts du Gabon: Les arts plastiques du bassin de l'Ogooué* (Paris: Éditions de l'ORSTOM, 1979), 142.

23 For an early twentieth-century example, see description of a cult of ancestors among the Fang in Raponda-Walker and Sillans. *Rites et croyances*, 146–54.

24 MacGaffey, *Kongo*, 80.

25 The names of charms often designated the entire therapeutic and cult complex. For instance, in the nineteenth century, the generic Fang word *biang* (pl. *mebi-ang*) comprised the round drums and boxes made out of tree bark in which the skulls of ancestors were preserved (*nsuk bieri*), the anthropomorphic figures topping them (*mwan biang*, lit. "children of medicine"), and the rituals that activated the agency of the relics. Fernandez, *Bwiti*, 253 sqq.

26 MacGaffey, *Kongo*, 90–96.

27 Today, scholars remind us about the free circulation of charms, and the fact that their agency endures away from ritual chains: "By contrast, the *nkisi* is not linked to the person of the *nganga*, because [as the proverb says] 'the *nganga* can die, but the *nkisi* endures.' . . . The acquisition of a *minkisi* is done by purchase, by legacy or by initiation." Mulina Habi Buganza, "Le Nkisi dans la tradition Woyo du Bas-Zaire," in *Fétiches: Objets enchantés, mots réalisés*. Special issue of *Systèmes de pensée en Afrique noire*, no. 8 (1985): 204 and 210.

28 Pietz, "Problem of the Fetish: I," 5–17.

29 Nicolas Villault, *Relation des costes d'Afrique, appellées Guinée* (Paris: Thierry, 1669), 221, translated and quoted by William Pietz, "The Problem of the Fetish, IIIa: Bosman's Guinea and the Enlightenment Theory of Fetishism," *RES: Anthropology and Aesthetics*, no. 16 (autumn 1988): 110n9.

30 The notion was theorized a century later by Charles de Brosses, *Du culte des dieux fétiches, ou Parallèle de l'ancienne Religion de l'Egypte avec la Religion actuelle de Nigritie* (Geneva, 1760).

31 Dionigi Carli, *La Mission au Kongo des pères Michelangelo Guatari and Diogini Carli (1668)*, trans. Alix du Cheyron d'Abaz (Paris: Editions Chandeigne, Librairie portugaise, 2006), 87.

32 John Thornton, *The Kingdom of Kongo: Civil War and Transition, 1641–1718* (Madison: University of Wisconsin Press, 1983), 62. Anne Hilton, *The Kingdom of Kongo* (Oxford: Clarendon Press, 1985), 18.

33 Vansina, *Paths*, 98, 217, 298.

34 The purchase of African medicine in Lisbon is documented with certainty in the eighteenth century, but probably occurred earlier. On the coast of Guinea, talismanic pouches were called *bolsas de mandingas* and contained scrolls of paper with Arabic scripts from the Koran, or orations from the Bible, attesting to the hybrid power and probably circulation of these objects across diverse religious and geographic boundaries. James Sweet, *Recreating Africa: Culture, Kinship, and Religion in the African-Portuguese World, 1441–1770* (Chapel Hill: University of North Carolina Press, 2003), 185. See also Jane Guyer on the wide availability

of charms for sale: "Wealth in People and Self-Realization in Equatorial Africa," *Man* 28, no. 2 (1993): 247.

35 Carli, *La Mission au Kongo*, 113.

36 Carli, *La Mission au Kongo*, 143.

37 "They send us their children with alms consisting in a couple of squares of raffia fibers, or 3500 small shells (this is their currency, called *zimbi* in the local language). . . . They also bring a bit of salt on a leaf, so that we can bless the water, and they give us all these gifts so we can baptize their children, and if they have nothing to offer, we do it for the love of God." Carli, *La Mission au Kongo*, 100–101.

38 Patrick J. Geary, *Furta Sacra: Theft of Relics in the Central Middle Ages* (Princeton, N.J.: Princeton University Press, 1982). On relics and the objectification of the holy in Antiquity, see Peter Brown, *Society and the Holy in Late Antiquity* (Berkeley: Los Angeles: University of California Press, 1982).

39 In the Tio Kingdom, the high priest in charge of the national spirit could pick anything that went ashore from the Congo River and make an *ibili* charm with it. One could go to the priest and acquire an *ibili* against payment. Anyone, moreover, could become a *ngaa* by purchasing the charm *kaa* from an instructor. Vansina, *Paths*, 330; and Jan Vansina, *The Tio Kingdom of the Middle Congo, 1880–1892* (London: Oxford University Press, 1973), 75, 175–77, and 182–83.

40 Jan Vansina, *How Societies Are Born: Governance in West Central Africa before 1600* (Charlottesville: University of Virginia Press, 2004) 167, 190, and 242.

41 Circa 1820, the leaders of the Orungu polity on the Gabon coast stole the skull of the founder of a rival Nkomi polity and placed it as a bounty among their own ancestral relics (oMyènè: *alumbi*). Joseph Ambouroué-Avaro, *Un Peuple gabonais à l'aube de la civilisation: Le Bas-Ogooué au XIXe siècle* (Paris: Karthala, 1981), 147; and Raponda-Walker, *Notes d'histoire*, 113–14.

42 For comparison, in Madagascar, missionaries rejoiced when the Merina abandoned their "idols" (*sampy*), failing to realize that *sampy* were always disposable and renewable. Maurice Bloch, *From Blessing to Violence: History and Ideology in the Circumcision Ritual of the Merina of Madagascar* (Cambridge: Cambridge University Press, 1986).

43 Perrois, *Arts du Gabon*, 35, 41, 111, and 188–89, fig. 39. See also figures composed with potent medicine in a bundle (Perrois, *Arts du Gabon*, 306 and 308). When a clan split in branches that settled in different locales, the communal relics were redistributed among the diverging groups.

44 Fleuriot de Langle, "Croisières à la côte d'Afrique (1868)," in *Le Tour du Monde: Nouveau Journal des Voyages*, vol. 31 (Paris: Librairie Hachette, 1876), 266.

45 Paul Du Chaillu, *Explorations and Adventures in Equatorial Africa: With Accounts of the Manners and Customs of the People, and of the Chace [sic] of the Gorilla, Crocodile, Leopard, Elephant, Hippopotamus, and Other Animals* (London: John Murray, 1861), 337.

46 According to Louis Perrois, this is probably the oldest such recorded purchase in Gabon. Perrois traces the second purchase to 1867, when American trader B. Walker bought a Vili or Gisira mask in central Gabon (now in the Pitt Rivers Museum). Louis Perrois, "The Western Historiography of African Reliquary Sculpture," in *Eternal Ancestors: The Art of the Central African Reliquary*, edited by Alisa LaGamma (New York: Metropolitan Museum of Art / New Haven, Conn.: Yale University Press, 2007), 63–77. During a visit to Orungu country, however, Du Chaillu failed to buy "idols" for twenty dollars; the king told him that he would not sell them even for one hundred slaves. Du Chaillu, *Explorations and Adventures*, 148.

47 Ethelreda Lewis, *Trader Horn: Being the Life and Works of Alfred Aloysius Horn* (New York: The Library Guild of America, 1927), 135.

48 Mariette Portet, *En blanc sur les cartes* (Condé-sur-Noireau, France: Imprimeur-Editeur Ch. Corlet, 1969). Graux started his career in Lambaréné and in 1883 moved to Libreville as principal agent for the trading company Daumas, Béraud et Cie. Every other year, he sailed to France with boxes of local objects that he had collected for the "benefit of history."

49 Johannes Fabian, *Out of Our Minds: Reason and Madness in the Exploration of Central Africa* (Berkeley: University of California Press, 2000), 190–97.

50 Perrois, "Western Historiography," 63–65, and 212, fig. 51.

51 The Brazza mission to West Africa in 1883–85 collected many more objects in the Haut-Ogooué that were later deposited in the Museum of Man in Paris. Perrois, "Western Historiography," 65–67. Alissa LaGamma, ed., *Eternal Ancestors: The Art of the Central African Reliquary* (New York: Metropolitan Museum of Art / New Haven, Conn.: Yale University Press, 2007), fig. 75, 248–49, features a Kota reliquary ensemble in the form of a basket filled with sacra, and covered with a dense fringe of hide filaments. It was acquired in the mid-1880s by Charles Vital Roche, district officer at Franceville, who gave it to the Trocadero Ethnography Museum in 1897. James Fernandez found that, by the 1940s, the decorative figures used to top the reliquaries themselves started to change status: the Fang placed increased value on the sculptures themselves, in which they introduced pieces of crania to protect them against the missionary and administrative appropriation of relics. Fernandez, *Bwiti*, 266.

52 Günther Tessman, *Die Pangwe: Völkerkundliche Monographie Eines Westafrikanischen Negerstammes; Ergebnisse Der Lübecker Pangwe-expedition, 1907–1909 und Früherer Forschungen, 1904–1907* (Berlin: E. Wasmuth, A.-G., 1913).

53 Kathleen Bickford Berzock and Christa Clarke, eds., *Representing Africa in American Art Museums: A Century of Collecting and Displaying* (Seattle: University of Washington Press, 2011).

54 Perrois, *Arts du Gabon*, 9–11; and Perrois, "Western Historiography," 74–77. In the Congo Free State, Presbyterian and Catholic missions started to buy curios in the 1890s and to sell them for export in Leopoldville and in Europe. Jan Van-

sina, *Being Colonized: The Kuba Experience in Rural Congo, 1880–1960* (Madison: University of Wisconsin Press, 2010), 227–28 and 275–76.

55 Christopher Steiner, *African Art in Transit* (Cambridge: Cambridge University Press, 1994), 162–64. For an example of the high prices reached by "authentic" (e.g., religious) artifacts from Gabon, see how, in June 2006, a Fang mask originally worn by members of the Ngil judicial association reached the unprecedented price of 5.9 million euros (approximately US$7.5 million) at an auction house in Paris. See "African mask takes record $7.5 million at Paris auction, article in *USA Today*, 18 June 2006: http://usatoday30.usatoday.com/news/world /2006–06–18-african-mask_x.htm. Accessed 09/16/2013.

56 Griffon du Bellay, "Croisières à la côte d'Afrique (1861–1864)," *Le Tour du Monde: Nouveau Journal des Voyages*, vol. 12 (Paris: Librairie Hachette, 1865), 296–97, glossed over such motives: "One day, I bought for a few tobacco leaves one of these baroque figures one can find in every village, with a piece of glass encased in the chest, and feathers surrounding the head. The transaction was a long and difficult one, as the grotesque divinity, stuck at the extremity of a pole, was a great war-fetish whose many accomplishments had long proved its value. . . . It is easy to understand that the lucky owner of such a talisman hesitated to part with it. He finally relinquished it, but in no circumstances would have he sold it to a Black. He was ready to surrender an invincibility that I could not benefit from, but he would have consented to foolishly give up such a fortunate privilege to any black who could, one day, changed into an enemy."

57 See Gehne's photograph in Christaud M. Geary, "Photographic Practice in Africa and Its Implications for the Use of Historical Photographs as Contextual Evidence," in *Fotographia e storia dell'Africa*, ed. Alessandro Triulzi (Napoli, Istituto Universitario Orientale1995), 107 and 122.

58 Günther Tessman, 1913, quoted in Geary, "Photographic Practice," 107. Alisa Lagamma, "The Body Eternal: The Aesthetics of Equatorial African Reliquary Sculpture," in LaGamma, *Eternal Ancestors*, 101. For earlier refusals, see Du Chaillu's description of another failure to buy a "goddess" from King Damagondai of the Anenge people, in Du Chaillu, *Explorations and Adventures*, 239.

59 LaGamma, *Eternal Ancestors*, 128.

60 Perrois, *Arts du Gabon*, 286–87.

61 "Mission du Gabon," *Bulletin* CSSP, no. 150, July 1899, 115–16. Catholic missionaries also observed an intensifying of local worshiping in Sette Cama in 1910. "Communauté de St-Benoit-Labre à Ngalé (Sette Cama)," *Bulletin* CSSP tome 25, 278, April 1910, 477–78.

62 Procès-verbal d'interrogatoire no 770, 24 September 1955, affaire Moutsinga, ANG/Fonds provincial, Ndendé, 26, "Justice et commissions rogatoires."

63 Procès-verbal d'interrogatoire no. 278, 20 May 1957, affaire Nzaboule Belo, ANG/ Fonds provincial, Ndendé 16, "Justice et commissions rogatoires."

64 Daniel Bounje, an elderly Shamaye man living southeast of the town of Makokou, interview reproduced in Jean-Christophe Matimi, "Tradition et innovations
dans la construction de l'identité chez les Shamaye (Gabon) entre 1930 et 1990"
(PhD thesis, Université Laval, 1998), vii.

65 Interview with Mr. Diata, Mouila, June 2002.

66 "La défense magique," manuscript signed by Jérôme Adam (future bishop of
Gabon), n.d. (probably from the 1890s), Archives CSSP, 271-Dos. B-IV.

67 Letter from André Raponda-Walker, Sindara, 19 March 1934 to Mgr. Leroy,
Archives CSSP, 271-Dos B-IV. Leroy authored an influential study on the *Religion
of the Primitive Peoples* (1925).

68 "Communauté de Donghila," *Bulletin* CSSP, Tome 25, no. 275, January 1910, 398.

69 L. Lejeune, "Station St François à Lambaréné dans l'Ogooué," Annales CSSP,
1899, 55–57.

70 Monseigneur Carrie, quoted in Jean Delcourt, *Au Congo français, Monseigneur
Carrie, 1842–1904* (Pointe-Noire: Évêché, no date [1935?]), 433–34.

71 "Communauté de St Dominique à Bata," *Bulletin* CSSP, tome 18 (1896–1898), 502.

72 Jeanne-Françoise Vincent, "Le Mouvement Croix-Koma: Une nouvelle forme
de lutte contre la sorcellerie en pays Kongo," *Cahiers d'études africaines* 6, no. 24
(1966): 561. Cinnamon, "Ambivalent Power"; and Tonda, *La Guérison divine.*

73 Rapport du chef de district de Mouila-Ndendé au chef de région de la Ngounié,
no. 785, 22 September 1948, ANG/FP 101.

74 Rapport du chef de district de Mouila-Ndendé au chef de région de la Ngounié,
no. 785, 22 September 1948, ANG/FP 101. *Moulimfou* was possibly connected
with the first foray of Pentecostalism in Gabon, the *réveil* (revival) initiative
introduced in northern Gabon in 1935 by Swiss Protestant missionaries Gaston
Vernaud and Samuel Galley. Whenever they preached and blessed the converts,
Vernaud and Galley seemed to have observed a conventional reliance on the
vocabulary of fetishes, fetishism, and fetish-men (*féticheurs*). Preeminent in their
sermons was the Holy Spirit, rather than the Devil or witchcraft. André Perrier,
Gabon: Un réveil religieux, 1935–1937 (Paris: L'Harmattan, 1988).

75 Rapport du gouverneur du Gabon sur les sociétés secrètes, c. 1950, Archives
d'outre-mer 5D 64. Lettre du gouverneur du Gabon aux chefs de région, no. 262/
APS, 9 May 1950, ANG/FP 36. M.-O. Nkogho-Mve, from Mindili (Franceville),
"Djobi. Nouveau-né des fétiches du Haut-Ogooué," *Liaison*, no. 49–50 (1955):
52–54.

76 Matimi, "Tradition et innovations," 93 sqq.

77 Fernandez, *Bwiti*, 230–35. Three versions of the foundational myth of Mademoiselle exist in Gabon; see Tonda, *La Guérison divine*, 63–98. A branch of the movement spread around Makokou after Joseph Ndende witnessed a white woman
rising from water. She gave him a stick of ebony with a carved ivory cap, and
asked him to build a shrine to protect villages and to replace the "dirty bones"
people were keeping.

78 Circulaire du gouverneur du Gabon Yves Digo aux chefs de région et de district, no. 634 bis/AP, 12 July 1956, ANG Mitzic 2D J III-9–2. The report, however, explains that Mademoiselle belonged to a series of cleansing movements starting in the early 1940s: Koula from Kellé (1943), Mandoukou from Kellé (1945), Njobi from Franceville via Okondja (1950), and Dombakessa, which came from Kellé and suppressed Njobi, and was itself entirely destroyed by Mademoiselle in 1955.

79 In the Galoa language, people say "Go pangu'imounda"—to make the fetish (*imounda*) work, to activate it. The verb *go panga* means "to make," "to create," but it also has the simpler meaning "to work at a job." Lionel Ikogou-Renamy, personal communication, October 10, 2015. For a rich study of the meaning of *travail* (work/labor) in Gabon, see Guy Rossatanga-Rignault, *Le Travail du Blanc ne finit jamais: L'Africain, le temps et le travail moderne* (Libreville: Éditions Raponda-Walker, 2007).

80 Otto Gollnhofer, "Boduku: Ethno-histoire ghetsogho" (thèse de l'École Pratique des Hautes Études, Paris, 1967), 103. *Maghanga* included male and female initiation and therapeutic societies (Ya-Mwei and Boo), and the cult of ancestral relics (Bwete).

81 Among Fang speakers, people activate a charm (*biang*) with a specific taboo (*eki*) and with the fee given to obtain the medicine. Philippe Laburthe-Tolra, *Initiations et sociétés secrètes au Cameroun: Essai sur la religion bëti* (Paris: Karthala 1985), 139.

82 *Evu/kundu* can be translated today as witchcraft substance. For a detailed history, see chapter 4.

83 Achieved leadership means that a person does not inherit the quality from descent or institutions. Vansina, *Paths in the Rainforest*, 73. Correctly diagnosed, the affection compelled the patient to be initiated in the service of a divine entity, and become a specialized *nganga*.

84 Interview with Ta Mouketou, Cap Esterias, 30 June 2000.

85 The power of a *nganga* is always ambivalent and can be suspected to harm rather than to heal. To avoid the accusation of poisoning, Ta Mouketou told us he always drank a part of the potions and medicines he prescribed. For the same reason, he never kept patients in his home for more than a day. This way, he avoided rumors or accusations that he might have cursed or bewitched a person trusted to his care. Interview with Ta Mouketou, Cap Esterias, 30 June 2000.

86 Laburthe-Tolra, *Initiations*, 141. Ta Mouketou made us understand that he had not performed a special transaction with spirits and ancestors by sacrificing a relative.

87 Colonial texts often mentioned that experts (*nganga*) carefully shielded their knowledge from the curiosity of ordinary people. For instance; "Notes d'ethnologie: Le Ngo, société secrète du Haut Ogooué," unsigned, Fonds Pouchet, Archives CSSP, 2D 60 8a3; and Jacques Eckendorf, "Notes sur les coutumes bawanji," Fonds Pouchet, Archives CSSP, 2D 60 8a3.

88 Chapter 7 elaborates on white *puissance* and the fact that it comprises modern science and technology.

89 Conversation with Mme Njoni, Nombakele, Libreville, 23 June 2000.

90 Interview with Mme Marcelle, Quaben, Libreville, 19 June 2000.

91 In 2000, I listened to *C'est la Vie* for several days. Fieldwork, Libreville, Summer 2000.

92 Afrika, No 1, *C'est la Vie*, shows on 22 June 2000.

93 Nguéma-Ndong said that his grandfather, a reputable *nganga*, had spit some cola nuts on him when he was a baby. Although he did not use the term *bénédiction*, the anecdote suggested that he had received some special mystical talent with the blessing. Interview with Patrice Nguéma-Ndong, Libreville, 26 June 2000.

94 The term *tradi-praticiens* appeared in the 1990s; it means healers and doctors who practice their craft publicly, with the approval of the state.

95 Tonda, *La Guérison divine*.

96 On poisoners in colonial Libreville, see Jeremy Rich, *A Workman Is Worthy of his Meat: Food and Colonialism in the Gabon Estuary* (Lincoln: University of Nebraska Press, 2007), 31–33.

97 Only in the 1950s did administrators try to use French provisions on the "illegal practice of medicine" to contain the proliferation of healers and prophets. They failed to popularize the legal device in courts, however. Circulaire du gouverneur général de l'AEF sur la "médecine indigène," no. 104/AG, 1943, ANG/FP 525.

98 Alain Rey, *Dictionnaire historique de la langue française* (Paris: Dictionnaires Le Robert, 2000), 1:420.

99 Joseph Coignard, "Etudes sur les principaux fétiches et sociétés occultes du pays eshira, apinji, isogho," St-Martin de Mouila, Archives CSSP, Fonds Pouchet, 2D 60 9b4.

100 De Brosses, *Du culte des Dieux Fétiches*.

101 Catholic priests in Southern Gabon wrote that "pagan customs are falling into disuse" and "the most worshipped fetishes are starting to be ridiculed." "Ste Anne des Eschiras," *Bulletin* CSSP, no. 20–158, April 1900, 372; "Donguila," *Bulletin* CSSP, no. 24–244, June 1907, 191.

102 Brian Larkin, *Signal and Noise. Media, Infrastructure, and Urban Culture in Nigeria* (Durham, N.C.: Duke University Press), 6–9 and 39. Larkin does not look at the ways in which missionaries in southern Nigeria participated in the colonial sublime.

103 "Sette Cama," *Bulletin* CSSP, tome 16, 1891–1893, 479.

104 Robert H. Nassau, *Fetishism in West Africa: Forty Years' Observation of Native Customs and Superstitions* (London: Duckworth, 1904), 271.

105 Décret du 17 juillet 1944 instituant un code pénal indigène, *Journal officiel de l'Afrique équatoriale française* [Official journal of French Equatorial Africa] (hereinafter *JOAEF*), 15 October 1944, 800. In 1947, a decree defined again *charlatanisme* as a legal misdemeanor. Article 64, paragraph 9, in Décret No. 47–2248 du 19 novembre 1947 modifiant des articles du code pénal applicable en AEF, *JOAEF*,

15 December 1947, 1611–13. The 1936 decree on native justice listed the following crimes: intentional attacks against persons and against life; pillaging; arson; rape; kidnapping; poisoning of wells, cisterns, and springs; preparing and administrating poison ordeals; mutilation; slave trade; and anthropophagy; it did not include any mention of sorcery or witchcraft.

106 To my knowledge, *charlatan* first appeared in Gabonese writing in a 1955 article signed by M.-O. Nkogho-Mve (Franceville) in the monthly cultural journal *Liaison*, sponsored by the French colonial authorities. The author criticized the spreading of the Njobi cleansing movement in the Haut-Ogooué Province. "Nos charlatans," *Liaison*, no. 49–50 (1955): 54.

107 Fiche mensuelle d'activités, no. 10/CF, January 1962, signed Thomas Mouecoucou, ANG/Archives provinciales Ndendé, 14.

108 Because of these ideas, *sorcellerie* (witchcraft/sorcery) emerged in general colonial parlance only in the late 1920s. In the early 1950s, it still lagged far behind the repertoire of *fétichisme* (fetishism). Florence Bernault, "Witchcraft and the Colonial Life of the Fetish," in *Spirits in Politics: Uncertainties of Power and Healing in African Societies*, ed. Barbara Meier and Arne S. Steinforth (Frankfurt am Main: Campus Publishers, 2013), 53–74.

109 Bulletin de renseignements no 74 à gouverneur du Gabon, signé par le chef région du Haut Ogooué, 29 February 1948, ANG/FP 44. See also Florence Bernault, "De la modernité comme impuissance: Fétichisme et crise du politique en Afrique équatoriale et ailleurs," *Cahiers d'Études africaines*49–3, no. 195 (2009): 747–74.

110 Peter Worsley, *The Trumpet Shall Sound: A Study of "Cargo" Cults in Melanesia*, 3rd ed. 1957; New York: Schocken, 1968); and Arjun Appadurai, *The Social Life of Things: Commodities in Cultural Perspective* (Cambridge: Cambridge University Press, 1986), 51–52. For a metacritique of the notion, see Lamont Lindstrom, *Cargo Cult: Strange Stories of Desire from Melanesia and Beyond* (Honolulu: University of Hawai'i Press, 1993).

111 Robert H. Milligan, *Fetish Folk of West Africa* (1912; New York: AMS Press, 1970), 223. Yet neither colonial administrators nor missionaries provided free services to the Gabonese. Missionaries, in particular, charged a fee for procuring medicines and cures to the Gabonese. In 1893, a Catholic priest candidly explained, "The Blacks . . . find our medicine excellent. One advantage is that can be afforded by most. Meanwhile, the *nganga* sell their ruckus for a 'piece,' that is $20 worth of fine cloth." "Sette Cama," Bulletin CSSP, tome 16, 1891–93, 481.

112 "Instructions aux chefs de quartier sur la population flottante, les féticheurs et les mpindis," du chef de quartier Félix Rapontchombo, Glass, 18 January 1943, ANG/ FP, 1634.

113 In 1952, the tribunal of the Seine Department in France sentenced him to two years in prison and a large fine. Circulaire du gouverneur du Gabon, no. 1621, signed Y. Digo, 12 December 1953, ANG/FP 36.

114 Ruchpaul's most expensive items were lucky wristwatches (5,900 francs) and special talismans to protect against evil attacks (up to 12,000 francs). Lucky

charms cost only 150 francs. Extrait des minutes du Greffe du Tribunal de première instance du Département de la Seine, Paris, 2 February 1952, ANG/FP 36.

115 Order form from Mme Arika, 24 March 1954, ANG/FP 36. Lettre du Procureur
de la République près le tribunal de première instance de Port-Gentil au Gouverneur du Gabon, no. 21/C/53, signed J. Fouquet, 20 February 1953, ANG/FP 36.

116 In the 1950s, for instance, a "Professor Salomon" based in Port-Gentil was sending numerous advertising letters and dozens of packets by the post, prompting
the governor general to lament the "gullibility" of the Gabonese. Lettre du
procureur de la République à Port Gentil, no. 21/C/53, signed J. Fouquet, 20
February 1953; circulaire du gouverneur général de l'AEF sur la lutte contre le
charlatanisme, no. 1725/API, 13 October 1953, ANG/FP 36; circulaire du gouverneur du Gabon sur la lutte contre le charlatanisme, no. 1621/AP.AG. AS, 12
December 1953, ANG/FP 36; rapport politique de Fougamou, 1953, signed F.
Barbus, 11 January 1954, AGN/FP 35. These reports were likely prompted by a
1953 *circulaire* from the French minister of the colonies who encouraged administrators in Gabon to try and curb the influence of magicians. He recommended
that French civil authorities scrutinize the mail and organized lectures to educate
the Gabonese public on the nefarious effects of such commerce in magic. Lettre
du Governeur général de l'AEF aux gouverneurs des colonies, no. 1725/API, 13
October 1953, and Circulaire, Ministère de la France d'outre-mer, no. 6631, October 1953, ANG/FP 36.

117 John Janzen has documented in the Kongo region in the 1960s how crazy spells
were often interpreted as an illness following the purchase and use of powerful
fetishes (*minkisi*) without observing the correct prescriptions. People said that
the fetishes had "burned the fingers" of the careless user. A young man who
wanted to transform into a French-speaking white Belgian man had ordered
medicine from France and became mad. He was cured by throwing all his European possessions into the river before the ancestors. Janzen and Arkinstall, *Quest
for Therapy*, 182–83. On more recent incidents with defective biopharmaceutical
drugs ordered online, see Patrice Yengo, "Médicaments, pratique de soin, lien
social. La question de la médicalité en Afrique centrale," unpublished research
project, 2010. Author's archives.

118 Fernandez, *Bwiti*, 215 sqq.

119 Interview with Raphaël Tsande, Mouila, 6 June 2002. *Maboulisme* comes from
the French slang *maboule* or *maboul*, "crazy."

120 This is in the vein of Wyatt MacGaffey's idea that charms and medicines can
work properly if used only in an agentive chain of rituals managed by a *nganga*.
MacGaffey, "Aesthetics."

121 Fieldwork, Libreville, 19 June 2000.

122 According to Joseph Tonda, in Gabon and in Congo-Brazzaville, the word
médicament means a biomedical drug as well as poison, and a "fetish," in other
words, any product of nature or society that is invested with an extraordinary

power." Joseph Tonda, *Le Souverain moderne: Le Corps du pouvoir en Afrique centrale (Congo, Gabon)* (Paris: Karthala, 2005), 143 and 167.

123 Janzen and Arkinstall, *Quest for Therapy.*

CHAPTER 3 ⁏ Carnal Fetishism

1 For references on ritual murders and organ trafficking in Africa, see footnote 99 and 101.

2 On the fetish as a composite assemblage of contradictory values, see Giorgio Agamben, *Homo Sacer: Sovereign Power and Bare Life* (Stanford, CA: Stanford University Press, 1998), 99. In a colonial context, see Anne McClintock, *Imperial Leather: Race, Gender, and Sexuality in the Colonial Contest* (New York: Routledge, 1995), 217.

3 For pioneering analyses on death and graves as a colonial battleground, see Achille Mbembe, *La Naissance du maquis dans le Sud-Cameroun* (Paris: Karthala, 1996), 1–36; Filip De Boeck, "Beyond the Grave: History, Memory and Death in Postcolonial Congo/Zaire," in *Memory and the Postcolony: African Anthropology and the Critique of Power,* ed. Richard Werbner (London: Zed Books, 1998); and Sandra Greene, *Sacred Sites: A History of Meaning and Memory in Ghana* (Bloomington, Indiana University Press, 2002).

4 Fleuriot de Langle, "Croisières à la côte d'Afrique (1868)," *Le Tour du Monde: Nouveau Journal des Voyages,* vol. 31 (Paris: Librairie Hachette, 1876), 275.

5 Paul Du Chaillu, *A Journey to Ashango-Land: And Further Penetration into Equatorial Africa* (New York: D. Appleton, 1867), 31, 132, and 321. P. Payeur-Didelot, *Trente mois au continent mystérieux: Gabon-Congo et côte occidentale d'Afrique* (Paris: Berger-Levrault, 189), 127, 139–40, 151, 160.

6 Philippe Ariès, *Western Attitudes towards Death: From the Middle Ages to the Present* (Baltimore, Md.: Johns Hopkins University Press, 1974), 85–88.

7 Ariès, *Western Attitudes,* 101.

8 Terence Ranger, "Taking Hold of the Land: Holy Places and Pilgrimages in Twentieth Century Zimbabwe," *Past and Present,* no. 117 (1987): 158–94; Florence Bernault, "Colonial Bones: The 2006 Burial of Savorgnan De Brazza," *African Affairs* 109 (July 2010): 367–90.

9 Extraits du journal de la Mission St Martin des Apindjis, Père Guyader, 10 December 1904, Archives CSSP, Fonds Pouchet, 2D60–6–2. To my knowledge, this was the last episode that Europeans discussed of Africans cannibalizing a white person.

10 Lettre du chef de circonscription Rousselot, no. 70, 20 July 1910, Sette Cama. ANG/FP, 551.

11 Rapport de tournée de l'Adjudant-Chef Chèvre dans la circonscription de la Karagoua-Koudou (Djouah), no. 12, 10 September 1920, ANG/FP 878.

12 Cornelius Castoriadis, *The Imaginary Institution of Society* (Cambridge: Polity, 1987).

13 In the seventeenth century, Loango chiefs forbade the burial of white foreigners in their sacred grounds because they saw them as witches, an anecdote that confirmed indigenous ideas about the magic power of white flesh. Andrew Battell et al., *The Strange Adventures of Andrew Battell of Leigh, in Angola and the Adjoining Regions* (1625) (London: Hakluyt Society, 1901), 51.

14 "Sainte-Marie du Gabon," *Bulletin* CSSP 14, July 1885–December 1887, 385. The governor of Gabon adopted a series of decrees in 1881, 1887, 1900, and 1903 based on a French law voted in 1881.

15 Arrêté du gouverneur du Gabon, August 1910, ANG/FP 551.

16 Circulaire du gouverneur général du Gabon Guyon aux chefs de circonscription sur la détermination des emplacements de cimetières, no. 49, 11 April 1916, ANG/FP, 551.

17 Chef de Circonscription de l'Okano, Avis à la population, 14 August 1916, ANG/FP 551. Circulaire du gouverneur général du Gabon Guyon aux chefs de circonscription sur la détermination des emplacements de cimetières, no. 49, 11 April 1916, ANG/FP, 551. A *commodo et incommodo* investigation summarizes the practicality and impracticalities of a project.

18 Lettre du chef de la circonscription de Bongo au gouverneur du Gabon, 20 March 1916, no. 155, ANG/FP 551.

19 Rapport du chef de la région des Adoumas sur la création de deux cimetières à Koula Moutou, no. 88, 29 December 1949, ANG/FP 1790.

20 The failure to bury people in official cemeteries was sanctioned by a maximum of fifteen days in prison and a one-hundred-franc fine. Décret du 31 mai 1910 portant règlement sur l'indigénat en Afrique équatoriale française, and Arrêté déterminant les infractions spéciales à l'indigénat, article 21, *Journal officiel de l'Afrique equatoriale française* [Official journal of French Equatorial Africa] (hereinafter JOAEF), 1910, 377–78 and 485.

21 Some colonial administrators seemed to tolerate a standard, two-day exposition of the corpse. Procès-verbal d'enregistrement de plainte, affaire Djibo-Bouéza, circonscription du Djouah, 11 May 1942, ANG/FP, 629.

22 In nineteenth-century Gabon, burial techniques generally displayed the status of the deceased: the graveyards for powerful and wealthy people differed from those of commoners. Children and important family members were customarily buried next to the household. Members of founding clans were usually buried in the village they created, thus sustaining later claims over land. See Paul Du Chaillu, *Voyages et aventures dans l'Afrique équatoriale: Moeurs et coutumes des habitants, chasses au gorille, au crocodiles, au léopard, à l'éléphant, à l'hippopotame, etc., etc.* (Paris: M. Lévy frères, 1863), 90–91; Abbé Walker, "Les cimetières de famille au Gabon," undated manusc., Archives CSSP, Fonds Pouchet, 2D 60–14-A3; and François Gaulme, *Le Pays de Cama: Un Ancien état côtier du Gabon et ses origines* (Paris: Karthala, 1981), 214.

23 Décret relatif à la répression de l'anthropophagie en Afrique occidentale et en Afrique équatoriale française, JOAEF, 15 June 1923, ANG/FP 629. I examine the law in further details in chapter 6.

24 André Raponda-Walker and Roger Sillans, *Rites et croyances des peuples du Gabon: Essai sur les pratiques religieuses d'autrefois et d'aujourd'hui* (Paris: Présence africaine, 1983), 115–21. Although no reliable statistics exist on the frequency of ritual autopsies during the colonial period in Equatorial Africa, Jean-Pierre Warnier and Matthieu Salpêteur have recently documented the revival of ritual autopsies in Cameroon; Matthieu Salpêteur and Jean-Pierre Warnier, "Looking for the Effects of Bodily Organs and Substances through Vernacular Public Autopsy in Cameroon," *Critical African Studies* 5, no. 3 (2013): 154–73.

25 For instance, télégramme-lettre du chef de la région Haut-Ogooué, Franceville, 6 February 1948, ANG/FP, 44.

26 Rapport sur la situation politique, Minvoul, 1938, unsigned, ANG/FP 213.

27 Joseph Ambouroué-Avaro, *Un Peuple gabonais à l'aube de la colonisation: Le Bas-Ogowe au XIXe siècle* (Paris: Karthala, 1981), 23.

28 Ambouroué-Avaro, *Un Peuple gabonais*, 71 and 93. *Ngul* is often called *puissance* today. On this latter concept, see chapter 2.

29 Ambouroué-Avaro, *Un Peuple gabonais*, is the prime inspiration for this idea.

30 I borrow the expression "shady body" from the French rendering of the Fang word *nsisim* as *"ombre,"* or *"part ombreuse"* in Philippe Laburthe-Tolra, *Initiations et sociétés secrètes au Cameroun: Essai sur la religion bëti* (Paris: Karthala, 1985), 45 and 53. West Equatorial Africans' beliefs in multiple bodies are rich and diverse, and cannot be summarized under a single formula.

31 In the 2000s, informants told me that one could recognize "shady-" or "witch-bodies" because they were naked and never clothed. They also avoided light and other objects associated with human civilization. Interview with Paul Mba Aubame, Libreville, 20 July 2000. With the exception of scholars and social scientists at the Université Omar Bongo Onbimba (hereinafter UOB) in Libreville, and Father Zacharie Péron (now deceased), I use pseudonyms for all my informants.

32 Email conversation with Lionel Ikogou-Renamy, 11 November 2015. To talk about a witch, Galoa speakers use either *olovalovi* or *ognyèmba*.

33 In Europe, by contrast, the body had been rendered ontologically inert and physically univocal. The use of a single term, "body" (French: *corps*), to talk about an organism indiscriminately before and after death illustrated this narrowing. In turn, the word "body" gives a reducing image of the ways in which Bantu languages described different aspects or phases in the life of a person. Among the Fang, for instance, the living body was called *nyól*, and the cadaver *mbim*. Often, the Fang would call the cadaver *mod*, or "man," avoiding the connotation of "animal carcass" contained in the term *mbim*. If a dead person had been consecrated as an ancestor, the Fang would also call his or her body *ebembe* (ancestor). Laburthe-Tolra, *Initiations*, 45; and Victor Largeau, *Encyclopédie pahouine, Congo français: Éléments de grammaire et dictionnaire français-pahouin* (Paris: E. Leroux, 1901), 149–50. South of Gabon, Kongo speakers at the beginning of the twentieth century used several terms to define the composite parts of the body, such

as *vuvudi* (the shell), *mvumbi* (the invisible part of the person), *kivumunu* (the life-giving organ) *mwela* (the breath), *mooyo* (life or belly), *peeve* (spirit or wind), *nsala* (the principle of life). Karl Laman, *The Kongo* (Uppsala, Sweden: Almqvist & Wiksell), 1962, 3:1–6. See also Albert Doutreloux, *L'Ombre des fétiches: Société et culture yombe* (Louvain: Nauwelaerts, 1967), 234–38; and Simon Bockie, *Death and the Invisible Powers: The World of Kongo Belief* (Bloomington: Indiana University Press, 1993), 129–30.

34 In Fang, *evus* (also *evu, evur, ngwel*) means "life force" and "witch-substance." The word was probably a recent innovation formed from the Fang term for the second stomach of ruminants, **-pù* (Jan Vasina, personal communication, 12 April 2007). For description of modern beliefs in *evus*, see Laburthe-Tolra, *Initiations*, 59–121. In other Gabonese languages, the witch-substance was called *inyamba* (oMyènè), *likundu, dikundu* (Masango, Gisir, Balumbu, iPunu, iVili), all three formed from the proto-Bantu roots **-jemba* and **-kundú*, this second root meaning "stomach." For distribution, see Jan Vansina, *Paths in the Rainforests: Toward a History of Political Tradition in Equatorial Africa* (Madison: University of Wisconsin Press, 1990), 299–300. Precolonial equatorial societies also possessed a practical and detailed knowledge of the body and its organic functions.

35 James Fernandez explains the "circularity" of the witch-substance among the Fang: if *evu* was considered as an agent of men's intention, men's intentions were also believed to be a consequence of the nature of their *evu*. He also qualifies the witch-substance as a way for the Fang of representing to themselves hidden or uncertain aspects of capacity. James Fernandez, *Bwiti: An Ethnography of the Religious Imagination in Africa* (Princeton, NJ: Princeton University Press, 1982), 210–14 and 220–21. I do not have room to explore the diverse and complex angles pertaining to the relationship between the notion of "person" and "body," nor gendered ideas about *evus*.

36 However, many societies believed that the witch-substance could grow again and that its invisible "root" never left the body.

37 Laburthe-Tolra, *Initiations*, 62–63, warns that one should not oppose social and antisocial *evus* in a simplistic way.

38 Vansina, *Paths*, 97. On the power of death common to chiefs and witches, and *kundu* as witch-substance, see Wyatt MacGaffey, "The Religious Commissions of the Bakongo," *Man* 5, no. 1 (March 1970): 27–38, particularly 30–34; and Laburthe-Tolra, *Initiations*, 162–63.

39 They could also decipher traces of witch attacks in the victim's body after death: a ritual autopsy found traces of internal wounds inflicted by the witch. On ritual autopsies in contemporary Cameroon, see Salpêteur and Warnier, "Looking."

40 Georges Dupré described the burning and dispersal of the bones of a criminal in the late 1960s among the Beembé in Congo-Brazzaville, in *Les Naissances d'une société espace et historicité chez les Beembé du Congo* (Paris: Éditions de l'ORSTOM, 1985), 89.

41 Günther Tessman, *Die Pangwe*, French translation in Philippe Laburthe-Tolra and Christiane Falgayrettes-Leveau, *Fang* (Paris: Musée Dapper, 1991), 240.

42 The emergence of Christian relics in Late Antiquity derived from similar imaginaries. Peter Brown, *The Cult of the Saints: Its Rise and Function in Latin Christianity* (Chicago, IL: University of Chicago Press, 1981).

43 On Christian (mis)interpretations of indigenous ideas of shady and mystical bodies as "soul," see, for instance, how Raponda-Walker and Sillans describe ancestors as "disembodied souls" (*âmes désincarnées*); Raponda-Walker and Sillans, *Rites*, 2. The confusion came perhaps from Christianized African informants trying to fit their worldviews into European categories.

44 Wyatt MacGaffey, *Kongo Political Culture: The Conceptual Challenge of the Particular* (Bloomington: Indiana University Press, 2000).

45 The cult of ancestors helped to create social hierarchies among male elders. For a broadly applicable example in Fang societies in the twentieth century, see Georges Balandier, *Sociology of Black Africa: Social Dynamics in Central Africa* (New York: Praeger Publishers, 1970), 205.

46 Laburthe-Tolra, *Initiations*, 339.

47 "Invocation of the fetishes among the Duma people," drawing by Edouard Riou based on a sketch by Jacques de Brazza between Madiville-Lastoursville and Masuku-Franceville, around 1883. Jacques accompanied his brother Pierre on his third expedition to central Africa. Published in Pierre Savorgnan de Brazza, "Voyages dans l'Ouest Africain." *Le Tour du Monde: Nouveau journal des voyages* 54, no. 1402 (1887): 329. Also available in the James J. Ross Archives of African Images, Yale University, no. 1608. Among the Kota, relics were often kept in a net hanging in the clan leader's house, as explained by Louis Perrois, *Arts du Gabon: Les Arts plastiques du bassin de l'Ogooué* (Paris: Éditions de l'ORSTOM, 1979), 142.

48 For instance, *bekon* in Fang means both "relics" and "ancestors." Relics were also used to empower the sacred compounds and enclosures of initiation societies. *Bwiti* experts buried the skulls of powerful initiates under the main pillar of new *bwiti* chapels, while members of the female initiation society Njembe buried the remains of powerful women in their sacred compound. Raponda-Walker and Sillans, *Rites*, 153–54.

49 Tessman, *Die Pangwe*, 284–85.

50 On contagion, see Laburthe-Tolra, *Initiations*, 197; the Fang-Bëti cleansed the community by charging the cadaver with all its impurities. The same fear of contagion explains that autopsies were sometimes performed by slaves and outcasts. "Cimetières mpongwés," unsigned notes, Archives CSSP, Fonds Pouchet, 2D60–8B6.

51 The slave trade fueled considerable African rumors about white cannibals and witches who used the body of captives for processing commodities such as cheese, gunpowder, and textiles. Among many studies, see Rosalind Shaw, "The Production of Witchcraft/Witchcraft as Production: Memory, Modernity and

the Slave Trade in Sierra Leone," *American Ethnologist* 24, no. 4 (1996): 856–76; and John Thornton, "Cannibals, Witches, and Slave Traders in the Atlantic World," *William and Mary Quarterly* 60, no. 2 (2003): 273–94. On accusations of witchcraft against leaders and *nganga*, see Tessman, *Die Pangwe*, 285 and 295; Laburthe-Tolra, *Initiations*, 339 and 354; and Philippe Laburthe-Tolra, *Les Seigneurs de la forêt: Essai sur le passé historique, l'organisation sociale et les normes éthiques des anciens Bëti du Cameroun* (Paris: Karthala, 1981), 340–42.

52 Yet the very term "sacrifice" often obscures this reality, as it comes from a Western tradition powerfully informed by Christian images of destruction, especially when applied to non-Christian societies. Luc de Heusch, *Sacrifice in Africa: A Structuralist Approach* (Manchester, UK: Manchester University Press, 1985).

53 Joseph Tonda, personal communication, 27 October 2015.

54 Peter Geschiere, *The Modernity of Witchcraft: Politics and the Occult in Postcolonial Africa* (Charlottesville: University Press of Virginia, 1997), 65.

55 Laburthe-Tolra, *Initiations*, 111–21, reports anecdotes on the "extraordinary cruelty" (*méchanceté extraordinaire*) of "murderous leaders" (chefs assassins) and "criminal healers" (*guérisseurs criminels*) among the Fang-Bëti.

56 Mikhail Bakhtin, *Rabelais and His World* (Bloomington: Indiana University Press, 1984), 18–19. See also Ernst Kantorowicz, *The King's Two Bodies: A Study in Medieval Political Theology* (Princeton, NJ: Princeton University Press, 1957); and Carolyn Walker Bynum, *The Resurrection of the Body in Western Christianity, 200–1336* (New York: Columbia University Press, 1995).

57 Michel Foucault, *Naissance de la clinique: Une Archéologie du regard médical* (1963) (Paris: Presses Universitaires de France, 2009); Brian S. Turner, *The Body and Society: Explorations in Social Theory* (Thousand Oaks, CA: Sage Publications, 1996), 36, and 55–56; and David Le Breton, *Anthropologie du corps et modernité*, 2nd ed. (Paris: Presses universitaires de France, 2001). On how Christian missionaries partook in medical and secular views of the body, see Jean Comaroff and John Comaroff, *Of Revelation and Revolution* (Chicago, IL: University of Chicago Press, 1997), 1:252.

58 Antoine de Baecque, *The Body Politic: Corporeal Metaphor in Revolutionary France* (Stanford, CA: Stanford University Press, 1993).

59 Pierre Bourdieu, *Distinction: A Social Critique of the Judgment of Taste* (Cambridge, MA: Harvard University Press, 1984); and Marcel Mauss, "Techniques of the Body," *Economy and Society* 2, no. 1 (1973): 70–88.

60 Michel Foucault, *Discipline and Punish: The Birth of the Prison* (New York, Vintage Books, 1979); and Michel Foucault, "*Il faut défendre la société*": *Cours au Collège de France (1975–1976)* (Paris: Seuil/Gallimard, 1997), 213–35.

61 On similar ideas, see the recent work of Joseph Tonda, *L'Impérialisme postcolonial: Critique de la société des éblouissements* (Paris: Karthala, 2015).

62 Xavier Frass, "Monographie de la Côte-Nord du Gabon," 1908, 12, ANG/FP 3788.

63 Du Chaillu, *Journey to Ashango-Land*, 436.

64 Résumés des rapports mensuels, Franceville, November–December 1911, ANG/
FP, 48. Xavier Frass, "Monographie de la Cote-Nord du Gabon," 1908, 12, ANG/
FP, 4015. Monsignor Augouard, "L'anthropophagie dans le bassin de l'Oubanghi,"
Annales apostoliques de la Congrégation du Saint-Esprit (July 1890), 97–98, argued
that the continuous presence of Europeans led to the decline of anthropophagy
as the natives became "ashamed" of their cannibal practices.

65 Soeur Marie Germaine and Louis Marin, *Le Christ au Gabon* (Louvain: Museum
Lessianum, 1931), 114. Homi Bhabha has famously analyzed mimicry as a colonial
paradox that prescribed Africans to imitate colonizers at the same time as it se-
cured an irreparable difference between rulers and ruled ("not quite, not white").
Yet it also served as a weapon for the colonized, who could return the gaze of
the colonialists and shatter their unity. Homi K. Bhabha, "Of Mimicry and Man:
The Ambivalence of Colonial Discourse," in *The Location of Culture* (London:
Routledge, 1994), 85–92.

66 Interview with Father Zacharie Péron, Mouila, 6 June 2002. I have found a single
mention of saintly relics in Gabon, in May 1955, in the Catholic mission at Oyem,
where the local priests installed some bones of Thérèse of Lisieux in a new
church dedicated to the saint. Martin Ndong, "Consécration de l'Église Sainte-
Thérèse d'Oyem," *Semaine de l'AEF*, no. 142, 21 May 1955, 2.

67 Lettre pastorale de son Excellence Monseigneur le Vicaire apostolique sur le
fétichisme, Carême 1952. Archives CSSP, 4J1–6b4.

68 The bishop wrote that Christian relics were venerated as signs and symbols but
had no power of their own. In life, the body of the saints had been "the temples
of the Holy Spirit and would resuscitate on Judgment Day. . . . We show them to
God so He, in memory of the love of Saints, can answer the prayers of the faithful." Lettre pastorale de son Excellence Monseigneur le Vicaire apostolique sue le
fétichisme, Carême 1952, Archives CSSP, 4J1–6b4.

69 Lettre à l'administrateur du poste de Mossaka, Moyen-Congo, no. 1712, 2
May 1917, n.s. Archives d'outre-mer, Aix en Provence, 5D33.

70 Catherine Coquery-Vidrovitch, *Le Congo au temps des grandes compagnies concessionnaires, 1898–1930* (Paris: La Haye, Mouton, 1972), 78–82.

71 Including my own *History of Prisons and Confinement in Africa* (Portsmouth, NJ:
Heinemann, 2003).

72 The Maloundou case is part of a series, preserved in the national archives of
Gabon of thirty-five trials ending in the death penalty between 1912 and 1945.
In case of death penalty, a higher court in Brazzaville needed to confirm the
sentence of any tribunal in the colonies of French Equatorial Africa.

73 Procès-verbal d'exécution de Maloundou Ma I Biatsi, signed by Yvan Larrieu,
chef de la subdivision de Mouila, 14 January 1931, and lettre du bureau des affaires
civiles à chef de la subdivision de Mouila, nb 563, 9 February 1931, ANG/FP, 699.
The report does not mention Maloundou's crime.

74 This was a usual provision at the time. Arrêté fixant les règles d'application du Décret du 22 juillet 1939 qui supprime la publicité des exécutions capitales, no. 688/AP, 26 February 1940, ANG/FP 699.

75 Colonial legislation on death penalty provided that the corpse should not be given to the family but be immediately buried in official grounds. Article 52 du Décret portant règlement sur le service de place, 7 October 1909, and circulaire du gouverneur général de l'AEF sur les exécutions capitales, July 16, 1931, ANG/FP, 699.

76 Rapport sur l'assassinat de Mme Pierre Izac à Nkogo, signed by administrator Boutin, 18 December 1917, and Télégramme officiel au gouverneur général du Gabon, signed by Thomann, 15 December 1917, ANG/FP, 1696.

77 In 1917, international opinion was aware that private militias and colonial troops had cut off the hands of Africans in the Belgian Congo. Coquery-Vidrovitch, *Le Congo*; and Adam Hochschild, *King Leopold's Ghost: A Story of Greed, Terror, and Heroism in Colonial Africa*, 1st Mariner Books ed. (Boston, MA: Houghton Mifflin, 1999).

78 Likewise, in Joseph Conrad's 1899 masterpiece, *Heart of Darkness* (New York: Norton, 1988), commercial agent Kurtz creates a kingdom in the rainforest where he engages in slave trading and, to civilize the natives, kills and beheads them.

79 Rapport sur l'assassinat de Mme Pierre Izac à Nkogo, signed by administrator Boutin, 18 December 1917, and télégramme officiel au gouverneur général du Gabon, signed by Thomann, December 14, 1917, ANG/FP, 1696.

80 Jean-François Bayart and Romain Bertrand coined the term "hegemonic transactions" (*transactions hégémoniques*) in "De quel 'legs colonial' parle-t-on?," *Esprit* 12, no. 330 (2006): 154–60.

81 Colonial texts documented the point until late in the 1950s. See, for instance, Georges A. Heuse, "La Psychologie des Noirs africains," *Liaison* (published in Brazzaville), no. 56 (March–April 1957): "White rulers must be frank. They should tell the Blacks that they want to exploit the riches of African land because they need them and Blacks do not have the psycho-technical abilities or the technical means to do it. But in return, [the white ruler] must . . . compensate largely the Black for his work, secure his food and health, respect his traditions and his entire personality, give him a choice between self-government and participation to a European Union, or a total autonomy" (27).

82 Payeur-Didelot, *Trente mois*, 53 and 355.

83 Report on the economy of Gabon signed by E. Drogue, director of the Agricultural Services of French Equatorial Africa, 9 April 1948, ANG/FP 521/AGR.

84 Conrad sailed up the Congo River for the British Merchant Navy in 1890. The novella *An Outpost of Progress* appeared in a volume of short stories titled *Tales of Unrest* (London: T. Fisher Unwin, 1898). Conrad later described the novella as "the lightest part of the loot I carried off from Central Africa, the main portion being of course 'The Heart of Darkness.' Other men have found a lot of quite dif-

ferent things there and I have the comfortable conviction that what I took would not have been of much use to anybody else. And it must be said that it was but a very small amount of plunder. All of it could go into one's breast pocket when folded neatly. As for the story itself it is true enough in its essentials. The sustained invention of a really telling lie demands a talent I do not possess." Author's note in Joseph Conrad, *Tales of Unrest* (Garden City, NY: Doubleday, Page, 1923).

85 Georges Simenon, *Le Coup de lune: Roman inédit* (Paris: A. Fayard, 1933).

86 Simenon, *Le Coup de lune*, 37.

87 On colonial fear of disease, contamination, and miscegenation, see Philip Curtin, "Medical Knowledge and Urban Planning in Colonial Tropical Africa," *American Historical Review* 90, no. 3 (1985): 594–613; and Ann Laura Stoler, "Sexual Affronts and Racial Frontiers: European Identities and the Cultural Politics of Exclusion in Colonial Southeast Asia," *Comparative Studies in Society and History* 34, no. 3 (1992): 514–51.

88 Marcel Rondet-Saint, preface to Maurice Rondet-Saint, *L'Afrique équatoriale française* (Paris: Plon-Nourrit, 1911), 1. In 1875, the Marquis de Compiègne quoted "L'Afrique nécrologique," a list published in the *Bulletin of Geographical Society* that compiled the "martyrs of science" who scattered (*jalonner*) with their cadavers the road they traced in Africa." Louis-Alphonse-Victor du Pont de Compiègne, *L'Afrique équatoriale: Okanda, Bangouens, Osyéba* (Paris: Plon, 1875), 284. The theme continued to animate colonial debates at the peak of the colonial period. In 1938, a fellow senator celebrated the "vibrant soul," the "heroic faith and the sacrifice of our explorers and soldiers in French Equatorial Africa." Lucien Hubert, preface to Georges Bruel, *L'Afrique Équatoriale Française (A.E.F.)* (Paris: Larose, 1930), 2.

89 For instance, Robert Milligan, *The Fetish Folk of West Africa* (1912; New York: AMS Press, 1970), 18–20; Alexandre Le Roy, *La Religion des primitifs.* 5th ed. Paris: G. Beauchesne, 1925, 306; Georges Renouard, *L'Ouest africain et les Missions Catholiques: Congo et Oubanghi* (Paris: H. Oudin, 1904), 181; Jean Dybowski, *Le Congo méconnu* (Paris: Librairie Hachette, 1912), 44; and Henri Trilles, *Mille Lieux dans l'inconnu: En Pleine forêt équatoriale: Chez les Fang anthropophages* (Bruges: Librairie de l'Œuvre Saint-Charles, 1935), 135.

90 Dybowski, *Le Congo méconnu*, 44.

91 Schweitzer's career was recognized in 1952 when he won the Nobel Peace Prize.

92 Marcel Mauss and Henri Hubert theorized the formula in 1898, basing their demonstration both in non-Western and in Christian examples. Henri Hubert and Marcel Mauss, *Sacrifice: Its Nature and Function* (London: Cohen & West, 1964).

93 Joseph Tonda, *Souverain moderne: Le Corps du pouvoir en Afrique centrale (Congo, Gabon)* (Paris: Karthala, 2005), 134–36.

94 Délicat Chérubin, "La Mission catholique de Mayumba" (master's thesis, UOB, Libreville, 1984), 119. On the traffic of relics in medieval Europe, see Patrick Geary, *Furta Sacra: Thefts of Relics in the Central Middle Ages* (Princeton, N. J.: Princeton University Press, 1990), and his chapter "Sacred Commodities: The

Circulation of Medieval Relics," in Arjun Appadurai, ed., *The Social Life of Things: Commodities in Cultural Perspective* (Cambridge: Cambridge University Press, 1986), 169–91.

95 I examine these episodes in more details in chapter 6.

96 Interview in Eric Gilles Dibady Mandendi, "Stations missionaires et postes administratifs dans la Ngounié nord (1850–1959)" (Master's thesis, UOB, Libreville, 1991), 164.

97 In the 1960s, for example, an uninitiated Bëti denounced that members of the Melan, a secret society traditionally in charge of protecting the community through the cult of the dead, had stolen the buried corpses of his parents. Laburthe-Tolra, *Initiations*, 348–49.

98 The dustcarts of SOVOG, the Libreville company in charge of garbage collection, came to discharge their products.

99 Lionel Cédrick Ikogou-Renamy, "L'Or blanc: Le Marché occulte et illégal du corps humain à Libreville" (PhD thesis, UOB, Libreville, 2014).

100 Usually several hundred thousand francs XFA. Ikogou-Renamy, "L'Or blanc."

101 Fieldwork, 1998–2012. For historical approaches to ritual murders, see Colin Murray and Peter Sanders, *Medicine Murder in Colonial Lesotho: The Anatomy of a Moral Crisis* (Edinburgh: Edinburgh University Press, 2005); and David Pratten, *The Man-Leopard Murders: History and Society in Colonial Nigeria* (Bloomington: Indiana University Press, 2007).

102 "Ritual" here is a double misnomer: instead of a sanctioned rite performed by trusted experts, it defines here an immoral, outdated, and evil fetish ceremony and crime contrasting with Christianity.

103 *Commanditaire* in French shares significant etymology with *commandant*, the local French-Gabonese term for district officers and, beyond, for all French colonialists. For a general discussion on *commandement* as a postcolonial mode of governance in Equatorial Africa, see Achille Mbembe, *On the Postcolony* (Berkeley: University of California Press, 2001), 24–61.

104 See a description by Jean Elvis Ebang Ondo, president of the Association against Ritual Crimes (Association de lutte contre les crimes rituels, ALCR), Discourse in Geneva, 13 March 2013, accessed 4 June 2014, http://partenia2000.over-blog .com/article-les-crimes-rituels-au-gabon-l-alcr-a-geneve-116113711.html.

105 Florence Bernault, "Carnal Technologies and the Double Life of the Body in Gabon," *Critical African Studies* 5, no. 3 (2013): 175–94.

CHAPTER 4 ⁑ The Value of People

1 "Au Gabon, c'est l'argent . . . Donne-moi l'argent!" Discussion with Elise Ekang-Mve, Lambaréné, 27 June 2007. I use pseudonyms for the names of all informants with the exception of academic and public figures.

2 *Bouffer* is an old slang term in metropolitan French that can be translated as "to grub." In Gabon, however, *bouffer* has the narrower meaning of eating money.

"Here, everybody grubs around" (*Ici, tout le monde bouffe*), truck driver Moham-med Tall told me on the road to Mouila, 26 June 2007, as we were chatting about local corruption.

3   Jean Comaroff and John Comaroff, "Occult Economies and the Violence of Abstraction: Notes from the South African Postcolony," *American Ethnologist* 26, no. 2 (May 1999): 279–303; Nancy Scheper-Hughes, "The Global Traffic in Human Organs," *Current Anthropology* 41, no. 2 (April 2000): 191–224; Isak Niehaus, "Coins for Blood and Blood for Coins: From Sacrifice to Ritual Murder in the South African Lowveld," *Etnofoor* 13, no. 2 (2000): 31–54; Nancy Scheper-Hughes and Loïc Wacquant, eds., *Commodifying Bodies* (Thousand Oaks, CA: Sage Publications, 2002); Lesley Sharp, *Strange Harvest: Organ Transplants, Denatured Bodies, and the Transformed Self* (Berkeley: University of California Press, 2006).

4   Jonathan Parry and Maurice Bloch, eds., *Money and the Morality of Exchange* (Cambridge: Cambridge University Press, 1989), 2–7.

5   "The body was the plane where the commodity met the self"; in Jean Comaroff and John Comaroff, *Of Revelation and Revolution* (Chicago, IL: University of Chicago Press, 1997), 2:60.

6   Lit. "price for (of) blood."

7   Circulaire concernant le nouveau tarif à appliquer au "prix du sang," no. 40/AG, 20 March 1944, signed Pierre Vuillaume, ANG/FP 57.

8   The only mention I found in the *Journal officiel de l'Afrique équatoriale française* [Official journal of French Equatorial Africa] (hereinafter JOAEF) of something akin to blood money was a 1927 decree. It stipulated that, in addition to standard sentences, the convicted party could be condemned to pay "restitution" to the victim. The decree did not offer further details. Décret du 5 mars 1927 détermi-nant les pouvoirs du gouverneur général en ce qui concerne l'action de la justice, JOAEF, 1 May 1927, 310–12.

9   Most records are preserved in the Fonds présidentiel (Presidential Fund) of the National Archives of Gabon in Libreville (hereinafter ANG/FP). A few are kept in the Archives d'outre-mer in Aix-en-Provence (hereinafter ANOM).

10 Colonial authors often mentioned *prix du sang* prior to 1940. Fleuriot de Langle told how Fang warriors, after wounding French troops, offered to give two sheep to the commanding officer for "blood money." Fleuriot de Langle, "Croisières à la côte d'Afrique (1868)," *Le Tour du Monde: Nouveau Journal des Voyages*, vol. 31 (Paris: Librairie Hachette, 1876), 267. See also Victor Largeau, *Encyclopédie pahouine, Congo français: Éléments de grammaire et dictionnaire français-pahouin* (Paris: E. Leroux, 1901), 355–57; and Georges Le Testu, *Notes sur les coutumes bapounou dans la circonscription de la Nyanga* (Caen, France: J. Haulard la Brière), 1918, 199.

11 The term *prix du sang* was not used in the record of the trial. Procès-verbal d'audience publique, Affaire Charles Graystock, handwritten copy signed Turenne, 12 August 1922, ANG/FP 461. In 1926, a court compared *prix du*

sang to a "customary retribution." Jugements de la cour d'appel, Chambre d'homologation, Affaire Ibonbo Issoumbo, Nyanga, 26 February 1926, ANOM, 5 D64.

12 "Considering that the custom provides that blood money must be paid to the family of the victim, the tribunal must follow this custom and order the guilty party to pay an indemnity." Dossier no. 293, minutes du greffe de la cour d'appel sur le jugement du 11 mai 1925, 9 September 1925, ANOM, 5D 64. In 1933, again, the higher homologation court in Brazzaville distinguished between *prix du sang* and retribution. Observations relatives au jugement no. 8 du tribunal du 2ème degré du Bas-Ogooué, no. 2528/AC, 26 July 1933, signed Marchessou, ANG/FP 394.

13 Observations relatives au jugement no. 8 du tribunal du 2ème degré du Bas-Ogooué, no. 2528/AC, 26 July 1933, signed Marchessou, ANG/FP 394. Affaire Bepigue, tribunal du 1er degré de Boué, no. 29, 6 October 1941, ANG/FP 87. Affaire Moutsinga Boumba, Mayumba, no. 1, 1943, ANG/FP 841. Affaire Paul Bekalé, Lettre du Gouverneur Vuillaume, no. 867, 22 August 1944, ANG/FP 567.

14 In a 1936 case of a miscarriage resulting from witchcraft practices, the court asked the guilty party for "civil incidental damages" (*réparations civiles*). Affaire Issoumba, 1936, ANG/FP 129. In 1937, another court gave a sentence of five hundred French francs to serve as "customary indemnity." Rapport politique 1937, Ngounié, unsigned, ANG/FP 35. In 1942, a sentence for the murder of a child in a case of alleged anthropophagy led to "a fine" (*amende*) of one hundred French francs for the "prejudice" (*damage*), "considering that the custom provided for this civil reparation." Affaire Nzolo, no. 140, 1942, Archives provinciales, Nzobo, ANG, 8. In 1943, in a hearing concerning a poisoning attempt, the court provided five hundred French francs to the victim's family for "incidental damages" (*dommages et intérêts*). Affaire Mkui Mondo et Esseng Abiang, 1943, ANG/FP 841. Oftentimes, too, the courts failed to provide such payment, even in cases of second-degree murder. For instance, Affaire O. Niang, Tribunal du 2d degré de la circonscription du Bas-Ogooué, 3 August 1938, ANG/FP 811. *Prix du sang* did not appear in the penal codes of 1936 or 1944, nor in the law on native justice in 1947.

15 In 1910, a law encouraged tribunals to use local "customs" as long as they were not contrary to the principles of French civilization. Arrêté du 13 septembre 1910 portant réorganisation de la justice en AEF, *JOAEF*, 15 October 1910, 527–52.

16 On European sentences seeking to convert African "customs," see Florence Bernault, "The Shadow of Rule: Colonial Power and Modern Punishment in Africa," in *Cultures of Confinement: A Global History of the Prison in Asia, Africa, the Middle-East and Latin America*, ed. Frank Dikötter (London: Christopher Hurst, 2007), 77–83.

17 See note 50.

18 I did not find any evidence, however, that colonialists used blood money to break down the human body into cash-valued organs and limbs.

19 See chapter 6.

20 Loi no. 21–63 portant code pénal, *Journal officiel de la République du Gabon*, 25 July 1963, 583–611.

21 E. E. Evans-Pritchard first introduced the notions of "blood-feud" and "blood-guilt" in the mid-1950s in *Nuer Religion* (Oxford: Clarendon Press, 1956), 293–96. His study likely influenced anthropologists of Equatorial Africa: he described how priests can settle a "blood-feud" between two families after one man has killed another. If the killer seeks refuge in the priest's compound, the priest draws the point of a fishing spear in the man's arm to draw blood, and then performs the sacrifice of a cow. In contrast with the Nuer, Equatorial African societies did not use the blood of the guilty party, and even less the mediation of cattle. Yet several anthropologists of the region referred to the notion as an obvious one. French anthropologist George Dupré used "blood money" (without explaining the notion) for translating the *lébumi* payment in marked iron currencies that people used for bride-wealth, for buying slaves, and for compensating for the murder or the premature death of a wife, among the Nzabi people in Congo-Brazzaville. George Dupré, *Un Ordre et sa destruction* (Paris: ORSTOM, 1982), 133, 155, 192, 207, and 249. See also Georges Dupré, *Les Naissances d'une société: Espace et historicité chez les Beembé du Congo* (Paris: Éditions de l'ORSTOM, 1985), 324.

22 Jean-Marie Aubame, *Les Bëti du Gabon et d'ailleurs* (Paris: L'Harmattan, 2002), 2:252. Aubame says that uncles can claim the *prix du sang* from the paternal family when one of their nephews dies.

23 "[A Fang man's] private property was composed of his wives and children, his personal house, his tools for hunting framing and fishing, and the poultry and sheep that he had given in loan to relatives. The wife's private property included her house, trees and garden, the plantation cleared by her husband, cooking tools, and whatever gifts she had gotten from her family." Léon Mba, "Essai de droit coutumier pahouin," *Bulletin de la société de recherches congolaises*, no. 25 (1938): 5–47.

24 The quote dates from 1967 and is taken from Philippe Laburthe-Tolra, *Les Seigneurs de la forêt: Essai sur le passé historique, l'organisation sociale et les normes éthiques des anciens Bëti du Cameroun* (Paris: Publications de la Sorbonne, 1981), 362 and 372–73.

25 Among the Fang Bëti in contemporary Gabon, the father of the groom provides the bride with a new name that often reflects on the wealth she represents, for instance *nkuma* (rich), or *nda auma* (to bear a large number of children). If the groom's family is "poor," i.e., has only one or two male children, the bride can receive the name of *elikh akuma*, which means "legacy," e.g., a "heritage" rich in human potentiality. Aubame, *Les Bëti du Gabon*, 197–98.

26 In Ndumu, *Ikàba' dore* means to spend money. *Ikàba mùtù* literally "to spend a man," has several other meanings: to send a person in slavery, to detach him or her from the household, and to compensate another family for a crime. Gabriel Bounda, "La Morphologie de la répression chez les Ndumu du Haut-Ogooué"

(Master's thesis, Université Omar Bongo Onbimba (hereinafter UOB), Libreville, 1983), 14.

27 Arielle Ekang-Mve, "Famille Nzébi et stérilité (Gabon)," (Master's thesis, UOB, Libreville, June 2006), 22–23.

28 In 1952, an administrative report quoted a public Gabonese rumor according to which a mining company, SOREDIA, was "wasting" (*gaspillait*) the country. Rapport politique de Mbigou, no. 26/CF, 1952, unsigned, ANG/FP 94.

29 The term *gaspiller*, "to waste," is a departure from the colloquial French *gâter*, "to spoil" or "to waste." Today, *gaspiller les femmes* (to waste women) describes how one "spoils" female relatives by giving them too many gifts. In a recent cartoon about the birthday of Gabon's first lady, Edith Bongo, titled "Bonne fête Maman Edith!," Omar Bongo (the president of Gabon) exclaims, "But who has spoiled our women like that?" (*Mais qui a gaspillé nos femmes comme ça?*). *Le Nganga*, 24 May 2002, 2. In nearby Congo-Brazzaville, during the recent civil war (1997–2003), *gaspiller les enfants* (to waste the children) meant three things: their killing by the militias' random fire, their dying from the horrendous living conditions that they experienced as refugees in the wilderness, and the fact that their productive social potential was "wasted" (destroyed) by their participation in the destructive violence of the militias.

30 See Bounda, "La Morphologie de la répression," 14, and interview no. 4, 17 April 2005, in Ekang-Mve, "Famille Nzébi et stérilité," 22–23.

31 Interview with Mr. Fulgence Mboukou, Mouila, 2 June 2002. Mwiri used to be the main male initiation society that organized the coming of age of iPunu-speaking residents. It is today almost defunct.

32 Joseph Miller, *Way of Death: Merchant Capitalism and the Angolan Slave Trade, 1730–1830* (Madison: University of Wisconsin Press, 1988), 149.

33 In the mid-nineteenth century, an annual average of fifty thousand guns arrived in West Equatorial Africa. Jan Vansina, *The Tio Kingdom of the Middle Congo, 1882–1892* (London: Oxford University Press, 1973), 269.

34 I use "foreign" here in the sense of traders who did not belong to local societies. Yet many slavers were Afro-Europeans of mixed descent, born in Africa and educated in the Atlantic world (Europe, Brazil, and the Caribbean). Likewise, middlemen in the hinterland came from Gabon or from the coastal regions of Equatorial Africa.

35 Miller, *Way of Death*, 40–70.

36 Robert Harms, *River of Wealth, River of Sorrow: The Central Zaire Basin in the Era of the Slave and Ivory Trade, 1500–1891* (New Haven, CT: Yale University Press, 1981).

37 Harms, *River of Wealth*, 237.

38 I follow classic historians of Equatorial Africa who borrowed the term "big men" from Melanesian studies. Marshall Sahlins first conceptualized the notion to define men of influence and wealth who were not "chiefs" and did not hold

institutional positions in society. Although it was later criticized, in particular by Marilyn Strathern and Maurice Godelier, the notion of big men works well for precolonial Equatorial African societies in which people achieved rather than inherited positions of wealth and leadership. Marshall Sahlins, "Poor Man, Rich Man, Big Man, Chief: Political Types in Melanesia and Polynesia," *Comparative Studies in History and Society* 5, no. 3 (April 1963): 285–303. For critique and elaboration on the notion, see Maurice Godelier and Marilyn Strathern, eds., *Big Men and Great Men: Personifications of Power in Melanesia* (Cambridge: Cambridge University Press, 1991). On usage in Equatorial African history, see Jan Vansina, *Paths in the Rainforests: Toward a History of Political Tradition in Equatorial Africa* (Madison: University of Wisconsin Press, 1990), 275.

39 On slavery and the value of the person, see Claude Meillassoux, *Maidens, Meal, and Money: Capitalism and the Domestic Community* (Cambridge: Cambridge University Press, 1981). See also Suzanne Miers and Igor Kopytoff, eds., *Slavery in Africa: Historical and Anthropological Perspectives* (Madison: University of Wisconsin Press, 1977). The emphasis on wealth-in-people for Equatorial Africa came originally from Miller, *Way of Death*, 40–70.

40 Jane Guyer, "Wealth in People and Self-Realization in Equatorial Africa," *Man* 28, no. 2 (1993): 243–65. Jane Guyer and Samuel Eno Belinga, "Wealth in People as Wealth in Knowledge: Accumulation and Composition in Equatorial Africa," *Journal of African History* 36, no. 1 (1995): 91–120.

41 House is the translation of the proto-Bantu *-ganda*, meaning the establishment of a big man. It comprises his household and the extended realm of clients and allies. Vansina, *Paths*, 74–77 and 268–70. A ruler skillfully composed immediate and delayed claims that he could assert on a complex network of clients and dependents.

42 As Guyer herself suggested in "Wealth in People and Self Realization," 246. Wyatt MacGaffey's concept of the "personhood of objects and the objecthood of people" shows that West Equatorial Africans saw both charms and the body to be suffused with the agency of ancestors and spirits. Wyatt MacGaffey, *Kongo Political Culture: The Conceptual Challenge of the Particular* (Bloomington: Indiana University Press, 2000). See also chapter 3 in this volume.

43 Paul and Laura Bohannan wrote the classic study on the separation between spheres of exchanges (and the respective currencies used in each) among the Tiv of Nigeria. Paul Bohannan, "Some Principles of Exchange and Investment among the Tiv," *American Ethnologist* 57: 60–69; and Paul Bohannan and Laura Bohannan, *Tiv Economy* (London: Longmans, 1968).

44 With the possible exception of very large and heavy currencies such as the *ngele* lances of the Eso; Nancy Rose Hunt, *A Colonial Lexicon of Birth Ritual, Medicalization, and Mobility in the Congo* (Durham, NC: Duke University Press, 1999), 36–37. Yet Colleen Kriger suggests that even these could be reworked into smaller units, and move back and forth from commodity to more restricted

markets. Colleen Kriger, *Pride of Men: Ironworking in 19th-Century West Central Africa* (Portsmouth, NH: Heinemann, 1999). On unrestricted exchanges among the Beembé in Congo-Brazzaville, see Dupré, *Les Naissances*, 118.

45 Vansina, *Tio Kingdom*, 293.

46 Vansina, *Tio Kingdom*, 305 and 88–89 (on bride-wealth).

47 Vansina, *Paths*, 206. For a later example, Georges Dupré wrote that the Beembé did not use marked currency to pay bride-wealth (*bila*). Dupré, *Naissances*, 223.

48 According to Jane Guyer, low thresholds characterized equatorial African spheres of exchanges: the "incremental valuation" between exchanged items meant that currencies worked as "open value receptors." They assessed both things and persons. Guyer, "Wealth in People and Self Realization." See also Harms, *River of Wealth*, 166.

49 Evans-Pritchard, in *Nuer Religion*, conceptualized the general principle of substitution. Among the Nuer, cattle substituted for people in sacrifices and to put an end to family feuds. For substitution strategies in Equatorial and Central Africa, see Luc de Heusch, *Sacrifice in Africa: A Structuralist Approach* (Manchester, UK: Manchester University Press, 1985).

50 In the 1970s among the Fang Bëti in southern Cameroon, objects and animals (a bundle of iron rods, goats, and sheep) still worked as substitute for a person. They served to pay for social payments and for sacred exchanges with ancestors and spirits. Philippe Laburthe-Tolra, *Initiations et sociétés secrètes au Cameroun: Essai sur la religion bëti* (Paris: Karthala, 1985), 304–7 and 378.

51 Vansina, *Tio Kingdom*, 366 and 378.

52 We do not know what happened. Procès-verbal d'interrogatoire de Pangangoy. Affaire Dalékolo, Booué, 1912, ANG/FP 61. Marriage currencies also symbolized departed kin members and stood as substitutes for a person. Among the Eso in Eastern Congo, for instance, *ngbele* lances really stood for the lost daughter and her husband, and represented them. Charged with social potential, they meant that the family could use them to further alliances by acquiring new wives for its sons and nephews. Hunt, *Colonial Lexicon*, 36 and sqq.

53 As theorized by Wyatt MacGaffey, objects could be charged with a person's inner strength. MacGaffey, *Kongo Political*, 78–96. See also Laburthe-Tolra, *Initiations et sociétés secrètes*, 8. In the Haut-Ogooué in the 1950s, people considered that the belongings of a deceased person that were exposed on his or her tomb stood as a form of individuality. To use them was considered as calling death upon oneself. Jean-Baptiste Menié (a nurse from Okondja), "La Crainte des morts dans le Haut-Ogooué," *Liaison*, no. 36 (June 1953): 46–47.

54 Florence Bernault, "Aesthetics of Acquisition: Gabonese Spectacles and the Transactional Life of Bodies and Things," *Comparative Studies in Society and History* no. 3 (July 2015): 753–77.

55 Miller, *Way of Death*, 42–43.

56 On symbolic tributes, see Miller, *Way of Death*, 47–53. Equatorial Africans did not consider commercial partners as autonomous equals brought momentarily

together to acquire a product and its countervalue. Instead, they saw trading as a mediating procedure that produced social relations, and mutual bonds of obligation between commercial partners. The imaginary endured during the Atlantic trade.

57 Farmers often considered hunter-gatherers as the ultimate debtors. Roy Grinker, *Houses in the Rain Forest: Ethnicity and Inequality among Farmers and Foragers in Central Africa* (Berkeley: University of California Press, 1994).

58 Vansina, *Paths*, 152. Robert Harms calls the notion that riches existed in limited quantity a "zero sum game," borrowing from George Foster. Harms, *River of Wealth*. George Foster, "Peasant Society and the Image of the Limited Good," *American Anthropologist*, no. 62 (1965): 293–315.

59 James Fernandez, "Christian Acculturation and Fang Witchcraft," *Cahiers d'études africaines* 2, no. 6 (1961): 245–46.

60 Fernandez, "Christian Acculturation," 247. However, several houses could get together for defensive or commercial alliances.

61 Bruce Berman and John Lonsdale famously argued for the case of a "moral economy" in precolonial Kenya and among the Gikuyu, where agrarian solidarity elevated rights to subsistence over commercial profit or capital accumulation. Bruce Berman and John Lonsdale, *Unhappy Valley: Conflict in Kenya and Africa* (London: James Currey, 1992). See also Thomas Spear, *Mountain Farmers: Moral Economies of Land and Agricultural Development in Arusha and Meru* (Oxford: James Currey, 1997); and Parker Shipton, *Mortgaging the Ancestors: Ideologies of Attachment in Africa* (New Haven, CT: Yale University Press, 2009).

62 "Partout la vie humaine est comptée pour peu de chose"; Fleuriot de Langle, "Croisières," 1876, 304. Victor de Compiègne wrote that the Fang sold their children out of cupidity. Louis-Alphonse-Victor du Pont de Compiègne, *L'Afrique équatoriale: Gabonais, Pahouins, Gallois* (Paris: Plon, 1876), 160. To a wandering adventurer like Casimir Castellani, the "savage Bacota's only goal in life [was] to conduct business." Charles Castellani, *Les Femmes au Congo* (Paris: Flammarion, 1898), 83. See also P. Payeur-Didelot, *Trente mois au continent mystérieux: Gabon-Congo et côte occidentale d'Afrique* (Paris: Berger-Levrault, 1899), 187.

63 "The wars where they sell and eat each other" (*la guerre où l'on se vend et se mange*); Adolphe Cureau, *Les Sociétés primitives de l'Afrique équatoriale* (Paris: Armand Colin, 1912), 204–5. Georges Renouard, *L'Ouest africain et les Missions catholiques: Congo et Oubanghi* (Paris: H. Oudin, 1904), 20 and 118–21: "Adouma people sell each other" (*les Adoumas se vendent les uns les autres*); and Payeur-Didelot, *Trente mois*, 187.

64 Jane Guyer, "Indigenous Currencies and the History of Marriage Payments: A Case Study from Cameroon," *Cahiers d'études africaines* 26, no. 104 (1986): 577–610; and "Bridewealth and Dowry Revisited: The Position of Women in Sub-Saharan Africa and North India," *Current Anthropology* 30, no. 4 (1989): 413–35. See also Nancy Rose Hunt on coins and bride-wealth in the Belgian Congo; Hunt, *Colonial Lexicon*, 63–79.

In 1912, Catholic writer Georges Renouard wrote that no true family feeling could exist between a black man, his wives, and children since women were traded in marriage like an object in a commercial "deal," and were treated like "an animal that works and pays." Renouard, *L'Ouest africain*, 118–25.

65 Colonial authors denounced Gabonese "fake marriages," in which the wife left her husband after a brief period of time, and returned to her parents who kept the marriage payment and could marry their daughter again. Jean Dybowski, *Le Congo méconnu* (Paris: Hachette, 1912), 219.

66 Maurice Briault, *Dans la forêt du Gabon: Etudes et scènes africaines* (Paris: Bernard Grasset, 1930), 62. After 1946, the colonial prejudice that husbands married for greed and undeserved profits was briefly revived by the adoption of welfare policies (*allocations familiales*, or family social security and benefits) in the French colonies. Jacques Hubert, "Esquisse de la coutume bapounou et généralités sur la dégradation des coutumes au Gabon," ANG/FP 52, 12.

67 On *otangani*, see Guyer and Belinga, "Wealth in People"; and Fernandez, "Christian Acculturation." For a recent analysis, see Joseph Tonda, *Le Souverain moderne: Le Corps du pouvoir en Afrique centrale (Congo, Gabon)* (Paris: Karthala, 2005), 173.

68 Joseph Conrad's novella *Heart of Darkness* (1899; New York: Norton, 1988) dramatized the fact with Kurtz's insane "kingdom" on the upstream Congo River. See also the colonial myth that administrators were the "kings of the bush" (*rois de la brousse*). Hubert Deschamps, *Roi de la brousse: Mémoires d'autres mondes* (Paris: Berger-Levrault, 1975).

69 Such colonial forms of sovereignty have been famously coined by Sara Berry as "hegemony on a shoestring." Sara Berry, "Hegemony on a Shoestring: Indirect Rule and Access to Land," *Africa, Journal of the International African Institute* 62, no. 3 (1992): 327–55.

70 In the 1890s, an Assango entrepreneur mimicked the recruiting agents of traders, factory agents, and civil servants who paid for portage. He gathered men in a village and promised that they would be paid exorbitant salaries for carrying commodities. Twenty men agreed to follow him and never came back. Administrator Maclatchy, monographie de la subdivision de Mimongo, 20 March 1936, 61, Archives CSSP, Fonds Pouchet, 273-A-II. See also Catherine Coquery-Vidrovitch, *Le Congo au temps des grandes companies concessionaires* (Paris: Mouton, 1972). Christopher Gray, *Colonial Rule and Crisis in Southern Gabon, ca. 1850–1940* (Rochester, NY: University of Rochester Press, 2002), esp. chapters 5 and 6.

71 Rapport sur la Circonscription du Como, 1er semestre, February 1913, ANG/FP 246. Nicolas Metegue N'Nah, *Histoire du Gabon: Des Origines à l'aube du XXe siècle* (Paris: L'Harmattan, 2006), 100, signals how the Enenga chief Rampole detained trader R. N. B. Walker for several months.

72 "Résumé de l'Affaire Maguibou, Ragnonona," in réponse au questionnaire de la Société esclavagiste pour fait de traite, no. 118, signed by le chef de la subdivision de Sindara, 16 February 1923, and by the president of the court, Le Testu, ANG/FP 820.

73 Agents forcibly collected twenty-one tons of rubber in 1942–43. Rapport politique de la Ngounié, 1943, signed F. Boraschi, ANG/FP 418.

74 Rapport politique de 1944 de la Ngounié, unsigned, and Rapport politique de Mbigou du second semestre 1948, signed Chevallier, ANG/FP 344.

75 In 1929, the administration estimated that 25,000 men worked in the timber industry in Gabon. Gray, *Colonial Rule*, 185–89. Christopher Gray and François Ngolet, "Lambaréné, Okoumé and the Transformation of Labor along the Middle Ogooué (Gabon), 1870–1945," *Journal of African History* 40, no. 1 (1999): 105.

76 Such regrouping had already begun in the 1910s for reasons of surveillance, census, and tax collection. The French systematized the effort in the 1930s and 1950s. Gilles Sautter, *De l'Atlantique au fleuve Congo: Une géographie du sous-peuplement, République du Congo, République gabonaise* (Paris: La Haye, Mouton, 1966); Georges Balandier, *The Sociology of Black Africa: Social Dynamics in Central Africa* (New York: Praeger Publishers, 1970); and Roland Pourtier, *Le Gabon*, 2 vols. (Paris: L'Harmattan, 1989).

77 For comparison, see Phyllis Martin, *Catholic Women in Congo-Brazzaville: Mothers and Sisters in Troubled Times* (Bloomington: Indiana University Press, 2009), 44–50; Fiona Bowie, Deborah Kirkwood, and Shirley Ardener, *Women and Missions, Past and Present: Anthropological and Historical Perceptions* (Providence, RI: Berg, 1993).

78 André Raponda-Walker, "Comment la Mission de N. D. de l'équateur a sauvé deux Eshiras condamnés à périr par le feu," Mission des Eshiras, Imprimerie Ste Marie. Archives CSSP, 2D60.8b1. In 1917, in the Alima region of Congo-Brazzaville, desperate Mbochi parents sold their daughters to the Catholic mission in Boundji so they could get cash to pay taxes. The priests purchased twenty-two girls for forty francs each. Georges Mazenot, *La Likouala-Mossaka: Histoire de la pénétration du Haut Congo, 1878–1920* (Paris: La Haye, Mouton, 1970), 334.

79 Père Lejeune, "La condition de la femme chez les Pahouins," 86, *Annales* CSSP, July 1891.

80 Rapport sur la Mission Ste Anne de Libreville 1894–1897, *Bulletin* CSSP, tome 18, 1894–1897, 496–501. The fathers had now "a deal" with local families: by paying bride-wealth for girls, they "got more children than [they] could accept." They also rejoiced in the support offered by the district officer, Mr. Foret. In Lambaréné, the priests bought five male slaves between 1902 and 1905. Rapport sur la Mission St-François-Xavier à Lambaréné, *Bulletin* CSSP, tome 23, No. 23, 1905–06, 59–60. In Lastourville in 1895, the Catholic fathers complained that, because of the competition of Protestant missionaries, they had to pay "dearly" the parents to secure the children's attendance to school. Rapport de la Mission St Pierre Claver à Lastourville, *Bulletin* CSSP, tome 18, 1894–97, 536.

81 Protestant missionaries also tried to create stable Christian communities by securing plenary control over some of their pupils. White families settled at the Bongolo mission, in southern Gabon, provided room and board to students "so

the children would be sheltered from pagan temptations." In 1948, they tried to adopt the children and pressured the parents to renounce all rights on their offspring. The local French administration found the procedure illegal. Lettre du chef de la région de la Ngounié-Nyanga au gouverneur du Gabon, no. 746/CF, 21 July 1948. ANG/FP 52. See also Rapport politique du premier semestre 1948, district de Mouila, ANG/FP 52.

82 The story, probably apocryphal, encouraged parishioners in European churches to donate to the Catholic missions in Africa. Rapport de la Mission des Eshiras (Mouila), *Bulletin* CSSP, tome 21, no. 185, July 1902, 500.

83 Rapport sur la Mission St-François-Xavier à Lambaréné, *Bulletin* CSSP, tome 23, no. 23, 1905–1906, 59–60.

84 Faits de traite relevés sur la frontière du Gabon, Lieutenant-gouverneur P. I. du Moyen Congo au Lieutenant-Gouverneur du Gabon, signed Thomann, no. 348, 19 April 1922, ANG/FP 820.

85 The etymology of *acheter* (to buy) comes from the popular Latin *ad captare* (and possibly from *acceptare*), "to capture something and bring it closer to oneself." *Vendre* (to sell) comes from *emere* (to procure), the root of the word "redemption," and in medieval Latin, it also meant special judicial procedures. In the thirteenth century, a third meaning emerged for *emere*: "to free a captive with a ransom." Alain Rey, *Dictionnaire historique de la langue française* (Paris: Dictionnaires Le Robert, 2000), 1:15.

86 Mongo Beti fictionalized this African perspective in *The Poor Christ of Bomba* (Paris: Présence africaine, 1956).

87 People exchanged slaves against precious commodities (salt, imported goods), not standardized currencies.

88 Yet *otangani* is a social rather than a strictly racial term: it can also apply to rich and greedy black Gabonese.

89 Fieldwork with Joseph Tonda, Mouila, Summer 2002.

90 The CFA franc (ISO code: XAF) was introduced to the French colonies in Equatorial Africa in 1945 to replace the French Equatorial African franc. It still serves today as the currency for Cameroon, Central African Republic, Chad, the Republic of the Congo, Equatorial Guinea, and Gabon and is issued by the BEAC (Banque des États de l'Afrique Centrale, or Bank of the Central African States). CFA stands for Coopération financière en Afrique centrale ("Financial Cooperation in Central Africa").

91 In Gabon and in Congo-Brazzaville, I often heard people say, "Whites are people who count, they are counted" (*les blancs comptent; ils sont comptés*), meaning that the state keeps a record and must protect them. The French verb *compter* expresses an action (to count) and a status (to matter).

92 Tonda, *Le Souverain moderne*, 132–34.

93 On money as medicine, see Joseph Tonda, *La Guérison divine en Afrique centrale (Congo, Gabon)* (Paris: Karthala, 2002), 51.

94 Kriger, *Pride of Men*, 89.

95 Traders also provided local rulers with "certificates of honor" destined to enhance the commercial reputation of the latter and prevent foreign monopolies
on Gabonese markets. Paul Du Chaillu, *Voyages et aventures dans l'Afrique équatoriale: Moeurs et coutumes des habitants, chasses au gorille, au crocodile, au léopard, à
l'éléphant, à l'hippopotame, etc., etc.* (Paris: M. Lévy frères, 1863), 14–17.

96 Du Chaillu, *Voyages*, 86–87 and 98–99.

97 Georges Dupré, "The History and Adventures of a Monetary Object of the
Kwélé of the Congo: Mezong, Mondjos, and Mandjong," in *Money Matters:
Instability, Values, and Social Payments in the Modern History of West African
Communities*, ed. Jane Guyer (Portsmouth, NH: Heinemann, 1995), 77–96. Also
Kriger, *Pride of Men*, 236. Mazenot, *La Likouala-Mossaka*, 179 and 194, attests that
people still used *mitako* in northern Congo-Brazzaville in the 1900s.

98 On how foreign commercial firms and agents progressively destroyed the Gabonese networks of middle men, see chapter 2 of this volume. For an excellent
demonstration that the presence of money does not in itself have the power to
revolutionize society and economic exchanges, see Parry and Bloch, *Money*, 3.

99 By "free-floating currencies" I mean national coins backed by independent
nation-states such as Germany, Austria, Great Britain, the United States, and so
on, such as the silver dollars, Austrian thalers, and many other coins that circulated in Equatorial Africa.

100 Coquery-Vidrovitch, *Le Congo*, 158–59. In 1908 on the northern coast of Gabon,
the French paid Fang workers in kind only, assessed at one French franc per day.
The wage was smaller than the food ration and the .75 francs in cash that workers
obtained on the Loango coast. Xavier Frass, Monographie de la côte nord du
Gabon, 1908, 44, ANG/FP 3788.

101 As rightly suggested by Adeline Masquelier in the case of colonial Niger: "Narratives of Power, Images of Wealth: The Ritual Economy of Bori in the Market,"
in Jean Comaroff and John Comaroff, eds., *Modernity and Its Malcontents: Ritual
and Power in Postcolonial Africa* (Chicago, IL.: University of Chicago Press, 1993),
3–33.

102 On coupons, see Mary Douglas, "Primitive Rationing: A Study in Primitive
Exchange," in *Themes in Economic Anthropology*, ed. Raymond Firth (Oxon:
Routledge, 2004), 119–47.

103 According to the author, the paper cash issued by the mission looked "somewhat
like the tickets formerly given in Sabbath schools as rewards of merit." Joseph H.
Reading, *The Ogowe Band: A Narrative of African Travel* (Philadelphia, PA: Reading, 1890), 248. Although the story concerns the Benita Station, the coupons
reproduced in the book were from the larger Baraka Station in Libreville.

104 Reading, *Ogowe Band*, 248.

105 For a brilliant analysis of the role of paper (*mukanda*) in the new language of
power and colonial modernity in the Belgian Congo, see Pedro A. G. Monaville,
"Decolonizing the University: Postal Politics, The Student Movement, and
Global 1968 in the Congo" (PhD thesis, University of Michigan, 2013), 51–52.

106 Coquery-Vidrovitch, *Le Congo*, 124–30. Gray, *Colonial Rule*, 150–69. In 1916 near Mimongo, eight agents from the Société du Haut-Ogooué concessionary company launched an armed assault against the village Nzoula, where the inhabitants refused to collect rubber, and collected 3,900 French francs in tax. Administrator Maclatchy, monographie de la subdivision de Mimongo, 20 March 1936, 4, Archives CSSP Pouchet 273-A-II.

107 In 1918–19, the administrator recorded 792 deaths for a population of 7,371. Rapports de la Mission de Donghila, Mouny et St Pierre de Ndjolé, *Bulletin* CSSP, tome 30, 1921–22, 659–64, 671, and 705.

108 In their reports, colonial administrators converted the value of collected goods in French francs, a written abstraction that masked the concrete violence that presided to taxation. Emmanuel Pascotte, rapport sur les territoires concédés, 1917, ANG/FP 137. See also rapport manuscrit du capitaine Le Canu, chef de la circonscription de l'Ivindo au gouverneur du Gabon, Makokou 10 September 1913, ANG/FP 954. French administrator Maclatchy in Mimongo wrote that "cash only started to be used as currency by 1919. Banknotes have no value." Rapport sur la subdivision de Mimongo en 1936, 93 pages, signed Maclatchy, Archives CSSP, Fonds Pouchet 273-A-II. See also Coquery-Vidrovitch, *Le Congo*, 135–38.

109 Gray, *Colonial Rule*, 153 and 158. Rapport du chef de la subdivision de Djambani, signed Bideaux, 28 May 1914, AOM, 5D 32.

110 Coquery-Vidrovitch, *Le Congo*, 162–64. When cash circulation was grossly insufficient, and Africans refused to use bank notes, the government resorted to mint *jetons-monnaies*. It is not clear what these monies looked like.

111 Maclatchy, informations politiques de la Ngounié, August 1948, ANG/FP 52.

112 Félix Éboué, *La Nouvelle politique indigène pour l'Afrique équatoriale française* (Paris: Office français d'édition, 1940), 19–20.

113 The notebooks had some of the following comments on local chiefs: "mediocre," "old," "worthless" (*incapable*), "alcoholic and lazy," "blind," "impotent." Arrêté sur l'organisation des chefferies indigènes de l'AEF, 28 December 1936, *Journal officiel de l'Afrique équatoriale française*, 15 January 1937. In 1945, in Sindara, the chiefs received five hundred to seven hundred French francs wages per trimester. Rapport politique du second semestre 1944, Fougamou/Sindara, 13 January 1945, ANG/FP 35.

114 In 1848, the French signed a treaty of protection with the Mpongwe leaders of the Gabon Estuary. In 1942, the French government gave ten thousand French francs in cash and goods to forty-six chiefs including the traditional rulers of the Gabon Estuary, Denis, Quaben, Glass and Louis, in order to compensate for the loss of their land. K. David Patterson, *The Northern Gabon Coast to 1875* (Oxford: Clarendon Press, 1975), 110; and Elikia M'Bokolo, *Noirs et Blancs en Afrique équatoriale: Les sociétés côtières et la pénétration française (vers 1820–1874)* (Paris: Editions de l'Ecole des Hautes Études en Sciences Sociales, 1981), 141–44.

115 Rapport politique du second semestre 1944, Fougamou/Sindara, 13 January 1945, ANG/FP 35. For an earlier example, see how the district chief of Ndjolé in 1905,

after a violent rebellion among the Issoghos (Mitsogho), reported that he lacked money to create intelligence and "secure some loyalty" among them. Lettre du commandant de Ndjolé, 17 January 1905, no. 201, ANG/FP 207.

116   For instance, for the Fourteenth of July ceremony in 1955, the chief of the canton of Bapounou Nord, near Mouila, received 2,000 French francs. The canton chief of Lebamba received 3,600 French francs to cover the expenses of the visit of the governor of Gabon. Décisions nos. 19, 20, and 21, 13–24 August 1955, signed by district chief M. Blin, ANG/Archives provinciales Ndendé, 15. In Ndendé, the French authorities gave 5,000 French francs to the Catholic and the Protestant mission for a *messe d'action de grâce* to be celebrated on 17 August 1961, the first celebration of Gabon independence. Fiche d'activités, district de Ndendé, no. 51/CF, August 1961, ANG/Archives provinciales Ndendé, 14.

117   Bernault, "Aesthetics of Acquisition."

118   Although it is difficult to know when colonial authorities started using *jetons*, they are widely attested in the archives from 1913 onward. The earliest document dates from 1913; it records the number of tax tokens delivered by the district chief to people who had paid taxes: "In August [I gave] 106 tax tokens, in September 134, but none in December." Lieutenant Fichepain, commandant of the post of Mikongo (Moyen-Ogooué), "Situation des jetons d'impôts au 31 décembre 1913," ANG/FP 203. I was unable to find any visual trace of *jetons d'impôt* in Gabon.

119   In 1910–11 in the Ngounié, missionaries complained of famine and inundation. Yet, they wrote, the authorities raised the head tax from three to five French francs (equivalent to one hundred kilograms of palm nuts). As a result, they wrote, people fled the villages and lived in the forest. Colonial *tirailleurs* arrested and chained all farmers who did not carry the tax token. Rapport de la Mission Notre-Dame-des-Apindjis, Janvier 1913, *Bulletin* CSSP, vol. 26, no. 311, 981–82.

120   Mission du Gabon: St-Martin-Des-Apindjis, *Bulletin* CSSP tome 26, 1911–1913, 981–82. In 1918 in neighboring Congo, militia troops arrested a dozen men on their way to a market in Brazzaville who failed to exhibit tax tokens, and forced them to pay taxes a second time. The district officer warned the militias that a fresh shipment of tokens had not yet reached the post, and instructed them to release the men. Lettre du chef de circonscription des Bakongo au Lieutenant-Gouverneur du Congo, 27 February 1918, AOM, 5D 33.

121   Arrêté fixant les modifications apportées aux Arrêtés du 30 décembre 1916 et du 11 octobre 1920 sur les conditions de perceptions de la capitation, 9 October 1931, quoted by Coquery-Vidrovitch, *Le Congo*, 140n6. See also Gray, *Colonial Rule*, 152. Although I did not find archival traces of this, the policy certainly increased a black market for tax tokens, allowing some chiefs to give the precious medals to certain people for certain services.

122   The collection of laws and decrees in the *Journal officiel de l'Afrique équatoriale française* did not record the end of the practice. To my knowledge, no scholarly study of tax tokens has been published.

123 The *symbole* worked as "a fetish-object punishing those who dared to speak the forbidden language of the fetishes." Joseph Tonda, "Fétichisme et sorcellerie: La Force de mort du pouvoir souverain moderne en Afrique centrale," unpublished paper. Author's archives. See also description of how delinquent Gabonese pupils had to wear the skull of a monkey, in Mabik-ma-Kombil, *Parlons Yipunu: Langue et culture des Punu du Gabon-Congo* (Paris: L'Harmattan, 2001), 1.

124 Rémy Bazenguissa-Ganga, *Les Voies du politique au Congo: Essai de sociologie historique* (Paris: Karthala, 1997).

125 Compagnie de l'Ibenga au gouverneur du Congo, 26 August 1906, quoted by Coquery-Vidrovitch, *Le Congo*, 117.

126 Jacques Hubert, "Mémoire sur les coutumes Bapunu," ca. 1950, Archives CSSP Fonds Pouchet, 2D60 8a5.

127 Rachel Jean-Baptiste, *Conjugal Rights: Marriage, Sexuality, and Urban Life in Colonial Libreville, Gabon* (Athens: Ohio University Press, 2014).

128 First of all by Joseph Tonda, who shows that the social body of these women transforms into a "body-sex" (*corps-sexe*). Tonda, *Le Souverain moderne*, 208–19.

129 *Pèmba* means the color white, associated to the kaolin powder used for rituals; *motètè* means both "debt" and "wealth." Amélie Mogoa Boussengui, "Pemba Motete, ou dispositif de la conquête du pouvoir et de subjectivation de la femme mitsogho," unpublished paper, 2017, author's archives.

130 Ekang-Mve, "Famille Nzèbi et stérilité," 25.

131 Interview with Mme Njoni, Quartier Nombakele, Libreville, 23 June 2000.

132 Frank Christopher Nzamba, "La Sorcellerie dans les conflits d'héritage en milieu urbain chez les Punu: Cas de Libreville" (Master's thesis, UOB, Libreville, 2005), 31–32.

133 For further examples, see Tonda, *Le Souverain moderne*, 188–93.

CHAPTER 5 ⁝ Cannibal Mirrors

Epigraph: Fernand Rouget, *L'Expansion coloniale au Congo français* (Paris: E. Larose, 1906), 347.

1 For a detailed critique of the myth, see James Fernandez, *Bwiti: An Ethnography of the Religious Imagination in Africa* (Princeton, NJ: Princeton University Press, 1981).

2 Among the few exceptions, Joseph Conrad allocated the charge of cannibalism to Kurz, the white antihero. At the beginning of *Heart of Darkness*, Marlow remarks that the remains of a gentle captain killed in a scuffle, although "grass [was] growing through his ribs," were "all there." Joseph Conrad, *Heart of Darkness* (1899; New York: Norton & Company, 1988), 7.

3 I examine these idioms in chapter 6. On the pervasiveness of the cannibal trope among explorers in Equatorial Africa, see Johannes Fabian, *Out of Our Minds: Reason and Madness in the Exploration of Central Africa* (Berkeley: Los Angeles: University of California Press, 2000), 221–26.

4 Rosalind Shaw, "The Production of Witchcraft/Witchcraft as Production: Memory, Modernity and the Slave Trade in Sierra Leone," *American Ethnologist* 24, no. 4 (1996): 856–76. For the transposing of the thought in the context of late capitalism, see Peter Geschiere, *The Modernity of Witchcraft: Politics and the Occult in Postcolonial Africa* (Charlottesville: University Press of Virginia, 1997); Jean Comaroff and John Comaroff, eds., *Modernity and its Malcontents: Ritual and Power in Postcolonial Africa* (Chicago, IL: University of Chicago Press, 1993); and John Thornton, "Cannibals, Witches, and Slave Traders in the Atlantic World," *William and Mary Quarterly* 60, no. 2 (2003): 273–94.

5 Francisco Damião Cosme, Luanda, 1770, in Luís de Pina, ed. "Tractato das queixas endemicas, e mais fataes nesta Conquista," *Studia*, no. 20–22 (1967): 119–268, quoted in Joseph Miller, *Way of Death: Merchant Capitalism and the Angolan Slave Trade, 1730–1830* (Madison: University of Wisconsin Press, 1988), 389. For a more recent approach, see John Thornton, *Africans in the Making of the Atlantic World, 1400–1800* (Cambridge: Cambridge University Press, 1998), 316.

6 Joshua Oliver-Mason, "These Blurred Copies of Himself: T. H. Huxley, Paul Du Chaillu, and the Reader's Place among the Apes," *Victorian Literature and Culture* 42 (2014): 102.

7 Nancy Rose Hunt, *Colonial Lexicon of Birth Ritual, Medicalization, and Mobility in the Congo* (Durham, NC: Duke University Press, 1999); and Benjamin N. Lawrance, Emily L. Osborn, and Richard L. Roberts, eds., *Intermediaries, Interpreters, and Clerks: African Employees in the Making of Colonial Africa* (Madison: University of Wisconsin Press, 2006).

8 Other thirds included the hypersexualized African woman, the "degenerate" tribes of the coast, and "pygmies" (hunter-gatherer communities).

9 Paul Du Chaillu, *The Country of the Dwarfs* (New York: Harper and Brothers, 1872), frontispiece and 43–45. Artist unknown, illustration signed C. R. S. Public domain.

10 Paul Du Chaillu, *Adventures in the Great Forest of Equatorial Africa and the Country of the Dwarfs,* abridged and popular ed. (New York: Harper, 1899), 474. Augustus Collodon, *Congo Jake: The Story of My Adventurous Life* (London: Sampson Low, Marston, 1932), 116–26, 185–86, and 195–96.

11 Francis Barker, Peter Hulme, and Margaret Iversen, eds. *Cannibalism and the Colonial World* (Cambridge: Cambridge University Press, 1998), 16–17.

12 Hans Staden, *Hans Staden's True History: An Account of Cannibal Captivity in Brazil* (c. 1557) (Durham, NC: Duke University Press, 2008); André Thévet, *The New Found Worlde or Antarctike* (London: Henrie Bynneman for Thomas Hacket, 1568); and Jean de Léry, *Journal de Bord de Jean de Léry en la Terre de Brésil, 1557* (Paris: Editions de Paris, 1957).

13 For a detailed analysis, see Quentin Buvelot, Dante Martins Teixeira, and Elly de Vries, *Albert Eckhout: A Dutch Artist in Brazil* (Zwolle, Netherlands: Waanders, 1999).

14 Thomas Huxley's *Man's Place in Nature* (1863) appeared just after Du Chaillu's work. George W. Stocking Jr., *Victorian Anthropology* (New York: Free Press, 1987).

15 In 1493, Diego Álvarez Chança, Columbus's physician, declared that the Caribs used their beach dwellings as veritable "human butcher-shops" after examining four or five human bones that an officer had found in a deserted hut on the island. Barker, Hulme, and Iversen, *Cannibalism*, 16. This important intellectual moment pushed the figure of the cannibal away from the core of European myths (ogres, witches, and werewolves) off to distant "savage" nations, and created *cannibalism* as a habitual, communal, and ritual fact performed by pagan savages.

16 I borrow the concept "dream-books" from Ben Grant, "'Interior Explorations': Paul Belloni Du Chaillu's Dream Book," *Journal of European Studies* 38, no. 4: 407–19. Although I do not agree with the general critique of William Arens against the existence of cannibalism, the current anthropological consensus about Gabon argues that anthropophagy did not exist in the region. See Fernandez, *Bwiti*; and William Arens, *The Man-Eating Myth: Anthropology and Anthropophagy* (Oxford: Oxford University Press, 1980).

17 This paragraph follows the detailed biography of Du Chaillu by K. David Patterson, "Paul B. Du Chaillu and the Exploration of Gabon, 1855–1865," *International Journal of African Historical Studies* 7, no. 4 (1974): 647–67. During his 1852–55 sojourn in the United States, Du Chaillu obtained American citizenship.

18 Paul B. Du Chaillu, *Explorations and Adventures in Equatorial Africa: With Accounts of the Manners and Customs of the People, and of the Chace [sic] of the Gorilla, Crocodile, Leopard, Elephant, Hippopotamus, and Other Animals* (London: John Murray, 1861); reprinted in New York: Negro University Press, 1969, 103–4. He wrote a different version of the scene in *Recent Remarkable Discoveries in Central Africa* (Philadelphia, PA: Barclay, 1867), 59–60. Despite his critique of Du Chaillu, Richard Burton copied the scene in *Two Trips to Gorilla Land and the Cataracts of the Congo* (London: Sampson Low, Marston, 1876), 1:212.

19 Du Chaillu, *Explorations and Adventures*, 104 and 120. He added the term "*scene infernale*" (scene from Hell) in the French translation published two years later. Paul Du Chaillu, *Voyages et aventures dans l'Afrique équatoriale: Moeurs et coutumes des habitants, chasses au gorille, au crocodile, au léopard, à l'éléphant, à l'hippopotame, etc., etc.* (Paris: M. Lévy frères, 1863), 165.

20 Du Chaillu, *Explorations and Adventures*, 280–81.

21 Louis-Alphonse-Victor du Pont de Compiègne, *L'Afrique équatoriale: Gabonais Pahouins, Gallois* (Paris: Plon, 1876). See also Griffon Du Bellay, "Le Gabon, 1861–1864," in *Le Tour du Monde: Nouveau Journal des Voyages* (Paris: Librairie Hachette, 1865), vol. 12, no. 2:273–320. Almost simultaneously published in German (1874), in English, and in French (1875), August Georg Schweinfurth's *Au coeur de l'Afrique: Trois ans de voyages et d'aventures dans les régions inexplorées*

de l'Afrique centrale, vol. 1 (Paris: Hachette, 1875), hinted a possible link between the Fan and the Niam Niam (Mangbetu) tribes of the Western Nile. The case garnered immediate attention among imperial milieus, and triggered diffusionist theories on the spread of cannibal tribes from the Sudan to West Africa.

22 Burton, *Two Trips*, 210–12.

23 Burton, *Two Trips*, 217.

24 Mary Kingsley, *Travels in West Africa Congo Français, Corisco, and Cameroons* (London: Macmillan, 1897), 331.

25 Sigmund Freud, *The Interpretation of Dreams* (1899; New York: Chelsea House Publishers, 1987).

26 Excerpts from diary of Father Guyader, Catholic mission of Saint-Martin-des-Apindjis, 1903–1905, Archives CSSP, Fond Pouchet, 2D60–9a1.

27 Entry from 26 May 1904, diary of Father Guyader, Catholic mission of Saint-Martin-des-Apindjis, 1903–1905, Archives CSSP, Fond Pouchet, 2D60–9a1.

28 Joseph Blache, *Vrais noirs et vrais blancs d'Afrique au 20e siècle* (Orléans, France: M. Caillette, 1922), 93–95. Soeur Marie Germaine and Louis Marin mentioned the story in *Le Christ au Gabon* (Louvain: Museum Lessianum, 1931), 86–87, as did George Balandier in *Sociologie actuelle de l'Afrique noire* (Paris: Presses universitaires de France, 1950), 222n1.

29 One symptom of this irrational and speculative imaginary lies in the failure of the repertoire of "anthropophagy" to compete with and displace that of cannibalism. Although anthropophagy had emerged in the sixteenth century to help Westerners distinguish between unthinkable behavior (cannibalism) and ritual practice (anthropophagy), the term never took hold in Gabon. Derived from the Latin *anthropophagus* (itself a borrowing from the Greek *anthrôpophagos*), *anthropophagie* and *anthropophages* spread in France in the sixteenth century. Alain Rey, ed., *Dictionnaire historique de la langue française* (Paris: Dictionnaire Le Robert, 2000), vol. 1:92. André Thévet was the first to distinguish between *cannibalisme* as a horrible and inhuman act, and *anthropophagie* (or *andropaphagie*) as a ritual practice limited to the ingestion of enemies. André Thévet, *Singularitez de la France antartique* (1557) and *Cosmographie universelle* (1775), quoted in Frank Lestringant, *Cannibals: The Discovery and Representation of the Cannibal from Columbus to Jules Verne* (Berkeley: University of California Press, 1997), 44–49. Gananath Obeyesekere warns, however, of the lack of conceptualization of the difference between the two terms, in *Cannibal Talk: The Man-Eating Myth and Human Sacrifice in the South Seas*, Berkeley (Los Angeles: University of California Press, 2005), 14–15.

30 Diverse archives mention isolated tiger-men murderers in 1904, 1906, and 1908. In April 1904, Father Guyader commented on the murder of a native woman by a tiger-man. He explained that the tiger-man fetish had "seized" three men passing near the crime scene: they had rushed to the cadaver to consume a chunk of human meat. In December of that same year, the fetish cursed the chief of a village, who helped the tiger man to cut up the corpse of a child. Excerpts

from Father Guyader's diary at Catholic mission of Saint Martin of the Apindjis, 1903–1905, Archives CSSP, Fond Pouchet, 2D60–9a1.

31 "Tiger" is a misnomer, as only leopards live in Gabon. On tiger-men in Gabon, see Christopher Gray, *Colonial Rule and Crisis in Equatorial Africa: Southern Gabon ca. 1850–1940* (Rochester, NY: University of Rochester, 2002), 195–224.

32 Thirty years later, the governor of Gabon, Yves Digo, mentioned that the report figured among the three most quoted studies on tiger-men. Lettre du chef de territoire Yves Digo au gouverneur général de l'AEF, no. 956/AP-AG, 20 July 1953, Archives nationales d'outre mer (hereafter ANOM), 5D 64.

33 Journal du poste de Mekambo (1924–30), ANG/FP 108. In the national archives in Gabon and the ANOM in France, I collected over seventy-five cases and mentions of cases of tiger-men from 1904 to 1940, and approximately fifteen from 1941 to 1951. This conservative estimate is based on attested cases I found in the archives. However, administrative reports mention, if only in passing, a much larger number of cases and convictions.

34 The last mention of a tiger-man murder in the national archives of Gabon dates from 1951.

35 Rapport de Monsieur Hippolyte Charbonnier, Adjoint des Services Civils, Chef de la Subdivision de Tchibanga, à Monsieur l'Administrateur Bourdil, Chef de la Circonscription de la Nyanga (typescript copy), 26 November 1914, Archives CSSP 2D60.9a1. Charbonnier's report was also published in *Bulletin de la Société des Recherches Congolaises*, no. 6, 1925, 171–81. Christopher Gray mentions that the *Annales apostoliques* reproduced the report in 1921, but I could not verify this fact. Gray, *Colonial Rule and Crisis*, 219n22.

36 Charles Zika, *The Appearance of Witchcraft: Print and Visual Culture in Sixteenth-Century Europe* (London: Routledge, 2007), 75.

37 The genre of detective stories in France (*romans policiers*) emerged progressively after Eugène Francois Vidocq, the former chief of the French Police between 1812 and 1827, published his memoirs in 1828. Elsa de Lavergne, *La Naissance du roman policier français: Du Second Empire à la Première Guerre mondiale* (Paris: Classiques Garnier, 2009). At the end of the banquet, Charbonnier asserted, little traces of the cannibal orgy survived: the leopard-men crushed and dispersed the victim's remains with a large stone, hid the knife in the *marmite*, and buried the pot in a secret spot marked by a piece of dead wood.

38 Rapport de Monsieur Hippolyte Charbonnier, Adjoint des Services Civils, Chef de la Subdivision de Tchibanga, à Monsieur l'Administrateur Bourdil, Chef de la Circonscription de la Nyanga (typescript copy), 26 November 1914, Archives CSSP 2D60.9a1.

39 Lettre de René Berlan à Le Testu, from Mimongo, 6 August 1917, CSSP, Fonds Pouchet, 2D60–9a1.

40 Aymard ruled over a *circonscription* (in the colony, the smaller administrative unit, below the "region") of forty thousand souls. Le Testu noted that some administrators had criticized Charbonnier's report. Rapport de Georges Le Testu,

"Sur quelques coutumes indigènes du Gabon," 31 October 1942, Archives CSSP, Fonds Pouchet, 2D60 9a1. In French West Africa, the anthropologist Lucien Lévy-Bruhl, member of the special Commission of Enquiry on the Social Conditions in the Colonies led by Henri Guernut in 1937, asked governors in French West and Equatorial Africa to send him trial records and reports on sorcery, ritual anthropophagy, and secret societies. In the ANOM and National Archives of Gabon, several questionnaires and the answers written by local administrators survive, but Lévy-Bruhl did not seem to have written a final report on his investigations. William Cohen, *Rulers of Empire: French Colonial Services in Africa* (Washington, DC: Hoover Institution Press, 1972), 371; and Sophie Dulucq, "La mentalité cannibale," post no. 19, accessed 14 December 2017, *Anthropophagie et Histoire: Enquête sur une répression coloniale en Afrique*, https://anthist .hypotheses.org/325.

41 For the early story on British sailors captured and eaten on the Como River in 1839–40, see Fleuriot de Langle, "Croisières à la côte d'Afrique (1868)," in *Le Tour du Monde: Nouveau Journal des Voyages* (Paris: Librairie Hachette, 1876), 31:257–304. Henri Trilles repeated the story in "Le Gabon catholique, 1844–1894," manuscript s.d. (c. 1895), Archives du Centre Culturel Français Libreville, GA 266-TRI. See also the profanation of a nun's tomb in Gabon; Compiègne, *L'Afrique équatoriale: Gabonais*, 352.

42 Du Chaillu, *Explorations and Adventures*, 37 and 120.

43 Du Chaillu, *Explorations and Adventures*, 104 and 120. There is a similar idea in Georges Bruel, *La France équatoriale africaine: Le Pays, les habitants, la colonisation, les pouvoirs public* (Paris: Larose, 1935), 168–69.

44 Du Chaillu, *Explorations and Adventures*, 127.

45 There was also a reversal from civilized man to cannibal savage: once Du Chaillu ate a dish prepared by a chief's wife and became nauseated by the thought that "a trick was being played upon me, having recently become acquainted with an Africa custom, of which I had not previously heard, and which consisted in serving, in dishes given to a guest, powder from the skull of a deceased ancestor, with a view to soften his heart in the matter of parting presents." Du Chaillu, *Adventures in the Great Forest*, 400. See also John Miller, "Meat, Cannibalism and Humanity in Paul Du Chaillu's *Explorations and Adventures in Equatorial Africa*; or, What Does a Gorilla Hunter Eat for Breakfast?," *Gothic Studies* 16, no. 1 (May 2014): 70–84.

46 Early exceptions are found in Du Chaillu, *Explorations and Adventures*, 120; and in Louis-Alphonse-Victor du Pont de Compiègne, *L'Afrique équatoriale: Okanda, Bangouens, Osyéba* (Paris: Plon, 1875), 155–57. According to Compiègne, the Fang of Gabon sold their dead and unburied cadavers to prepare them as food.

47 Megan Vaughan, *Curing Their Ills: Colonial Power and African Illness* (Cambridge: Polity Press, 1991), 33–35.

48 Anne McClintock, *Imperial Leather: Race, Gender, and Sexuality in the Colonial Contest* (New York: Routledge, 1995), 71–74, 245–46, and 270–73. See also Bill

Ashcroft, *On Post-colonial Futures: Transformations of Colonial Culture* (London: Continuum, 2001), 36–53.

49 Du Bellay, "Le Gabon," 315; and Victor Largeau, *Encyclopédie pahouine, Congo français: Éléments de grammaire et dictionnaire français-pahouin* (Paris: E. Leroux, 1901), 10.

50 On pollution, see Mary Douglas, *Purity and Danger: An Analysis of Concepts of Pollution and Taboo* (London: Routledge and Kegan Paul, 1976).

51 Du Chaillu, *Explorations and Adventures*, 120; Compiègne, *L'Afrique équatoriale: Okanda*, 155; Adolphe Louis Cureau, *Les Sociétés primitives de l'Afrique équatoriale* (Paris: Armand Colin, 1912), 202–8; and Bruel, *La France équatoriale africaine*, 165–70. "The Fans eat the cadavers fished from rivers," wrote P. Payeur-Didelot in 1899, in *Trente mois au continent mystérieux: Gabon-Congo et côte occidentale d'Afrique* (Paris: Berger-Levrault, 1899), 161. Robert Hamill Nassau described how the Fang "[dug] up dead bodies to feast on their flesh"; Robert Hamill Nassau, *Fetishism in West Africa: Forty Years' Observation of Native Customs and Superstitions* (London: Duckworth, 1904), 235 and 246. Nassau, a Presbyterian missionary and a medical doctor (he had obtained his MD from the University of Pennsylvania Medical School in 1861), was first appointed in 1862 on Corisco Island off the coast of Gabon. He then served throughout the colony in Benita, Belambla, Kangwe (later known as Lambaréné), Talaguga, Baraka (Libreville), and Batanga. He returned to the United States in 1906.

52 Georges Renouard, *L'Ouest africain et les Missions Catholiques: Congo et Oubanghi* (Paris: H. Oudin, 1904), 134–36, professed that African cannibals would immerse a child in a river so his flesh would "macerate" and "tenderize." On the "Bond-jos" in Ubangi, see also Mgr. Alexandre Le Roy, *La Religion des primitifs*, 5th ed. (Paris: G. Beauchesne, 1925), 353; Cureau, *Les Sociétés primitives*, 37–38; and Henri Trilles, *Mille Lieux dans l'inconnu: En Pleine forêt équatoriale chez les Fang anthropophages* (Bruges, Belgium: Desclée de Brouwer, 1935), 28.

53 Fernand Grébert, *Au Gabon (Afrique équatoriale française)* (Paris: Société des Missions évangéliques de Paris, 1922), 80.

54 Le Roy, *La Religion des primitifs*, 317–18. The book won a prize from the Académie française.

55 On pornotropics, see McClintock, *Imperial Leather*, 21–24. See also Marina Warner, "Fee Fie to Fum: The Child in the Jaws of History," in Barker, Hulme, and Inversen, *Cannibalism*, 165. Warner shows that the erotic fantasies in the imperial lore of cannibalism expressed the danger of control versus autonomy, annihilation versus possession, and social binding versus individuality.

56 The passage continues, "Fifteen years later, it was not a dream anymore, but 'reality.' We were in the midst of savages, much more hideous and mean that we had ever imagined them. Sometimes a knife was hold on my head, I saw the fire and the skewer up close as I came indeed to be interested in them personally. I was taken a prisoner once, too: it was much less funny that in my childhood!" Henri Trilles, *Fleurs noires et âmes blanches* (Lille: Desclée, De Brouwer, 1914), 8.

57 Carol Summers, "Intimate Colonialism: The Imperial Production of Reproduction in Uganda, 1907–1925," *Signs* 16, no. 4 (summer 1991): 787–807. For a recent study of this topic in Gabon, see Rachel Jean-Baptiste, *Conjugal Rights: Marriage, Sexuality, and Urban Life Colonial Libreville, Gabon, 1849–1960* (Athens: Ohio University Press, 2014).

58 Karl Marx coined "social reproduction" to explain the transmission of social inequality in *Das Kapital* (1867; first French edition 1872). Karl Marx, *Das Kapital: Kritik Der Politischen Ökonomie* (Berlin: Dietz, 1983).

59 Arthur de Gobineau, *Essai sur l'inégalité des races humaines* (Paris: Didot, 1855). Gobineau's aim was "to bring history in the family of natural sciences" (*faire entrer l'histoire dans la famille des sciences naturelles*). He was the first theorist of the Aryan race with Georges Vacher de la Pouge, *L'Aryen, son rôle social, cours libre de science politique, professé à l'Université de Montpellier (1889–1890)* (Paris: A. Fontemoing, 1899).

60 Gustave Le Bon, *Les Premières civilisations* (Paris: Bibliothèque Camille Flammarion, 1889), 122. Charles Darwin used the term "primitive horde" to refer to the simplest form of a social group of mammals.

61 Griffon du Bellay, "Le Gabon," 278 and 308. Cureau, *Les Sociétés primitives,* v–vi.

62 Renouard, *L'Ouest africain*, 97–98. Georges Montandon, *La Race, les races: Mise au point d'ethnologie somatique* (Paris: Payot, 1933), 161. In 1865, Griffon Du Bellay had already noted the Gabonese taste for "debased diets" such as snakes, insects, or spoiled meats. Griffon du Bellay, "Le Gabon," 278 and 308.

63 Le Roy, *La Religion des primitifs,* 95–96.

64 Georges Bruel, *L'Afrique Équatoriale Française (A.E.F.)* (Paris: Larose, 1930), 23.

65 Yet Europeans had long pondered on this dimension of anthropophagy. In 1899, French sociologists Marcel Mauss and Henri Hubert theorized cannibalism anew in a seminal article on the religious nature and function of sacrifice. Henri Hubert and Marcel Mauss, "Essai sur la nature et la fonction du sacrifice," *Année sociologique*, no. 2 (1899): 29–138.

66 Nassau, *Fetishism in West Africa*, 139 and 235. For Milligan, a Presbyterian missionary from the United States who served six years in Gabon, mostly at the Baraka station in Libreville, "fetishism" served only to conceal primal terrors toward the supernatural and gross appetites for material profit. In the first case, cannibalism derived from "a last desperate resort of fear seeking fetish protection. Robert H. Milligan, *The Fetish Folk of West Africa* (New York: AMS Press, 1970) [orig. pub. 1912], 241.

67 Trilles, *Fleurs noires*, 175–79.

68 Claude Lévi-Strauss, *The Elementary Structures of Kinship* (Boston, MA: Beacon Press, 1969); and Michel Foucault, *Abnormal: Lectures at the Collège de France* (New York: Picador, 1999), 78.

69 Payeur-Didelot, *Trente mois*, 227. Renouart wrote, "Anthropophagy is indissociable from slavery"; Renouart, *L'Ouest africain* 133.

70 Du Chaillu, *Explorations and Adventures*, 492. See also Bruel, *La France équato-riale française*, 191.

71 Administrator Maclatchy, Monographie de la subdivision de Mimongo, 20 March 1936, CSSP Pouchet 273-A-II, 23.

72 *Les enfants livrés ainsi comme otages sont rarement libérés et passent de maîtres à maîtres; du rôle d'animaux utiles et apprivoisés qu'ils jouent d'abord, ils ne tardent pas à descendre, dans la suite à celui de bêtes malfaisantes. Car non seulement l'esclave s'est abruti et a perdu toute fierté, tout ressort, mais il a contracté toutes sortes de vices au cours de ses ventes successives.* Soeur Marie-Germain, *Le Christ au Gabon*, 11–12. See also Cureau, *Les Sociétés primitives*, v–vi.

73 Du Chaillu, *Explorations and Adventures*, 98.

74 Compiègne, *L'Afrique équatoriale: Gabonais*.

75 Compiègne, *L'Afrique équatoriale: Gabonais*; Trilles, *Le Totémisme*, 123.

76 The Fang's perceived invasion toward the coast presumably compensated for their decentralized structures. Trilles, *Le Totémisme*, 123. In 1947, Edouard Trézenem argued that they represented "the most cohesive fraction of the Gabo-nese population." *L'Afrique équatoriale française: Le Cameroun* (Paris: Société d'éditions géographiques, maritimes et coloniales, 1947), 54.

77 The Hamitic hypothesis, popular until the 1960s, argued that some African races descended from Semites, or "Hamites," the branch started by Ham, the cursed son of Noah. Charles Seligman, *Races in Africa*, 4th ed. (London: Oxford University Press, 1966), 136. On the Hamitic hypothesis in the Great Lakes region, see Jean-Pierre Chrétien, "Hutu et Tutsi au Rwanda et au Burundi," in *Au cœur de l'ethnie*, ed. Elikia M'Bokolo et Jean-Loup Amselle, 2d ed. (Paris: La Découverte, 1999), 129–65.

78 Louis Franc, *De l'origine des Pahouins: Essai de résolution de ce problème ethno-logique* (Paris, Maloine, 1905). The absence of slave trading among the Fang, when not blamed on cannibalism, became a sign of moral and racial purity by contrast with the "decadence" of coastal tribes. Leighton Wilson, "Pangwe People," *Missionary Herald*, Vol. 39–6 (June 1843): 238–39.

79 At the International Congress for the History of Religions in Basel, Protes-tant missionary E. Allégret compared Fang beliefs in the spirit of the dead, to that of Achilles in Homer. "Les idées religieuses des Fangs," *Revue d'Histoire des Religions* 50 (1904): 219. Günther Tessman linked the Fang cosmology to that of ancient Egyptians. Tessman, *Die Pangwe: Völkerkundliche Monogra-phie Eines Westafrikanischen Negerstammes; Ergebnisse Der Lübecker Pangwe-expedition, 1907–1909 und Früherer Forschungen, 1904–1907* (Berlin: E. Wasmuth, A.-G., 1913), translated in *Fang*, ed. Philippe Laburthe-Tolra and Christiane Falgayrettes-Leveau (Paris: Musée Dapper, 1991), 296. Father Henri Trilles compared the Fang language and totems to those of ancient Egyptians; Trilles, *Le Totémisme*, 4, 46, 115, and 309–7. "Like the Jews," Pastor Grébert observed, "children are taught the genealogy of their father and their tribe"; Grébert, *Au Gabon*, 54.

80 Thomas Savage first named it *Troglodydes gorilla*. Today, the taxonomy for the Western gorilla of West Central Africa is *Gorilla gorilla*.

81 Patterson, "Paul B. Du Chaillu," 655 and 662.

82 In chapters 20 and 21, Du Chaillu signaled the "vast chasm [that] lies between even the most inferior forms of the human race and the most superior of the apes"; Du Chaillu, *Explorations and Adventures*, 388–429. In the French edition, two plates compared human and gorillas' skulls; Du Chaillu, *Voyages et aventures*, 415.

83 Mary Louise Pratt, *Imperial Eyes: Travel Writing and Transculturation* (London: Routledge, 1992), 208–10, argues that the discovery in the late 1850s was so ideologically charged that Westerners had to reenact it at regular intervals ever since.

84 Du Chaillu, *Explorations and Adventures*, 101. On page 86, Du Chaillu wrote, "I protest I felt like almost like a murderer when I saw the gorilla this first time. As they ran—on their hind-legs—they looked fearfully like hairy men; their heads down, their bodies inclined forward, their whole appearance like men running for their lives."

85 Du Chaillu, *Explorations and Adventures*, 98; and Robert Hamill Nassau, *In an Elephant Corral, and Other Tales of West African Experiences* (1912; New York: Negro Universities Press, 1969), 112.

86 Compiègne, *L'Afrique équatoriale: Okandas*, 85.

87 Schweinfurth, *Au coeur de l'Afrique* (1874), 1:296. Payeur-Didelot, *Trente mois*, 116.

88 Tessman, "Die Pangwe," in Falgeyrettes-Leveau and Laburthe-Tolra, *Fang*, 263.

89 Léon Poutrin, *Travaux scientifiques de la Mission Cottes au Sud-Cameroun (1905–1908): Anthropologie, ethnographie, linguistique* (Paris: Ernest Leroux, 1911), 69–71.

90 Montandon wrote that the "Negro" of Equatorial Africa was "more primitive, more simian than other human races," and that the "Negroes" descended from a man "less Negro than him, the Negroid. . . . The [contemporary] Negro thus becomes—unless cross-breeding (*métissage*) or intentional domestication occurs—always more Negro"; Montandon, *La Race*, 114, 128, and 156.

91 Early texts always wrote of gorillas in a cluster with man-eaters. See Griffon du Bellay, "Le Gabon," 307–9. Richard Burton's 1876 account of his single-day visit to a Fang village ended with a short transition summarizing his failure to encounter a gorilla (chapter 10) and a final, elaborate description of "Mr., Mrs., and Master Gorilla" (chapter 11). Burton, *Two Trips*, 197–261. Mary Kingsley described her first encounter with gorillas right after her initial meeting with the Fang; Kingsley, *Travels*, 267–68.

92 Burton, *Two Trips*, 250–51. Trilles, *Mille Lieux*, 79–80. Robert Hamill Nassau also examines the rumor of cannibal gorillas in *My Ogowe: Being a Narrative of Daily Incidents during my Sixteen years in Equatorial West Africa* (New York: Neale, 1909), 99. See also Du Chaillu, *Voyages et aventures*, 292.

93 Joseph H. Reading, *The Ogowe Band: A Narrative of African Travel* (Philadelphia, PA: Reading, 1890), 227.

94 Maurice Briault, *Sur les pistes de l'AEF*, 2nd ed. (Paris: Editions Alsatia, 1948), 21, records the following exchange: "The facies [of the gorilla we killed yesterday] has something human, but monstrous: it really is a horrible beast! Although its meat tastes good and its aroma is not too strong, few of our Senegalese ate some. 'It's almost a man!,' they said. But the villagers did not leave anything! And as one of them told me, it is good, it is very good indeed, however it is not as good as a man. 'So you ate man?' I asked. 'Oh, not much, just to taste it.' 'And how many men did you taste?' 'Very few indeed! I did not sample more than fifty. And looking at me with a lusty eye:—The Whites must taste much better.' I myself ate of the gorilla, and found it quite good, although a bit strong in flavor."

95 Du Chaillu, *Explorations and Adventures*, 71.

96 Du Chaillu, *Explorations and Adventures*, 63.

97 The passage was so evocative that it prompted the author to add a prudish footnote at the bottom of the page, reverting to the pronoun "it": "I have no hesitation in saying that the gorilla is the most horrible wild animal I have seen [and that it gives] a feeling of horrible disgust on account of its hideousness of appearance." Kingsley, *Travels*, fn268.

98 The prejudice came, partly, from the popular idea that the African brain stopped developing after puberty. Milligan for instance (*Fetish Folk of West Africa*, 1912, 181), contrasted the cunning, seriousness, and intelligence of the African boy, "who bears the strongest stamp of humanity" with the behavior of the adolescent African, who becomes stupidly happy." According to Cureau, *Les Sociétés primitives* (1912), two distinct stages characterized the Negro's intellectual life: at sexual maturity, it brutally stopped and "slightly regressed." In 1935, Bruel's encyclopedic description of French Equatorial Africa reproduced Cureau's theory with much admiration. Bruel, *L'Afrique Équatoriale française*, 174.

99 Du Chaillu, *Adventures in the Great Forest*, 152 sqq. Later, Du Chaillu's assistants bring him a wounded mother with a baby. He writes, "Her death was like of a human being, and afflicted me more than I could have thought possible. Her child clung to her and tried to obtain milk from her breast after she was dead. I photographed them both when the young one was resting on his mother's lap." He kept the gorilla alive for three days, feeding him with goat milk. Du Chaillu, *Adventures in the Great Forest*, 159–61.

100 Paul Belloni Du Chaillu, *Recent Remarkable Discoveries in Central Africa* (Philadelphia, PA: Barclay, 1867), 95. The same anecdote was distilled in a book for children featuring Du Chaillu's pet chimpanzee, Master Tommy: "He was growing so accustomed to civilized life that I began to have great hopes of carrying him alive to America." Paul B. Du Chaillu, *Stories of the Gorilla Country: Narrated for Young People* (New York: Harper and Brothers, 1872), 291.

101 Payeur-Didelot, *Trente mois*, 248. In the 1890s, R. L. Garner, an American researcher, came to Gabon to work the hypothesis that the gorilla had an articulate language. Jeremy Rich, *Missing Links: The African and American Worlds of R. L. Garner, Primate Collector* (Athens: University of Georgia Press, 2012).

102 Gabrielle Vassal, *Mon séjour au Congo français* (Paris: Pierre Roger, 1925), 156. See also the description of the "ape-like" underling of a colonialist's cook in Brazzaville in the late 1930s in Mary Motley, *Devils in Waiting* (London: Longmans, 1959), 34–35.

103 Sigmund Freud, *Totem and Taboo: Some Points of Agreement between the Mental Lives of Savages and Neurotics* (1913; New York: Norton, 1950). See also Erdem Pulcu, "An Evolutionary Perspective on Gradual Formation of Superego in the Primal Horde," *Frontiers in Psychology* 5, no. 8 (January 2014): [n.p.], published online, accessed 14 March 2015: https://www.ncbi.nlm.nih.gov/pmc/articles /PMC3900855/.

104 In Du Chaillu's texts, the most repeated qualification for male gorillas was their size ("big," "huge," "immense") and their posture ("terrific," "horrid," "frightful"). He never used these terms for female gorillas.

105 Du Chaillu, *Explorations and Adventures*, 98.

106 Paul Du Chaillu, *Lost in the Jungle: Narrated for Young People*. New York: Harper & Brothers, 1875, 136.

107 Trilles, *Mille Lieux*, 80. Grébert, *Au Gabon*, 36.

108 Du Chaillu, *Lost in the Jungle*, 51. But Alfred Marche insisted that gorillas preferred to flee than to attack hunters. Albert Marche, *Trois voyages dans l'Afrique occidentale: Sénégal, Gambie, Casamance, Gabon, Ogooué* (Paris: Librairie Hachette, 1882), 150–51.

109 Du Chaillu, *Lost in the Jungle*, 129–31, the text reads, "The poor brave fellow, who had gone off alone, was lying on the ground in a pool of his own blood, and, I at first thought, quite dead. Beside him lay his gun; the stock was broken, and the barrel bent almost double. In one place it was flattened, and it bore plainly the marks of the gorilla's teeth. . . . [The poor fellow said,] "As I raised my gun to fire, the gorilla, which was quite close to me, stretched out his long and powerful arm, and dashed the gun from my grasp. It struck the ground with great violence and went off. Then, in an instant, and with a terrible roar, the animal raised his arm and came at me with terrific force. I was felled to the ground by a heavy blow from his immense open paw. . . . He cut me in two; and while I lay bleeding on the ground, the monster seized my gun, and I thought he would dash my brains out with it. That is all I remember. I know that I am going to die."

110 Du Chaillu, *Explorations and Adventures*, 434. For an analysis of similar illustrations, see Christopher Steiner, "Travel Engravings and the Construction of the Primitive," in *Prehistories of the Future, Primitivist Project and the Culture of Modernism*, ed. Elazar Barkan and Ronald Bush (Stanford, CA: Stanford University Press, 1996), 202–25.

111 Du Chaillu, *Explorations and Adventures*, 287.

112 Du Chaillu, *Stories of the Gorilla Country*, 81.

113 Du Chaillu, *Explorations and Adventures*, 243.

114 "The capture of an infant gorilla by Du Chaillu and the African hunters who accompanied him." Wood engraving from a newspaper account of Du Chaillu's

travels, 1867, origin unknown, last access date 13 December 2017, available online at Granger Historical Picture Archive, www.granger.com/results.asp?inline =true&image=0037401&wwwflag=4&itemx=42&screenwidth=1366.

115 Circulaire du Ministère des colonies, signed Pietri, 10 June 1930, ANG/FP 57. Rapport du Directeur de l'agriculture de l'AEF, signed Drogue, 9 April 1948, no. 521/AGR, ANG/FP 57.

116 Fleuriot de Langle, "Croisières," 281–82.

117 Nassau, *In an Elephant Corral*, 104–5.

118 On colonizers' guilt and usurpation, see Albert Memmi, *Portrait du colonisé: Précédé du portrait du colonisateur* (Paris: Buchet/Chastel, 1957).

119 When Jacques died of consumption, Fleuriot de Langle gave the cadaver to Sir Charles Lyell, a close friend of Darwin and a geologist interested in the theory of evolution. Fleuriot de Langle, Croisières, "Croisières," 282.

120 Compiègne, *L'Afrique équatoriale: Okanda*, 191–92 and 210; and Marche, *Trois voyages*, 250. There is a similar tale in Payeur-Didelot, who put the "little orphan's cadaver" in a barrel of white alcohol and sent it to France; Payeur-Didelot, *Trente mois*, 251. The fact that Anatole's remains did not keep well allowed Du Chaillu, twelve years later, to achieve fame with the specimens he shipped to New York and London.

121 Leonard G. Wilson, "The Gorilla and the Question of Human Origins: The Brain Controversy," *Journal of the History of Medicine and Allied Sciences* 51 (1996): 184–207; Amanda Hodgson, "Defining the Species: Apes, Savages and Humans in Scientific and Literary Writing of the 1860s," *Journal of Victorian Culture* 4, no. 2 (1999): 228–51; Dan Bivona, "Human Thighs and Susceptible Apes: Self-Implicating Category Confusion in Victorian Discourse on West Africa," *Nineteenth-Century Prose* 32, no. 2 (2005): 81–121; and John Miller, *Empire and the Animal Body, Violence, Identity and Ecology in Victorian Adventure Fiction* (London: Anthem Press, 2014).

122 Burton, *Two Trips*, 243.

123 Collodon, *Congo Jake*, 200. William Winwood Reade bought a freshly killed gorilla from African traders; William Winwood Reade, *Savage Africa; Being the Narrative of a Tour in Equatorial, Southwestern and Northwestern Africa* (New York: Harper & Brothers, 1864), 76–77. In 1876, Nassau was looking for gorilla skeletons in Galoa and Nkomi country. He refused many that were incomplete as, he came to regret, he "failed to appreciate that even an imperfect skeleton would, at that time, had been value in America." The value of these incomplete items possibly amounted probably to US$100. Nassau, *My Ogowe*, 155.

124 Nassau, *In an Elephant Corral*, 91–132.

125 Du Chaillu, *Lost in the Jungle*, 52. In *Adventures in the Great Forest*, Du Chaillu describes one of his assistants, Igala, as his right-hand man: "He was also my taxidermist, for I had taught him to skin and preserve animals" (368–69).

126 Du Chaillu, *Explorations and Adventures*, 109.

127 Du Chaillu, *Recent Remarkable Discoveries*, 92; and Du Chaillu, *Explorations and Adventures*, 76. Several large chests full of cloth, tobacco, and beads served to buy gorilla skins and animal carcasses from local sellers.

128 Nassau lived in Talagouga, the largest Protestant mission in central Gabon, near the Ogooué River.

129 Nassau, *In an Elephant Corral*, 109–10.

130 Nassau, *In an Elephant Corral*, 130–31. He gave the contents of the jar to Dr. Morton for microscopic examination.

131 Du Chaillu, *Adventures in the Great Forest*, 442 and 474.

132 Jan Vansina, *Paths in the Rainforests: Toward a History of Political Tradition in Equatorial Africa* (Madison: University of Wisconsin Press, 1990), 74, 78, 276–77.

133 Tamara Giles-Vernick and Stephanie Rupp, "Visions of Apes, Reflections on Change: Telling Tales of Great Apes in Equatorial Africa," *African Studies Review* 49, no. 1 (April 2006): 51–73.

134 Collodon, *Congo Jake*, 116–26, 185–86, and 195–96. One of the most famous episodes of political usurpation in Gabon occurred when the Nkomi people crowned Reverend Bichet, a catholic missionary, their king. Auguste Foret, "Le Lac Fernan-Vaz," *Bulletin de la société de géographie* 19, no. 308 (1898): 308–27; and François Gaulme, "Un Problème d'histoire du Gabon: Le Sacre du P. Bichet par les Nkomi en 1897," *Revue française d'histoire d'outre-mer* 61, no. 224 (1974): 395–416.

135 "Carnaval des Colons à Madingou," *La Semaine de l'AEF*, no. 180 (11 November 1956), 4.

136 For Payeur-Didelot, two "cannibal races," the Baholi and the Mbondjo, were "remarkable for their herculean height, bulging muscles, and simian faces." Payeur-Didelot, *Trente mois*, 239. Countless stories featured male gorillas kidnapping black women in feasts both erotic and cannibalistic. Du Chaillu wrote, "Two Mbondemo women were walking together through the woods, when suddenly an immense gorilla stepped into the path and, clutching one of the women, bore her off in spite of the screams struggles of both. . . . A few days afterwards she returned to her home [and] related that the gorilla had forced her to submit to his desires"; Du Chaillu, *Explorations and Adventures*, 86–87. See also Reade, *Savage Africa*, 184. Other writers used the rumors to animalize African women: "One has to have singular appetites [to consume them]," wrote Charles Castellani in 1898, in *Les Femmes au Congo* (Paris: Flammarion, 1898), 17, 28–31, 39.

137 Susan D. Bernstein, "Ape Anxiety: Sensation Fiction, Evolution, and the Genre Question," *Journal of Victorian Culture* 6, no. 2 (2001): 250–71.

138 Arthur Conan Doyle, *The Case-Book of Sherlock Holmes* (London: Wordsworth Editions, 1995), first published in *Strand Magazine* October 1921–April 1927.

139 Serge Voronoff, *Quarante-trois greffes du singe à l'homme* (Paris: Librairie Octave Douin, 1924). Nine professors of medicine from France, Italy, Brazil, and Peru, and more than 120 physicians, Voronoff claimed, attended his procedures. Seven of his patients were themselves doctors of medicine.

140 He sent them to the British Museum and Dr. Owen. Appendix 1, in Paul Belloni Du Chaillu, *A Journey to Ashango-Land: And Further Penetration into Equatorial Africa* (New York: D. Appleton, 1867), 439–60.

141 Du Chaillu, *Recent Remarkable Discoveries*, 63.

142 Du Chaillu, *Recent Remarkable Discoveries*, 71.

143 Du Chaillu, *Adventures in the Great Forest*, 442–46. To reassure the women, he said, he tried to measure one of his Ashango guides, who refused. Colonial administrators routinely measured local Gabonese. In 1936, for instance, the district chief Maclatchy listed the height of several Babongo (Pygmy) women he had measured at the administrative post in Mimongo (Ngounié). Administrator Maclatchy, Monographie de la subdivision de Mimongo, 20 March 1936, 32, CSSP Pouchet 273-A-II.

144 Marche, *Trois voyages*, 109.

CHAPTER 6 ⁝ Eating

1 The Gabonese use the French expression *pièces détachées* for human organs harvested on a murdered body. It has the same double meaning of mechanical devices and replacement parts as "body parts" in English. It is very common for mechanics in Gabon to hang a sign reading "*Pièces détachées*" in front of their workshops.

2 Verbs for eating derive from the proto-Bantu *-dia-. Contemporary verbs for bewitching derive from the proto-Bantu *-dog-. See, for instance, the Fang expression of *adzi nlem* ("to eat the heart," "to eat the life force").

3 A prime inspiration for this idea is Joseph Ambouroué-Avaro, *Un Peuple gabonais à l'aube de la colonisation: Le Bas-Ogowe au XIXe siècle* (Paris: Karthala, 1981).

4 For comparison, see Rosalind Shaw, *Memories of the Slave Trade: Ritual and the Historical Imagination in Sierra Leone*. Chicago, IL: University of Chicago Press, 2002.

5 Jan Vansina, *Paths in the Rainforests: Towards a History of Political Tradition in Equatorial Africa* (Madison: University of Wisconsin Press, 1990), 299.

6 Ambouroué-Avaro, *Un Peuple gabonais*; also see chapter 3 of this volume.

7 Joseph Tonda was the first to insist on the dyad of absorption and regurgitating; Joseph Tonda, *Le Souverain moderne: Le Corps du pouvoir en Afrique centrale (Congo, Gabon)* (Paris: Karthala, 2005), 200–201 and 209–13.

8 Likewise, Fang Bëti speakers thought that the mother cooked the initial fat and the fetus to humanize it until it became a child. Philippe Laburthe-Tolra, *Les Seigneurs de la forêt: Essai sur le passé historique, l'organisation sociale et les normes éthiques des anciens Bëti du Cameroun* (Paris: Publications de la Sorbonne, 1981), 281.

9 Laburthe-Tolra, *Les Seigneurs de la forêt*, 289–90.

10 On ritual autopsies, see Matthieu Salpêteur and Jean-Pierre Warnier, "Looking for the Effects of Bodily Organs and Substances through Vernacular Public

Autopsy in Cameroon," *Critical African Studies* 5, no. 3 (fall 2013): 153–74. Several cults, including Bwiti, prescribed initiates to absorb a hallucinatory drink so they could see ancestors.

11 That *evu* itself, as a substance detachable from the body, probably came as a late innovation, maybe starting among the Fang-speaking groups, reinforces the point. Jan Vansina, personal communication, 12 April 2007.

12 However, some pupils regarded *kundu* as "coveting flesh." The term might result from Laman's translation. Karl Laman, *The Kongo* (Uppsala, Sweden: Studia Ethnographica Upsaliensia, 1962), 3:216 and 3:223.

13 Laman added that some people grew it in the intestines, and some in the liver, the stomach, the heart, or the lungs. Laman, *Kongo* 3:242.

14 Günther Tessman, *Die Pangwe: Völkerkundliche Monographie Eines Westafrikanischen Negerstammes; Ergebnisse Der Lübecker Pangwe-expedition, 1907–1909 und Früherer Forschungen, 1904–1907* (Berlin: E. Wasmuth, A.-G., 1913), translated in *Fang*, ed. Philippe Laburthe-Tolra and Christiane Falgayrettes-Leveau (Paris: Musée Dapper, 1991), 292.

15 Field notes, 30 June 2007.

16 Colleen E. Kriger, *Pride of Men: Ironworking in 19th-Century West Central Africa* (Portsmouth, NH: Heinemann, 1999), 100.

17 Administrator Maclatchy, monographie de la subdivision de Mimongo, 20 March 1936, 48, Archives CSSP Pouchet 273-A-II.

18 Louis-Alphonse-Victor du Pont de Compiègne, *L'Afrique équatoriale: Gabonais Pahouins, Gallois* (Paris: Plon, 1876), 287.

19 Mabik-ma-Kombil, *Parlons Yipunu: Langue et culture des punu du Gabon-Congo* (Paris: L'Harmattan, 2001), 129. According to Luc Moreau, a Mpongwe informant, "A *fusil nocturne* is almost invisible, it looks like a leaf. You can put it on the ground, and when the person walks on it, he or she gets hurt." Interview with Luc Moreau, Libreville, 19 June 2000. Names of informants, unless otherwise noted, have been anonymized.

20 Richard Lynch Garner, "Heathen Rites to Heathen Gods, III. Buiti—Revelations of the Prophet," Richard Lynch Garner Papers, National Anthropological Archives, Smithsonian Institution, Washington, DC. I thank Jeremy Rich for sending me a copy of this document.

21 Rapport d'Hippolyte Charbonnier, adjoint des services civils, chef de la subdivisison de Tchibanga, à Monsieur l'administrateur Bourdil, chef de la circonscription de la Nyanga, November 26, 1916, Archives CSSP, 2D 60.9a1. For an enduring French use of marmites to qualify secret associations, see R. P. Briault, *Dans la forêt du Gabon: Études et scènes africaines* (Paris: Bernard Grasset, 1930), 148–52; and André Raponda-Walker and Roger Sillans, *Rites et croyances des peuples du Gabon: Essai sur les pratiques religieuses d'autrefois et d'aujourd'hui* (Paris: Présence africaine, 1962), 182.

22 For details on the colonial repertoire of secret societies, see Florence Bernault, "Witchcraft and the Colonial Life of the Fetish," in *Spirits in Politics: Uncertainties*

of Power and Healing in African Societies, eds. Barbara Meier and Arne S. Steinforth (Frankfurt am Main: Campus Publishers, 2013), 53–74.

23 Conversation with Luc Moreau, Libreville, 28 June 2000.

24 Interview with Raphaël Tsande, Mouila, 6 June 2002. On marmites, see also note 77.

25 Kajsa Elkhom Friedman, "Liberating the State from the People: Class, Power and Magic in Congo," unpublished manuscript, authors' archives, 1994, 107.

26 This was out of 206 criminal cases I found in the archives, approximately 61 percent. The average frequency is to be taken with caution, however. The cases occurred unevenly, with many taking place during the tiger-men waves of murder in the 1920s and 1930s, and it is possible that the French kept more records of cannibal cases than of other cases.

27 This is how Christopher Gray interprets the surge of tiger-men affairs in Gabon. Christopher Gray, *Colonial Rule and Crisis in Equatorial Africa: Southern Gabon, ca. 1850–1940* (Rochester, NY: University of Rochester Press, 2002), 195–224.

28 Chambre d'homologation de l'AEF, Procès-verbal et interrogatoires, 21 March 1925, Dossier 213, Archives nationales d'outre-mer (hereinafter ANOM) 5D 64.

29 Interrogatoire du témoin Samona, Chambre d'homologation de l'AEF, Procès-verbal et interrogatoires, 21 March 1925, Dossier 213, ANOM 5D 64.

30 Procès-verbal d'arrestation de Moubokounou Mathieu, signed Henri Ambayrac, 19 March 1955, ANG/FP 25.

31 In matrilineal societies, the maternal uncle is the primary protector and authority of children, but he is also a prime suspect when his kin suffer witchcraft attacks.

32 Procès-verbal d'audition de témoin et déposition du sergent de la garde régionale Amady So, 21 March 1925, Mocabe, ANOM, 2D 64.

33 The French transcript of Moubokoumou's testimony used the word *médicaments* and *remèdes* (English: medicines, remedies) for the healer's substances. Procès-verbal d'arrestation de Moubokoumou Mathieu, signed Henri Ambayrac, 19 March 1955, ANG/FP 25.

34 Personal communication with Joseph Tonda, October 2015.

35 Tessman, *Die Pangwe,* 284–85.

36 Report on tiger-men by Hippolyte Charbonnier, Adjoint des services civils, chef de la subdivision de Tchibanga, dated 26 November 1916, Archives CSSP, Fond Pouchet, 2D60–9a1.

37 See chapter 5, fn 38, for more details.

38 Notice relating administrator Banister's voyage, Archives of the Musée de l'Homme, 39.33 DT/Oswald Wirth, quoted by Raponda-Walker and Sillans, *Rites et croyances,* 193.

39 Both suspects were sentenced to eight years in prison. Audience publique du tribunal du second degré de la circonscription du Bas-Ogooué, Lambaréné, 3 August 1938, ANG/FP 811.

40 Documents typed by African clerks often displayed an accent on a silent *e*. The mistake, rare among metropolitan writers, corresponds to the Gabonese pronunciation of the vowel as *é*.

41 A few days later, according to the transcript, Dinga brought Kombila and a few accomplices to a *mpindi* (seasonal camp), where a man named Mangari was tending his field. The gang kidnapped Mangari, cut his throat with a small scythe, and quartered the body. Young Kombila got the hand, while the others shared the head, the shoulder, and the right arm of the victim. Lettre du chef de la subdivision de Mouila au lieutenant-gouverneur du Gabon, no. 25, 14 February 1922; and audience du tribunal indigène de la subdivision de Mouila en matière répressive, 4 November 1920, ANG/FP 1609.

42 Père Jean Bonneau, *Grammaire pounoue et lexique pounou-francais* (Brazzaville: French Equatorial Africa: Imprimerie Charité, 1956), 122; Mabik-ma-Kombil, *Parlons Yipunu*, 170

43 "To eat" is *-nia* in Omyènè, and *-ji* in iPunu. "To bewitch" is *-loga* in iPunu. "To poison" is *-lomba*. "Witch" is *mulosi* (plur. *balosi*) in iPunu. Urbain Teissères, *Méthode pratique pour apprendre l'Omyènè* (Paris: Société des Missions Evangéliques de Paris, 1957). François Nsuka-Nkutsi, *Éléments de description du Punu* (Lyon, France: Université Lyon 2, 1980).

44 In French colonies, the law punished manslaughter and first-degree murder without premeditation with forced labor only. Décret relatif à la répression de l'anthropophagie en Afrique occidentale et en Afrique équatoriale française, JOAEF, 15 June 1923, 282. In 1937, cannibalism came under further scrutiny when the French Parliament launched a wide-scale inquiry on the social conditions in the colonies. Henry Gernut organized a commission with members such as Lucien Lévy-Bruhl and André Gide, but the project failed, together with the Front Populaire government. Lévy-Bruhl, however, wrote an important report on cannibalism in West and Equatorial Africa. Ghislaine Lydon, "The Unraveling of a Neglected Source: A Report on Women in Francophone West Africa in the 1930s," *Cahiers d'études africaines* 37, no. 147 (1997): 561.

45 Most of them were connected to tiger-men affairs. Between 1904 and 1923, I found mentions of only seven death sentences in the archives, which is an underestimation: many trials are incomplete and do not include the sentence.

46 Meiss had obviously overstepped his duty as district officer and president of the local tribunal: only second-degree courts could try crimes and pronounce the death penalty. But the higher court (*chambre d'homologation*) in Brazzaville acquitted him of the charge in 1931. Lettre de Pierre Duverge au lieutenant-gouverneur du Gabon, 27 February 1931; lettre de J.-F. Bernard au gouverneur général de l'AEF à Brazzaville, n. d.; rapport, signed by Hutinel, 24 March 1930, M'Vadhi; and procès-verbaux d'interrogation de témoins no. 7, 13, 20, 21, and 24 January 1931, ANG/FP 811.

47 A final article added the possibility of banishing the guilty parties from their residential district for five to twenty years. Although trials show that the 1923

decree derived from earlier colonial jurisprudence, early regulations are difficult to trace; they originated in the governor general's office in the form of letters and *circulaires,* and were seldom published in the *Journal officiel de l'Afrique équatoriale française.* The 1923 decree survived after World War II. In 1946, the legislator added a special article (264) to the general French penal code that now applied to all Africans. It concerned people who traded in human bones or who practiced sorcery, magic, or charlatanism. The crime was punished by one to five years of prison and ten years of exile.

48 The court sentenced N'Dong M'Ba to two years of prison and five years of exile. Audience publique du Tribunal de second degré de l'Estuaire, no. 34, 8–9 May 1941, Affaire N'Dong M'Ba, ANG/FP, Estuaire 835. After World War II, however, some administrators started to recognize the legitimacy of family cults, especially among the Fang. In 1951, a man accused of keeping human bones in his house got "attenuating circumstances for only perpetuating a Fang custom"; the judge pronounced a suspended sentence of one year in prison. In 1955, a case of "grave desecration" in the Fang region of Mitzic ended up in three months of prison. Registre des jugements du Tribunal de Mitzic, affaire no. 8, 6 July 1951, ANG/FP 509; registre des jugements du Tribunal de Mitzic, and Audience des flagrants délits, affaire no. 75, 12 February 1955, ANG/FP 509.

49 The chief also insinuated that Boueza had committed two previous murders. He ended his testimony by asking the officer "to punish Boueza with the utmost severity, or more crimes would occur." Procès-verbal d'enregistrement de plainte de Djibo, 11 May 1942, Tribunal indigène de Mékambo, Djouah, and Audience publique du Tribunal de second degré du Djouah, Mékambo, no. 44, 8 October 1942, ANG/FP, 629.

50 Procès-verbal d'enregistrement de plainte de Djibo, 11 May 1942.

51 For a detailed analysis of the combining of Catholic rites with cannibal images in the Tooro Kingdom of Western Uganda, see Heike Behrend, *Resurrecting Cannibals: The Catholic Church, Witch-Hunts, and the Production of Pagans in Western Uganda* (Woodbridge, UK: Boydell & Brewer, 2011).

52 Bekale in particular talked of "The Eternal Lord in his vengeance [who] remembers the blood that has been shed and He will not forget the cries of the afflicted [Psalms, IX, 13]." Pierre Bekale quoted in James Fernandez, "Christian Acculturation and Fang Witchcraft," *Cahiers d'études africaines* 2, no. 6 (1961): 244–70.

53 People also call them *Ota Mpolo* (the Big Table). Interview with Raphaël Tsande, Mouila, 6 June 2002. In iPunu, the ordinary term for table is *tavulu,* from the French *table* and English "table."

54 In 1910, an obituary for the carpenter at the mission St-Martin-des-Apindjis, close to Mouila where I interviewed Raphael Tsande, explained that "the last work of the brother, a communion table, was done for God; we firmly trust that the Father of the Family will welcome him to his table, at the banquet of Eternal Life." Mission du Gabon: St-Martin-Des-Apindjis," *Bulletin* CSSP, tome 26, 1911–1913, 980.

55 Since the Reformation, violent conflicts and contention on the nature of the holy host and the resurrection of Christ's body have torn Western Christendom. Frank Lestringant, *Une sainte horreur, ou, le voyage en Eucharistie: XVIe–XVIIIe siècles* (Paris: Presses universitaires de France, 1996). Missionaries also saw the sacrifice of Christ as the act of God himself, not a ritual initiated by any person or "expert."

56 I worked with anthropologist Lionel Ikogou-Renamy to determine how Protestant missionaries used to translate the Gospel in the vernacular. Our investigation shows that they were careful not to use the vernacular for meat (*nyama*) or flesh (*ozyonli, ebanda*) when talking of the Last Supper. In the Mpongwè version of the New Testament from 1852, for instance, "the body of Christ" is translated as *mpemba y Yesu* (the bread of Jesus), and "blood" as *ntyini*. Missionaries of the American Board of Commissioners for Foreign Missions, *The Gospel according to St John, Translated into the Mpongwe Language* (New York: American Bible Society, 1852).

57 Pentecostal churches also helped to popularize the term *magie noire* (black magic). André Perrier, *Gabon: Un Réveil religieux* (Paris: L'Harmattan, 1988); and André Mary, "La Diabolisation du sorcier et le réveil de Satan," *Religiologiques*, no. 18 (1998): 53–77.

58 The Very Bad Heart of the Devil carries the older view that the witch-substance is located in the heart, not the belly.

59 People usually translate vampire in the vernacular with the same terms they use for witch-substance: *kundu, evu,* and *inyèmba*.

60 Yet, a few months before the conversation, one of my friends had suffered accusations of being a witch. His vampire (read his "brains," "publications," and "academic success") had provoked tremendous jealousy among his peers.

61 Luise White, *Speaking with Vampires: Rumor and History in Colonial Africa* (Berkeley: University of California Press, 2000).

62 Polidori's story was adapted in dozens of plays, illustrations, and novellas until 1897, when Bram Stoker's *Dracula* took over. Both stories depict the vampire as an "undead" man, a foreign aristocrat who rises from the grave and sustains his life by drinking the blood of young victims, mostly women. The evil hero is a frightening parody of the resurrection of Jesus and the promise of Christian salvation.

63 "The white man represents, in the eyes of the Blacks of equatorial Africa, either a *Ouenga*, or a *Nkou*. . . . *Ouenga* represents vampirism. In its quality of incarnate being, it participates from human life and supernatural life, like anthropophagi [*anthropophage*]." Fleuriot de Langle, "Croisières à la côte d'Afrique (1868)," in *Le Tour du Monde: Nouveau Journal des Voyages* (Paris: Librairie Hachette, 1876), 31:277–78.

64 Kongo pupils recorded such pictures by 1900. "The *kundu* is said to be like the *mpeeve* (wind or spirit), that flies to and fro to catch things"; Laman, *Kongo* 3:216. See also Tessman, *Die Pangwe*, 295: "During the night, when the witch sleeps, his

evus go away and leave the body to wander and look for accomplices. Their sign of rally is the cry of the owl, or the sound that comes out of a large snail's shell in which witches blow. They fly to and fro, and for a short period, can rest on tree branches."

65 Victor Largeau, *Encyclopédie pahouine, Congo français: Éléments de grammaire et dictionnaire français-pahouin* (Paris: E. Leroux, 1901), 374. See chapter 3 for the ability of *evu/kundu* to creep out of the graves of deceased people in the form of a small animal.

66 Henri Lavignotte, *L'Évur: Croyance des pahouins du Gabon* (Paris, Société des Missions évangéliques, 1936), 18 and 80. See also Henri Lavignotte, "L'Évus chez les Pahouins du Gabon," manuscript s. d., Archives CSSP 4J 1.8b2, 273-B-II. For a counterexample, see Robert Hamill Nassau, *In an Elephant Corral: And Other Tales of West African Experiences* (1912; New York: Negro Universities Press, 1969): the chapter "Owenga the Vampire" does not mention blood or blood sucking. *Desmodontinae*, or blood sucking bats, are not native of Africa; they live only in the Americas. Tessman described *evu* as a form of energy and compared it to a fire. He reported a Fang tale of witches that lacerated the body of the victim, drank his blood in banana leaves, and told him that he would die in a few days. Tessman, *Die Pangwe*, 136. Maurice Briault wrote that Africans sucked blood, and sometimes made figurines in the image of Christ by combining human blood and red soil into a sort of dough that they mixed with bones, nails, and hair. Maurice Briault, "Les Hommes-tigres (récit gabonais)," n.d., 8 and 10, Archives CSSP, 2d60.9a3. dos. 5.

67 On blood brotherhood, see Vansina, *Paths*, 94.

68 Richard Lower, a British surgeon, successfully performed a blood transfusion on a dog in 1665. A similar attempt by French Jean-Baptiste Denys in 1667, this time transfusing blood between two humans, convinced the French Parliament to ban transfusions in 1670. British physicians dared to repeat the technique and publish the result of their experiments only in the 1820s and 1830s.

69 Visit at Lambaréné hospital and estate of Schweitzer, summer 2007.

70 Report on tiger-men by Hippolyte Charbonnier, Adjoint des services civils, chef de la subdivision de Tchibanga, dated 26 November 1916, Archives CSSP, Fond Pouchet, 2D60–9a1.

71 In 1950, an article in the *évolués* journal *Liaison* made several references to blood and witch-eating (compared to the female mosquito that cannot hatch without blood) without ever bringing up the term vampire. Jean Malonga, "La Sorcellerie et l' 'ordre' du Lemba chez les Laris," *Liaison* 62 (March–April 1958), 47–48.

72 The text was partly published by Fernandez in "Christian Acculturation."

73 Memorandum titled "Taolac-Intérêt personel par amour-propre," unsigned and undated, 21 Archives CSSP, Fond Pouchet, 2D60–9B5. The text probably dates from the 1940s–1950s: Father Pouchet collected it during his tenure in Gabon (1935–57) as an example of the insanity of "detribalized" Africans.

74 Bekale explains that before flying to the banquet, the witches strip down and become white. He wrote that genuine white people also attend the feast, but they always refrain from eating or drinking. They are present only to witness the crimes so they will be able to testify on Judgment Day.

75 On the prevalence in vernacular imaginaries, of *evu/kundu* as small, crawling animals, see Ambouroué-Avaro, *Un Peuple gabonais*, 77.

76 The text calls the Devil the "black Oronéom."

77 The text continues: By a supernaturally criminal influence, the *vampireux* kills and invisibly sucks the blood from human flesh. . . . Man being blood, the malefic person, every time it is possible to get a person, makes an invisible animal from the blood of his prey. The *vampireux* cuts it and cooks the meat in an invisible cooking pot called (*ntchouanayo-gwera*). (Truth of which precise details must be asked from old experienced blacks). Memorandum titled "Taolac-Intérêt perso-nel par amour-propre," unsigned and undated, 21 Archives CSSP, Fond Pouchet, 2D60–9B5.

78 In the 1960s and 1970s, however, vampire images spread uncritically in the anthropological and scholarly literature on African witchcraft. Raponda-Walker and Sillans, *Rites et croyances*, 82, reproduced missionary writings on the vampire. Philippe Laburthe-Tolra, *Initiations et sociétés secrètes au Cameroun: Essai sur la religion bëti* (Paris: Karthala, 1985), 77–78, invoked witches' "vampirism" and thirst for blood but did not support his translation with examples. Eric de Rosny, who practiced ritual healing in Cameroon in the 1980s, said that the men who possessed *tok*, a witch substance located in the liver, "are called *nthum* (a word that corresponds, with the same terrifying connotation, to the French word vampire). . . . Invisible, the vampires get out at night to go suck the blood of their victims until death. . . . This sorcery [is] a form of anthropophagy." Eric de Rosny, *Les yeux de ma chèvre* (Paris, Plon, 1981), 91 and 239.

79 Among the Fang, for instance, goat milk and raw chicken eggs (nicknamed "the blood of the hen") could be used to cure a wounded *evu*. Raponda-Walker and Sillans, *Rites et croyances*, 115 sqq. Laburthe-Tolra, *Initiations*, 78; and Henri Lavignotte, "L' evus chez les Pahouins du Gabon," dactyl., 18–20, Archives CSSP, 273-B-II. Lavignotte also wrote that the Fang used the blood of a sacrificed goat when they wished to plant an *evu* in a baby.

80 Bonneau, *Grammaire pounoue*, 20.

81 Laman, *Kongo* 3:217–19, 3:222, and 3:237: "Men cut up the meat, and they cook it in human skulls, or in new pots. Women bring the flesh in a basket and cook it." A story reported by Father Raponda-Walker in the early 1960s, but supposedly dating from 1901, claimed that murderers took the brain from the victim, drank his blood mixed with palm-wine, and made medicine with bits of flesh taken out of the cadaver. Raponda-Walker and Sillans, *Rites et croyances*, 182.

82 Rapport de l'audience publique du tribunal indigène de la subdivision de Mouila, matière répressive, 1920, ANG/FP 1609.

83 Mariani, "Assassinat par le feu, hommes panthères, anthropophagie, race ban-jabis. Rapport sur une affaire d'assassinat aux fins d'anthropophagie," *Bulletin de la société de recherches congolaises*, no. 10 (1929): 134. Christopher Gray percep-tively analyzed the case in *Colonial Rule*, 200.

84 V. C. Aymard, "De l'homme-tigre chez les Massango, dans la subdivision de Mbigou," handwritten report, July 1926. Archives CSSP, 2D 60. 9a1.

85 For an exhaustive social anthropology of Bwiti in northern Gabon, see James Fernandez, *Bwiti: An Ethnography of the Religious Imagination in Africa* (Prince-ton, NJ: Princeton University Press, 1981). For a recent study of Bwiti initiation, see Julien Bonhomme, *Le Miroir et le crâne: Parcours initiatique du Bwete Misoko (Gabon)* (Paris: CNRS: Fondation de la maison des sciences de l'homme, 2006).

86 André Mary, *Le Défi du syncrétisme: Le Travail symbolique de la religion d'eboga (Gabon)* (Paris, Editions de l'EHESS, 1999), 482–85.

87 See René Bureau on other versions of Benzoghe's myth; he reports that the mur-derers drank her blood and likens the chewing of *eboga* to eating Benzoghe and the flesh of Christ. René Bureau, *Bokayé!: Essai sur le Bwiti fang du Gabon* (Paris: L'Harmattan, 1996), 80 and 333.

88 Bureau, *Bokayé!*, 295.

89 In this regard, the story is quite comparable to many myths of origin that func-tion around a dyad of normative and transgressive acts.

90 Audience publique du tribunal de second degré du Département de l'Estuaire, no. 35, 9 May 1941, ANG/FP 835.

91 Lettre de l'Administrateur Lieutenant-Gouverneur du Gabon L. Vingarassamy au Gouverneur général de l'AEF, no. 246, 25 August 1931, AOM 5D 69. Mba was sent to prison from 1 August 1931 until his release and exile to Oubangui-Chari in 1934. For lack of evidence, the courts dismissed the accusation of poisoning in July 1932.

92 Florence Bernault, *Démocraties ambigues en Afrique centrale: Congo-Brazzaville, Gabon: 1940–1965* (Paris, Karthala, 1996), 219–21. Upon his release, the governor of Gabon exiled Mba and placed him under house arrest in Oubangui-Chari for ten years (1934–46). Arrêté fixant la peine d'interdiction de séjour de Léon Mba, no. 485, 6 April 1934 signed by Governor Antonetti, ANOM 5D 69, Dossier I (C-7).

93 French administrators privately warned their colleagues about Léon Mba's "witchcraft practices" and his affiliation to the "fetishistic sect of the Bwitists." Lettre d'Astier de Pompignan, chef du département de l'Estuaire au gouverneur du Gabon, no. 180/C, 21 October 1939; and lettre de Louis Bonvin, Président du tribunal de 2d degré de Libreville, n. d., ANOM 5D 69.

94 Bernault, *Démocraties*, 218. One territorial in 1956, impressed by Léon Mba, discussed the affair with an African priest, Abbé Théodore Kwaou. He wrote in his monthly report that "this affair of human flesh [*chair humaine*] had been tied to a religious rather than a mercantile business." Rapport politique de Ndende, signed Rege, 31 January 1956, no. 7/CF, ANG/ Fonds provincial 14.

95 Mikeni Dienguesse, "Après l'avoir drogué à l' "Iboga," le charlatan tue et fait jeter son patient dans un ravin," *L'Union*, no. 3682, 15 April 1988, 3.

96 Mikeni Dinguesse, "Assassinat de Ondo Ndong André: Des témoignages émouvants," *L'Union*, no. 3683, 22 April 1988, 3; and Louis Bravo and Mikeni Dinguesse, "Mba Ntem avoue avoir déjà mangé six personnes," *L'Union*, no. 3686, 26 April 1988, 1 and 3. According to the journalist, Mba Ntem sent the sexual organs by driver to Essono Mba Filomeno, the "pope" of the Mvoe Ening Bwiti sect who lived in Equatorial Guinea.

97 The investigation lasted nineteenth months, and showed important inconsistencies. For instance, Mba Ntem confessed that he had "eaten" six people before Ono Ndong, one of them an unborn fetus in his wife's womb: the fact suggests that the suspect used the verb "to eat" in a mystical sense. In November 1989, the tribunal of Oyem sentenced Mba Ntem to death for killing the victim by suffocation and for performing anthropophagy; his brother-in-law and main accomplice; Mve Owono, to life in prison and forced labor; and his wife, Abogo-Owono Florence, to five years in prison. Fidel Biteghe, "Affaire Mba: le procès s'ouvre demain," *L'Union*, 22 November 1989; "La thèse de l'assassinat se précise," *L'Union*, 29 November 1989, 7; and "Mba Ntem reconnu coupable de l'assassinat du professeur et condamné à mort," *L'Union*, 6 December 1989, 3.

98 "Organs of Power" (*Les organes du pouvoir*), produced by the TV Show *L'effet Papillon*, TV Channel Canal Plus, aired on 8 April, 2012.

99 Shaw, *Memories of the Slave Trade*, 219.

Conclusion

Epigraphs: Patriote le Mort-Vivant, "Le Tam Tam revient," *Le Patriote*, no. 8 (November 1976): 4; Le Costo, "La Mort: Une industrie fructueuse," *Echo de Missamba*, no. 21 (26 June 2012): 7; Murielle Ndong, "Sorcellerie et Charlatanisme: L'Avion mystique," *L'Union*, 20 May 2016; Jean Ndouanis, "Le Régime des Bongo-ondimba est le commanditaire des crimes rituels," Le Blog de Jean Ndouanis, accessed March 2015, http://jean-ndouanis.blogspot.com/2015/03 /les-crimes-rituels-de-bongo-ondimba-ali.html.

1 See "illicit cohabitation" in Achille Mbembe, *On the Postcolony* (Berkeley: University of California Press, 2001), 110.

2 The expression "too shameful for words" comes from Esther Rashkin, *Unspeakable Secrets and the Psychoanalysis of Culture* (Albany, NY: SUNY Press, 2008), 19.

3 Postcolonial scholars developed these concepts to retrieve the agency of the colonized. Gayatri Spivak and Edward Saïd, quoted in Robert Young, *Colonial Desire: Hybridity in Theory, Culture, and Race* (London: Routledge, 1995), 161–62.

4 My idea is close to Michael Taussig's analysis of the colonial culture of terror in Amazonia, and the ways in which the mirroring of colonizers' and colonized's fears and fantasies led to horrific excesses. Michael Taussig, "Culture of Terror,

Space of Death: Roger Casement's Putamayo Report and the Explanation of Torture," *Comparative Studies in Society and History* 26 (1984): 467–97.

5 Among the few who pioneered this approach are Luise White, *Speaking with Vampires: Rumor and History in Colonial Africa* (Berkeley: University of California Press, 2000); and the historical anthropology of Heike Behrend, *Resurrecting Cannibals: The Catholic Church, Witch-Hunts, and the Production of Pagans in Western Uganda* (Woodbridge, UK: Boydell & Brewer, 2011).

6 David M. Gordon, *Invisible Agents: Spirits in a Central African History* (Athens: Ohio University Press, 2012).

7 Consider how two specialists of medical anthropology explain that, in order for bodies to be made alienable, they must first be visualized as detachable and thing-like, while the mystical essence of body fluids, organs, and tissues must be dissipated and reconceptualized as objects available for commodification. Margaret M. Lock and Vinh-Kim Nguyen, *An Anthropology of Biomedicine* (Chichester, UK: Wiley-Blackwell, 2010), 244.

8 Biomedical transplants of organs and surgical interventions do regularly occur in Gabon, a country equipped with modern medical facilities, and with a strong trust in biomedicine.

9 Ann Laura Stoler, *Carnal Knowledge and Imperial Power: Race and the Intimate in Colonial Rule* (Berkeley: University of California Press, 2002). Christopher J. Lee, "The 'Native' Undefined: Colonial Categories, Anglo-African Status and the Politics of Kinship in British Central Africa, 1929–38," *Journal of African History* 46, no. 3 (2005): 457–78.

10 Peter Geschiere gives an illuminating analysis of kinship and intimate betrayal in *Witchcraft, Intimacy, and Trust. Africa in Comparison* (Chicago, IL: University of Chicago Press, 2013).

11 Only after completing this manuscript did I become aware of Harish Trivedi's pioneering study of colonial transactions in the field of literary exchanges between Great-Britain and India. I hope this volume provokes new conversations about the notion of transactions. Harish Trivedi, *Colonial Transactions: English Literature and India* (New York: Manchester University Press, 1995).

12 Pierre Bourdieu, *Outline of a Theory of Practice*, Cambridge: Cambridge University Press, 1977, and *Distinction: A Social Critique of the Judgment of Taste* (Cambridge, MA: Harvard University Press, 1984). Joseph Tonda transferred and reworked the idea of capital in Equatorial Africa to explain how people imagine power, technology, and knowledge. Joseph Tonda, *Le Souverain moderne: Le Corps du pouvoir en Afrique centrale (Congo, Gabon)* (Paris: Karthala, 2005).

13 Arjun Appadurai, "Introduction: Commodities and the Politics of Value," in *The Social Life of Things: Commodities in Cultural Perspective* (Cambridge: Cambridge University Press, 1986), 3–63; and Arjun Appadurai, "Commodities and the Politics of Value," in *The Future as Cultural Fact: Essay on the Global Condition* (London: Verso, 2013), 9–60.

14 Florence Bernault, "Carnal Technologies and the Double Life of the Body in Gabon," *Critical African Studies* 5, no. 3 (2013): 175–94.

15 Steve Feierman, "African Histories and the Dissolution of World History," in *Africa and the Disciplines: The Contributions of Research in Africa to the Social Sciences and the Humanities*, ed. Robert H. Bates, Valentin Mudimbe, and Jean O'Barr (Chicago, IL: University of Chicago Press, 1993), 167–212. On folk epistemologies, see Elizabeth Isischei, *Voices of the Poor in Africa: Moral Economy and the Popular Imagination* (Rochester NY: University of Rochester Press, 2002). For a more pessimistic diagnosis on how African scholarship can generate global analytical tools, see Florence Bernault, "L'Afrique et la modernité des sciences sociales," *Vingtième Siècle, Revue d'histoire* 70, no. 70 (2001): 127–38.

16 Paul Gilroy, *The Black Atlantic: Modernity and Double Consciousness* (Cambridge, MA: Harvard University Press, 1993).

BIBLIOGRAPHY

À la jeunesse francaise: L'Appel de la France extérieure. Paris: Frazier-Soye, 1930.

Abu-Lughod, Lila. "Writing against Culture." In Anthropology and Theory: Issues in Epistemology, edited by Henrietta Moore and Todd Sanders, 466–79. 2nd ed. Chichester, UK: John Wiley & Sons, 2014.

Adas, Michael. Machines as the Measure of Men: Science, Technology, and Ideologies of Western Dominance. Ithaca, NY: Cornell University Press, 1989.

Agamben, Giorgio. Homo Sacer: Sovereign Power and Bare Life. Stanford, CA: Stanford University Press, 1998.

Agamben, Giorgio. Opus Dei: Archéologie de l'office. Paris: Seuil, 2012.

Alexandre, Pierre, and Jacques Binet. Le groupe dit pahouin (Fang, Boulou, Bëti). Paris: Presses universitaires de France, 1958.

Allégret, E. "Les idées religieuses des Fangs." Revue d'Histoire des Religions 50 (1904): 214–33.

Allman, Jean, and John Parker. Tongnaab: The History of a West African God. Bloomington: Indiana University Press, 2005.

Ambouroué-Avaro, Joseph. Un Peuple gabonais à l'aube de la colonisation: Le Bas-Ogowe au XIXe siècle. Paris: Karthala, 1981.

Ambrière, Francis. Afrique centrale: Les républiques d'expression française. Les Guides bleus. Paris: Hachette, 1962.

Anderson, Benedict. Imagined Communities: Reflections on the Origin and Spread of Nationalism. Rev. ed. London: Verso, 1991.

Anderson, Warwick, Deborah Jenson, and Richard Keller, eds. Unconscious Dominions: Psychoanalysis, Colonial Trauma, and Global Sovereignties. Durham, NC: Duke University Press, 2011.

Andersson, Efraim. Messianic Popular Movements in the Lower Congo. Uppsala, Sweden: Almqvist & Wiksells, 1958.

Appadurai, Arjun. "Commodities and the Politics of Value." In The Future as Cultural Fact: Essay on the Global Condition, 9–60. London: Verso, 2013.

Appadurai, Arjun. Modernity at Large: Cultural Dimensions of Globalization. Minneapolis: University of Minnesota Press, 1996.

Appadurai, Arjun. *The Social Life of Things: Commodities in Cultural Perspective.* Cambridge: Cambridge University Press, 1986.

Arens, William. *The Man-Eating Myth: Anthropology and Anthropophagy.* Oxford: Oxford University Press, 1980.

Ariès, Philippe. *Western Attitudes toward Death: From the Middle Ages to the Present.* Baltimore, MD: Johns Hopkins University Press, 1974.

Ashcroft, Bill. *On Post-colonial Futures: Transformations of Colonial Culture.* London: Continuum, 200.

Ashforth, Adam. *Witchcraft, Violence, and Democracy in South Africa.* Chicago, IL: University of Chicago Press, 2005.

Aubame, Jean-Marie. *Les Bëti du Gabon et d'ailleurs.* 2 vols. Paris: L'Harmattan, 2002.

Augé, Marc, ed. *La construction du monde: Religion, représentations, idéologie.* Paris: François Maspero, 1974.

Bakhtin, Mikhail M. *Rabelais and His World.* Bloomington: Indiana University Press, 1984.

Balandier, Georges. *Sociologie actuelle de l'Afrique noire.* Paris: Presses universitaires de France, 1950.

Balandier, Georges. *The Sociology of Black Africa: Social Dynamics in Central Africa.* New York: Praeger, 1970.

Balandier, Georges, and Jean-Claude Pauvert. *Les villages gabonais: aspects démographiques, économiques, sociologiques, projets de modernisation.* Brazzaville: Institut d'études centrafricaines, 1952.

Barker, Francis, Peter Hulme, and Margaret Iversen, eds. *Cannibalism and the Colonial World.* Cambridge: Cambridge University Press, 1998.

Barringer, Tim, and Tom Flynn. *Colonialism and the Object: Empire, Material Culture, and the Museum.* London: Routledge, 1998.

Barth, Fredrick. "On the Study of Social Change." *American Anthropologist,* no. 69 (1967): 661–69.

Battell, Andrew, et al. *The Strange Adventures of Andrew Battell of Leigh, in Angola and the Adjoining Regions.* 1625. London: Hakluyt Society Reprint, 1901.

Baumann, Hermann, and Diedrich Westermann. *Les peuples et les civilisations de l'Afrique.* Paris: Payot, 1948.

Bayart, Jean-François. *L'État au Cameroun.* Paris: Karthala, 1979.

Bayart, Jean-François. *L'État en Afrique: La Politique du ventre.* Paris: Fayart, 1989.

Bayart, Jean-François. *The State in Africa: The Politics of the Belly.* New York: Longman, 1993.

Bayart, Jean-François, and Romain Bertrand. "De quel 'legs colonial' parle-t-on?" *Esprit* 12, no. 330 (2006): 154–60.

Bazenguissa-Ganga, Rémy. *Les Voies du politique au Congo: Essai de sociologie historique.* Paris: Karthala, 1997.

Behrend, Heike. *Resurrecting Cannibals: The Catholic Church, Witch-Hunts, and the Production of Pagans in Western Uganda.* Woodbridge, UK: Boydell & Brewer, 2011.

Bekker, Simon, and Laurent Fourchard, eds. *Governing Cities in Africa: Politics and Policies.* Cape Town, South Africa: HSRC Press, 2013.

Benveniste, Emile. *Le Vocabulaire des institutions indo-européennes.* Vol. 1, *Économie, parenté, société.* Vol. 2, *Pouvoir, droit, religion.* Paris: Éditions de Minuit, 1969.

Berman, Bruce, and John Lonsdale. *Unhappy Valley: Conflict in Kenya and Africa.* London: James Currey, 1992.

Bernault, Florence. "Aesthetics of Acquisition: Gabonese Spectacles and the Transactional Life of Bodies and Things." *Comparative Studies in Society and History* 57, no. 3 (July 2015): 753–77.

Bernault, Florence. "Carnal Technologies and the Double Life of the Body in Gabon." *Critical African Studies* 5, no. 3 (2013): 175–94.

Bernault, Florence. "Colonial Bones: The 2006 Burial of Savorgnan De Brazza." *African Affairs* 109 (July 2010): 367–90.

Bernault, Florence. "De la modernité comme impuissance: Fétichisme et crise du politique en Afrique équatoriale et ailleurs." *Cahiers d'Études africaines* Vol. 49–3, no. 195 (2009), 747–74.

Bernault, Florence. *Démocraties ambiguës en Afrique centrale: Congo-Brazzaville, Gabon, 1940–1965.* Paris: Karthala, 1996.

Bernault, Florence. "L'Afrique et la modernité des sciences sociales." *Vingtième Siècle, Revue d'histoire* 70, no. 70 (2001): 127–38.

Bernault, Florence. *A History of Prisons and Confinement in Africa.* Portsmouth, NJ: Heinemann, 2003.

Bernault, Florence. "The Shadow of Rule: Colonial Power and Modern Punishment in Africa." In *Cultures of Confinement: A Global History of the Prison in Asia, Africa, the Middle-East, and Latin America,* edited by Frank Dikötter, 77–83. London: Christopher Hurst, 2007.

Bernault, Florence. "Suitcases and the Poetics of Oddities: Writing History from Disorderly Archives." *History in Africa,* vol. 42: 269–77.

Bernault, Florence. "Witchcraft and the Colonial Life of the Fetish." In *Spirits in Politics: Uncertainties of Power and Healing in African Societies,* edited by Barbara Meier and Arne S. Steinforth, 53–74. Frankfurt am Main: Campus Publishers, 2013.

Berne, Eric. *Games People Play.* New York: Grove Press, 1964.

Bernstein, Susan D. "Ape Anxiety: Sensation Fiction, Evolution, and the Genre Question." *Journal of Victorian Culture* 6, no. 2 (2001): 250–71.

Berry, Sara. "Hegemony on a Shoestring: Indirect Rule and Access to Land." *Africa, Journal of the International African Institute* 62, no. 3 (1992): 327–55.

Berzock, Kathleen Bickford, and Christa Clarke. *Representing Africa in American Art Museums: A Century of Collecting and Display.* Seattle: University of Washington Press, 2011.

Bhabha, Homi K. *The Location of Culture.* London: Routledge, 1994.

Biaya, T. K. "La Mort et ses métamorphoses au Congo-Zaire." *Cahiers africains,* no. 31–32 (1998): 101–4.

Birmingham, David, and Phyllis M. Martin. *History of Central Africa.* 2 vols. London: Longman, 1983.

Birmingham, David, and Phyllis M. Martin. *History of Central Africa: The Contemporary Years since 1960.* London: Longman, 1998.

Bivona, Dan. "Human Thighs and Susceptible Apes: Self-Implicating Category Confusion in Victorian Discourse on West Africa." *Nineteenth-Century Prose* 32, no. 2 (2005): 81–121.

Blache, Joseph. *Vrais noirs et vrais blancs d'Afrique au 20e siècle.* Orléans, France: M. Caillette, 1922.

Bloch, Maurice. *From Blessing to Violence: History and Ideology in the Circumcision Ritual of the Merina of Madagascar.* Cambridge: Cambridge University Press, 1986.

Bockie, Simon. *Death and the Invisible Powers: The World of Kongo Belief.* Bloomington: Indiana University Press, 1993.

Bohannan, Paul. "Some Principles of Exchange and Investment among the Tiv." *American Ethnologist* 57 (1955): 60–69.

Bohannan, Paul, and Laura Bohannan. *Tiv Economy.* London: Longmans, 1968.

Bond, George C., and Diane M. Ciekawy. *Witchcraft Dialogues: Anthropological and Philosophical Exchanges.* Athens: Ohio University Press, 2001.

Bonhomme, Julien, *Le Miroir et le crâne: Parcours initiatique du Bwete Misoko (Gabon).* Paris: CNRS: Fondation de la maison des sciences de l'homme, 2006.

Bonneau, Jean. *Grammaire pounoue et lexique pounou-francais.* Brazzaville, French Equatorial Africa: Imprimerie Charité, 1956.

Bouët Willaumez, Louis Edouard. *Commerce et traite des Noirs aux Côtes occidentales d'Afrique.* Paris: Imprimerie Nationale, 1848.

Bounda, Gabriel. "La Morphologie de la répression chez les Ndumu du Haut-Ogooué." Master's thesis, Université Omar Bongo Onbimba, Libreville, 1983.

Bourdieu, Pierre. *Distinction: A Social Critique of the Judgment of Taste.* Cambridge, MA: Harvard University Press, 1984.

Bourdieu, Pierre. *Outline of a Theory of Practice.* Cambridge: Cambridge University Press, 1977.

Bowie, Fiona, Deborah Kirkwood, and Shirley Ardener. *Women and Missions, Past and Present: Anthropological and Historical Perceptions.* Providence, RI: Berg, 1993.

Brazza, Pierre Savorgnan de, and Henri Brunschwig. *Brazza explorateur: L'Ogooué, 1875–1879.* Paris: La Haye, Mouton, 1966.

Brazza, "Pierre Savorgnan de. Voyages dans l'Ouest Africain." *Le Tour du Monde: Nouveau journal des voyages* 54, no. 1402 (1887): 289–336.

Briault, Maurice. *Dans la forêt du Gabon: Études et scènes africaines.* Paris: Grasset, 1930.

Briault, Maurice. *Sous le zéro équatorial: Études et scènes africaines.* Paris: Bloud & Gay, 1927.

Briault, Maurice. *Sur les pistes de l' A.E.F.* 2nd ed. Paris: Éditions Alsatia, 1948.

Brower, M. Brady. *Unruly Spirits: The Science of Psychic Phenomena in Modern France.* Urbana: University of Illinois Press, 2010.

Brown, Peter. *The Cult of the Saints: Its Rise and Function in Latin Christianity.* Chicago, IL: University of Chicago Press, 1981.

Brown, Peter. *Society and the Holy in Late Antiquity.* Berkeley: University of California Press, 1982.

Bruel, Georges. *La France Équatoriale Africaine: Le pays, les habitants la colonisation, les pouvoirs publics.* Paris: Larose, 1935.

Bruel, Georges. *L'Afrique Équatoriale Française (A.E.F.).* Paris: Larose, 1930.

Bry, Théodore de. *Americae, Omnia Elegantibus Figuris in Aes Expressa a T. de Bry.* Frankfurt am Main: Theodor de Bry, 1590–1634.

Buakasa Tulu Kia Mpansu. *L'Impensé du discours: "Kindoki" et "nkisi" en pays Kongo du Zaïre.* Kinshasa: Faculté de Théologie catholique, 1980.

Bureau, René. *Bokayé!: Essai Sur le Bwiti fang du Gabon.* Paris: L'Harmattan, 1996.

Burke, Timothy. *Lifebuoy Men, Lux Women: Commodification, Consumption, and Cleanliness in Modern Zimbabwe.* Durham, NC: Duke University Press, 1996.

Burroughs, Edgar Rice. *Tarzan of the Apes.* 1914. New York: Ballantine Books, 1963.

Burton, Richard Francis. *Two Trips to Gorilla Land and the Cataracts of the Congo.* Vol. 1. London: Sampson Low, Marston, 1876.

Butler, Judith. *The Psychic Life of Power.* Stanford, CA: Stanford University Press, 1997.

Bynum, Caroline Walker. *The Resurrection of the Body in Western Christianity, 200–1336.* New York: Columbia University Press, 1995.

Carli, Dionigi. *La Mission au Kongo des pères Michelangelo Guatari and Dionigi Carli (1668).* Translated by Alix du Cheyron d'Abaz. Paris: Editions Chandeigne, Librairie portugaise, 2006.

Castellani, Charles Jules. *Les Femmes au Congo.* Paris: Flammarion, 1898.

Castoriadis, Cornelius. *The Imaginary Institution of Society.* Cambridge: Polity, 1987.

Castoriadis, Cornelius. *L'Institution imaginaire de la société.* 4th ed., revised and corrected. Paris: Seuil, 1975.

Césaire, Aimé. *Discourse on Colonialism.* New York: Monthly Review Press, 2000.

Chavannes, Charles de. *Avec Brazza: Souvenirs de la Mission de l'Ouest-Africain (Mars 1883–Janvier 1886).* 3rd ed. Paris: Librairie Plon, 1935.

Chrétien, Jean-Pierre. "Hutu et Tutsi au Rwanda et au Burundi." In *Au cœur de l'ethnie,* edited by Elikia M'Bokolo et Jean-Loup Amselle, 129–65. 2nd ed. Paris: La Découverte, 1999.

Cinnamon, John. "Ambivalent Power: Anti-Sorcery and Occult Subjugation in Late Colonial Gabon." *Journal of Colonialism and Colonial History* 3, no. 3 (2002): n.p.

Cinnamon, John. "Of Fetishism and Totemism: Missionary Ethnology and Academic Social Science in Early-Twentieth-Century Gabon." In *The Spiritual in* the Secular: Missionaries and Knowledge about Africa, edited by Patrick Harries and David Maxwell, 100–134. Grand Rapids, MI: W. B. Eerdmans, 2012.

Clist, Bernard. *Gabon: 100 000 ans d'histoire*. Libreville, Gabon: Centre Culturel Français Saint-Exupéry, 1995.

Cohen, William. *Rulers of Empire: French Colonial Services in Africa*. Washington, DC: Hoover Institution Press, 1972.

Collodon, Augustus C. *Congo Jake: The Story of My Adventurous Life*. London: Sampson Low, Marston, 1932.

Comaroff, Jean, and John L. Comaroff, eds. *Modernity and Its Malcontents: Ritual and Power in Postcolonial Africa*. Chicago, IL: University of Chicago Press, 1993.

Comaroff, Jean, and John Comaroff. "Occult Economies and the Violence of Abstraction: Notes from the South African Postcolony." *American Ethnologist* 26, no. 2 (May 1999): 279–303.

Comaroff, Jean, and John L. Comaroff. *Of Revelation and Revolution*. 2 vols. Chicago, IL: University of Chicago Press, 1991 and 1997.

Compiègne, Louis-Alphonse-Victor du Pont de. *L' Afrique équatoriale: Gabonais, Pahouins, Gallois*. Paris: Plon, 1876.

Compiègne, Louis-Alphonse-Victor du Pont de. *L' Afrique équatoriale: Okanda, Bangouens, Osyéba*. Paris: Plon, 1875.

Conan Doyle, Arthur. *The Case-Book of Sherlock Holmes and His Last Bow*. London: Wordsworth Editions, 1995.

Conklin, Alice L. *A Mission to Civilize: The Republican Idea of Empire in France and West Africa, 1895–1930*. Stanford, CA: Stanford University Press, 1997.

Conrad, Joseph. *Heart of Darkness*. 1899. New York: Norton, 1988.

Conrad, Joseph. *Tales of Unrest*. 1898. Garden City, NY: Doubleday, Page, 1923.

Cooper, Frederick. *Citizenship between Empire and Nation: Remaking France and French Africa, 1945–1960*. Princeton, NJ: Princeton University Press, 2014.

Cooper, Frederick. *Colonialism in Question: Theory, Knowledge, History*. Berkeley: University of California Press, 2005.

Cooper, Frederick. "Conflict and Connection: Rethinking Colonial African History." *American Historical Review* 99, no. 5 (December 1994): 1516–45.

Cooper, Frederick. *Decolonization and African Society: The Labor Question in French and British Africa*. Cambridge: Cambridge University Press, 1996.

Cooper, Frederick, and Ann Laura Stoler, eds. *Tensions of Empire: Colonial Cultures in a Bourgeois World*. Berkeley: University of California Press, 1997.

Coquery-Vidrovitch, Catherine. *Le Congo au temps des grandes compagnies concessionnaires, 1898–1930*. Paris: Mouton, 1972.

Corbey, Raymond, and Bert Theunissen. *Ape, Man, Apeman: Changing Views since 1600*. Leiden: University of Leiden, 1995.

Cornish, Charles J. *The People's Natural History: Embracing Living Animals of the World and Living Races of Mankind*. New York: University Society, 1903.

Cottes, Augustin. *La Mission Cottes au sud-Cameroun (1905–1908): Exposé des résultats scientifiques, d'après les Travaux des divers membres de la Section fran-*

çaise de la Commission de délimitation entre le Congo français et le Cameroun (frontière méridionale) et les documents étudiés au Muséum d'histoire naturelle. Paris: E. Leroux, 1911.

Cureau, Adolphe Louis. Les Sociétés primitives de l'Afrique équatoriale. Paris: Armand Colin, 1912.

Cureau, Adolphe Louis, and E. Andrews. Savage Man in Central Africa: A Study of Primitive Races in the French Congo. London: T. F. Unwin, 1915.

Curtin, Philip D., ed. Africa and the West: Intellectual Responses to European Culture. Madison: University of Wisconsin Press, 1972.

Curtin, Philip D. "Medical Knowledge and Urban Planning in Colonial Tropical Africa." American Historical Review 90, no. 3 (1985): 594–613.

Daney, Pierre. "Sur les croyances des indigènes de la circonscription de Sindara (Gabon, A.E.F.)." Revue anthropologique, no. 34 (1924): 272–82.

Darwin, Charles. On the Origin of Species by Means of Natural Selection, or the Preservation of Favoured Races in the Struggle for Life. London: John Murray, 1859.

De Baecque, Antoine. The Body Politic: Corporeal Metaphor in Revolutionary France, 1770–1800. Stanford, CA: Stanford University Press, 1997.

De Boeck, Filip. "Beyond the Grave: History, Memory and Death in Postcolonial Congo/Zaire." In Memory and the Postcolony: African Anthropology and the Critique of Power, edited by Richard Werbner, 21–55. London: Zed Books, 1998.

De Boeck, Filip. "Borderland Breccia: The Mutant Hero in the Historical Imagination of a Central African Diamond Frontier." Journal of Colonialism and Colonial History 1, no. 2 (winter 2000).

De Brosses, Charles. Du culte des dieux fétiches, ou Parallèle de l'ancienne Religion de l'Egypte avec la Religion actuelle de Nigritie. Geneva: no publisher name [n.p.]1760.

Dedet, Christian. La Mémoire du fleuve: L'Afrique aventureuse de Jean Michonet. Paris: Éditions Phébus, 1984.

Delcourt, Jean. Au Congo français, Monseigneur Carrie, 1842–1904. Paris: S. I., no date [n.d.] [1935?].

Délicat, Chérubin. "Recherches sur la Mission Catholique du Saint Esprit de Mayumba de 1888 à 1960." Bachelor's thesis, Université Omar Bongo Onbimba, Libreville, 1983.

Delisle, F. "La Fabrication du fer dans le Haut-Ogooué observée par Léon Guiral, membre de la mission de l'Ouest africain." Revue d'ethnographie, (1884): 465–73.

Denis, Maurice Eugène. Histoire militaire de l'Afrique équatoriale française. Paris: Imprimerie nationale, 1931.

Deschamps, Hubert. Quinze ans de Gabon: Les Débuts de l'établissement français, 1839–1853. Paris: Société française d'histoire d'outre-mer, Maisonneuve et Larose, 1965.

Deschamps, Hubert. Traditions orales et archives au Gabon: Contribution à l'ethnohistoire. Paris: Berger-Levrault, 1962.

Deschamps, Hubert. *Roi de la brousse: Mémoires d'autres mondes*. Paris: Berger-Levrault, 1975.

Devauges, Roland. *L'Oncle, le ndoki et l'entrepreneur: La Petite entreprise congolaise à Brazzaville*. Paris: Travaux et Documents de l'ORSTOM, 1977.

Dirks, Nicholas B., ed. *Colonialism and Culture*. Ann Arbor: University of Michigan Press, 1992.

Dorlin, Elsa. *La Matrice de la race: Généalogie sexuelle et coloniale de la nation française*. Paris: Éditions La Découverte, 2006.

Douglas, Mary. "Primitive Rationing: A Study in Primitive Exchange." In *Themes in Economic Anthropology*, edited by Raymond Firth, 119–47. Oxon: Routledge, 2004.

Douglas, Mary. *Purity and Danger: An Analysis of Concepts of Pollution and Taboo*. London: Routledge and Kegan Paul, 1976.

Douglas, Mary, and Baron Isherwood. *The World of Goods*. New York: Basic Books, 1979.

Doutreloux, Albert. *L'Ombre des fétiches: Société et culture yombe*. Louvain: Nauwelaerts, 1967.

Drewal, Henry. "Mami Wata and Santa Marta: Imag(in)ing Selves and Others." In *Images and Empire: Visuality in Colonial and Postcolonial Africa*, edited by Paul Landau and Deborah Kaspin, 193–211. Berkeley: University of California Press, 2002.

Du Berrie, Jéuan. *Under the Cannibal Curse*. London: Stanley Paul, 1938.

Du Chaillu, Paul Belloni. *A Journey to Ashango-Land and Further Penetration into Equatorial Africa*. New York: D. Appleton, 1867.

Du Chaillu, Paul Belloni. *Adventures in the Great Forest of Equatorial Africa and the Country of the Dwarfs*. Abridged and popular ed. New York: Harper, 1890.

Du Chaillu, Paul Belloni. *The Country of the Dwarfs*. New York: Harper and Brothers, 1872.

Du Chaillu, Paul Belloni. *Explorations and Adventures in Equatorial Africa: With Accounts of the Manners and Customs of the People, and of the Chace* [sic] *of the Gorilla, Crocodile, Leopard, Elephant, Hippopotamus, and Other Animals*. London: John Murray, 1861; reprinted in New York: Negro University Press, 1969.

Du Chaillu, Paul Belloni. *Lost in the Jungle: Narrated for Young People*. New York: Harper & Brothers, 1875.

Du Chaillu, Paul Belloni. *Recent Remarkable Discoveries in Central Africa*. Philadelphia, PA: Barclay, 1867.

Du Chaillu, Paul Belloni. *Stories of the Gorilla Country: Narrated for Young People*. New York: Harper and Brothers, 1872.

Du Chaillu, Paul Belloni. *Voyages et aventures dans l'Afrique équatoriale: Moeurs et coutumes des habitants, chasses au gorille, au crocodile, au léopard, à l'éléphant, à l'hippopotame, etc., etc.* Paris: M. Lévy frères, 1863.

Dulucq, Sophie. "La mentalité cannibale." Post no. 19. *Anthropophagie et Histoire: Enquête sur une répression coloniale en Afrique*. Accessed 14 December 2017. https://anthist.hypotheses.org/325.

Dupré, Georges. "The History and Adventures of a Monetary Object of the Kwele." In *Money Matters: Instability, Values, and Social Payments in the Modern History of West African Communities*, edited by Jane Guyer, 77–96. Portsmouth, NH: Heinemann, 1995.

Dupré Georges. "Le Commerce entre sociétés lignagères: Les Nzabi dans la traite à la fin du XIXe siècle (Gabon-Congo)." *Cahiers d'études africaines* 12, no. 48 (1972): 616–58.

Dupré, Georges. *Les Naissances d'une société: Espace et historicité chez les Beembé du Congo*. Paris: Éditions de l'ORSTOM, 1985.

Dupré, Georges. *Un Ordre et sa destruction*. Paris: Editions de l'ORSTOM, 1982.

Durkheim, Émile. *The Elementary Forms of the Religious Life*. 1915. New York: Free Press, 1965.

Dybowski, Jean. *Le Congo méconnu*. Paris: Hachette, 1912.

Ebang Ondo, Jean Elvis. *Manifeste contre les crimes rituels au Gabon*. Paris: L'Harmattan, 2010.

Éboué, Félix. *La Nouvelle politique indigène pour l'Afrique équatoriale française*. Paris: Office français d'édition, 1940.

Eboussi Boulaga, F. *Christianity without Fetishes: An African Critique and Recapture of Christianity*. Maryknoll, NY: Orbis Books, 1984.

Edema, Atibakwa Baboya. *Dictionnaire bangála-français-lingála*. Saint Maur, France: Sépia Éditions, 1994.

Eggers, Nicole. "Kitawala in the Congo: Politics, Religion, Health and Healing in 20th Century Central Africa," PhD thesis, University of Wisconsin-Madison, May 2013.

Eggers, Nicole. "Mukombozi and the Monganga: The Violence of Healing in a Kitawalist Uprising in 1944." *Africa*, no. 85 (2015): 417–36.

Ekang-Mve, Arielle. "Famille Nzébi et stérilité (Gabon)." Master's thesis, Université Omar Bongo Onbimba, Libreville, June 2006.

Elias, Norbert. *La Civilisation des moeurs*. French translation. Paris: Calmann-Lévy, 1973.

Elkhom Friedman, Kajsa. "Liberating the State from the People: Class, Power and Magic in Congo." Unpublished manuscript, 1994, author's archives.

Ellis, Stephen, and Gerrie ter Haar. *Worlds of Power: Religious Thought and Political Practice in Africa*. New York: Oxford University Press, 2004.

Emirbayer, Mustapha, and Ann Mische. "What Is Agency?" *American Journal of Sociology* 103, no. 4 (January 1998): 962–1023.

Engels, Dagmar, and Shula Marks, eds. *Contesting Colonial Hegemony: State and Society in Africa and India*. London: British Academic Press, 1994.

Evans-Pritchard, E. E. *Nuer Religion*. Oxford: Clarendon Press, 1956.

Fabian, Johannes. *Out of Our Minds: Reason and Madness in the Exploration of Central Africa*. Berkeley: University of California Press, 2000.

Fanon, Frantz. *Les damnés de la terre*. 2nd ed. Paris: F. Maspero, 1961.

Favret-Saada, Jeanne. *Les Mots, la mort, les sorts*. Paris: Gallimard, 1977.

Feierman, Steven. "African Histories and the Dissolution of World History." In *Africa and the Disciplines: The Contributions of Research in Africa to the Social Sciences and the Humanities*, edited by Robert H. Bates, Valentin Mudimbe, and Jean O'Barr, 167–212. Chicago, IL: University of Chicago Press, 1993.

Feierman, Steven. *Peasant Intellectuals: Anthropology and History in Tanzania.* Madison: University of Wisconsin Press, 1990.

Feierman, Steven. "Colonizers, Scholars, and Invisible Histories." In *Beyond the Linguistic Turn: New Directions in the Study of Society and Culture*, edited by Victoria E. Bonnell and Lynn Hunt, 182–216. Berkeley: University of California Press, 1999.

Ferme, Mariane C. *The Underneath of Things: Violence, History, and the Everyday in Sierra Leone.* Berkeley: University of California Press, 2001.

Fernandez, James W. *Bwiti: An Ethnography of the Religious Imagination in Africa.* Princeton, NJ: Princeton University Press, 1981.

Fernandez, James. "Christian Acculturation and Fang Witchcraft." *Cahiers d'études africaines* 2 no. 6 (1961): 244–70.

"Fétiches: objets enchantés, mots réalisés." Special issue of the journal *Systèmes de pensée en Afrique noire*, no. 8 (1985).

Fields, Karen E. *Revival and Rebellion in Colonial Central Africa: Revisions to the Theory of Indirect Rule.* Princeton, NJ: Princeton University Press, 1985.

Fleuriot de Langle. "Croisières à la côte d'Afrique (1868)." In *Le Tour du Monde: Nouveau Journal des Voyages.* Vol. 31. Paris: Librairie Hachette, 1876, 257–304.

Foret, Auguste. "Le Lac Fernan-Vaz." *Bulletin de la société de géographie* 19, no. 308 (1898): 308–27.

Foster, George. "Peasant Society and the Image of the Limited Good." *American Anthropologist*, no. 62 (1965): 293–315.

Foucault, Michel. *Abnormal: Lectures at the Collège de France.* New York: Picador, 1999.

Foucault, Michel. *Discipline and Punish: The Birth of the Prison.* New York: Vintage Books, 1979.

Foucault, Michel. *"Il faut défendre la société": Cours au Collège de France (1975–1976).* Paris: Seuil/Gallimard, 1997.

Foucault, Michel. *Naissance de la clinique: Une Archéologie du regard médical.* 1963. Paris: Presses Universitaires de France, 2009.

Franc, Louis. *De l'origine des Pahouins: Essai de résolution de ce problème ethnologique.* Paris: Maloine, 1905.

Frank, Frederick. *Days with Albert Schweitzer: A Lambaréné Landscape.* London: Peter Davies, 1959.

Freud, Sigmund. *The Interpretation of Dreams.* 1899. New York: Chelsea House Publishers, 1987.

Freud, Sigmund. *Totem and Taboo: Some Points of Agreement between the Mental Lives of Savages and Neurotics.* New York: Norton, 1950.

Freud, Sigmund, and Peter Gay. *The Freud Reader.* New York: W. W. Norton, 1995.

Gallagher, Catherine, and Thomas Walter Laqueur. *The Making of the Modern Body: Sexuality and Society in the Nineteenth Century.* Berkeley: University of California Press, 1987.

Gardinier, David E. *Historical Dictionary of Gabon.* 2nd ed. Metuchen, NJ: Scarecrow Press, 1994.

Gaulme, Francois. "Le Bwiti chez les Nkomi: Association cultuelles et évolution historique sur le littoral gabonais." *Journal des africanistes* 49, no. 2 (1979): 37–87.

Gaulme, François. *Le Gabon et son ombre.* Paris: Karthala, 1988.

Gaulme, François. *Le Pays de Cama: Un Ancien état côtier du Gabon et ses origines.* Paris: Karthala, 1981.

Gaulme, François. "Un Problème d'histoire du Gabon: Le sacre du Bichet par les Nkomi en 1897." *Revue française d'histoire d'outre-mer* 61, no. 224 (1974): 395–416.

Geary, Patrick J. *Furta Sacra: Thefts of Relics in the Central Middle Ages.* Princeton, NJ: Princeton University Press, 1990.

Geary, Christraud M. "Photographic Practice in Africa and Its Implications for the Use of Historical Photographs as Contextual Evidence." In *Fotographia e storia dell' Africa,* edited by Alessandro Triulzi. Napoli: I.U.O., 1995.

Geary, Patrick J. "Sacred Commodities: The Circulation of Medieval Relics." In *The Social Life of Things: Commodities in Cultural,* edited by Arjun Appadurai, 169–91. Cambridge: Cambridge University Press, 1986.

Gell, Alfred. "Technology and Magic." *Anthropology Today* 4, no. 2 (1988): 6–9.

Geschiere, Peter. *The Modernity of Witchcraft: Politics and the Occult in Postcolonial Africa.* Charlottesville: University of Virginia Press, 1997.

Geschiere, Peter. *Witchcraft, Intimacy, and Trust: Africa in Comparison.* Chicago, IL: University of Chicago Press, 2013.

Giles-Vernick, Tamara. *Cutting the Vines of the Past: Environmental Histories of the Central African Rainforest.* Charlottesville: University of Virginia Press, 2002.

Giles-Vernick, Tamara, and Stephanie Rupp. "Visions of Apes, Reflections on Change: Telling Tales of Great Apes in Equatorial Africa." *African Studies Review* 49, no. 1 (April 2006): 51–73.

Gilroy, Paul. *Against Race: Imagining Political Culture beyond the Color Line,* Cambridge, MA: Harvard University Press, 2000.

Gilroy, Paul. *The Black Atlantic: Modernity and Double Consciousness.* Cambridge, MA: Harvard University Press, 1993.

Glassman, Jonathan. *Feasts and Riot: Revelry, Rebellion, and Popular Consciousness on the Swahili Coast, 1856–1888.* Portsmouth, NH: Heinemann, 1996.

Gluckman, Max. "Analysis of a Social Situation in Modern Zululand." *Bantu Studies* 40, no. 1 (1940): 1–30.

Gobineau, Arthur de. *Essai sur l'inégalité des races humaines.* Paris: Didot, 1855.

Godbout, Jacques T., and Alain Caillé. *L'Esprit du don.* Paris: La Découverte, 1992.

Godelier, Maurice, and Marilyn Strathern, eds. *Big Men and Great Men: Personifications of Power in Melanesia*. Cambridge: Cambridge University Press, 1991.

Gollnhofer, Otto. "Boduku: Ethno-histoire ghetsogho." Thèse de l'École Pratique des Hautes Études, Paris, 1967.

Gollnhofer, Otto. "Les rites de passage de la société initiatique du Bwete chez les Mitsogho: La Manducation de l'iboga." Thèse de doctorat de troisième cycle, École Pratique des Hautes Études, Paris, 1974.

Gollnhofer, Otto, and Roger Sillans. *La Mémoire d'un peuple: Ethno-histoire des Mitsogho, ethnie du Gabon central*. Paris: Présence africaine, 1997.

Gondola, Charles Didier. *Villes miroirs: Migrations et identités urbaines à Brazzaville et Kinshasa, 1930–1970*. Paris: L'Harmattan, 1997.

Goody, Jack. *Death, Property, and the Ancestors: A Study of the Mortuary Customs of the Lodagaa of West Africa*. London: Tavistock, 1962.

Gordon, David M. *Invisible Agents. Spirits in a Central African History*. Athens: Ohio University Press, 2012.

Gramsci, Antonio. *Selections from the Prison Notebooks of Antonio Gramsci*. Edited and translated by Quintin Hoare and Geoffrey Nowell Smith. New York: International, 1971.

Grant, Ben. "'Interior Explorations': Paul Belloni du Chaillu's Dream Book." *Journal of European Studies* 38, no. 4:407–19.

Gray, Christopher J. *Colonial Rule and Crisis in Equatorial Africa: Southern Gabon ca. 1850–1940*. Rochester, NY: University of Rochester Press, 2002.

Gray, Christopher. "Territoriality, Ethnicity and Colonial Rule in Southern Gabon, 1850–1960." PhD thesis, Indiana University, Bloomington, 1995.

Gray, Christopher, and François Ngolet. "Lambaréné, Okoumé and the Transformation of Labor along the Middle Ogooué (Gabon), 1870–1945." *Journal of African History* 40, no. 1 (1999): 87–107.

Great Britain Naval Intelligence Division. *French Equatorial Africa and Cameroons*. London: Naval Intelligence Division, 1942.

Grébert, Fernand. *Au Gabon (Afrique équatoriale française)*. Paris: Société des Missions évangéliques de Paris, 1922.

Grébert, Fernand, Claude Savary, and Louis Perrois. *Le Gabon de Fernand Grébert, 1913–1932*. Geneva: Musée d'ethnographie de Genève, 2003.

Greene, Sandra E. *Sacred Sites and the Colonial Encounter: A History of Meaning and Memory in Ghana*. Bloomington: Indiana University Press, 2002.

Griffon du Bellay. "Le Gabon, 1861–1864." In *Le Tour du Monde: Nouveau Journal des Voyages*, 273–320. Vol. 12, no. 2. Paris: Librairie Hachette, 1865.

Grinker, Roy Richard. *Houses in the Rain Forest: Ethnicity and Inequality among Farmers and Foragers in Central Africa*. Berkeley: University of California Press, 1994.

Groves, Colin. "A History of Gorilla Taxonomy." In *Gorilla Biology: A Multidisciplinary Perspective*, edited by Andrea B. Taylor and Michele L. Goldsmith, 15–34. Cambridge, NY: Cambridge University Press, 2002.

Guernier, Eugène. *Afrique équatoriale française*. Paris: Encyclopédie coloniale et maritime, 1950.

Guha, Ranajit. *A Subaltern Studies Reader, 1986–1995*. Minneapolis: University of Minnesota Press, 1997.

Guiral, Léon. *Le Congo français du Gabon à Brazzaville*. Paris: E. Plon, Nourrit, 1889.

Guthrie, Malcolm. *Comparative Bantu*, 4 vols. Farnham, UK: Gregg Press, 1967–1971.

Guyer, Jane I. "Indigenous Currencies and the History of Marriage Payments: A Case Study from Cameroon." *Cahiers d'Études Africaines* 26, no. 104 (1986): 577–610.

Guyer, Jane I. "Bridewealth, and Dowry Revisited: The Position of Women in Sub-Saharan Africa and North India." *Current Anthropology* 30, no. 4 (1989): 413–35.

Guyer, Jane I. *Marginal Gains: Monetary Transactions in Atlantic Africa*. Chicago, IL: University of Chicago Press, 2004.

Guyer, Jane I., ed. *Money Matters: Instability, Values, and Social Payments in the Modern History of West African Communities*. Portsmouth, NH: Heinemann, 1995.

Guyer, Jane I. "Wealth in People and Self-Realization in Equatorial Africa." *Man* 28, no. 2 (1993): 243–65.

Guyer, Jane I., and Samuel M. Eno Belinga. "Wealth in People as Wealth in Knowledge: Accumulation and Composition in Equatorial Africa." *Journal of African History* 36, no. 1 (1995): 91–120.

Haraway, Donna. *Primate Visions: Gender, Race, and Nature in the World of Modern Science*. New York: Routledge, 1989.

Harms, Robert W. *River of Wealth, River of Sorrow: The Central Zaire Basin in the Era of the Slave and Ivory Trade, 1500–1891*. New Haven, CT: Yale University Press, 1981.

Hecht, Gabrielle. *Radiance of France: Nuclear Power and National Identity after World War II*. Boston, MA: MIT Press, 1998.

Hendricks, Thomas. "Work in the Rainforest: Labour, Race and Desire in a Congolese Logging Camp." PhD thesis, Institute for Anthropological Research in Africa, Catholic University of Leuven, 2013.

Heusch, Luc de. *Sacrifice in Africa: A Structuralist Approach*. Manchester, UK: Manchester University Press, 1985.

Heywood, Linda M., and John K. Thornton. *Central Africans, Atlantic Creoles, and the Making of the Foundation of the Americas, 1585–1660*. New York: Cambridge University Press, 2007.

Hilton, Anne. *The Kingdom of Kongo*. Oxford: Clarendon Press, 1985.

Hochschild, Adam. *King Leopold's Ghost: A Story of Greed, Terror, and Heroism in Colonial Africa*. Mariner Books. Boston, MA: Houghton Mifflin, 1999.

Hodgson, Amanda. "Defining the Species: Apes, Savages and Humans in Scientific and Literary Writing of the 1860s." *Journal of Victorian Culture* 4, no. 2 (1999): 228–51.

Horn, Trader, and Ethelreda Lewis. *Trader Horn: Being the Life and Works of Alfred Aloysius Horn*. New York: Library Guild of America, 1927.

Houlet, Georges. *Les guides bleus: Afrique centrale: Les républiques d'expression française*. Paris: Librairie Hachette, 1962.

Howard, Allen M., and Richard M. Shain, eds. *The Spatial Factor in African History: The Relationship of the Social, Material, and Perceptual*. Leiden: Brill, 2005.

Hubert, Henri, and Marcel Mauss. *Sacrifice: Its Nature and Function*. London: Cohen & West, 1964.

Hunt, Nancy Rose. *A Colonial Lexicon of Birth Ritual, Medicalization, and Mobility in the Congo*. Durham, NC: Duke University Press, 1999.

Hunt, Nancy Rose. *A Nervous State: Violence, Remedies, and Reveries in Colonial Congo*. Durham, NC: Duke University Press, 2016.

Hutchinson, Sharon Elaine. *Nuer Dilemmas: Coping with Money, War, and the State*. Berkeley: University of California Press, 1996.

Huxley, Thomas Henry. *Man's Place in Nature: And Other Anthropological Essays*. New York: D. Appleton, 1919.

Idiata, Daniel Franck. *Les langues du Gabon: Données en vue de l'élaboration d'un atlas linguistique*. Paris: L'Harmattan, 2007.

Ikogou-Renamy, Lionel Cédrick. "L'Or blanc: Le Marché occulte et illégal du corps humain à Libreville." PhD thesis, Université Omar Bongo Onbimba, Libreville, 2014.

Isischei, Elizabeth. *Voices of the Poor in Africa: Moral Economy and the Popular Imagination*. Rochester NY: University of Rochester Press, 2002.

Janzen, John M., and William Arkinstall. *The Quest for Therapy in Lower Zaire*. Berkeley: University of California Press, 1978.

Jean-Baptiste, Rachel. *Conjugal Rights: Marriage, Sexuality, and Urban Life Colonial Libreville, Gabon, 1849–1960*. Athens: Ohio University Press, 2014.

Jewsiewicki, Bogumil. *Mami Wata: La Peinture Urbaine au Congo*. Paris: Gallimard, 2003.

Johnson, Walter. "On Agency." *Journal of Social History* 37, no. 1 (autumn 2003): 113–24.

Kantorowicz, Ernst. *The King's Two Bodies: A Study in Mediaeval Political Theology*. Princeton, NJ: Princeton University Press, 1957.

Kapferer, Bruce. *Strategy and Transaction in an African Factory: African Workers and Indian Management in a Zambian Town*. Manchester, UK: Manchester University Press, 1972.

Kapferer, Bruce. *Transaction and Meaning: Directions in the Anthropology of Exchange and Symbolic Behavior*. Philadelphia, PA: Institute for the Study of Human Issues, 1976.

Kialo, Paulin. *Anthropologie de la forêt: Populations pové et exploitants forestiers français au Gabon.* Paris: L'Harmattan, 2007.

Kingsley, Mary Henrietta. *Travels in West Africa Congo Français, Corisco, and Cameroons.* London: Macmillan, 1897.

Klieman, Kairn A. *"The Pygmies Were Our Compass": Bantu and Batwa in the History of West Central Africa, Early Times to c. 1900 C.E.* Portsmouth, NH: Heinemann, 2003.

Koumba, Monique. "Contribution à l'histoire de Mouila des origines à 1971." Master's thesis, Université Omar Bongo Onbimba, Libreville, 1984.

Koumba, Micheline. "Le Dibur-Simbu et la naissance du Mwi Bapunu." Bachelor's thesis, Université Omar Bongo Onbimba, Libreville, 1985.

Koumba-Mamfoumbi, Monique. "La Mission Saint Martin des Apindji (1900–1954): Étude de cas sur l'histoire de l'évangélisation du Gabon." Master's thesis, Université Omar Bongo Onbimba, Libreville, 1983.

Koumba-Mamfoumbi, Monique. "Les Punu du Gabon des origines à 1899." PhD thesis, Université Paris 1-Sorbonne, 1987.

Kriger, Colleen E. *Pride of Men: Ironworking in 19th-Century West Central Africa.* Portsmouth, NH: Heinemann, 1999.

Laburthe-Tolra, Philippe. *Initiations et sociétés secrètes au Cameroun: Essai sur la religion bëti.* Paris: Karthala, 1985.

Laburthe-Tolra, Philippe. *Les Seigneurs de la forêt: Essai sur le passé historique, l'organisation sociale et les normes éthiques des anciens Bëti du Cameroun.* Paris: Publications de la Sorbonne, 1981.

Laburthe-Tolra, Philippe. *Vers la lumière ou Le désir d'Ariel: À propos des Bëti du Cameroun: Sociologie de la conversion.* Paris: Karthala, 1999.

Laburthe-Tolra, Philippe, Christiane Falgayrettes-Leveau, and Günther Tessmann. *Fang.* Paris: Musée Dapper, 1991.

LaGamma, Alisa. "The Body Eternal: The Aesthetics of Equatorial African Reliquary Sculpture." In *Eternal Ancestors: The Art of the Central African Reliquary,* edited by Alisa Lagamma, 3–32. New York: Metropolitan Museum of Art/New Haven, CT: Yale University Press, 2007.

LaGamma, Alisa, ed. *Eternal Ancestors: The Art of the Central African Reliquary.* New York: Metropolitan Museum of Art / New Haven, CT: Yale University Press, 2007.

Laman, Karl E. *The Kongo.* 4 vols. 1953; repr., Uppsala, Sweden: Almqvist & Wiksell, 1962.

Landau, Paul Stuart, and Deborah D. Kaspin. *Images and Empires: Visuality in Colonial and Postcolonial Africa.* Berkeley: University of California Press, 2002.

Laplanche, Jean, and Jean-Bertrand Pontalis. *Vocabulaire de la psychanalyse.* 5th ed. Paris: Presses universitaires de France, 2007.

Largeau, Victor. *Encyclopédie pahouine, Congo français: Éléments de grammaire et dictionnaire français-pahouin.* Paris: E. Leroux, 1901.

Larkin, Brian. "The Politics and Poetics of Infrastructure." *Annual Review of Anthropology* 42 (2013): 327–43.

Larkin, Brian. *Signal and Noise: Media, Infrastructure, and Urban Culture in Nigeria*. Durham, NC: Duke University Press, 2008.

Larson, Pier. "Capacities and Modes of Thinking: Intellectual Engagements and Subaltern Hegemony in the Early History of Malagasy Christianity." *American Historical Review* 102, no. 4 (1997): 969–1002.

Latour, Bruno. *Sur le culte moderne des dieux faitiches, suivi de Iconoclash*. Paris: La Découverte, 2009.

Lavergne, Elsa de. *La Naissance du roman policier français: Du Second Empire à la Première Guerre mondiale*. Paris: Classiques Garnier, 2009.

Lavignotte, Henri. *L'Évur: Croyance des pahouins au Gabon*. Paris: Société des Missions évangéliques, 1936.

Lawrance, Benjamin N., Emily L. Osborn, and Richard L. Roberts. *Intermediaries, Interpreters, and Clerks: African Employees in the Making of Colonial Africa*. Madison: University of Wisconsin Press, 2006.

Le Bon, Gustave. *The Crowd: A Study of the Popular Mind*. 1896. New York: Penguin Books, 1977.

Le Bon, Gustave. *Les Premières civilisations*. Paris: Bibliothèque Camille Flammarion, 1889.

Le Bon, Gustave. *L'Homme et les sociétés—Leurs origines et leur histoire*. Paris: J. Rothschild, 1881.

Le Bon, Gustave. *Lois psychologiques de l'évolution des peuples*. Paris: Félix Alcan, 1895.

Le Breton, David. *Anthropologie du corps et modernité*. 2nd ed. Paris: Presses universitaires de France, 2001.

Le Roy, Alexandre. *La Religion des primitifs*. 5th ed. Paris: G. Beauchesne, 1925.

Le Testu, Georges. *Notes sur les coutumes bapounou dans la circonscription de la Nyanga*. Caen, France: J. Haulard la Brière, n.d.

Lee, Christopher J. "The 'Native' Undefined: Colonial Categories, Anglo-African Status and the Politics of Kinship in British Central Africa, 1929–38." *Journal of African History* 46, no. 3 (2005): 457–78.

Leroi-Gourhan, André, and Jean Poirier. *Ethnologie de l'Union française (territoires extérieurs)*. Paris: Presses universitaires de France, 1953.

Léry, Jean de. *Journal de Bord de Jean de Léry en la Terre de Brésil, 1557*. Paris: Editions de Paris, 1957.

Lestringant, Frank. *Cannibals: The Discovery and Representation of the Cannibal from Columbus to Jules Verne*. Berkeley: University of California Press, 1997.

Lestringant, Frank. *Une Sainte horreur, ou, le voyage en Eucharistie: XVIe–XVIIIe siècle*. Paris: Presses universitaires de France, 1996.

Lévi-Strauss, Claude. *The Elementary Structures of Kinship*. Boston, MA: Beacon Press, 1969.

Lévi-Strauss, Claude. *The Savage Mind*. Chicago, IL: University of Chicago Press, 1966.

Lewis, Ethelreda, *Trader Horn: Being the Life and Works of Alfred Aloysius Horn*. New York: Library Guild of America, 1927.

Lindstrom, Lamont. *Cargo Cult: Strange Stories of Desire from Melanesia and Beyond*. Honolulu: University of Hawai'i Press, 1993.

Lock, Margaret M., and Vinh-Kim Nguyen. *An Anthropology of Biomedicine*. Chichester, UK: Wiley-Blackwell, 2010.

Lonsdale John. "Kenya: Home Country and African Frontier." In *Settlers and Expatriates: Britons over the Seas*, edited by Robert Bickers, 74–111. Oxford: Oxford University Press, 2010.

Lydon, Ghislaine. "The Unraveling of a Neglected Source: A Report on Women in Francophone West Africa in the 1930s." *Cahiers d'études africaines* 37, no. 147 (1997): 555–84.

Mabik-ma-Kombil, *Parlons Yipunu: Langue et culture des Punu du Gabon-Congo*. Paris: L'Harmattan, 2001.

MacGaffey, Wyatt. "Aesthetics and Politics of Violence in Central Africa." *Journal of African Cultural Studies* 13, no. 1 (June 2000): 63–75.

MacGaffey, Wyatt. "Changing Representations in Central African History." *Journal of African History* 46, no. 2 (2005): 189–207.

MacGaffey, Wyatt. "Kongo and the King of the Americans." *Journal of Modern African Studies* 6, no. 2 (1968): 171–81.

MacGaffey, Wyatt. *Kongo Political Culture: The Conceptual Challenge of the Particular*. Bloomington: Indiana University Press, 2000.

MacGaffey, Wyatt. *Modern Kongo Prophets: Religion in a Plural Society*. Bloomington: Indiana University Press, 1983.

MacGaffey, Wyatt. *Religion and Society in Central Africa: The Bakongo of Lower Zaire*. Chicago, IL: University of Chicago Press, 1986.

MacGaffey, Wyatt. "The Religious Commissions of the Bakongo." *Man* 5, no. 1 (March 1970): 27–38.

MacGaffey, Wyatt, and al. *Astonishment and Power*. Washington, DC: Published for the National Museum of African Art by the Smithsonian Institution Press, 1993.

Mallart Guimera, L. *Ni dos ni ventre: Religion, magie, et sorcellerie Evuzok*. Paris: Société d'ethnographie, 1981.

Mamfoumbi, Christian. "L'Évolution des sociétés secrètes chez les Gisir du Gabon." Master's thesis, Université Omar Bongo Onbimba, Libreville, 1981.

Mandendi, Eric Gilles Dibady. "Stations missionaires et postes administratifs dans la Ngounié nord (1850–1959)." Master's thesis, Université Omar Bongo Onbimba, Libreville, 1991.

Manghady Manghady, José Hervé. "Le Commerce inter-ethnique au Gabon: Le Cas des Nzébi et des Punu du sud Ngounié dans la seconde moitié du XIXe siècle." Master's thesis, Université Omar Bongo Onbimba, Libreville, 1997.

Mann, Gregory. *Native Sons: West African Veterans and France in the Twentieth Century*. Durham, NC: Duke University Press, 2006.

Marche, Alfred. *Trois voyages dans l'Afrique occidentale: Sénégal—Gambie—Casamance—Gabon—Ogooué.* 2nd ed. Paris: Librairie Hachette, 1882.

Marie-Germaine, Soeur, and Louis Marin. *Le Christ au Gabon.* Louvain: Museum Lessianum, 1931.

Martin, Phyllis M. *Catholic Women of Congo-Brazzaville: Mothers and Sisters in Troubled Times.* Bloomington: Indiana University Press, 2009.

Martin, Phyllis M. *The External Trade of the Loango Coast, 1576–1870: The Effects of Changing Commercial Relations on the Vili Kingdom of Loango.* Oxford: Clarendon Press, 1972.

Martin, Phyllis M. "Family Strategies in Nineteenth-Century Cabinda." *Journal of African History* 28, no. 1 (1987): 65–86.

Martin, Phyllis M. *Leisure and Society in Colonial Brazzaville.* Cambridge: Cambridge University Press, 1995.

Mary, André. "La Diabolisation du sorcier et le réveil de Satan." *Religiologiques,* no. 18 (1998): 53–77.

Mary, André. *Le Défi du syncrétisme: Le Travail symbolique de la religion d'Eboga, Gabon.* Paris: Éditions de l'École des Hautes Études en Sciences Sociales, 1999.

Marx, Karl. *Das Kapital: Kritik Der Politischen Ökonomie.* Berlin: Dietz, 1983.

Masquelier, Adeline. "Narratives of Power, Images of Wealth: The Ritual Economy of Bori in the Market." In *Modernity and Its Malcontents: Ritual and Power in Postcolonial Africa,* edited by Jean and John Comaroff, 3–33. Chicago, IL: University of Chicago Press, 1993.

Matimi, Jean-Christophe. "Tradition et innovations dans la construction de l'identité chez les Shamaye (Gabon) entre 1930 et 1990." PhD thesis, Université Laval, 1998.

Mauss, Marcel. *The Gift: Forms and Functions of Exchange in Archaic Societies.* New York: Norton, 1990.

Mauss, Marcel. "Techniques of the Body," *Economy and Society* 2, no. 1 (1973): 70–88.

Mazenot, Georges. *La Likouala-Mossaka: Histoire de la pénétration du Haut Congo, 1878–1920.* Paris: La Haye, Mouton, 1970.

Mba, Léon. "Essai de droit coutumier pahouin." *Bulletin de la société de recherches congolaises,* no. 25 (1938): 5–47.

Mbembe, Achille. *Afriques indociles: Christianisme, pouvoir et état en société postcoloniale.* Paris: Karthala, 1988.

Mbembe, Achille. "La Colonie, son petit secret et sa part maudite." *Politique africaine,* no. 102 (June 2006): 101–27.

Mbembe, Achille. *La Naissance du maquis dans le Sud-Cameroun (1920–1960): Histoire des usages de la raison en colonie.* Paris: Karthala, 1996.

Mbembe, Achille. "La Prolifération du divin en Afrique sub-Saharienne." In *Les politiques de Dieu,* edited by Gilles Kepel, 177–201. Paris: Karthala, 1993.

Mbembe, Achille. *On the Postcolony.* Berkeley: University of California Press, 2001.

Mbembe, Achille. "Provisional Notes on the Postcolony." *Africa*, 62, no. 1 (1992): 3–37.

M'Bokolo, Elikia. *Noirs et blancs en Afrique équatoriale: Les Sociétés côtières et la pénétration française, vers 1820–1874.* Paris: Editions de l'Ecole des Hautes Études en Sciences Sociales, 1981.

McClintock, Anne. *Imperial Leather: Race, Gender, and Sexuality in the Colonial Contest.* New York: Routledge, 1995.

Meillassoux, Claude. *Maidens, Meal, and Money: Capitalism and the Domestic Community.* Cambridge: Cambridge University Press, 1981.

Memmi, Albert. *The Colonizer and the Colonized.* Boston, MA: Beacon Press, 1967.

Memmi, Albert. *Portrait du colonisé: Précédé du portrait du colonisateur.* Paris: Buchet/Chastel, 1957.

Meteghe-N'Nah, Nicolas. *Histoire du Gabon: Des Origines à l'aube du XXIe siècle.* Paris: L'Harmattan, 2006.

Meteghe-N'Nah, Nicolas. "Imaginaire populaire, croyances et établissement de la domination coloniale au Gabon au XIXe siècle." *Annales de la Faculté des Lettres, Arts et Sciences Humaines,* Université d'Abomey-Calavi, Bénin, no. 8 (December 2002): 79–92.

Meteghe-N'Nah, Nicolas. *L'Implantation coloniale au Gabon: Résistance d'un peuple.* Paris: L'Harmattan, 1981.

Meteghe-N'Nah, Nicolas. *Mariage morganatique et intégration sociale chez les peuples matrilinéaires du Gabon précolonial: L'Exemple punu.* Libreville: Éditions des Annales de la Faculté des Lettres et Sciences Humaines, 2005.

Meyer, Birgit. "Mediation and Immediacy: Sensational Forms, Semiotic Ideologies and the Question of the Medium." *Social Anthropology*, no. 19 (2011): 23–39.

Meyer, Birgit, and Peter Pels, eds. *Magic and Modernity: Interfaces of Revelation and Concealment.* Stanford, CA: Stanford University Press, 2003.

Miers, Suzanne, and Igor Kopytoff, eds. *Slavery in Africa: Historical and Anthropological Perspectives.* Madison: University of Wisconsin Press, 1977.

Miller, John. *Empire and the Animal Body: Violence, Identity, and Ecology in Victorian Adventure Fiction.* London: Anthem Press, 2014.

Miller, John. "Meat, Cannibalism and Humanity in Paul du Chaillu's *Explorations and Adventures in Equatorial Africa*; or, What Does a Gorilla Hunter Eat for Breakfast?" *Gothic Studies* 16, no. 1 (May 2014): 70–84.

Miller, Joseph C. *Way of Death: Merchant Capitalism and the Angolan Slave Trade, 1730–1830.* Madison: University of Wisconsin Press, 1988.

Milligan, Robert H. *The Fetish Folk of West Africa.* 1912. New York: AMS Press, 1970.

Milligan, Robert H. *The Jungle Folk of Africa.* 2nd ed. New York: F. H. Revell, 1908.

Missié, Jean-Pierre. "Signification et influence des enseignes à caractère religieux dans le domaine commercial à Brazzaville." *Annales de l'Université Marien Ngouabi* 8, no. 1 (2007): 57–72.

Missionaries of the American Board of Commissioners for Foreign Missions. *The Gospel according to St John, translated into the Mpongwe Language.* New York: American Bible Society, 1852.

Missioumbou, Paul. "Héritage, contradictions et changements socio-culturels chez les Nzébi: Contribution à l'analyse de la crise de l'institution familiale au Gabon." Master's thesis, Université Omar Bongo Onbimba, Libreville, 1999.

Monaville, Pedro A. G. "Decolonizing the University: Postal Politics, the Student Movement, and Global 1968 in the Congo." PhD thesis, University of Michigan, 2013.

Monroe, John Warne. *Laboratories of Faith: Mesmerism, Spiritism, and Occultism in Modern France.* Ithaca, NY: Cornell University Press, 2008.

Montandon, Georges. *La Race, les races: Mise au point d'ethnologie somatique.* Paris: Payot, 1933.

Motley, Mary. *Devils in Waiting.* London: Longmans, 1959.

Mouguiama-Daouda, Patrick. *Remplacement, extinction et mélange des langues: Situation gabonaise et perspectives théoriques.* Paris: L'Harmattan, 2006.

Mulina, Habi Buganza, "Le Nkisi dans la tradition Woyo du Bas-Zaïre." *Fétiches: Objets enchantés, mots réalisés.* Special issue of *Systèmes de pensée en Afrique noire*, no. 8 (1985): 201–20.

Murray, Colin, and Peter Sanders. *Medicine Murder in Colonial Lesotho: The Anatomy of a Moral Crisis.* Edinburgh: Edinburgh University Press, 2005.

Nassau, Robert Hamill. *Crowned in Palm-Land: A Story of African Mission Life.* Philadelphia, PA: J. Lippincott, 1874.

Nassau, Robert Hamill. *Fetishism in West Africa: Forty Years' Observation of Native Customs and Superstitions.* London: Duckworth, 1904.

Nassau, Robert Hamill. *In an Elephant Corral: And Other Tales of West African Experiences.* 1912. New York: Negro Universities Press, 1969.

Nassau, Robert Hamill. *My Ogowe: Being a Narrative of Daily Incidents during my Sixteen years in Equatorial West Africa.* New York: Neale, 1914.

Ndaywel à Nziem, Isodore. "Du Zaïre au Congo: La Vierge du Désarmement et la guerre de libération." *Canadian Journal of African Studies* 33, no. 2 (1999): 500–529.

Ngolet, François. "Ideological Manipulations and Political Longevity: The Power of Omar Bongo in Gabon since 1967." *African Studies Review* 43, no. 2 (2000): 55–71.

Niehaus, Isak. "Coins for Blood and Blood for Coins: From Sacrifice to Ritual Murder in the South African Lowveld." *Etnofoor* 13, no. 2 (2000): 31–54.

Nsuka-Nkutsi, François. *Éléments de description du Punu.* Lyon, France: Université Lyon 2, 1980.

Nzamba, Frank Christopher. "La Sorcellerie dans les conflits d'héritage en milieu urbain chez les Punu: Cas de Libreville." Master's thesis, Université Omar Bongo Onbimba, Libreville, 2005.

Obengui, Guy Donald Adjoï. "Njobi et pouvoir politique chez les Mbede." Master's thesis, Université Omar Bongo Ondimba, Libreville, 2008.

Obeyesekere, Gananath. *Cannibal Talk: The Man-Eating Myth and Human Sacrifice in the South Seas*. Berkeley: University of California Press, 2005.

Obyesekere, Gananath. *The Work of Culture: Symbolic Transformation in Psychoanalysis and Anthropology*. Chicago, IL: University of Chicago Press, 1990.

Oliver-Mason, Joshua. "These Blurred Copies of Himself: T. H. Huxley, Paul du Chaillu, and the Reader's Place among the Apes." *Victorian Literature and Culture* 42 (2014): 99–122.

Ostergaard-Christensen, Lavrids. *At Work with Albert Schweitzer*. London: George Allen & Unwin, 1962.

Parry, Jonathan, and Maurice Bloch, eds. *Money and the Morality of Exchange*. Cambridge: Cambridge University Press, 1989.

Patterson, K. David. "Paul B. Du Chaillu and the Exploration of Gabon, 1855–1865." *International Journal of African Historical Studies* 7, no. 4 (1974): 647–67.

Patterson, K. David. *The Northern Gabon Coast to 1875*. Oxford: Clarendon Press, 1975.

Payeur-Didelot, P. *Trente mois au continent mystérieux: Gabon-Congo et côte occidentale d'Afrique*. Paris: Berger-Levrault, 1899.

Perrier, André. *Gabon: Un Réveil religieux, 1935–1937*. Paris: L'Harmattan, 1988.

Perrois, Louis. *Arts du Gabon: Les Arts plastiques du bassin de l'Ogooué*. Paris: Éditions de l'ORSTOM, 1979.

Perrois, Louis. *Byeri Fang: Sculptures d'ancêtres en Afrique*. Marseille, France: Musées de Marseille, Réunion des Musées Nationaux, 1992.

Perrois, Louis, ed. *L'Esprit de la forêt. Terres du Gabon*. Bordeaux, France: Musée d'Aquitaine / Paris: Somogy Éditions d'art, 1997.

Perrois, Louis. "The Western Historiography of African Reliquary Sculpture." In *Eternal Ancestors: The Art of the Central African Reliquary*, edited by Alisa LaGamma, 63–77. New York: Metropolitan Museum of Art/New Haven, CT: Yale University Press, 2007.

Pietz, William. *Le Fétiche. Généalogie d'un problème*. Paris: Kargo & L'éclat, 2005.

Pietz, William. "The Problem of the Fetish: I." *RES: Anthropology and Aesthetics*, no. 9 (spring 1985): 5–17.

Pietz, William. "The Problem of the Fetish, II: The Origin of the Fetish." *RES: Anthropology and Aesthetics*, no. 13 (spring 1987): 23–45.

Pietz, William. "The Problem of the Fetish, IIIa: Bosman's Guinea and the Enlightenment Theory of Fetishism." *RES: Anthropology and Aesthetics*, no. 16 (autumn 1988): 105–24.

Portet, Mariette. *En blanc sur les cartes*. Condé-sur-Noireau, France: Imprimeur-Editeur Ch. Corlet, 1969.

Pourtier, Roland. *Le Gabon*. 2 vols. Paris: L'Harmattan, 1989.

Poutrin, Léon. *Travaux scientifiques de la Mission Cottes au Sud-Cameroun, 1905–1908: Anthropologie, ethnographie, linguistique*. Paris: E. Leroux, 1911.

Pratt, Mary Louise. *Imperial Eyes: Travel Writing and Transculturation*. London: Routledge, 1992.

Pratten, David. *The Man-Leopard Murders: History and Society in Colonial Nigeria*. Bloomington: Indiana University Press, 2007.

Pulcu, Erdem. "An Evolutionary Perspective on Gradual Formation of Superego in the Primal Horde." *Frontiers in Psychology* 5, no. 8 (January 2014): n.p., published online.

Ranger, Terence. "Taking Hold of the Land: Holy Places and Pilgrimages in Twentieth-Century Zimbabwe." *Past and Present*, no. 117 (1987): 158–94.

Raponda-Walker, André. *Au pays des Ishogos: Simple récit de voyage*. Libreville: Fondation Raponda Walker, 1994.

Raponda-Walker, André. *Contes Gabonais*. Nouvelle édition revue et augmentée. Paris: Présence africaine, 1967.

Raponda-Walker, André. *Éléments de grammaire ébongwé (langue des pygmées)*. Libreville: Fondation Raponda Walker, n.d. [1937].

Raponda-Walker, André. *Éléments de grammaire fang*. Libreville: Fondation Raponda Walker, 1995.

Raponda-Walker, André. *Éléments de grammaire ghetsogho*. Libreville: Fondation Raponda Walker, n.d.

Raponda-Walker, André. *Notes d'histoire du Gabon, Suivi de: Toponymie de l'Estuaire Libreville et Toponymie du Fernan Vaz Port Gentil*. 1960. Libreville: Éditions Raponda-Walker, 1996.

Raponda-Walker, André, and Roger Sillans. *Rites et croyances des peuples du Gabon: Essai sur les pratiques religieuses d'autrefois et d'aujourd'hui*. Paris: Présence africaine, 1983.

Rashkin, Esther. *Unspeakable Secrets and the Psychoanalysis of Culture*. Albany, NY: SUNY Press, 2008.

Reade, William Winwood. *Savage Africa; Being the Narrative of a Tour in Equatorial, Southwestern and Northwestern Africa*. New York: Harper & Brothers, 1864.

Reading, Joseph H. *The Ogowe Band: A Narrative of African Travel*. Philadelphia, PA: Reading, 1890.

Renouard, Georges. *L'Ouest africain et les Missions Catholiques: Congo et Oubanghi*. Paris: H. Oudin, 1904.

Reste, Jean-François. *À l'ombre de la grande forêt*. 7th ed. Paris: Stock, Delamain & Boutelleau, 1943.

Rey, Alain, ed. *Dictionnaire historique de la langue française*. 2 Vols., Paris: Dictionnaires Le Robert, 2000.

Rey, Pierre-Philippe. "Articulation des modes de dépendance et des modes de reproduction dans deux sociétés lignagères (Punu et Kunyi du Congo-Brazzaville)." *Cahiers d'études africaines* 9, no. 35 (1969): 415–40.

Rey, Pierre-Philippe. *Colonialisme, néo-colonialisme et transition au capitalisme: Exemple de la Comilog au Congo-Brazzaville*. Paris: F. Maspero, 1971.

Rich, Jeremy. *Missing Links: The African and American Worlds of R. L. Garner, Primate Collector*. Athens: University of Georgia Press, 2012.

Rich, Jeremy. *A Workman Is Worthy of His Meat: Food and Colonialism in the Gabon Estuary*. Lincoln: University of Nebraska Press, 2007.

Rondet-Saint, Maurice. *L'Afrique Équatoriale Française*. Paris: Plon-Nourrit, 1911.

Rosny, Eric de. *Les Yeux de ma chèvre: Sur les pas des maîtres de la nuit en pays Douala (Cameroun)*. Paris: Librairie Plon, 1981.

Rossatanga-Rignault, Guy. *Le Travail du Blanc ne finit jamais: L'Africain, le temps et le travail moderne*. Libreville: Éditions Raponda-Walker, 2007.

Rouget, Fernand. *L'Expansion coloniale au Congo français*. Paris: E. Larose, 1906.

Rupture-Solidarité, Collectif. *Le Gabon malgré lui*. Paris: Karthala, 2005.

Rupture-Solidarité, Collectif. *Rites et dépossessions*. Paris: Karthala, 2004.

Sahlins, Marshall. "Poor Man, Rich Man, Big Man, Chief: Political Types in Melanesia and Polynesia." *Comparative Studies in History and Society* 5, no. 3 (April 1963): 285–303.

Salpêteur, Matthieu, and Jean-Pierre Warnier. "Looking for the Effects of Bodily Organs and Substances through Vernacular Public Autopsy in Cameroon." *Critical African Studies* 5, no. 3 (fall 2013): 154–73.

Sautter, Gilles. *De l'Atlantique au fleuve Congo: Une géographie du sous-peuplement, République du Congo, République gabonaise*. Paris: La Haye, Mouton, 1966.

Schatzberg, Michael G. *Political Legitimacy in Middle Africa: Father, Family, Food*. Bloomington: Indiana University Press, 2001.

Scheper-Hughes, Nancy. "The Global Traffic in Human Organs." *Current Anthropology* 41, no. 2 (April 2000): 191–224.

Scheper-Hughes, Nancy, and Loïc Wacquant, eds. *Commodifying Bodies*. Thousand Oaks, CA: Sage Publications, 2002.

Schweinfurth, August Georg. *Au coeur de l'Afrique: Trois ans de voyages et d'aventures dans les régions inexplorées de l'Afrique centrale*. Vol. 1. Paris: Hachette, 1875.

Schweitzer, Albert. *African Notebook*. 1939. Bloomington: Indiana University Press, 1958.

Schweitzer, Albert. *The Primeval Forest*. 1931. Baltimore, MD: Johns Hopkins University Press, 1998.

Seligman, Charles. *Races in Africa*. 4th ed. London: Oxford University Press, 1966.

Sharp, Lesley A. *Strange Harvest: Organ Transplants, Denatured Bodies, and the Transformed Self*. Berkeley: University of California Press, 2006.

Shaw, Rosalind. *Memories of the Slave Trade: Ritual and the Historical Imagination in Sierra Leone*. Chicago, IL: University of Chicago Press, 2002.

Shaw, Rosalind. "The Production of Witchcraft/Witchcraft as Production: Memory, Modernity and the Slave Trade in Sierra Leone." *American Ethnologist* 24, no. 4 (1996): 856–76.

Sheppard, William H. *Pioneers in Congo*. Louisville, KY: Pentecostal Publishing, 1917.

Shipton, Parker M. *Mortgaging the Ancestors: Ideologies of Attachment in Africa.* New Haven, CT: Yale University Press, 2009.

Simenon, Georges. *Le Coup de lune: Roman inédit.* Paris: A. Fayard, 1933.

Sinda, Martial. *Le Messianisme congolais et ses incidences politiques: Kimbanguisme, matsouanisme, autres mouvements.* Paris: Payot, 1972.

Spear, Thomas. *Mountain Farmers: Moral Economies of Land and Agricultural Development in Arusha and Meru.* Oxford: James Currey, 1997.

Spear, Thomas. "Neo-Traditionalism and the Limits of Invention in British Colonial Africa." *Journal of African History* 44, no. 1 (2003): 3–27.

Staden, Hans. *Hans Staden's True History: An Account of Cannibal Captivity in Brazil* (c. 1557). Durham, NC: Duke University Press, 2008.

Steiner, Christopher Burghard. *African Art in Transit.* Cambridge: Cambridge University Press, 1994.

Stocking Jr., George W. *Victorian Anthropology.* New York: Free Press, 1987.

Stoker, Bram. *Dracula.* New York: Barnes & Noble, 1992.

Stoler, Ann Laura. *Along the Archival Grain: Epistemic Anxieties and Colonial Common Sense.* Princeton, NJ: Princeton University Press, 2009.

Stoler, Ann Laura. *Carnal Knowledge and Imperial Power: Race and the Intimate in Colonial Rule.* Berkeley: University of California Press, 2002.

Stoler, Ann Laura. "In Cold Blood: Hierarchies of Credibility and the Politics of Colonial Narratives." *Representations*, no. 37 (1992): 151–89.

Stoler, Ann Laura. "Sexual Affronts and Racial Frontiers: European Identities and the Cultural Politics of Exclusion in Colonial Southeast Asia." *Comparative Studies in Society and History* 34, no. 3 (1992): 514–51.

Suchman, Lucy A. *Human-Machine Reconfigurations: Plans and Situated Actions.* 2nd ed. Cambridge: Cambridge University Press, 2007.

Summers, Carol. "Intimate Colonialism: The Imperial Production of Reproduction in Uganda, 1907–1925." *Signs* 16, no. 4 (summer 1991): 787–807.

Sweet, James H. *Recreating Africa: Culture, Kinship, and Religion in the African-Portuguese World, 1441–1770.* Chapel Hill: University of North Carolina Press, 2003.

Swiderski, Stanislaw. "Notes biographiques sur les fondateurs et les guides spirituels des sectes syncrétiques au Gabon." *Anthropologica* 15, no. 1 (1973): 37–87.

Taussig, Michael T. "Culture of Terror, Space of Death. Roger Casement's Putamayo Report and the Explanation of Torture." *Comparative Studies in Society and History* 26 (1984): 467–97.

Taussig, Michael T. *Shamanism, Colonialism, and the Wild Man: A Study in Terror and Healing.* Chicago, IL: University of Chicago Press, 1986.

Taylor, Mark C. *Critical Terms for Religious Studies.* Chicago, IL: University of Chicago Press, 1998.

Teissères, Urbain. *Méthode pratique pour apprendre l'Omyènè.* Paris: Société des Missions Evangéliques de Paris, 1957.

Tempels, Placide. *La Philosophie Bantoue.* 2nd ed. Paris: Éditions africaines, 1948.

Tessmann, Günther. *Die Pangwe: Völkerkundliche Monographie Eines Westafrikanischen Negerstammes; Ergebnisse Der Lübecker Pangwe-expedition, 1907–1909 und Früherer Forschungen, 1904–1907*. Berlin: E. Wasmuth, A.-G., 1913. Partial translation in French in *Fang*, edited by Philippe Laburthe-Tolra and Christiane Falgayrettes-Leveau, 167–314. Paris: Musée Dapper, 1991.

Thévet, André. *The New Found Worlde or Antarctike*. London: Henrie Bynneman for Thomas Hacket, 1568.

Thomas, Lynn M. "The Modern Girl and Racial Respectability in 1930s South Africa." *Journal of African History* 47, no. 3 (2006): 461–90.

Thompson, Robert Farris, and Joseph Cornet. *The Four Moments of the Sun: Kongo Art in Two Worlds*. Washington, DC: National Gallery of Art, 1981.

Thornton, John K. *Africa and Africans in the Making of the Atlantic World, 1400–1800*. 2nd ed. Cambridge: Cambridge University Press, 1998.

Thornton, John. "Cannibals, Witches, and Slave Traders in the Atlantic World." *William and Mary Quarterly* 60, no. 2 (2003): 273–94.

Thornton, John K. *The Kingdom of Kongo: Civil War and Transition, 1641–1718*. Madison: University of Wisconsin Press, 1983.

Thornton, John K. *The Kongolese Saint Anthony: Dona Beatriz Kimpa Vita and the Antonian Movement, 1684–1706*. Cambridge: Cambridge University Press, 1998.

Tonda, Joseph. "Fétichisme et sorcellerie: La Force de mort du pouvoir souverain moderne en Afrique centrale." Unpublished paper, author's archives.

Tonda, Joseph. *La Guérison divine en Afrique centrale (Congo, Gabon)*. Paris: Karthala, 2002.

Tonda, Joseph. *Le Souverain moderne: Le Corps du pouvoir en Afrique centrale (Congo, Gabon)*. Paris: Karthala, 2005.

Tonda, Joseph. *L'Impérialisme postcolonial: Critique de la société des éblouissements*. Paris: Karthala, 2015.

Trézenem, Edouard. *L'Afrique équatoriale française: Le Cameroun*. Paris: Société d'éditions géographiques, maritimes et coloniales, 1947.

Trézenem, Édouard, and Bertrand Lembezat. *La France Équatoriale: L'Afrique équatoriale française: Le Cameroun*. Paris: Société d'éditions géographiques, maritimes et coloniales, 1947.

Trial, Georges. *Le roman du gorille*. Paris: Gallimard, 1936.

Trilles, Henri. *Chez les Fang, ou Quinze années de séjour au Congo français*. Lille: Société Saint-Augustin & Desclée, De Brouwer, 1913.

Trilles, Henri. *Fleurs noires et âmes blanches*. Lille: Desclée, De Brouwer, 1914.

Trilles, Henri. *Le Totémisme chez les Fân*. Münster, Germany: Aschendorff, 1912.

Trilles, Henri. *Mille Lieues dans l'inconnu: En pleine forêt équatoriale; chez les Fang anthropophages*. Bruges: Librairie de l'Œuvre Saint-Charles, 1935.

Trivedi, Harish. *Colonial Transactions: English Literature and India*. New York: Manchester University Press, 1995.

Tsing, Anna Lowenhaupt. *Friction: An Ethnography of Global Connection*. Princeton, NJ: Princeton University Press, 2005.

Turner, Bryan S. *The Body and Society: Explorations in Social Theory*. Thousand Oaks, CA: Sage Publications, 1996.

Urquhart, Clara. *With Doctor Schweitzer in Lambaréné*. London: George G. Harrap, 1957.

Urry, John. *Mobilities*. Cambridge, UK: Polity, 2007.

Vacher de la Pouge, Georges. *L'Aryen, son rôle social, cours libre de science politique, professé à l'Université de Montpellier (1889–1890)*. Paris: A. Fontemoing, 1899.

Vansina, Jan. *Art History in Africa: An Introduction to Method*. London: Longman, 1984.

Vansina, Jan. *Being Colonized: The Kuba Experience in Rural Congo, 1880–1960*. Madison: University of Wisconsin Press, 2010.

Vansina, Jan. *How Societies Are Born: Governance in West Central Africa before 1600*. Charlottesville: University of Virginia Press, 2004.

Vansina, Jan. *Paths in the Rainforests: Toward a History of Political Tradition in Equatorial Africa*. Madison: University of Wisconsin Press, 1990.

Vansina, Jan. "Peoples of the Forest." In *History of Central Africa*, edited by David Birmingham and Phyllis M. Martin, 75–117. Vol. 1. London and New York: Longman, 1983.

Vansina, Jan. *The Tio Kingdom of the Middle Congo, 1880–1892*. London: Oxford University Press, 1973.

Vassal, Gabrielle. *Mon séjour au Congo français*. Paris: Pierre Roger, 1925.

Vassal, Gabrielle, and Joseph Vassal. *Français, Belges et Portugais en Afrique équatoriale: Pointe-Noire, Matadi, Lobito*. Paris: Roger, 1931.

Vaughan, Megan. *Curing Their Ills: Colonial Power and African Illness*. Cambridge, UK: Polity Press, 1991.

Vellut, Jean-Luc. "Quelle profondeur historique pour l'image de la Vierge Marie au Congo? " *Canadian Journal of African Studies* 33 no. 2 (1999): 530–47.

Villault, Nicolas. *Relation des costes d'Afrique, appellées Guinée*. Paris: Thierry, 1669.

Vincent, Jeanne-Françoise. "Le Mouvement Croix-Koma: Une nouvelle forme de lutte contre la sorcellerie en pays Kongo." *Cahiers d'éudes africaines* 6, no. 24 (1966): 527–63.

Voronoff, Serge. *Quarante-trois greffes du singe à l'homme*. Paris: Librairie Octave Doin, 1924.

Vromen, Ariadne, Katharine Gelber, and Anika Gauja. *Powerscape: Contemporary Australian Politics*. Sydney, Australia: Allen & Unwin, 2009.

Wannyn, Rob L. *L'art ancien du métal au Bas-Congo*. Champles par Wavre, Belgium: Éditions du Vieux Planquesaule, 1961.

Warner, Marina. "Fee Fie to Fum: The Child in the Jaws of History." In *Cannibalism and the Colonial World*, edited by John Barker, Peter Hulme and Margaret Inversen, 165. Cambridge: Cambridge University Press, 1998.

Weiner, Annette B. *Inalienable Possessions: The Paradox of Keeping-While-Giving*. Berkeley: University of California Press, 1992.

White, Luise. *The Assassination of Herbert Chitepo: Texts and Politics in Zimbabwe.* Bloomington: Indiana University Press, 2003.

White, Luise. *Speaking with Vampires: Rumor and History in Colonial Africa.* Berkeley: University of California Press, 2000.

White, Luise. *Unpopular Sovereignty: Rhodesian Independence and African Decolonization.* Chicago, IL: University of Chicago Press, 2015.

Wickers, Serge. *Contribution à la connaissance du droit privé des Bakongo.* Bordeaux, France: Taffard, 1954.

Wilson, Leighton. "Pangwe People." *Missionary Herald,* June (1843): 238–39.

Wilson, Leonard G. "The Gorilla and the Question of Human Origins: The Brain Controversy." *Journal of the History of Medicine and Allied Sciences* 51 (1996): 184–207.

Wing, Joseph van. *Études Bakongo: Sociologie—Religion et Magie.* 2nd ed. Brussels: Desclée de Brouwer, 1959.

Worsley, Peter. *The Trumpet Shall Sound: A Study of "Cargo" Cults in Melanesia.* 3rd ed. 1957. New York: Schocken, 1968.

Yengo, Patrice. *Les Mutations sorcières dans le bassin du Congo: Du ventre et de sa politique.* Paris: Karthala, 2016.

Yengo, Patrice. "Médicaments, pratique de soin, lien social: La question de la médicalité en Afrique centrale." Unpublished research project, 2010, author's archives.

Young, Robert. *Colonial Desire: Hybridity in Theory, Culture, and Race.* London: Routledge, 1995.

Zantop, Susanne. *Colonial Fantasies: Conquest, Family, and Nation in Precolonial Germany, 1770–1870.* Durham, NC: Duke University Press, 1997.

Zika, Charles. *The Appearance of Witchcraft: Print and Visual Culture in Sixteenth-Century Europe.* London: Routledge, 2007.

INDEX

abject, theory of, 149–50, 195–96
Adam, Jérome, 84
"The Adventure of the Creeping Man"
  (Doyle), 165
affiliation, 7, 196, 200, 219n21
agency: capacity and, 3–4, 30–32, 55, 135;
  of charms, 10, 14, 69–70, 74–75, 77–79,
  85, 87–88, 94–95, 234n27; defined, 2–3;
  extraordinary, 2–3, 69, 74, 96, 184, 233n13;
  fetish, 7, 22, 196; immaterial, 14, 30, 148;
  introduction to, 1–5, 7–12, 14, 18, 22, 25;
  material, 14, 30, 85, 108, 148, 182; new
  forms of, 200–201, 203; of spirits, 27,
  30–33, 49, 54–55, 58, 65–67, 74, 233n13;
  transaction and, 8–11, 30, 69, 85
airplane, 1, 199
Ambouroué-Avaro, Joseph, 102
ancestors: agency of, 14, 74, 233n13; bones
  of, 23, 105, 167, 176–77, 187, 190, 235n41,
  284n48; convertibility and, 125–26; hierarchy and, 247n45; material existence of,
  4; Murhumi as, 29, 32, 35, 39, 217n4; role
  of, 14; Simbu as, 29, 34–36, 40, 46, 50,
  218n20; substitution and, 125–26
animals: preservation of, 1, 163–64, 205n2;
  sacrifice of, 19, 184
anthropology, 2, 80, 94, 115, 122, 166, 173, 201
anthropophagy, 101–2, 152, 168, 268n16; cannibalism distinguished from, 269n29;
  decree against, 169, 180–81, 189
antiwitchcraft movements, 70–71, 85–87, 91,
  93, 226n126
anxiety. See fear

apes: as archaic fathers, 157–64; Du Chaillu
  and, 155–59, 161, 163–67, 275n82, 275n84,
  276nn99–100, 277n104, 277n109, 277n114,
  279n136; grafts from, 169; interspecies sex
  and, 157, 164–66; preservation of, 163–64,
  205n2; race and, 139, 155–57; transference,
  20, 139, 154–57, 275nn90–92, 276nn98–101,
  277n102
archaic father, 157–64
archives, 6, 19–20, 23–25, 45, 71–72, 84–85,
  92, 99, 112, 119–20, 125, 142, 144, 170;
  judicial, 174; oral, 22, 170
l'argent. See money
Atlantic era, 38–40, 60, 92, 106
autopsy, 4, 101–2, 247n50
awareness, 5, 154; of similarities, 201; of
  transgression, 117, 195–96, 201

Babongo, 37
baghisi. See water spirits
Bakhtin, Mikhail, 107
Bandombi (clan), 34, 40
banganga. See experts and healers
Bekale, Pierre, 186, 284n52, 287n74
belly, 73, 138, 171–72, 285n58
belly-womb (ventre), 27, 29, 217n4; charms,
  171; eating and, 169–72, 192, 199, 280n8
Benzoghe, myth of, 189, 288n87
Bhabha, Homi, 249n65
big men, 34, 123, 130, 256n38, 257n41
bilabi (gift ceremonies), 126–27
binding, 14, 74, 102, 168; with knots, 72;
  rope and, 110, 191

biomedicine, 185, 214n71, 290n8; autopsy in, 101–2; carnal fetishism and, 96–97, 100–102, 115, 117; dispensaries, 44; hospital in Mouila, 44

biopower/biopolitics, 51, 196; carnal fetishism and, 202; reproduction and, 151–52

Bissiélo, Anaclé, 16

black magic, 90, 285n57

blacksmiths, 36–38, 131–32, 219n32

blacksmith spirits, 37, 55, 62, 220n37

blood: increasing role of, 19, 23; transfusion, 185, 286n68; vampires and, 183–87, 286n66, 286n71, 287nn77–78

blood price, blood money (*prix du sang*): for body parts, 254n18; colonialism and, 119–22, 137, 198, 253n8, 253nn10–11, 254n12, 254n18, 255nn21–22

body: charms from, 1–2, 19, 68, 97, 99, 101–6, 114–15, 187, 190–91, 196–97; civilizations of, 102; European understanding of, 245n33; as fetish, 107–11; hygiene, 96–102; power in, 22, 96–97, 102–11, 115, 117, 187–88, 196–97, 199, 257n42; remains, 1–2, 96–102, 106, 114–17, 163, 166–68, 181, 191–92, 283n47; sacrifice and, 114–17; as sign, 107–11; white, 97, 99, 102, 108

body-of-the-shade (*nsisim*), 103–4, 245nn30–31, 247n43

body parts (*pièces détachées*), 114–17, 168, 192, 254n18, 280n1

Bombe, 42, 48, 50–51

Boncoeur, Jean Emane, 71, 86

bones: of ancestors, 23, 105, 167, 176–77, 187, 190, 235n41, 284n48; power in, 104–6, 115, 117, 167

Bongo, Omar, 16, 21, 216n91, 217n1, 231n176

boucherie (butchery), 1, 117, 186, 188, 268n15

Boueza, 180–81, 284n49

Bourdieu, Pierre, 107, 200

bricolage, 5, 8–9

bride-clans, 40

bridge, Ngounié River, 56–58

Bruel, Georges, 152, 276n98

Bumweli, 32, 34, 219n22

burials, 97–102, 244n13, 244nn20–22, 250n75

Burton, Richard, 144, 156, 275n91

butchery (*boucherie*), 1, 117, 186, 188, 268n15

Bwiti (healing cult), 213n63, 230n158, 247n48; Christianity and, 189; eating and, 189–92; high dignitaries of, 1, 70; literature on, 27

cannibalism: anthropophagy distinguished from, 269n29; archaic father and, 157–64; carnal fetishism and, 97, 101; colonialism and, 1, 138–41, 144–45, 148–67, 243n9, 268nn15–16, 268n21, 270n40, 271n41, 271nn45–46, 272nn51–52, 273n65, 283n44; Devil associated with, 183–84, 187; dreams and, 138–39, 142, 151, 154–55; Du Chaillu and, 139–44, 149, 153, 155–59, 161, 163–67, 271nn45–46, 279n136; eating and, 168–77, 179–90, 192–93, 287n81, 288n87; erotica, 148–51, 153; exoticized, 141–45; Fang and, 143–44, 150, 153–54, 178, 191, 271n46, 274n76, 274nn78–79; fear of, 22, 138, 146, 148–50, 155–56, 166; gorilla, 156, 275n92, 276n94; guilt and, 154–55, 158–59, 162, 166; imaginary of, 7, 138–39, 141, 145–46, 148, 151, 154–56, 168, 179, 195; law against, 19, 180–81; mirror of, 139–40, 143, 154; missionaries and, 150–51; monkey/ape transference and, 20, 139, 154–57, 275nn90–92, 276nn98–101, 277n102; Nassau and, 152, 163–64, 272n51, 275n91; race and, 138–39, 141–42, 151–52, 154–56, 166; raw flesh and, 188; self-destruction fantasies and, 151–53, 181, 247n51; slavery, 153, 247n51; tiger-men and, 139, 145–48, 173, 178–79, 185, 269n30, 270nn31–34, 270n37, 282nn26–27, 283nn44–45; transgressive hegemony and, 12; on trial, 148, 174–77, 184–85, 188, 283n45; white, 138, 141, 166–67, 247n51

capacity: agency and, 3–4, 30–32, 55, 135; of body, 97, 102–7; defined, 3; evil, 113; introduction to, 3–4, 8, 10, 18; powerscapes and, 52; transactions and, 195

Carli, Dionigi, 77–78

carnal fetishism: biomedicine and, 96–97, 100–102, 115, 117; biopower/biopolitics and, 202; cannibalism and, 97, 101; cemeteries and, 97–102, 115–17; colonialism

and, 96–102, 104, 107–15, 117; defined,
96–97, 117; fear and, 99, 101, 106, 108, 114;
grave robbing and, 99, 114–17; hegemonic transactions in, 111–14; imaginary
of, 7, 96–97, 107–8, 117; sacrifice in, 106,
108–9, 114–17

Castoriadis, Cornelius, 6, 201, 209n30

Catholic Church, 44–45, 49, 55–56; Congregation of the Holy Ghost, 108–9; Eucharist, 109, 181–83, 207n17, 285nn55–56;
Saint-Sulpician statues in, 61, 229n152

cauldrons, 172–74, 181. *See also marmite*

cemeteries, 97–102, 115–17, 244n13, 244n20,
244n22. *See also* grave robbing

Charbonnier, Hippolyte, 145–48, 178, 186,
270n37, 270n40

Charcot, Jean-Martin, 18

charlatans, 240n105, 241n106; charms and,
89–93; defined, 65, 89–92

charms: agency of, 10, 14, 69–70, 74–75,
77–79, 85, 87–88, 94–95, 234n27;
antiwitchcraft movements and, 85–87;
belly-womb, 171; from body, 1–2, 19, 68,
97, 99, 101–6, 114–15, 187, 190–91, 196–97;
charlatans and, 89–93; Christianity and,
10, 12, 61–62, 78, 83–85, 89–91, 108–9,
115, 197, 211n43, 235n37, 235n42, 236n54,
237n74; colonialism and, 69–70, 75–79,
83–85, 87, 89, 91–95, 97, 164; defined, 69,
74–75; early, 74–76; fetishes and, 75–81,
86–92; force in, 74, 106; making of, 1, 14,
177, 205n4, 213n59, 233nn13–16, 235n39,
235n43; *médicament*, 95, 136, 188, 220n40,
242n122; missionaries and, 10, 12, 61–62,
83–85, 108–9, 115, 197, 211n43, 235n37,
235n42, 236n54, 237n74; in museums,
81–82, 236n51; names of, 234n25; in
nineteenth century, 79–83; purchase of,
75, 77–83, 93–95, 234n34, 237nn55–56,
241n114; *symbole*, 135, 266n123; theft
of, 10, 79, 84, 95; transactions and, 69,
82–85, 87–88, 95, 106

Christianity: Bwiti and, 189; charms and, 10,
12, 61–62, 78, 83–85, 89–91, 108–9, 115, 197,
211n43, 235n37, 235n42, 236n54, 237n74;
destruction in, 248n52; Eucharist, 109,
181–83, 207n17, 285nn55–56; God of, 1,

16, 50, 92, 108–9, 114, 182, 230n157; Pentecostal, 91, 183, 238n74, 285n57; relics in,
78, 108, 247n42, 249n66, 249n68; saints,
50, 55–56, 59–64, 78, 249n66, 249n68;
witches in, 146–47. *See also* Catholic
Church; missionaries

Cinnamon, John, 70–71, 232n4

civil incidental damages (*réparations
civiles*), 254n14

civilization: archaic fathers and, 157–58;
of the body, 102; enslaving kin and, 40;
power of, 4, 9, 108, 195

clan (*kanda*), 34–35, 210n34, 219n21; in
Atlantic era, 38–40; colonial collaboration with, 45–50

Collodon, Augustus, 163, 165

colonialism, 17–18. *See also specific topics*

colonial kinship, 157, 199–200

commanditaire (patron), 65, 117, 168, 252n103

commensurability: of imaginaries, 201;
value, 5–7, 119, 124–26, 131, 135, 198

commodification: of magic, 118; of people,
96, 123, 130, 196–97, 253n5, 290n7; transactional value in, 4–5

commodity: category of, 119; exchanges of,
124, 262n87; fetish as, 201; metal objects,
172. *See also* goods

Compiègne, Louis-Alphonse-Victor du
Pont de, 112, 143–44, 154, 156, 162, 173,
259n62, 271n46

concessionary companies, 41–42, 132, 144,
222n65

Congregation of the Holy Ghost, 108–9

congruence, 195–96

congruent imaginaries, 6–8, 11, 201, 209n29

Conrad, Joseph: *Heart of Darkness*, 250n78,
250n84, 260n68, 266n2; *An Outpost of
Progress*, 112–14, 250n84

consumerism, 118

contagion, 106, 113, 149–50, 247n50

convertibility, 125–26

cook (*kolamba*), 177

cooked food, 187–88

cooking pot (*marmite*), 146–47, 172–74, 182,
186. *See also* cauldrons

Cooper, Frederick, 208n27, 210n39

Country of the Dwarfs (Du Chaillu), 139–40

Un Coup de lune (Simenon), 112–14
coupons, 132–33
craziness (*maboulisme*), 94, 242n119
crime rituel. See ritual crime

Darwin, Charles, 139, 141, 151, 273n60
debt, 41, 113, 266n129; crime, 125; of French
    people, 45; of hunter-gatherers, 259n57;
    loss and, 21; of recognition, 126; transac-
    tions in, 114, 126–28
Decree to Fight Anthropophagy (Décret
    sur la répression de l'anthropophagie),
    169, 180–81, 189
desire: archaic fathers and, 157–64; in
    colonialism, 11, 19, 21, 138–39, 151, 157–66;
    homoerotic, 19, 139, 151; interspecies
    sex and, 157, 164–66; of transgressive
    imaginaries, 21
destruction: colonial, 10, 85, 138, 151–54, 196;
    eating as, 168–69; in exchanges, 157–58,
    171, 179; replenishing and, 2; in sacrifice,
    211n42, 248n52; self-destruction, 151–53,
    181; symbolic, 168–69
Devil. *See* Satan/Devil
Dibur-Simbu: name of, 40, 217n6; Simbu as
    ancestor of, 29, 34–36, 40, 46, 50, 218n20;
    spirits and, 29, 32, 34–37, 39–40, 46,
    50–51, 53–54, 56–60, 64–66, 227n133
Dikakou, Nzaou, 66–67, 226n130
dismemberment, 21, 141, 163–64, 166, 191–92
diviner, 4, 88, 91, 214n71, 227n138. *See also*
    experts and healers
dogi. See witchcraft
domestication, 39–40
domination: in colonialism, 7–8, 10–11, 22,
    25, 44–45, 51, 54, 84, 91, 109, 111–12, 149,
    151, 162, 164, 194, 200–201, 211n43; imagi-
    naries of, 138; reversal of, 151; transaction
    creating, 5, 201; transgressive, 20; under-
    neath of, 11, 19
Doyle, Arthur Conan, 165
dream-book, 142, 268n16
dreams: cannibalism and, 138–39, 142, 151,
    154–55; spirits in, 35, 50, 52, 75, 83
Du Chaillu, Paul, 108, 236n46, 268n17,
    278n125, 280n143; apes and, 155–59, 161,
    163–67, 275n82, 275n84, 276nn99–100,

277n104, 277n109, 277n114, 279n136;
    cannibalism and, 139–44, 149, 153,
    155–59, 161, 163–67, 271nn45–46, 279n136;
    Country of the Dwarfs, 139–40; *Explora-
    tions and Adventures in Equatorial Africa,*
    79–80, 139, 155; Fougamou and, 37–38;
    human remains stolen by, 1, 166–67; *Lost
    in the Jungle,* 19–20
Dybowski, Jean, 113–14

eating (*manger*): belly-womb and, 169–72,
    192, 199, 280n8; Bwiti and, 189–92; can-
    nibalism and, 168–77, 179–90, 192–93,
    287n81, 288n87; cauldrons and, 172–74,
    181; colonialism and, 169, 171–86, 188–93;
    cooked food, 187–88; as destruction,
    168–69; evil and, 172, 181–82, 184, 186–87,
    199; fetishism and, 169, 173, 191, 273n66;
    god, 189; imaginaries of, 22–23, 168–70,
    172–73, 175, 179, 181, 183–85, 187, 192–93;
    literality of, 192–93; *marmites* and,
    172–74, 182, 186; misinterpretation of,
    177–79; money, 118, 252n2; power and,
    22, 138, 168–72, 174–75, 177, 179, 182–85,
    187–89, 192–93, 199; raw food, 187–88;
    symbolic meanings of, 168–71, 199; verbs
    for, 280n2; witch-substance and, 169–72,
    183–87, 192, 281nn11–13, 285n58, 285n64,
    286n66, 287n79
Eckhout, Albert, 141–43
economy, transactional, 10, 30, 69, 200
emasculation, 19–20, 158
Equatorial African tradition, 12, 94. *See also*
    West Equatorial African tradition
erotica, cannibal, 148–51, 153
ethnicity, 46–48, 224n95, 224nn99–101
Eucharist, 109, 181–83, 207n17, 285nn55–56
Evans-Pritchard, E. E., 255n21, 258n49
evil, 86, 91; borrowed figures of, 3; capacity,
    113; eating and, 172, 181–82, 184, 186–87, 199
evu. See witch-substance
Evus (prince), 181, 186
exchange: in colonial city, 43–45; of
    commodities, 124, 262n87; destruc-
    tive, 157–58, 171, 179; in eighteenth and
    nineteenth centuries, 32–36; of goods,
    30, 36, 110, 119, 170; lethal, 10; of people,

197; with *puissance*, 118; ritual, 30, 198; in sacrifice, 211n42; social meaning of, 127, 195; with spirit, 55, 65, 67; transaction contrasted with, 210n37

experts and healers (*nganga*; pl. *banganga*): ambivalent power of, 239n85; blacksmiths as, 36; decline of, 89; *evu/kundu* and, 103–4; fees charged by, 241n111; fetishes and, 72, 85, 87–91, 94–95, 234n27; knowledge of, 89, 239n87; politicians and, 1; role of, 14; seeing by, 37; specialized, 239n83; terms for, 213n60; witchcraft opposed to, 85

Explorations and Adventures in Equatorial Africa (Du Chaillu), 79–80, 139, 155

extraordinary agency, 2–3, 69, 74, 96, 184, 233n13

Fang: as cannibals, 143–44, 150, 153–54, 178, 191, 271n46, 274n76, 274nn78–79; relics, 81–85, 236n51; witch-substance and, 245nn33–35

farming, 33–34, 218n14, 222n71

father, archaic, 157–64

fear: of cannibalism, 22, 138, 146, 148–50, 155–56, 166; carnal fetishism and, 99, 101, 106, 108, 114; of emasculation, 20; of racial transmutation, 166; transgressions and, 195–96; of witchcraft, 106, 108

Feierman, Steven, 208n27, 211n44

Ferme, Mariane, 11, 212n49

Fernandez, James, 14, 94, 208n27, 236n51

fertility, 208n25

féticheurs (fetish-doctors), 91–93, 177, 238n74

fetish: agency, 7, 22, 196; body as, 107–11; charms and, 75–81, 86–92; as commodity, 201; cooking pot as, 146; defined, 69, 242n122; experts and, 72, 85, 87–91, 94–95, 234n27; illness from, 242n117; making of, 239n79; as material entity, 7, 109; *pèmba a motètè*, 136, 266n129; problem-idea of, 70; rethinking, 75–79; selling of, 72–73; *travailler les fétiches* and, 87–91; value of money, 131–34, 136, 198–99

fetish-doctors (*féticheurs*), 91–93, 177, 238n74

fetishism, 241n108, 252n102; colonialism and, 15, 42, 75, 77, 273n66; eating and, 169, 173, 191, 273n66. *See also* carnal fetishism

field research, 22, 25–26

Fleuriot de Langle, 79, 97, 127, 253n10, 278n119; gorillas adopted by, 161–62; on vampires, 184

force: in charms, 74, 106; as foreign term, 3; immaterial, 9, 16, 30, 50–51; invisible, 4, 54–55; life, 1–2, 102–3, 169

Foucault, Michel, 200

Fougamou, 37–39, 43, 175

free-floating currencies, 132, 263n99

French Revolution, 97, 107

Freud, Sigmund, 157, 216n93

Friedman, Kajsa Elkhom, 173

funerary rites, 97–102

fusil nocturne (nightly gun), 16, 173, 214n72, 281n19

Gabon: southern, 27–28, 32, 42–45; terrains, 12–16. *See also* Mouila

Garner, Richard, 142, 230n158, 276n101

gaspiller (waste), 123, 256nn28–29

Gehne, Hans, 81

genies (*mighesi*), 227n138

Germaine, Marie, 108

germ theory, 149, 185

Geschiere, Peter, 106, 205n7, 206n8, 290n10

gift ceremonies (*bilabi*), 126–27

Gilroy, Paul, 203

Gluckman, Max, 215n80

Gobineau, Arthur de, 51, 273n59

god: Christian, 1, 16, 50, 92, 108–9, 114, 182, 230n157; eating, 189

"going native," 113, 138, 165

goods: exchange of, 30, 36, 110, 119, 170; imported, 14, 38, 40–41, 71, 111, 123, 132, 136, 172; material, 29–30, 36, 38, 119, 123, 127, 197; people as, 122–23, 125–26; power of, 130

gorillas, 205n2, 275n80; as archaic fathers, 157–64; cannibal, 156, 275n92, 276n94; interspecies sex and, 157, 164–66; transference, 20, 139, 154–57, 275nn91–92, 276n99, 276n101

Graux, Emile, 80, 236n48

grave robbing: carnal fetishism and, 99, 114–17; remains stolen in, 1, 99, 114–17, 166–67, 190, 252n97. *See also* cemeteries

Grébert, Fernand, 150, 274n79

Guillaume, Paul, 81

guilt, 11–12, 171; cannibalism and, 154–55, 158–59, 162, 166; projection of, 196

guns, 16, 38, 41, 60, 131, 173, 214n72, 256n33, 281n19. *See also* nightly gun

Guyader, Father, 144–45, 269n30

Guyer, Jane, 124

Hamitic hypothesis, 154, 274n77

healers. *See* experts and healers

healing cult. *See* Bwiti

Heart of Darkness (Conrad), 250n78, 250n84, 260n68, 266n2

hegemony: defined, 211n44; on a shoe-string, 260n69; in transactions, 111–14, 210n36, 250n80; transgressive, 11–12

homoerotic desire, 19, 139, 151

Horn, Trader, 59, 80

hostages, 128–29

house, 14, 34, 66, 78, 101, 122–24, 127, 257n41; meeting house (*mbánjá*), 14, 33

human sacrifice, 36–37, 106, 109, 189–91, 220n40

hunger, interspecies sex and, 164–66

Hunt, Nancy Rose, 139, 208n25

hunter-gatherers, 58, 156, 259n57; Babongo, 33; as forest specialists, 35; as white people, 58. *See also* pygmies

husband-clans, 40

hybridity, 5, 59, 234n34

hygiene: germ theory and, 149, 185; magic and, 97–102

identity card, 54

Idumi (village), 35, 46

Ikogou-Renamy, Lionel, 115, 285n56

images, ambivalent status of, 55–56, 228n144

imaginaries: cannibalism, 7, 138–39, 141, 145–46, 148, 151, 154–56, 168, 179, 195; carnal fetishism, 7, 96–97, 107–8, 117; commensurable, 201; defined, 6, 201,

207n22, 209nn30–32; of domination, 138; of eating, 22–23, 168–70, 172–73, 175, 179, 181, 183–85, 187, 192–93; intro-duction to, 5–11, 18–23; of money, 131; of power, 5, 12, 29, 43, 192, 194, 197–98; practice of, 99; trading, 258n56; transac-tional, 7, 9–10, 40, 84, 195; transforma-tion of, 23, 40, 131, 193; transgressive, 21, 201

immaterial: agency, 14, 30, 148; eating and, 193; forces, 9, 16, 30, 50–51; spirits as, 4; symbol as, 107

imports: goods, 14, 38, 40–41, 71, 111, 123, 132, 136, 172; money, 131

initiation: ceremonies, 178; societies, 14, 34, 67, 89, 105, 108, 123, 247n48, 256n31

interspecies sex, 157, 164–66

intimacy, 17, 97, 149, 152, 208n25

invisibility: of force, 4, 54–55; science of, 29, 55, 67–68, 198; seeing and, 37–38, 49, 53–54, 60, 66, 197; of spirits, 32, 37–38, 52, 55–56; transformation from, 55

iron: cooking pots, 172; Fang and, 154; profits, 221n46; technology, 36–38, 55–57, 219n32, 219n34, 220n35; transacting, 36–38

irrationality, 4, 18, 269n29

Izac, Pierre, 110–11

Janzen, John, 95, 242n117

Jesus, Sacred Heart of, 181–83

jeton d'impôt (tax token), 134–35, 265nn118–22

jetons-monnaies, 264n106

kanda. See clan

Kingsley, Mary, 144, 156–57, 275n91

kinship: alliances, 7, 34, 40, 196; colonial, 157, 199–200; enslavement and, 40; fantasies of, 7

knots: binding with, 72; writing through, 18–23

knowledge: as capital, 200; esoteric, 38, 55, 68, 75, 88–89, 102; of moral failure, 196; of *nganga*, 89, 239n87; transmission of, 88–89, 102, 169

kolamba (cook), 177

Koumba, Monique, 58
kundu. See witch-substance

Laman, Karl, 171, 187–88, 281n13
land: control of, 32–35, 40–41, 194, 196, 199–200, 215n75; of desire, 157–64; powerscapes and, 51–53
languages, 206n13, 245n33
Largeau, Victor, 184
Lavignotte, Henri, 184
leaders: local, 15, 79, 123, 263n95; successful, 3, 103–4, 124, 199
leadership, 14, 79, 88, 164, 176, 239n83
Le Bon, Gustave, 151–52
Lenz, Oskar, 80
Leroy, Mgr., 150, 152
lethal exchange, 10
life force (*ngul*), 1–2, 102–3, 169
loss: debt and, 21; money replacing, 121; of power, 91, 167; saints and, 61, 64; in transactions, 9–10, 106
Lost in the Jungle (Du Chaillu), 19–20

maboulisme (craziness), 94, 242n119
MacGaffey, Wyatt, 74–75, 207n16, 230n164, 257n42, 258n53
Mademoiselle movement, 70–71, 86–87, 232n5, 238n77, 239n78
magic: black, 90, 285n57; commodification of, 118; hygiene and, 97–102; intrusion into, 2, 7; power and, 207n16
magicians (*magiciens*), 90–91, 242n116
Makita, Nyonda, 50
Mami Wata: in Atlantic era, 60; as global figure, 16; intrusion of, 200; Murhumi as, 27, 29, 31, 59–60; paintings, 55. *See also* water spirits
manger. See eating
Maquelle, Fernand, 54
marabouts, 1, 95
Marche, Alfred, 162, 167, 277n108
Marché Mont Bouët, 72–73
markets: Marché Mont Bouët, 72–73; missionaries establishing, 132; Samba-Magotsi, 39; therapeutic, 69, 80, 83, 93–95
marmite (cooking pot), 146–47, 172–74, 182, 186. *See also* cauldrons

marriage: social reproduction through, 6, 39, 195; value of, 125, 258n52, 259n64, 260nn65–66
Marx, Karl, 70, 209n30, 273n58
Mary, André, 189
mass visibility, 54
material: agency, 14, 30, 85, 108, 148, 182; eating and, 193; fetish as, 7, 109; goods, 29–30, 36, 38, 119, 123, 127, 197; spirits as, 4
materialism, 126
maternal uncle, 282n31
matrilineal descent, 29, 34, 40, 66–67; maternal uncle in, 282n31; rules of, 231n172
Mauss, Marcel, 58, 211n42, 251n92, 273n65
Mba, Léon, 15, 122, 190–91, 288nn91–94
Mba Ntem, Théophile, 191–92, 289n97
McClintock, Anne, 149
medical pluralism, 95
médicaments (medicine objects), 95, 136, 188, 220n40, 242n122
Meiss, Charles, 180, 283n46
Mère Mambu, 60, 64
mermaid, 29, 54–55, 59
metal objects, 36–38, 172
miasma contagion, 149
middle classes, 11, 211n46
middle figures, 139
mighesi (genies), 227n138
mimicry, 139, 165, 249n65
mining, 213n66
mirror: cannibal, 139–40, 143, 154; in colonial culture of terror, 289n4; concept of, 212n51
missionaries: cannibalism and, 150–51; charms and, 10, 12, 61–62, 83–85, 108–9, 115, 197, 211n43, 235n37, 235n42, 236n54, 237n74; Eucharist and, 182–83, 207n17, 285nn55–56; expectations of, 229nn148–49; fees charged by, 241n111; initiation societies attacked by, 108; money and, 132–33, 263n103; people bought by, 129–30, 261n81; slave trade and, 130; as sources, 25; vampires and, 184, 287n78; witchcraft and, 92
mistranslations, by colonialists, 179
misunderstanding, 5, 46, 174; creative misinterpretations, 208n27

money (l'argent), 257n44, 258nn47–48,
262n90; blood, 119–22, 137, 198, 253n8,
253nn10–11, 254n12, 254n18, 255nn21–22;
change from, 263n98; eating, 118, 252n2;
fetish value of, 131–34, 136, 198–99;
free-floating currencies, 132, 263n99;
imaginary of, 131; imported, 131; jetons-
monnaies, 264n106; loss replaced by,
121; missionaries and, 132–33, 263n103;
political significance of, 133–35; puissance
and, 135–37
money, as symbol, 121
monkeys, 1, 139–40, 154–57. See also apes
Montandon, Georges, 156, 275n90
moral economy, 259n61
moral norms, 12, 135
Motley, Mary, 17
Mougoungou, Ndinga, 52–53, 57
Mouila: colonial exchange in, 43–45; downtown, 52; economic stagnation in, 32–33;
ethnic groups, 46–48, 224n95, 224nn99–
101; military post in, 42; Murhumi in,
27–33, 54, 56–59, 62–67; race in, 44–45
Moulimfou (healing movement), 85–86,
237n74
mughisi. See water spirits
murder: punishment for, 283n44;
ritual crime, 96, 118, 122, 168, 191–93,
196–97; tiger-men and, 139, 145–48, 173,
178–79, 185, 269n30, 270nn31–34, 270n37,
282nn26–27, 283nn44–45
Murhumi: as ancestor, 29, 32, 35, 39, 217n4;
centrality of, 29; in crisis of symbolic
uncertainty, 32, 53–56, 67–68, 198; den
of, 53, 57; in eighteenth and nineteenth
centuries, 32–36; iron for, 36; as Mami
Wata, 27, 29, 31, 59–60; in Mouila, 27–33,
54, 56–59, 62–67; name of, 227n137; puissance of, 29, 32, 54–55, 58, 60, 65, 67; race
of, 55, 60; sacrifice and, 64–68, 230n163;
saints and, 59–64; shrine, 29–30, 54,
56–59, 64–65, 226n123, 227n133; as Siren,
29–31, 54, 59–65, 68, 227n135; Tailleurs
seeing, 53–56, 225n118; transfigurations
of, 30; as Virgin Mary, 27, 59, 60–64,
230n158; as water spirit, 27, 29–32, 34–36,
39, 48, 51–60, 62, 64–67

museums, 81–82, 236n51
mutability, 55
muviga (slave integrated to a lineage),
231n168
Mweli, 34, 46

Nassau, Robert Hamill, 278n123; cannibalism and, 152, 163–64, 272n51, 275n91; in
Talagouga, 92, 279n128
natural resources, 213n66
Ndende, Joseph, 86, 238n77
neem. See witch
negative transactions, 79, 95
nganga. See experts and healers
Ngoma, Florence, 70–71, 232nn5–6
Ngounié, 23–24, 27–68; bridge over the,
56–58, 226n128; river, 35, 39, 41, 43, 46,
48, 51, 56
Nguéma-Ndong, Patrice, 89–90, 240n93
ngul (life force), 1–2, 102–3, 169
night, 29, 57; body of the, 104; domain of
the, 16, 37, 50, 54–55, 58–60, 68, 71, 95,
103, 171; grave desecration at, 115; gun of
the, 214n72; rituals at, 105, 137, 178; tables
of the, 182; taxidermy at, 163–64; witch
activities, 183
nightly gun (fusil nocturne), 16, 173, 214n72,
281n19
Njobi, 67, 86, 231n176
nocturnal meat (viande de nuit), 188
norms, moral, 12, 135
nsisim (body-of-the-shade), 103–4,
245nn30–31, 247n43
Nzengui, Pierre, 31, 54, 67, 227n133

olovalovi. See witch
otangani (people who count), 127–31,
262n88, 262n91
An Outpost of Progress (Conrad), 112–14,
250n84

Parti Démocratique Gabonais, 20–21
patron (commanditaire), 65, 117, 168,
252n103
Payeur-Didelot, P., 112, 155, 157, 272n51,
279n136
pèmba a motètè, 136, 266n129

Pentecostal churches, 91, 183, 238n74, 285n57
Péron, Zacharie, 25, 108–9
Perrois, Louis, 83, 236n46
petits blancs (poor whites), 44
photography, 53–56, 81–82; African intelligence as, 108; identity, 54
pièces détachées (body parts), 114–17, 168, 192, 254n18, 280n1
pietà, 62, 230n157
Pietz, William, 70, 75, 77
politicians, 1, 3, 15–16, 66, 231n176
poor whites (*petits blancs*), 44
postcolonialism, 202–3
Pouchet, Father, 25, 92, 286n73
Poutrin, Léon, 156
pouvoir (power), 2–3, 9
poverty, 15–16, 214n69, 217n10
power: as ambivalent, 18, 239n85; biopower, 51, 151–52, 196, 202; in body, 22, 96–97, 102–11, 115, 117, 187–88, 196–97, 199, 257n42; in bones, 104–6, 115, 117, 167; of civilization, 4, 9, 108, 195; eating and, 22, 138, 168–72, 174–75, 177, 179, 182–85, 187–89, 192–93, 199; of goods, 130; imaginaries of, 5, 12, 29, 43, 192, 194, 197–98; introduction to, 1–12, 16–23, 25; loss of, 91, 167; magic and, 207n16; new lexicon of, 208n25; *pouvoir*, 2–3, 9; race and, 5–7; transactions in, 5, 7–11, 194–96, 200–201; transformation of, 3, 8–9, 23, 184, 189, 193; unusual channels of, 194; from wealth, 123–24. *See also puissance*
powerscapes, 51–53
presence, 200; politic of, 108–11; of spirits, 54
primal scene, 216n90
prix du sang. See blood price
projection, 6, 10, 21, 148, 196, 216n93
prosperity: in eighteenth and nineteenth centuries, 32–36; end of, 40–43
puissance (power): defined, 3, 29, 49–50; exchange with, 118; genealogy of, 3–4; imaginary of, 197–98; loss of, 91; modern, 46; money and, 135–37; of Murhumi, 29, 32, 54–55, 58, 60, 65, 67; powerscapes and, 51–53; theft of, 54,

114–15; of white people, 54–58, 65–67, 84, 89; witch-substance and, 197
Punu: reliquary bundle, 76; spirits and, 35–37, 39, 42, 46–50, 58, 219n22, 219n32, 224n100, 225n113
pygmies (*pygmées*), 33, 58, 156. *See also* hunter-gatherers

race: cannibalism and, 138–39, 141–42, 151–52, 154–56, 166; human remains and, 96–97, 100; in Mouila, 44–45; of Murhumi, 55, 60; power and, 5–7; recognition of similarities in, 7; taxonomy of, 46; triangular oppositions in, 202
racial transmutation, fear of, 166
Raponda-Walker, André, 61
Rashkin, Esther, 216n94, 289n2
rationality, 4, 18, 51, 147–48, 193
raw food, 187–88
Reading, Joseph H., 156
recognition: colonial, 5, 11, 18, 111, 201; debt of, 126; of racial similarities, 7; of white people as partners, 53
relics: Christian, 78, 108, 247n42, 249n66, 249n68; local, 10, 79, 81–85, 97, 101, 104–6, 115, 167, 176–78, 180–81, 187, 190, 193, 199, 234n25, 235n41, 235n43, 236n51, 247nn47–48
réparations civiles (civil incidental damages), 254n14
ritual autopsy, 4, 101, 245n24
ritual crime (*crime rituel*): historicized, 196–97; murder, 96, 118, 122, 168, 191–93, 196–97
ritual exchange, 30, 198
ritual stickiness, 75
rope, binding and, 110, 191. *See also* knots
rubber, 41, 221n60

Sacred Heart of Jesus, 181–83
sacrifice: animal, 19, 184; body parts and, 114–17; in carnal fetishism, 106, 108–9, 114–17; destruction in, 211n42, 248n52; economy, 125; exchange in, 211n42; human, 36–37, 106, 109, 176, 189–91, 220n40; reversing, 64–68; self-sacrifice, 113–14

saints: Christian, 50, 55–56, 59–64, 78, 249n66, 249n68; relics of, 78, 249n66, 249n68; Sirens and, 59–64

Saint-Sulpician statues, 61, 229n152

Samba-Magotsi market, 39; slaves named as, 38

Satan/Devil: cannibalism associated with, 183–84, 187; God and, 1; as snake, 64, 228n143; strength of, 50; vampires associated with, 184, 186–87, 192; Very Bad Heart of the Devil, 16, 183, 192, 199, 285n58

Schweitzer, Albert, 114, 185, 251n91

science, 9, 17

science of the invisible (science de l'invisible), 29, 55, 67–68, 198

science of the manifest (science du visible), 29, 55, 58, 67–68, 198

secrecy, of spirits, 37–38, 52, 55, 198

secret societies, 23, 146, 173, 186, 192, 252n97

self-destruction, fantasies of, 151–53, 181

self-sacrifice, 113–14

Seligman, Charles, 154

SHO (Société industrielle, commerciale et agricole du Haut Ogooué), 41–42, 128, 132, 144, 264n106

Simbu, 29, 34–36, 40, 46, 50, 218n20

Simenon, Georges, 112–14

Siren: Murhumi as, 29–31, 54, 59–65, 68, 227n135; saints and, 59–64. See also mermaid

slaves: commodities for, 262n87; muviga, 231n168; politicians as, 66

slave trade: abolished, 213n61; in Atlantic era, 38–40; cannibalism and, 153, 247n51; commodification of person in, 123; consumerism of, 118; engagement with, 14; Fang and, 274n78; by foreigners, 123, 256n34; iron and, 38; metal objects and, 172; missionaries and, 130; as transaction, 106–7

snakes, 60, 64, 228n143, 230n160

social reproduction: cannibal imaginary underwriting, 7, 138, 151; colonialism and, 7–10, 40, 138, 151–52, 176, 194–96, 200; defined, 273n58; through marriage, 6, 39, 195

social wealth, 172, 177; material goods and, 36, 38; value of, 119, 121, 125–27, 133, 136–37

Société industrielle, commerciale et agricole du Haut Ogooué (SHO), 41–42, 128, 132, 144, 264n106

Sociétés secrètes, 23, 173

sorcery (sorcellerie), 15, 85, 91, 196, 205n7, 241n108. See also witchcraft

Soubirous, Bernadette, 62

sources, 19, 23–26

Spear, Thomas, 208n26

spirits: agency of, 27, 30–33, 49, 54–55, 58, 65–67, 74, 233n13; in Atlantic era, 38–40; blacksmith, 37, 55, 62, 220n37; convertibility and, 125–26; Dibur-Simbu and, 29, 32, 34–37, 39–40, 46, 50–51, 53–54, 56–60, 64–66, 227n133; in dreams, 35, 50, 52, 75, 83; exchange with, 55, 65, 67; imbwiri, 59; invisibility of, 32, 37–38, 52, 55–56; iron smelting and, 220n35; as material and immaterial, 4; presence of, 54; Punu and, 35–37, 39, 42, 46–50, 58, 219n22, 219n32, 224n100, 225n113; role of, 14; secrecy of, 37–38, 52, 55, 198; substitution and, 125–26; transactions with, 32, 35–40, 65–66; water, 27, 29–32, 34–36, 39, 48, 51–60, 62, 64–67

statue, 30–31, 54–56, 58–59, 61–62, 64, 66–68, 72–74, 78, 80, 171, 197–98

Stoler, Ann Laura, 208n25, 209n30, 212n47

substitution, 125–26, 258n49

symbol: body as, 107–11; eating as, 168–71, 199; of emasculation, 19; as immaterial, 107; money as, 121; snakes as, 60, 64, 228n143, 230n160; worn around neck, 135, 266n123

symbole (symbol worn around neck), 135, 266n123

symbolic crisis, 32, 53–56, 67–68, 198

symbolic destruction, 168–69

symbolic systems, 212n48

syncretism, 27, 70, 208n25

tabernacle, 182, 199

table, 182, 284nn53–54

Tailleur, Mr. and Mrs., 53–56, 225n118, 232n179

Talagouga (Protestant Mission), 92, 279n128

taxes: colonial, 9, 41, 43, 119, 128, 133–36, 261n78, 264n108, 265nn118–22; tokens for, 134–35, 265nn118–22 technology, 22; bridge, 56–58; failure of, 194; iron, 36–38, 55–57, 219n32, 219n34, 220n35; transactional, 40

terror, colonial culture of, 289n4

Tessman, Günther, 80, 82, 104, 106, 178, 220n38; on apes, 155–56; on *evu*, 171, 286n66

theft: of charms, 10, 79, 84, 95; of human remains, 1, 96–97, 99, 106, 114–17, 166–67; of iron technology, 37; of *puissance*, 54, 114–15; with witchcraft, 127

therapeutic markets, 69, 80, 83, 93–95

thirds, colonial, 139, 153–54, 162, 202, 267n8

tiger-men: cannibalism and, 139, 145–48, 173, 178–79, 185, 269n30, 270nn31–34, 270n37, 282nn26–27, 283nn44–45; sources, 24–25; on trial, 148, 184–85, 283n45

Tonda, Joseph, 61, 214n73, 228n143, 266n128, 290n11; collaboration with, 26–27, 130–31; fetish defined by, 242n122

trading, imaginary, 258n56

tradi-praticiens (tradi-practitioners), 90, 240n94

tradition. *See* West Equatorial African tradition

transaction: concept of, 8–10, 210nn37–38; gone wrong, 8, 10. *See also specific topics*

transfiguration, 30, 35, 60

transformation: of imaginaries, 23, 40, 131, 193; from invisibility, 55; of power, 3, 8–9, 23, 184, 189, 193; transaction and, 8; in value of people, 131, 137

transgression: awareness of, 117, 195–96, 201; channels opened by, 194; in domination, 20; hegemony and, 11–12; imaginaries, 21, 201; *puissance* and, 197

travailler (work), 87–91

Trilles, Henri, 64, 151–52, 154, 156, 271n41, 274n79

usurpation, 139, 164–65, 200, 279n134

value: colonialism and, 118–22, 125–37; commensurable, 5–7, 119, 124–26, 131, 135, 198; fetish value of money, 131–34, 136,

198–99; of marriage, 125, 258n52, 259n64, 260nn65–66; of *otangani*, 127–31; of people, 22, 118–31, 137, 198–99, 255n23, 255nn25–26, 257n42, 258n50, 259n64, 261n80, 262n85, 262n87, 262n91, 264n113; of social wealth, 119, 121, 125–27, 133, 136–37; transactional, 126–27

vampires, 16, 65–66, 182, 285n60, 285nn62–63; blood and, 183–87, 286n66, 286n71, 287nn77–78; Devil associated with, 184, 186–87, 192; as witch-substance, 73, 183–87, 192, 230n163, 232n179

Vansina, Jan, 5, 60–61, 74, 123

Vassal, Gabrielle, 157

ventre. *See* belly-womb

Very Bad Heart of the Devil, 16, 183, 192, 199, 285n58

viande de nuit (nocturnal meat), 188

Villault, Nicolas, 77

Virgin Mary, 16; cults, 61, 228n145; intrusion of, 200; Mademoiselle-Minbara and, 70–71; Murhumi as, 27, 59, 60–64, 230n158; in pietà, 62, 230n157; snake crushed by, 64, 230n160

visibility: mass, 54; science of, 29, 55, 58, 67–68, 198; spirits and, 32, 37–38, 52, 55–56

Voronoff, Serge, 165–66, 279n139

Vuillaume, Pierre, 119

wages, 41, 119, 127, 134, 136, 263n100

waste (*gaspiller*), 123, 256nn28–29

water spirits (*mughisi*, pl. *baghisi*): images of, 55–56, 228n144; *imbwiri* (coastal water spirits), 59; Murhumi, 27, 29–32, 34–36, 39, 48, 51–60, 62, 64–67. *See also* Mami Wata

wealth, 266n129; through eating, 170; at expense of others, 127; in people, 119, 122–26, 137, 255n23, 255nn25–26; power from, 123–24; from slave trade, 106–7; social, 36, 38, 119, 121, 125–27, 133, 136–37, 172, 177

West Equatorial African tradition: Equatorial African tradition and, 94; legacy of, 5

White, Luise, 17, 183–84, 207n22, 212n47, 290n5

white cannibalism, 138, 141, 166–67, 247n51

white people: body of, 97, 99, 102, 108; as *magiciens*, 91; as *otangani*, 127–31, 262n88, 262n91; as partners, 53; *puissance* of, 54–58, 65–67, 84, 89

"whites," Gabonese: defined, 65–66; as *magiciens*, 91; *puissance* of, 65–66; as spiritual category, 230n164

witch (*neem, olovalovi*): cauldron of, 172–74, 181; in Christian folklore, 146–47; criminal, 107; defined, 104; flying, 1, 287n74; human remains and, 106

witchcraft (*dogi*): attacks, 1–2, 4, 246n39, 282n31; curing, 85–87; defined, 15, 85; fear of, 106, 108; historicized, 2, 196–97; movements against, 70–71, 85–87, 91, 93, 226n126; politics and, 1–2, 206n8; ritual autopsy and, 4, 101, 245n24; snakes in, 64; *sorcellerie* overlapping with, 15, 85, 91, 196, 205n7, 241n108; tables in, 182, 284nn53–54; as thievery, 127; transgressive hegemony and, 12

witch-substance (*evu/kundu*): defined, 14, 246n34; eating and, 169–72, 183–87, 192, 281nn11–13, 285n58, 285n64, 286n66, 287n79; experts and, 103–4; Fang and, 245nn33–35; *puissance* and, 197; revealed, 88; root of, 246n36; Tessman on, 171, 286n66; vampires as, 73, 183–87, 192, 230n163, 232n179

work (*travailler*), 87–91

World War I, 15, 42, 108, 128, 132

World War II, 42, 67, 128, 146

Yengo, Patrice, 26

Zenker, Georg August, 82